MEDIATING SPACES

Mediating Spaces

Literature, Politics, and the Scales of Yugoslav Socialism, 1870–1995

James M. Robertson

McGill-Queen's University Press
Montreal & Kingston • London • Chicago

© McGill-Queen's University Press 2024

ISBN 978-0-2280-2137-7 (cloth)
ISBN 978-0-2280-2187-2 (ePDF)
ISBN 978-0-2280-2188-9 (ePUB)

Legal deposit second quarter 2024
Bibliothèque nationale du Québec

Printed in Canada on acid-free paper that is 100% ancient forest free
(100% post-consumer recycled), processed chlorine free

This book has been published with the help of a Faculty Publication Support grant
from the University of California, Irvine Humanities Center.

We acknowledge the support of the Canada Council for the Arts.
Nous remercions le Conseil des arts du Canada de son soutien.

McGill-Queen's University Press in Montreal is on land which long served
as a site of meeting and exchange amongst Indigenous Peoples, including the
Haudenosaunee and Anishinabeg nations. In Kingston it is situated on the territory
of the Haudenosaunee and Anishinaabek. We acknowledge and thank the diverse
Indigenous Peoples whose footsteps have marked these territories on which peoples
of the world now gather.

Library and Archives Canada Cataloguing in Publication

Title: Mediating spaces : literature, politics, and the scales of Yugoslav socialism,
   1870–1995 / James M. Robertson.
Names: Robertson, William M. (Lecturer in history), author.
Description: Includes bibliographical references and index.
Identifiers: Canadiana (print) 20240333225 | Canadiana (ebook) 20240333284
   | ISBN 9780228021377 (hardcover) | ISBN 9780228021872 (ePDF) | ISBN
   9780228021889 (ePUB)
Subjects: LCSH: Socialism—Yugoslavia—History—19th century. | LCSH: Socialism
   Yugoslavia—History—20th century. | LCSH: Globalization—Yugoslavia—History
   19th century. | LCSH: Globalization—Yugoslavia—History—20th century. | LCSH:
   Socialism and literature—Yugoslavia. | LCSH: Literature and globalization
   Yugoslavia.| LCSH: Politics and literature—Yugoslavia.
Classification: LCC HX365.5.A6 R63 2c24 | DDC 335.00949709/04—dc23

This book was typeset in 10.5/13 Sabon.

In memory of Philippa Hetherington

Contents

Figures   ix

Acknowledgments   xi

Introduction   3

1 "A Cramped and Rusty Building": Globalization, Serbian Socialism, and the Limits of the Nation State, 1870–1914   25

2 Balkanizing Europe: The Early Comintern and the Yugoslav Avant-Gardes, 1918–26   44

3 Literary Capital in an Age of Global Crisis: The Political Economy of Translation on Europe's Periphery, 1928–34   66

4 The Popular Front, World Literature, and Rapprochement with Europe, 1934–38   98

5 The Slavic Vanguard of the Balkan Revolution: Race and Region in Yugoslav Stalinism, 1941–48   125

6 Cultural One-Worldism and the Geographies of Non-Alignment, 1948–68   158

7 The Cultural Spaces of Late Socialism: European Integration, Yugoslav Fragmentation, 1974–95   188

Conclusion   221

Notes   231

Index   295

Figures

1.1 The Balkans, 1910. Participants of the First Balkan Social Democratic Conference. 40

2.1 The Balkans, 1920. 47

3.1 *Nova literatura* 1, no. 4 (March 1929). Sig. 313/П, СВ1. Courtesy of Narodna biblioteka Srbije. 76

3.2 *Nova literatura* 1, nos. 5–6 (April–May 1929). Issue on "Contemporary Germany." Sig. 313/П, СВ1. Courtesy of Narodna biblioteka Srbije. 77

3.3 *Nova literatura* 1, no. 10 (September 1929). Issue on contemporary Soviet culture. Sig. 313/П, СВ1. Courtesy of Narodna biblioteka Srbije. 78

3.4 Portrait of Miroslav Krleža from the late1930s. Used with permission of the Muzej grada Zagreba. 88

3.5 Krsto Hegedušić, "Muži," from *Podravi motivi* (Zagreb: Minerva nakladna knjižara, 1933). 90

3.6 Pannonia in the 1930s. 93

5.1 The Slavic world in 1946. 132

5.2 Postage stamps issued to commemorate the 1946 All Slavic Conference. 145

6.1 States that sent representatives to the first Meeting of Non-Aligned Heads of State, 1961. 166

6.2 *Književne novine*, 15 February 1955, 1. Sig. 2180/Г, 1955. Courtesy of Narodna biblioteka Srbije. 183

7.1 European Economic Community, 1986. 193

Acknowledgments

Writing this book has incurred a number of debts that can never be repaid but should be acknowledged. The ideas here first began to take shape during my graduate studies at New York University, where I was lucky to be mentored by an incredible community of scholars. I doubt I would have survived the experience were it not for my advisor, Larry Wolff, whose infinite patience, wry humour, and healthy sense of perspective I appreciate more and more with age. Stefanos Geroulanos and Yanni Kotsonis compelled me to not just think more carefully but completely break down and reconstruct the foundations of my worldview, scholarly and otherwise. Zvi Ben Dor Benite continues to be a vital guide through the opacity of US academia. Jane Burbank, Katy Flemming, Manu Goswami, Stephen Gross, and Kristin Ross each, in different ways, helped shape this work. As formative as graduate school was, I would never have had the confidence to undertake it were it not for the early inspiration and support I received at the University of Sydney from Alison Moore, Dirk Moses, Glenda Sluga, and Shannon Woodcock. I have Dijana Mitrović and Radmila Gorup to thank for inspiring me with a love for the languages and literatures of the former Yugoslavia.

The seeds of this book were planted in the winter of 2007–08 in Belgrade, when Vladimir Unkovski-Korica gifted me a copy of Svetozar Marković's *Srbija na istoku*. In the years since that encounter I have continued to benefit from Vladimir's insights, as well as those of a network of intellectuals and activists in the former Yugoslav lands including Aranđel Bojanović, Ankica Čakardić, Stipe Ćurković, Adela Gjorgjioska, Stefan Gužvica, Andrew Hodges, Nikoleta Kosovac, Marko Kostanić, Primož Krašovec, Vladimir

Krstulović, Vladimir Marković, Domagoj Mihaljević, Andrea Milat, Goran Musić, Milena Ostojić, Jelena Petrović, Vladimir Simović, Igor Štiks, Mislav Stublić, Jelena Veljić, Ana Vilenica, Nikola Vukobratović, Vuk Vuković, and Mislav Žitko. These people have been invaluable interlocutors. Without their friendship, criticism, advice, and hospitality this book would not have been possible. I only hope that it contributes something of value to their current conjuncture.

During its convoluted composition, my research has been honed by the critical eyes of Yousuf Al-Bulushi, Jovana Babović, Ellen Elias-Bursać, Holly Case, Theodora Dragostinova, Sarah Farmer, Madigan Fichter, Emily Greble, Jovana Knežević, Tomislav Longinović, Susan Morrissey, Igor Štiks, and Marla Zubel. Their insights and generosity have been remarkable. Over the past decade Marina Antić, Johanna Bockman, Rossen Djagalov, Agnes Gagyi, Zsuzsa Gille, Mariya Ivancheva, Kole Kilibarda, Mary Taylor, and the crew around *LeftEast* have carved out a space in our field for critical revisions of Eastern Europe's socialist history and the dynamics of its capitalist present. The work that they achieved has provided the intellectual breathing room for this book. I am also indebted to the attentive readings and friendship of Miloš Jovanović, who has been a wonderful intellectual companion here in Southern California.

Since I joined the University of California Irvine, the work on this book has been buoyed by the warmth, humour, and counsel of a wonderful network of friends and colleagues including: Emily Baum, Tamara Beauchamp, Houri Berberian, Vinayak Chaturvedi, Ian Coller, David Fedman, Ben Garceau, Zina Giannopoulou, David Igler, Zoe Klemfuss, George Lang, Matthias Lehman, Mark Levine, Andrej Luptak, Joan Malczewski, Ted Martin, Annie McLanahan, Nancy McLoughlin, Tyrus Miller, Laura Mitchell, Miriam Mora-Quilon, Susan Morrissey, Nasrin Rahimieh, Renee Raphael, Chelsea Schields, Heidi Tinsman, and Jeff Wasserstrom. Emerald Archer and Doug Cremer at Woodbury University gave me my first break in academia and showed immeasurable generosity for which I will be forever grateful. Friends along the way have not only made this possible, but at times even fun: Shir Alon, Betty Banks, Joseph Blankholm, Muriam Haleh Davis, Oded Erez, Simcha Gross, Alexander Jabbari, Peter Jones, Felicity Palma, Victor Petrov, Jamie Phillips, David Rainbow, Liora Tamar, and Natasha Wheatley. Filip

Erdeljac is a brilliant scholar and critical thinker whose intellectual comradery and good humour has been the source of much joy. His retreat from academia is a sad reflection on the state of our field.

Richard Ratzlaff shepherded this project through the various hurdles of the publishing world, while Susan Glickman gave the text her care and attentiveness. Anna Briberih Slana and Vesna Vukelić at the Muzej grada Zagreba, Dragana Milunović and Suzana Rajić at the Narodna biblioteka Srbije, and Nancy Jachec were incredibly generous in helping me procure images. The meticulous Ben Pease helped to bring the geographies of my historical subjects to life. The keen eye and fastidiousness of Đorđe Božović were invaluable for large parts of this project.

Finally, in this endeavour I have been lucky enough to enjoy the dedication of a family whose global dispersion has not weakened their love. David Robertson's discipline and integrity continue to be a point of pride. Jane and Robert Robertson set me on the path to this career early on. Their love, support, and creativity are the foundation of every word I write. As this project entered its final stretch, my life was enriched with the arrival of Rania. Her energy and curiosity have been a respite from the demands of this book. Above all, Liron Mor has been a source of insights and inspiration. Her fidelity to youthful passions is a crucial provocation to the conformity and acquiescence of professional life. For me she is a vital reminder of Badiou's ethic: "Do all that you can to persevere in that which exceeds your perseverance. Persevere in the interruption. Seize in your being that which has seized and broken you."[1] I could not imagine a better person with whom to share this journey.

MEDIATING SPACES

Introduction

I grew up in a multi-national, multicultural and monoideological
community that had a future. I was not interested in politics. My
parents taught me nothing about it. The words "religion," "people,"
"nationality," or even "communism" and "the party" meant nothing
to me. I only ever wrote one "political" sentence (and I stole that from
a child): "I love my country because it is small and I feel sorry for it."
Dubravka Ugrešić, *The Culture of Lies*, 1995

In 1919, one of the first short stories by the Croatian modernist,
Miroslav Krleža (1893–1981), appeared in the Marxist journal
Plamen (The Flame). The story centres on a young Croat, Pero
Orlić, whose love for Europe leads him away from his native town
in the Balkan backwaters and onto the grand boulevards of Paris.
However, no sooner does the unfortunate protagonist arrive than his
faith in European civilization is shaken. Spurned by the Europeans
who mock his barbarous accent and believe that Croatia lies somewhere in Central Africa, Orlić is cast out into the streets. One evening, seeking shelter from the cold and the gendarmerie, he hides in
the Louvre where he accidentally awakens the corpse of an ancient
Elamite king, Hodorlahomor.[1] Disillusioned with the West, Orlić
prostates himself before the king of the ancient East and agrees to
be his guide in the new world. Asked by Hodorlahomor to account
for himself, Orlić explains that he is a Croat, from the Balkans, a
geographic marker that requires further explanation: "The Balkans,
if you please, are a peninsula of Europe. And Europe is, so to speak,
an insignificant peninsula of Asia. A superfluous appendix, so to
speak. Some sort of appendix, if Your Majesty knows what that is.
That appendix can be inflamed, and then you should see the trouble.

You lived in the heart of the world, and not in its appendix where it is dark and smelly. You lived in the heart and we in this poor extremity. And you were right, Your Majesty! To concern oneself with Europe is not worth the efforts."[2]

Wounded from his rejection by Europe, Orlić shifts his subservience to the East. Through the perspective of Hodorlahomor, the Croat rescales Europe, decentering the continent and recasting it as a "dark and smelly" appendix of Asia. However, the more familiar Orlić becomes with Hodorlahomor, the more disenchanted he becomes with the East as well. As the king begins to ape Parisian etiquette, his Croatian lackey bemoans his master's subservience to an effete, bourgeois Europe and the corruption of his savage virtue. Finally, renouncing his allegiance to both West and East, Orlić returns to his native Zagreb disillusioned and broken.

"Hodorlahomor the Great" had strong autobiographical overtones. Krleža had also grown up in thrall to an idealized Europe. Like his protagonist, Orlić, he felt stifled by the narrow horizons of his native Zagreb. "We live in a small city," the young Krleža lamented. "The bells, the ways of life, the mentality, the horizons: a pure province. But around us is open space. Great rivers, great cities, great seas. One must embark. Sail away."[3] In the spring of 1913 he set sail for Paris, but quickly became disillusioned, worn down by poverty, isolation, and his sense of inferiority. The experience coloured his literary and political outlook, imbuing him with a powerful sense that his Balkan origins excluded him from the ranks of European culture. "For these children of ours who thirst for Europe," he later observed, "the only things available are the stone benches of the parks in which we are not even shadows."[4]

Disillusioned with Europe, Krleža too turned away from the West. Like many Yugoslav nationalists in the Habsburg Empire at the time, he volunteered to fight for the Serbian army in the ongoing Balkan Wars. In June 1913 he left Paris, traveling first to Marseilles and then on to Thessaloniki, from where he made his way northwards to the Serbian command in the newly conquered town of Skopje. It was a fateful journey. The destruction wrought by Serbia's conquests dampened his enthusiasm for the war and its lofty ideals of national unity. Furthermore, his poor treatment at the hands of the Serbian authorities, who suspected him of being a Habsburg spy, undermined his faith in South Slavic brotherhood. Krleža went back to his Croatian province disheartened and lost.

Introduction

History, however, did not grant Krleža the same respite he accorded his dejected hero. The outbreak of World War I in the summer of 1914 urgently raised the problem of Croatia's place in a turbulent modern world. Mobilized to fight for an empire in which he felt himself to be a "second-class citizen," Krleža was hostile to the war effort. In May 1916, as he recovered from a bout of tuberculosis, he reflected on the fate of his homeland in the war: "I was lost in myself: Moscow, Istanbul, Belgrade, Vienna, Budapest, Berlin, Balkan, Slavdom, Illyria and right at the end, our poor Croatia, and it is only just today that it becomes clear to me what is wrong with her, with this hungry Croatia of ours. In Budapest I thought that I was a European, that things were clear to me; but I was actually a totally ordinary, confused fool ... Amidst these ordeals we are saddled with a still heavier burden: doubt in our own existence."[5] The passage, with its proliferation of overlapping and competing geographies, speaks to the ideological disorientation the war provoked. As the Habsburg Empire's war aims cut through ties of Slavic solidarity and as an ideal of Europe disappeared in the fog of artillery fire and poison gas, Krleža was cut adrift. No longer buoyed by childhood fantasies of Europe or militant ideals, he was lost and desperately cast about for a lifeline to the wider world.

That line arrived on the waves of revolution that cascaded into South East Europe from Russia in the years that followed October 1917. Communism promised to challenge the hierarchies of power and prestige in Europe and envisioned a revolutionary transformation of the continent's southeast. In the newly formed Kingdom of Serbs, Croats, and Slovenes, Krleža became one of communism's most prominent public figures. The movement's promise to remap the political and cultural space of Europe was central to his ideological commitment:

Today, when the imperial centres of Vienna and St. Petersburg are no more, we now find ourselves in the sphere of interest of Western European capitalism. With the Entente's redrawing of borders at Versailles they have created the Kingdom of Serbs, Croats and Slovenes in which we now live. Our people, for the first time in history have been unified in a single state. But the country is not yet free. What was once resolved over the telephone by imperial cabinets in Vienna or St. Petersburg is today resolved in London or Paris. But the old feudal principle remains the same: about us, but without us.

6   Mediating Spaces

> As maximalists, communists, bolsheviks, we are and want to be free Yugoslavs! ... [B]ut we are conscious of the fact that a single country cannot be free if it is not surrounded by other, equally free countries. To achieve this, our program emphasizes the idea of a free federation of Balkan states![6]

Through a program of regional unity, communism offered a means by which the small nations of South East Europe could pursue a path of economic and cultural development beyond the hegemony of Western Europe. Only through a Balkan federation, Krleža believed, could his people secure a future that lay neither on the cold stone benches of Western Europe nor at the feet of Eastern kings.

SUPRANATIONALISM IN THE AGE OF GLOBALIZATION

The Balkan federalism that framed Krleža's vision of national liberation is an example of what this book terms "mediating spaces": the supranational projects through which intellectuals, activists, and writers sought to nestle the nation in an effort to negotiate its integration into rapidly globalizing political, economic, and cultural horizons.[7] Such projects proliferated throughout Eastern Europe during the final half of the nineteenth century and permeated the political spectrum, appearing within radical, liberal, and conservative circles.[8] They were, however, especially pronounced on the revolutionary Left in the lands that would become Yugoslavia. From its emergence in the 1870s to the civil wars of the 1990s, Yugoslav socialism was animated by various projects of supranational unification: from regional projects of Balkan or Yugoslav federalism to more expansive visions of European unification or the Non-Aligned Movement. These projects sought to reconcile nationalist demands for self-determination with an understanding of capitalist modernity as increasingly global in scale and marked by profound asymmetries of wealth, power, and prestige. Recognizing the weakness of small nations within this global order, socialists on Europe's southeast periphery set out to secure political sovereignty, economic development, and cultural modernization at a scale between the national and the global. This book explores the history of these supranational visions, paying particular attention

Introduction

to the ways Yugoslav intellectuals mapped their political and cultural geographies in response to the shifting spatial dynamics of globalization over the long twentieth century.

The mediating spaces of Yugoslav socialism emerged from the pronounced spatial consciousness that characterized the experience of global capitalist modernity.[9] Yet, because historians have tended to approach supranationalism in South East Europe through the framework of the national question, this global context has been overlooked.[10] As this book demonstrates, however, the history of mediating spaces needs to be understood in a global framework.[11] The first projects of supranational consolidation in South East Europe were bound up with the territorial erosion of the Ottoman Empire and the struggle of European imperial states for strategic control in the region. As the empire's power waned, uprisings led by local elites and backed by European patrons established a series of autonomous or independent national states: Serbia (1804–17), Greece (1821–30), Romania (1877), Bulgaria (1908), and Albania (1913).[12] The integration of these new states into the periphery of a European economic zone, however, quickly hollowed them of whatever sovereignty their new political elites had hoped to enjoy. Reliant on the military, financial, and diplomatic support of great power patrons, they became quasi-states, territorial jurisdictions in which authority was dependent on the support of external powers.[13] For these states, liberation from the Ottoman Empire meant entrenching their dependence on the larger European powers and rendering their very existence precarious.[14]

Many observers at the time saw the weakness of these states as a consequence of the fragmentation of a once-unified Ottoman territory into a mosaic of tiny national kingdoms, a process that would come to be known as "balkanization."[15] This fragmentation ran counter to an emerging geopolitical paradigm that indexed states' wealth, power, and strategic capacity to jurisdiction over an expansive territory that could supply large populations, control strategic resources, and secure an economy of scale.[16] Observing the spread of this new paradigm, the German political geographer Friedrich Ratzel characterized it as the "law of the spatial growth of states."[17] Set against this paradigm, the kingdoms of South East Europe seemed woefully ill-prepared for the challenges of global capitalist modernity. Saddled with growing foreign debt and dependent on

European markets and capital, these small states appeared destined to become mere appendages of their imperial neighbours.[18]

Precisely to avoid this fate, intellectuals across Central, Eastern, and South East Europe set out to reconcile their aspirations for national self-determination with this new geopolitical paradigm. These intellectuals became convinced that national independence could only be secured within the framework of a larger territorial unit and this conviction led them to rescale problems of political sovereignty and economic development to a supranational level. Examples of these rescaling projects abound. We might think of the struggles of Lajos Kossuth and Nicolae Bălcescu to establish a Danubian confederation in the aftermath of the 1848 revolutions, or the efforts of Habsburg reformers like Oszkár Jászi or František Palacký to reorganize the empire as a federation of nation states.[19] We could point to the popularity of Balkan federalist ideas among Serbian and Bulgarian radicals from the 1870s onwards.[20] Pan-Slavism, too, offered a strategy for Slavic nations to secure their political, economic, and cultural existence within a larger territorial entity.[21] Even Austro-Marxism, typically noted for its *de*territorializing proclivities, was a project to reconcile national autonomy with the preservation of the Habsburg Empire's territorial integrity.[22] These examples point to a growing awareness that the political sovereignty, economic development, and cultural modernization of small nations could only be secured through expansive supranational polities that could mediate exposure to the destabilizing dynamics of globalization. Considered in this light, the mediating spaces of Yugoslav socialism are part of a wider history of political projects that sought to imagine forms of statehood and cultural community within configurations that exceeded the nation state.[23]

ON MEDIATING SPACES

The concept of mediating spaces is the central theoretical intervention of this book and requires a degree of elucidation up front. The concept offers an analytical framework for exploring the multiple strands of supranational thought that captured the imagination of Yugoslav socialists in the long twentieth century. The term "mediating spaces" describes those efforts to construct political or cultural projects that could interface between nationally-scaled sovereignties and global processes of integration and competition. Attentive to the weaknesses

Introduction 9

of small states in a rapidly globalizing world and recognizing the limits of national-territorial expansion in an ethnically diverse region, Yugoslav socialists sought to resolve problems of modern state-building at an intermediary scale, somewhere between the national and the global. Supranationalism, they believed, could strengthen their states' defensive capacities in a world of growing imperial predation. It could integrate disparate local markets into a larger, more viable economic zone. It fostered regional cosmopolitanism while remaining sensitive to the global asymmetries of power and prestige. By coordinating their activity at a supranational scale, Yugoslav socialists hoped to cohere spaces of mediation through which they could better negotiate their states' integration into global capitalist modernity.

Mediating spaces were a mode of what human geographers term "scalar politics": efforts to strategically deploy spatial scale to realize projects of social transformation.[24] This concept presupposes that spatial scales and their political or analytical salience are not ontologically given but socially constructed. And precisely because they are socially constructed, they can be understood as sites of political contestation. Yet scales are not infinitely malleable. They condition, constrain, or structure socio-spatial practices. Indeed, this relative fixity is what makes them a terrain of struggle; they serve as structures of both domination and resistance. Scale is, then, "both a product and a progenitor of social processes."[25]

As it is theorized in this book, the concept of mediating spaces is closely informed by Danny MacKinnon's theory of spatial scale as both inherited structure and emergent project. In MacKinnon's framework, scales are understood as accretions of previous socio-spatial processes whose sedimentation shapes the geographic present. Once cohered in institutions and established practices, inherited scales increasingly appear and act as material structures that organize socio-spatial activity into vertical hierarchies. This formulation acknowledges the materiality, durability, and relative historical fixity of spatial scales while also recognizing the possibility of their reconfiguration through conscious social action, i.e., through scalar politics. In moments of contestation or crisis, inherited structures can be transformed by emergent projects of scale-making.[26] This way of thinking about scale both clarifies how the scalar arrangements of a concrete historical situation at once condition, constrain, and direct social action and accounts for their malleability through political contestation.

Mediating Spaces uses the intellectual history of Yugoslav socialism over the long twentieth century to enrich the study of scalar politics by anchoring the concept in a historically detailed case study.[27] This allows the book to explore processes of scale-making over a broad period of time, extending the historical horizon to encompass the longer history of capitalist globalization.[28] Such a timeline offers a vantage point from which to better appreciate the respective fragility and durability of certain spatial scales, their dynamic interaction, and the viability of counterhegemonic politics. This case study also allows the book to complicate current assumptions about supranationalism by shifting focus away from the European core to its periphery. Because the European Union remains a paradigmatic example of supranationalism, this mode of scalar politics has often been narrowly understood as a means for capital to escape the regulative bounds of the nation state.[29] Focus on the European core, therefore, has tended to privilege the supranational as a scale of capital accumulation and technocratic governance. Shifting focus to the European periphery, however, reveals the ways in which supranational scalar politics could be deployed to counterhegemonic purposes.[30]

As they are theorized here, mediating spaces grew out of the tensions that emerged in the late nineteenth century between deepening processes of global integration and nationally articulated sovereignties. In this sense, the supranational should not be conceived as a clearly demarcated and stable scale of activity but rather as a dynamic field constituted and reconfigured by the frictions of globally and nationally scaled processes. As this book demonstrates, changing patterns of capitalist globalization prompted frequent recalibrations of state power in ways that inaugurated new fields of socio-spatial practice, including supranational politics. Understanding the supranational as an unstable and contingent field helps to explain the fragility of supranational projects and their sensitivity to the more durable processes of nationalism and globalization in the long twentieth century.

By theorizing supranational politics through the more capacious framework of mediating spaces, this book highlights the dynamic interaction of multiple registers of spatiality and integrates them into a holistic historical analysis. "Supranationalism," as it is used here, denotes a broad array of discourses, representations, practices, and organizations articulated at a scale between the national and the global. The mediating spaces of Yugoslav socialism were conceived and realized in multiple spatial forms, from territorial polities (the Socialist Federative Republic of Yugoslavia, the European Economic Community), to loose arrangements of political alliance or cultural affiliation (the Non-Aligned Movement, the new Slavic movement), to imagined spaces confined to the register of cultural production (the Balkans, Pannonia, Central Europe, or the Third World). Each of these were very different kinds of spaces, but in historical practice their conceptual borders were porous: imagined spaces could inform the creation of territorial polities, territorial polities could be frustrated and realized only as loose geopolitical alliances, etc. Framing these diverse spatialities through the concept of mediating spaces allows us to sidestep a priori distinctions between the political and the cultural, just as it does teleological assumptions that might distinguish between those projects realized and those failed.[31]

The ability to include multiple spatialities within the same analytical concept is critical in order to bridge the material and discursive registers of spatial production. This methodological intervention is of particular importance for Eastern European history, where scholars inspired by the work of Edward Said have focused solely on the discursive production of space. This scholarship has foregrounded the ways in which Eastern Europe and the Balkans were culturally constructed in opposition to Western Europeans' own notions of civility, order, and enlightenment.[32] While this work has been essential in deconstructing the cultural coordinates of these imagined spaces, it overlooks the material processes that shaped this region and structured its uneven integration into global capitalist modernity. The concept of mediating spaces integrates the material and discursive orders of spatial production, allowing us to track the relationship between the historical formation of discrete political and economic geographies and their cultural representations.[33]

A final word of clarification is required to fully flesh out the concept of mediating spaces. "Mediation" comes from the Latin *mediari*, meaning to intervene, to get between or in the middle. In English it describes an intervention with the purpose of negotiating or bringing about a settlement between two parties.[34] As deployed in this study, the term refers specifically to historical attempts to craft political, economic, or cultural projects that could negotiate or reconcile the tensions between the national and the global. In this sense, they were premised on an acknowledgement that the integrative tendencies of globalization were at once inexorable and represented a potential threat to the sovereignty of small nation states. Spatial mediation could be deployed to a number of strategic ends: to strengthen small states' defences in a hostile global order; to integrate local markets into a larger economic zone; to consolidate regional actors the better to project their geopolitical influence on the international stage; to resolve complex national questions. These diverse strategic modes also meant that existing mediating spaces could themselves become subjects of mediation. The Yugoslav federation, for instance, was a supranational polity that was at various times conceived within a larger mediating structure, including a Balkan federation, Slavdom, or the Non-Aligned Movement. The supranational, in other words, could itself be structured into vertical gradations of scale.

SPATIAL SCALES IN GLOBAL INTELLECTUAL HISTORY

In its account of the history of Yugoslav socialist thought, this book moves beyond the national framework that has dominated the field to consider the European periphery through the lens of global intellectual history.[35] The projects of supranational unification that animated Yugoslav socialists in the long twentieth century were shaped by the dynamic spatial history of capitalist globalization. Beginning in the second half of the nineteenth century, as David Harvey notes, capital "became embroiled in an incredible phase of massive long-term investment in the conquest of space."[36] The final waves of European imperial expansion, the thickened interweaving of world markets, the proliferation of telegraph, railway, and shipping networks, all structured a new globally-integrated system that facilitated the mobility of people, capital, and ideas to a historically unprecedented degree.[37] A central characteristic of this era of globalization was the diffusion, adaptation, and consequent morphology of radical doctrines of anarchism, socialism, and anticolonial nationalism that captured the imagination of intellectuals, students, and workers around the world. While products of this global transformation, these movements also came to be its most ardent critics, challenging the asymmetries of power, wealth, and prestige to which global capitalist modernity gave rise. The formation of modern radical thought, therefore, is evidence of globalization's capacity to generate novel intellectual systems.

The global turn in intellectual history has prompted a renewed interest in the history of radical thought.[38] This research has tended to explain the formation of globally interconnected political cultures with reference to the expansion of networks of trade, migration, transport, and communication.[39] However, important though it was, the increase of human mobility was only one factor in the formation of a new global consciousness. Globalization also overhauled the epistemological frameworks through which radical ideas were formed, fostering a greater sense of the simultaneity and interconnection of events and struggles around the world and shaping new understandings of political affiliation.[40] Departing from the focus on human mobility, this book details an approach to global intellectual history that shifts attention to the globalizing processes of spatial integration and geographical differentiation that generated new modes of human experience and conditioned the formation of modern radical thought. Specifically, it highlights how the production and reconfiguration of spatial scales transformed the conceptual frameworks and political horizons through which intellectuals plotted strategies of revolution and reform.

The rapid and violent integration of the globe during the wave of capitalist expansion in the final decades of the nineteenth century inaugurated a new era in the history of the production of space. As Neil Smith has argued, this period witnessed a profound change in the spatial dynamics of capitalist modernity: "As long as the absolute geographic expansion of capital continues, the contradictions which riddle the social fabric of capital can be cast in aspatial terms; space can be treated as external. When economic development is turned inward toward the acute internal differentiation of geographical space, the spatial dimension of contradiction not only becomes more apparent; it becomes more real in that space is drawn closer to the core of capital. Accordingly, where crises develop in the general system of capitalist production, these are manifested ever more directly (and visibly) in the geography of capitalism."[41] The globalization of the late nineteenth century, that is, marked not just a quantitative expansion of the area of the world capitalist system, but also a qualitative transformation of its spatial logic. Whereas capitalist forces could previously envision their infinite expansion into the supposedly empty, external spaces of the world beyond their domination, they were now forced to operate within a fixed planetary boundary. With the enclosure of capitalist production, a logic of infinite expansion was replaced by one of infinite production and reproduction of internally differentiated spaces.[42]

Spatial scale was critical to the new logic of geographic differentiation, organizing the vertical hierarchies by which the production of space and socio-spatial relations were structured.[43] The processes that shaped the geographies of global capitalist modernity – deterritorialization and reterritorialization, the disaggregation and reconcentration of energies and resources, the construction, deconstruction, or circumvention of governing institutions – were organized and embedded within historically specific scalar arrangements. These arrangements, in turn, conditioned the experience of globalization, structuring horizons of possibility, framing political or cultural imaginaries, and delineating the paths by which strategies of social change were envisioned and pursued. Spatial scales and their historical production and transformation are, therefore, a crucial methodological framework for theorizing the dialogue between global and intellectual history.

The paradigm of national developmentalism that emerged in the final decades of the nineteenth century offers a useful illustration of how spatial scale shaped the conceptual terrain of capitalist globalization. Charles Maier has described what he terms "the territorial rescaling of state power" during this period, which led statesmen to reconceive of territory as "a source of resources, livelihood, output, and energy … a decisive means of power and rule."[44] Faced with the global depression of the 1870s, reformers in industrializing states like Germany and Japan reorganized capitalist production by consolidating and repurposing the regulative state. This new spatial paradigm measured geopolitical power according to a state's capacity for territorial development and expansion, thereby strengthening an impulse towards imperial conquest.[45] This was not simply a reassertion of the nation state in response to global pressures but a recalibration of state power in response to a changing global environment. What matters for the argument here is that this recalibration recast the conceptual, political, economic, and cultural geographies of global capitalist modernity.[46]

The scalar transformations of late-nineteenth-century globalization were multiform. This was a period, Deborah Coen notes, in which "the scalar imagination was restless."[47] In the inter-imperial space of Eastern Europe, where intellectuals wrestled with new configurations of nationhood and empire, federalism became the chief conceptual framework through which they came to terms with scale as a political problem. The proliferation of federalist projects that sought to rearrange the political geography of the region during the late-nineteenth and early-twentieth centuries speaks to the growing preoccupation with the rescaling of statehood in the age of globalization. Analyzing this phenomenon, Holly Case has insightfully argued that federalist ideas captured the imagination of the nineteenth century because they corresponded to an "attitude of interrelation that the age engendered."[48] Federalism's unification of political spaces, that is, aligned with an increasingly pervasive intellectual procedure to conceptually aggregate the numerous political, social, and diplomatic questions that became widespread during this era.[49] This conceptual aggregation had obvious resonance at a moment of deepening global integration. Federalist projects sought to make sense of and navigate a world of ever widening and interconnecting scales of experience.

One final note is required to clarify the use of the term "Yugoslav socialism" in the chapters that follow. By this I refer to those currents of revolutionary leftist thought that developed in the lands that became the Kingdom of Serbs, Croats, and Slovenes in 1918. Geographically, this encompasses the pre-World War I territories of the Kingdom of Serbia, Ottoman Macedonia, and the southern regions of the Habsburg Empire. In this sense, Yugoslav socialism does not imply a historical periodization: the book begins in the 1870s, fifty years before the first Yugoslav state was formed, and concludes in the 1990s, as socialist Yugoslavia began to disappear from the map. In addition, the book uses the term "socialism" to describe a variety of strands of far-left thought, including social democracy, communism, anarchism, and Marxist humanism. When the argument necessitates sharper clarity, I use more precise terms. Relatedly, throughout the book I will generally use the term "Serbo-Croatian" as shorthand for the language that is today more cumbersomely denoted as Bosnian/Croatian/Serbian.

SOUTH EAST EUROPE IN THE WORLD LITERARY SYSTEM

The imagined spaces that animated Yugoslav socialism – Europe, the Balkans, Slavdom, the Third World – were first and foremost modes of cultural mapping. Borrowing Henri Lefebvre's theoretical framework, we can think of these geographies as representational spaces:

that is, as spaces experienced through their discursive representations or images. Often articulated in the field of cultural production, representational spaces are the bedrock of the social imaginary and offer a means of challenging the alienating abstraction of space that Lefebvre identified with capitalist production.[50] Such cultural geographies were crucial to sustaining the affective dimension of supranational projects, providing the landscapes upon which national differences could be bridged and new communities envisioned.[51]

Yugoslav socialism's mediating spaces were most pronounced in the realm of cultural production, especially in the literature of left-wing writers. There were three reasons for this. First, these supranational projects were, more often than not, speculative. They required leaps of the imagination that could best be sustained by poetic works capable of weaving meaning and fostering new modes of identification. This gave writers and artists important influence in shaping the contours of the supranational imaginary, cultivating its geographies of affiliation and affective dimensions. Second, supranational politics was infused with an awareness of global hierarchies of power that resonated with writers' and artists' own anxieties regarding the cultural hegemony of the West. Yugoslav writers, especially those on the Left, were deeply concerned with what many perceived to be the homogenizing tendencies of cultural globalization. These concerns drew them towards the antagonistic geopolitical imaginary that informed the supranationalism of the socialist movement. The more intellectuals rescaled problems of cultural development to these supranational platforms, the more their work gave life to these imagined geographies.

Finally, the pronounced cultural expression of Yugoslav socialism's mediating spaces was a consequence of the vicious repression of the communist movement by the interwar royalist government. This repression drove socialists into the relatively safer realm of culture, imbuing literary debates with broader questions of political ideology and facilitating the cross-pollination of political and cultural geographies. The conceptual synergy between the political-economic and cultural registers outlasted the repression of the interwar years and would remain a key element of Yugoslav socialist thought throughout the twentieth century. From 1919 until the wars of the 1990s, therefore, the mediating spaces of Yugoslav socialism typically found more direct and sustained expression in works of literature. The intellectual history of this movement is entangled with the history of its literary politics and Yugoslavia's place in the world literary field.

The idea of world literature has long been understood to be closely bound up with the history of capitalist globalization.[52] Already in the middle of the nineteenth century, Marx and Engels had spoken of the ways in which the global processes of capitalist expansion and integration of world space would erode cultural boundaries and create a single world literature.[53] By the end of the twentieth century, however, it was clear to literary theorists that just as capitalist integration had produced deeply differentiated economic geographies, so too had it established cultural hierarchies that elevated the national literatures of the West over those of the rest of the world.[54] Distinct textual traditions of the non-European world were recast as particular manifestations of a universal literature that only became legible with the rise and cultural dominance of Western Europe. This paradigm of "world literature" simultaneously rendered Western Europeans the guardians and privileged interpreters of past textual traditions and the vanguard of literary modernity.[55]

Pascale Casanova's work offers an especially productive lens for interrogating the hierarchies of world literature. Drawing inspiration from world systems theory, Casanova conceives of world literature as a field of domination and dependence in which writers from the periphery of the literary world compete for the recognition of the Western metropoles (Paris, London, New York). Authorized to speak on behalf of a supposedly "universal" literary aesthetics, the critics and publishers of the metropoles control the entrance of peripheral texts into global markets and decide on their consecration into the canon.[56] Casanova explains the dominance of these metropoles with reference to the principle of the autonomy of literature from politics. It was in those countries where literature had broken free from the political field, she argues, that writers, critics, and publishers could claim to represent a supposedly universal set of values. As such, it was typically those countries with a longer, more established literary heritage that were able to dominate the field of world literature as it expanded over the course of the nineteenth and twentieth centuries.[57]

The development of South East Europe's national literatures was profoundly shaped by their incorporation into this Western-dominated literary field. Unlike the textual traditions of Asia, which became part of a world canon through their appropriation by European Orientalists, South East Europe's integration over the nineteenth century was actively pursued by native intellectuals who sought Western recognition of their national cultures.[58] This dependence on the metropoles of Western Europe continued to shape Yugoslav literature into the twentieth century, and produced a sense of being at once proximate to and excluded from the borders of Europe. As Zoran Milutinović observes of Serbian writers, for instance: "the more they were culturally and intellectually integrated into Europe, the more opportunities they had to encounter stereotypes about themselves, and the greater the likelihood that they would internalize the foreigner's gaze."[59] This complex layering of identities was a marker of South East Europe's semi-peripherality in the world system, its liminal position as both sharing certain attributes with the core – white, Christian, geographically European – while experiencing the political, economic, and cultural subordination of the periphery.[60] This condition of semi-peripherality led Yugoslav writers, including those on the literary Left, to oscillate between embracing and rejecting a European identity.

Yugoslav socialists were acutely aware of the relations of domination and dependence that characterized the world literary system. This recognition reinforced the intellectual synergy between the political-economic and the cultural. As socialist writers in Yugoslavia became convinced of the need to modernize what they perceived as their underdeveloped national literatures, they transposed the language of economic development into a cultural register. The ensuing discussions drew intellectuals into a range of debates that turned on wider questions relating to the competition between modernism and realism, the role of translation and canon formation, the relationship between political and literary engagement, and their respective nations' places in the system.

But if Casanova's theory elucidates the dynamics of literary domination and dependence, it neglects the scope of supranational literature. Indeed, spatial scale has gone mostly untheorized in world literary theory, where the foundational works have largely carried over the national-global binary they inherited from world systems theory.[61] Owing to the centrality of language in the formation of the nation state, Casanova sees literary cultures as extensions of struggles for national independence.[62] The strategies peripheral writers employed in their struggle for recognition, therefore, are interpreted primarily with reference to their nations' positions within an asymmetrical world literary system.[63] This narrow binary of scale presumes a topographical alignment of political and cultural geographies that fuses the interstate system and the field of world literature in a way that reinscribes the nation as the dominant – if not sole – scale of activity below the global.[64] Such a binary of world and nation flattens out the multiple scalar arrangements that have structured global capitalist modernity and its cultural forms.

Just as Yugoslav socialists argued for the creation of supranational formations to secure political sovereignty and economic development, so too did many challenge the uneven geographies of prestige by rescaling strategies of cultural modernization within more expansive mediating spaces.[65] By so situating their project of national cultural development within supranational configurations, Yugoslav socialists demonstrated a variety of strategies that elude Casanova's account. Writers like Krleža, for instance, evoked regional landscapes that cut across ethnic communities, decentering the nation as the privileged site of cultural experience.[66] Others, such as August Cesarec, projected political solidarity between regional geographies that they sketched not with reference to a common language or cultural inheritance but rather a shared peripheral position within global space.[67] Meanwhile left-wing modernists, like the surrealist Marko Ristić, challenged the linear temporality that coded Western European literatures as more "modern" and instead eroded global cultural hierarchies by flattening conceptions of historical time.[68] Identifying these diverse literary strategies and reconstructing their rich history can only be done by attending to the mediating spaces within which they were conceived.

THE SPACES OF YUGOSLAV SOCIALISM

The supranational politics of Yugoslav socialism have typically been explored through the prism of the national question. This is especially true for studies of Balkan federalism and Yugoslavism, which have primarily framed these projects as efforts to resolve nationalist rivalries perceived as endogenous to the region.[69] The ways in which wider European or global dynamics shaped reconfigurations of political, economic, and cultural space in South East Europe have been largely overlooked.[70] Turning its gaze outwards, this book instead interprets the pronounced spatial consciousness of Yugoslav socialists as a product of and a strategic response to the shifting patterns of capitalist globalization. In so doing, it rethinks the history of these mediating spaces beyond the framework of the national question and instead situates them in relation to a broader matrix of political, economic, and cultural concerns that preoccupied socialist intellectuals in Europe's southeast periphery.

A key challenge to this approach is disentangling the history of Yugoslavism as it was envisioned as a program of unitarist nation-building or as a project of supranationalism. Ideas of Yugoslavism date back to the 1830s, when the Illyrian movement promoted cultural affiliation among the South Slavs. Following the 1848 revolutions, a program of Yugoslav national unity began to find greater reception among South Slavic activists in the Habsburg Empire, most notably Josip Juraj Strossmayer and Franjo Rački. The growing influence of Serbia over the middle of the nineteenth century saw a further spread of Yugoslavism as Serbian leaders began to promote the movement for South Slavic unity as a means to pursue their own project of territorial expansion.[71] From the outset, however, there was a deep ambiguity in the idea of Yugoslavia: Was this future country to be conceived as a politically unified and culturally homogenized South Slavic nation? Or was it to be a supranational structure in which the constituent national communities – Serbia, Croatia, Slovenia, Bulgaria – would continue to pursue their distinct paths of development? The tension between these two visions would dominate Yugoslav politics throughout the twentieth century. Yugoslavism, in other words, has at different moments in its history been envisioned as a project of national integration or a supranational mediating space. To the extent that this book offers a history of the Yugoslav idea, its goal is not to parse nationalist from supranationalist visions, but rather to relativize projects of Yugoslavism within the wider intellectual history of supranational thinking in the region.[72]

The book begins in the period 1870–1914, the decades when radical socialist ideas took root in Serbia. Through a close reading of the work of the agrarian socialist Svetozar Marković (1846–1875), and the chief theorist of the Serbian Social Democratic Party, Dimitrije Tucović (1881–1914), chapter 1 reconstructs their visions of a future Balkan federation. It argues that these projects of regional unification were shaped by new spatial paradigms produced by the accelerating processes of global integration and the deepening geopolitical rivalries among the great powers in the decades before World War I. These paradigms informed the effort of early socialist thinkers on Europe's periphery to prioritize the formation

Introduction

of supranational political projects as a means of securing political sovereignty and economic development. Unlike nationalist conceptions of Yugoslavism, these projects of Balkan federalism envisioned a future territorial polity based not on a shared ethnicity but on a common political-economic geography whose contours were delineated by the dynamics of an emerging imperialist world system.

The fallout of World War I profoundly transformed the spatialities of socialist thought in South East Europe. The destruction of the multi-ethnic empires that had dominated the region and the formation of the first Yugoslav state redrew political borders, while the impact of the Russian Revolution and rise of anticolonial movements in Asia opened new horizons of affiliation. Serbian socialists now formed part of a wider Yugoslav communist movement that was itself part of a world revolution that promised to remap political and cultural geographies at both regional and global scales. The swift repression of this burgeoning movement, however, drove much of its more radical intellectual ambitions into the safer realm of cultural production. Chapter 2 argues that during these years of upheaval and repression, the supranational politics of Yugoslav socialism came to be most visibly represented by the revolutionary avant-gardes. Transposing political-economic ideas of Balkan federalism into a political-aesthetic register, these avant-gardes reimagined South East Europe as a territory on the Comintern's map of world revolution. Eager to promote their cultural independence from Europe, radical writers like Miroslav Krleža, August Cesarec, Ljubomir Micić, and Srečko Kosovel crafted a geopoetics to unite the diverse populations of their region and promote affiliations with revolutionary movements across Eurasia. This conceptual transposition would have long-lasting consequences for Yugoslav socialism, ensuring that literature remained a key site for articulating the movement's supranational imaginary throughout the twentieth century.

The contours of those spaces, however, were sensitive to the changing configurations of the global economic and geopolitical system. This became clear when the shock of the great depression rapidly eroded the Balkan geography that had animated the revolutionary avant-gardes. Chapter 3 tracks this erosion through the literary polemics that erupted over the years 1928–34. These polemics were driven by underlying disagreements among Yugoslav intellectuals regarding national cultural development and the appropriate scale at which this was to be pursued. While adherents of the burgeoning social literature movement argued for integration into the Soviet-aligned proletarian literary movement, its opponents on both the Left and the Right insisted on more locally rooted, territorial strategies that they pursued at both national and supranational scales. The chapter demonstrates that the cultural debates that animated the literary Left around the world during this period – for example, the tension between creative freedom and political commitment or between literary modernism and realism – were, in Yugoslavia, infused with rivalries over the scalar politics of cultural development. These literary polemics therefore reflected a dislocation of the mediating spaces through which Yugoslav socialists sought to interface with an increasingly unstable global order.

Chapters 4 and 5 highlight the powerful influence of Soviet geopolitics on the contours of Yugoslav socialism's mediating spaces following the Stalinization of the Yugoslav Communist Party (KPJ) over the 1930s. If early ideas of Balkan federalism had been conceived as a mode of resistance to European hegemony, the years of the Popular Front (1935–39) witnessed a dramatic volte-face on the Yugoslav Left as communists embraced the idea of European belonging. Chapter 4 argues that this cultural reorientation towards Europe was set in motion by the Soviets' efforts to promote an antifascist alliance with France and Britain following the rise of Hitler. In line with this geopolitical alliance, communists across the continent were exhorted by Comintern leaders to defend a shared European civilization from fascist barbarism. Inspired by the ideas of the Hungarian Marxist Georg Lukács, writers on the Yugoslav Left aligned their national literatures with an increasingly Eurocentric conception of world literature. These theories, in turn, promoted a sense of belonging to a wider European cultural space. During this period, in other words, Yugoslav communists jettisoned their anticolonial Balkanism in favour of an antifascist Europeanism.

The outbreak of World War II precipitated a shift in Soviet geopolitical strategy and prompted officials in Moscow to seek an alliance of Slavic nations against Nazi Germany. During the war and in its immediate aftermath, the new Slavic movement fostered ideas of cultural affiliation and political solidarity as a means to promote Soviet influence throughout Eastern Europe. Chapter 5 argues that this Slavic ideology found especially fertile soil among Yugoslav communists, as it provided a conceptual framework for the party's policy of Yugoslav federalism. A supranational Yugoslav state, that is, was conceived as part of a wider Slavic geography of kinship that was understood to stretch from the Adriatic to the Pacific. Such a vision, however, was in sharp tension with the project of Balkan federalism that had enjoyed a revival during the war, and seemed to be close to realization as communist parties seized power across much of South East Europe. To reconcile the rival mediating spaces of Slavdom and the Balkans, Yugoslav intellectuals presented their country as a vanguard linking the Balkans to a wider Slavic socialist world. This ideological script helped to promote the prestige of the Yugoslav leadership across the region, which in turn provoked Stalin's suspicion that Yugoslavia posed a threat to Soviet hegemony.

The Tito-Stalin split of 1948, which saw Yugoslavia expelled from the Eastern bloc, again scrambled the scalar arrangements of Yugoslav socialism. With the dissolution of the new Slavic movement, and any plans for a Balkan federation abandoned, the quest for a new supranational configuration propelled Yugoslav socialists to an alliance with the Third World. From the mid-1950s, Yugoslavia became a leading member of the Non-Aligned Movement. Chapter 6 examines the cultural dimension of this reorientation towards the countries of Asia, Africa, and Latin America. During the 1950s and 1960s, Yugoslav intellectuals devised a modernist paradigm of cultural one-worldism through which they fostered cultural affiliation with the countries of the Third World. This paradigm was rooted in the idea of a common, longue durée humanity, and guided Yugoslav efforts to challenge global cultural hierarchies and familiarize local audiences with their newfound geopolitical allies. Through translations, travelogues, and cultural exchange, these efforts gave rise to what the chapter terms an "emergent geography of non-alignment."

Yugoslav socialism's Third World geographies, however, ran aground during the 1970s and 1980s as the economic turbulence of these decades gave rise to a new mode of radical globalization. The rolling crises of the 1970s – from the breakup of the Bretton Woods system in 1973 to the Volcker shock of 1979 – transformed the geographical coordinates of Yugoslav socialism, reorienting the country from a declining Third World and towards a rapidly integrating Europe.[73] Chapter 7 argues that this spatial reorientation produced new and competing cultural geographies that found expression in increasingly vitriolic polemics over the concept of Central Europe in the late 1980s. Eager to emphasize their belonging to an imagined Europe, critics renounced affiliations with the Third World and repudiated the anti-imperial politics that had been so central to Yugoslav socialist thought. The violent breakup of Yugoslavia and the celebrated integration of Europe, the chapter argues, were deeply interconnected events whose roots can be found in the global spatial reconfigurations of the 1970s. The wars of the 1990s decimated any remaining hopes for a revival of Yugoslav socialism, bringing it to a somber historical conclusion.

In her classic work of cultural criticism, Maria Todorova argued that the efforts to imagine the Balkans over the nineteenth and twentieth centuries constructed a lasting image of the region as violent, backwards, and barbaric. "Balkanism," as she termed this quasi-orientalist discourse, saturated the geography of South East Europe with these pejorative connotations to shore up a complementary image of Europe as rational, progressive, and civilized.[74] Departing from Todorova's account, this book excavates a very different intellectual history: one in which "Balkan" served not as the slander of Western observers but as a slogan of anti-imperialist and anticapitalist resistance.[75] The chapters that follow recover the emergence of this Balkan project in the late nineteenth century, trace its conceptual transpositions, morphologies, and decline, and interrogate its relation to those rival or adjacent geographies – Yugoslav, European, Slavic, Third Worldist – that structured alternative political and cultural affiliations. Disengaging from the dialogue with Said's *Orientalism* that has so long dominated the field, this book interprets these imagined spaces as counterhegemonic strategies generated by and in response to South East Europe's integration into global capitalist modernity.[76]

1

"A Cramped and Rusty Building"
Globalization, Serbian Socialism, and the Limits of the Nation State, 1870–1914

> Serbia is a state which, if it wants to live, must enter into the flow of European industry and civilization. If it does not do so, it will be sentenced to a completely peripheral and stationary life and will always have to be defending itself from a flood of European industry and civilization ... They have succeeded in making the world their market and are beginning to overcome the hindrances of time and space ... The waves of European trade are already lapping at the borders of Serbia.
>
> Nikola Pašić, Letter to the Minister of Education, 1872

I

On 3 October 1911, Italian forces opened fire on the Ottoman town of Tripoli. The attack marked the beginning of Italy's military campaign to seize the Ottoman Empire's last remaining territory in North Africa.[1] Italy's invasion was a further step in the kingdom's efforts to realize its colonial ambitions in Africa, thereby earning it a place among Europe's great powers. But for many observers the invasion of Tripolitania was a risky move, threatening to accelerate the disintegration of the Ottoman Empire and destabilize the balance of power in Europe. Critics worried whether Italy might serve as an irredentist model to the small national kingdoms of South East Europe which, having recently secured their independence from Istanbul, now looked to expand their territories at its expense. They were right to worry. On 8 October 1912, the kingdoms of Serbia, Montenegro, Bulgaria, and Greece declared war on the empire. The ensuing Balkan Wars would see the Ottomans lose the bulk of their European territory.[2] In the increasingly interconnected world of early-twentieth-century geopolitics, Italy's actions in North Africa had immediate ramifications in South East Europe.

The invasion of Ottoman Tripolitania did not just fuel the avarice of South East Europe's ruling elites; it also sparked waves of protest in solidarity with those North Africans who resisted the occupation of their lands. On 23 October 1911, social democrats throughout South East Europe called for mass demonstrations condemning Italy's invasion. Across Serbia, Bulgaria, and Greece, as well as several cities of the Ottoman Empire, thousands of protesters joined rallies demanding Italy's withdrawal. During these demonstrations, protesters reflexively drew parallels between the European conquest of North Africa and the dangers their own region faced. They pointed to the annexation of Bosnia and Herzegovina by the Habsburg Empire three years earlier as proof that South East Europe lay within the scope of Europe's appetites. While the ruling elites of the region might have seen in Italy a model to emulate, social democrats saw yet another imperial power that threatened their aspirations for national sovereignty, economic development, and peace.

During the protests of October 1911, social democrats leveraged the public's outrage over Italy's aggression to promote their demand for the unification of South East Europe. In the Ottoman city of Thessaloniki, for instance, a multi-ethnic crowd passed a resolution demanding the formation of a Balkan federation. This, they argued, was the only way to "enable the nations of the Balkans to ensure total development of culture and political independence."[3] Meanwhile, in the Serbian capital of Belgrade, the social democrat, Luka Pavićević, made a similar argument to a hall full of protesters: "Today Italy is doing to Tripoli what will be repeated to Albania tomorrow ... [T]he proletariat of the Balkans must find a radical means for its own protection ... a Balkan Democratic Federative Republic."[4] Similar demands for a Balkan federation echoed throughout the region.

These demands raise a curious question: Why did an Italian invasion of North Africa elicit calls for the political unification of South East Europe? What prompted social democrats to speak in terms of *geographic regions* rather than, say, nations or states? These questions indicate a new spatial consciousness that began to infuse radical political cultures over the late nineteenth and early twentieth centuries. This consciousness not only perceived the increasing

The Limits of the Nation State 27

interconnection of events around the world but also began to think in terms of geopolitical and geoeconomic zones.[5] Understood against this background, the invasion of Ottoman Tripolitania reverberated so widely precisely because the Italian Peninsula, North Africa, and South East Europe formed a triangular constellation within a broader geopolitical matrix that structured the conditions of political thought in the era of high imperialism. As this chapter argues, this new experience of global space made it possible for radical intellectuals to sketch the terrain of, ascribe political salience to, and perceive a commensurability between, distinct geographic regions. It was within this new spatial framework that ideas of Balkan federalism took root and proliferated during the first wave of capitalist globalization.

This chapter reconstructs the federalist imaginary of socialist thought in Serbia from the 1870s through to the outbreak of World War I. It focuses on two figures: the early agrarian socialist, Svetozar Marković (1846–1875) and the chief theorist of Serbian social democracy, Dimitrije Tucović (1881–1914). Through close readings of their work, it argues that the reconfigurations of global space during the final decades of the nineteenth century made possible new understandings of South East Europe as a discrete geography. Specifically, it shows how territorial paradigms that emerged through the process of capitalist globalization and the territorial erosion of the Ottoman Empire prompted radical intellectuals in South East Europe to conceive new forms of supranational unity. These regional geographies not only informed Serbian socialists' strategies for securing political self-determination and economic development, but also provided the conceptual framework for envisioning affiliations with anticolonial movements in Africa and Asia. Projects of regional federation, therefore, served Serbian socialists as a means for reimagining the Balkans not as a backwater of Europe but as a vanguard in the struggle against European imperialism.

II

The formation of a radical political culture in Serbia was a reaction to the entwined processes of state development and economic integration into a globalizing European capitalism over the late nineteenth and early twentieth centuries. These processes were, in turn, shaped by a shift in the spatial dynamics of the global system from what we will term a paradigm of circulation to one of concentration.

This shift in spatial paradigms was observed in the efforts of states to recalibrate their relationship to the global economy, the interstate system, and their own territories. If, during the boom years of the 1850s–60s, the spread of classical liberal models had promoted greater openness to and exchange with global circuits of capital, the onset of recession in the 1870s undermined faith in the deterritorializing logic of free market capitalism.[6] In these new circumstances of heightened competition and instability, states began to refortify national or imperial borders, to consolidate their rule over the territories these borders delineated, to standardize their administrative systems, to coordinate their economic forces, and to centralize political power.[7] While this spatial reconfiguration has typically been viewed through the experience of those second-tier powers that sought to challenge British hegemony, first and foremost Germany, it also had a profound impact on the small nations of South East Europe where it delimited the pathways for state building. Although from the 1840s to World War I the Serbian political class pursued a program of territorial expansion, the different articulations of this program were shaped by the global shift in spatial paradigms. Because it was against these expansionist programs that Serbian socialists devised their projects of regional federation, we must first reconstruct the history of Serbian state development in the wider context of nineteenth-century globalization.

In the middle decades of the nineteenth century, European states became more tightly linked through expanding networks of trade and finance. This expansion was driven, in part, by the British Empire's promotion of free market policies. Over the 1850s, Central European states moved towards the reduction of tariffs within their own borders, while international agreements increasingly sought to open major waterways, such as the Danube, to free international shipping.[8] The Cobden-Chevalier Treaty of 1860 marked a tipping point and in the two decades that followed, free (or freer) trade agreements proliferated across Europe, drawing in the multi-ethnic empires of Central Europe and, with them, the peripheral economies of the Balkans.[9] World space came to be understood as an expansive network of circulation, while economic development was presumed to be tied to states' openness to these global circuits.[10]

The critical stages of Serbian state development occurred during this period of commercial expansion and were shaped by its spatial dynamics. The modern Serbian state had its origins in the peasant insurgencies of 1804–15 that laid the foundation for a semi-autonomous principality in the Ottoman Empire. From the early 1840s onwards, Serbia's incipient political class, aided by a network of professionals from the Habsburg Empire, began to construct the modern Serbian state. Modernization, for this elite, meant the alignment of their new political institutions with those of the Habsburg Empire's expansive bureaucracy.[11] These mid-century state builders also wove their country into the expanding circuits of European trade, abolishing import-export restrictions, eroding the power of the guilds, standardizing the currency, and fostering free market policies.[12] These reforms facilitated the spread of Austrian credit into Serbia, further weaving the country's agrarian economy into the wider networks of European finance.[13] When the Kingdom of Serbia's independence was recognized at the Congress of Berlin in 1878, the tiny country was already integrated into the expanding circuits of global capitalism.

Serbia's integration, however, had been achieved through its incorporation into the economic periphery of the Habsburg Empire. An overriding concern of the country's political class was to escape this dependence. Their solution was a policy of territorial expansion, extending the country's borders to carve out a greater Serbia. In the middle third of the nineteenth century, Serbian expansionism was organized around the spatial paradigm of circulation. The 1844 *Načertanije (Draft)* of the young Interior Minister Ilija Garašanin, for instance, envisioned the Serbian principality as a pole of attraction for the South Slavic peoples of the region.[14] The expansion of Serbian influence, in Garašanin's view, was not to be achieved through force of arms but by public relations, building up a positive image of Serbia, fostering ties with neighbouring nationalities, and promoting Serbia as a centre of regional commerce. His plan emphasized the need for Serbia to open its borders to the wider region, the better to "incline" local populations towards her, and to establish strong commercial interests in the Adriatic.[15] This early project of state building resonated with the free market boom of the middle of the nineteenth century. Serbia, in Garašanin's plan, was to grow its influence by exploiting new networks of exchange, transport, and communication, opening itself up to expanding commercial circuits, and positioning itself as a nexus of trade between Europe and the Ottoman Empire.

The global depression of the 1870s inaugurated a second phase of capitalist globalization characterized by a marked realignment of the relationship of states to the global economy. When the prolonged nature of the depression eroded faith in the ability of markets to self-regulate, the British-led liberal order began to face a wave of defections and challenges to its hegemony. In 1879 Germany became the "epicenter of the protectionist counter-movement," imposing sweeping tariffs that triggered similar responses among neighbouring states.[16] A new spatial paradigm came to animate those economies that sought to compete in this more hostile global environment. This paradigm promoted the concentration of resources within national or imperial territories, the condensing of industrial and financial interests and their closer coordination with the state, the integration of civil society, in particular working and peasant classes, into the body politic, and new technologies of inclusion and exclusion designed to regulate the mobility of people and goods.[17]

This spatial paradigm of concentration posed sobering questions about the viability of small states like Serbia. From the 1880s onwards, the country witnessed its vital export trade with the Habsburg Empire constrict as Vienna threw up tariffs, eventually culminating in the infamous Pig Wars of 1906–08.[18] The rapid growth of foreign debt left Serbia increasingly dependent on European financial institutions, and compromised its economic sovereignty.[19] The country's expanding railroads were a stark symbol of its subordination, intended as they were not to facilitate Serbian trade but to link the Habsburg and German empires to Mediterranean and Middle Eastern markets.[20] Finally, the threat of Russian, Italian, or Habsburg expansion into South East Europe, made all the more real by the latter's annexation of Bosnia and Herzegovina in 1908, risked scuttling Serbian plans for territorial expansion. While the new spatial paradigm of concentration offered industrializing powers like Germany or Japan a means of state building and economic development, it accentuated the weaknesses of small agrarian states like Serbia. In the late nineteenth century, Serbia's political sovereignty seemed compromised by its crippling trade dependence, its growing foreign debt obligations, and the constraints imposed by the appetites of its more powerful neighbours.

No group expressed the newfound urgency of Serbia's plight better than the People's Radical Party and its charismatic leader, Nikola Pašić. Although a onetime student of the socialist Svetozar Marković, over the 1880s Pašić abandoned the Balkan federalism of his mentor and embraced Serbian nationalism. Pašić believed that the only way for Serbia to survive in the hostile global environment was its transformation into a modern state capable of mobilizing its population and resources with an eye to national economic development. To achieve this, he deployed a rhetoric of greater Serbian nationalism that could integrate the marginalized peasant population into the state and legitimate a project of aggressive territorial expansion.[21] Where Garašanin had seen the Serbian diaspora of the Balkans as a valuable resource for linking the principality into wider commercial networks, Pašić instead bemoaned the "dispersal" of the Serbian nation and insisted on the need for its political unification through territorial consolidation.[22] In the name of defending the Serbian peasant from foreign competition, Pašić pushed protectionism, attacked the railroads as symbols of foreign exploitation, and demanded that the state pursue a broad program of social welfare. Responding to the crisis of Serbian state building at the end of the nineteenth century, Pašić's populism was intended to concentrate the energies of the nation and dedicate them to a program of social improvement, economic development, and territorial expansion.[23]

The preceding account of Serbian state building serves our study of socialist thought in two ways. First, it demonstrates how the global spatial reconfigurations of the nineteenth century shaped the contours of political thought in Europe's southeast periphery. Specifically, the shift from a paradigm of circulation to one of concentration led to different ways of envisioning the nation and delimited different pathways of state building. This shift also informed the development of socialist thought in Serbia, marking the chief conceptual distinction between early socialist ideas of Balkan federalism and the Marxist theories of the fin de siècle social democrats. Second, these projects of Serbian territorial expansion were the foil against which socialists theorized their own projects of supranational unification. Although socialists diagnosed the same sets of problems as their nationalist rivals – imperial domination, trade dependence, and foreign debt – they proposed a very different strategy of territorial aggregation in the form of a supranational federation. As they assessed the asymmetries of the emerging global system, Serbia's socialists sought to craft a mediating space that could shield their region from the pressures of European imperial power and foster a project of local economic development.

III

The late 1860s and early 1870s were a period of enthusiasm for anarchist and socialist ideas in South East Europe. In these years a generation of young intellectuals, including Svetozar Marković in Serbia, Hristo Botev in Bulgaria, Zamfir Arbore in Romania, Panagiotis Panas and the Democratic Club of Patras in Greece, drew from the ideas of Proudhon, Bakunin and, later, Marx and Engels.[24] They were also inspired by the Paris Commune, the federalist experiments of the First Spanish Republic, and (less radically) the Swiss cantonal system, each of which offered captivating models for the revolutionary transformation of South East Europe.[25] For these early radicals, the goals of national self-determination, popular democracy, and social egalitarianism were bound up with the reorganization of the region's political-economic space.

The first major theorist of radical thought in Serbia was Svetozar Marković. An eclectic thinker, Marković's radicalism developed in the 1860s during his studies in Russia and Switzerland, where he was introduced to the populism of Nikolai Chernyshevskii, the anarchism of Proudhon and Bakunin, and the revolutionary socialism of Marx and Engels.[26] Enthused by Russian populism, committed to what he saw as the modern social sciences of Marxism and anarchism, and impressed by the democratic federalism of Switzerland, his work was the first to see the goal of Serbian national liberation as tied to a wider social revolution in South East Europe.[27]

Marković's thought was animated by his commitment to the simultaneity of national liberation and social revolution. The Serbian people's struggle for independence from the Ottoman Empire, he believed, needed to be pursued in tandem with the peasantry's emancipation from landlords, state officials, and usurers. This insistence on the simultaneity of national and social liberation coloured his critical view of nationalist movements in the Habsburg Empire that grounded their claims in the language of historical states rights.[28] These projects, Marković argued, would only lead to the creation of new aristocratic privileges at the expense of the people.[29] Any genuine project of national liberation would need to realize full social and economic equality and would, therefore, challenge the ruling elites of whatever nationality. This view also put him at odds with the Serbian political class and its policy of national expansion. Already in 1868, while studying in St Petersburg, Marković attacked

The Limits of the Nation State

the project of greater Serbia, which he characterized as a politics of conquest and bureaucratic domination. Such a policy, he argued, would leave the Serbian people "more impoverished and depleted than they are now."[30]

Marković also pointed to the limited scope of Serbian nationalism in the context of what he believed would be a regionwide social revolution. This paucity of nationalism was best evidenced in the antagonism between the expansionist aims of the Serbian state and the project of Bulgarian national liberation in the lands of "Southern Serbia" (today's Macedonia):

> The politics which delimit this "great and strong" Serbia,
> arouse suspicion in our natural allies on the Balkan Peninsula,
> the Bulgarians, and force them into a hostile camp. And so long
> as they are in this hostile camp, we cannot be free. From this
> follows the obvious point that Serbian national politics must
> be directed at the general liberation of the Balkan Peninsula.
> "Greater Serbia" is a cramped and rusty building from which
> it is not possible to defend Serbian national interests, just as
> a "Greater Bulgaria" would not secure the interests of the
> Bulgarian people. Only a Serbian-Bulgarian union (understood
> as established on the free will of both people) can secure the
> future of both people and of the whole of south-Slavdom.[31]

In this early effort to answer the national question, Marković articulated a vision of a future Balkan federation as a mediating space. The defence of Serbia's national interests, he argued, could not be undertaken at the scale of the nation state, which was too weak to challenge the will of its imperial neighbours. Instead, national liberation had to be secured at a supranational scale, in the form of a regional federation that could mediate exposure to the geopolitical pressures of the era. In the 1860s, Marković's vision of a future Balkan union was still confined to a South Slavic alliance of Serbia, Bulgaria, and Croatia. In this sense he had yet to go beyond the ethnic logic of pan-Slavism. But within a few years, his work would already demonstrate a sensitivity to the limitations of ethnic logics of community in South East Europe.

Marković's magnum opus was his 1872 *Srbija na istoku* (*Serbia in the East*). The book was an extended discussion of the history of the modern Serbian state, from the revolutions of 1804–15 through to what Marković characterized as their betrayal by the Obrenović dynasty and the new political class. The central thread of this book was the fate of the *zadruga*, the traditional institution of the Serbian peasantry that had formed the backbone of social and economic life in the countryside for centuries. These communes were made up of several extended families who collectively owned property and were largely self-sufficient. Almost certainly drawing from Herzen's interpretation of the Russian *obshchina*, Marković offered an idealistic portrayal of the *zadruga* as the kernel of a new social order based on egalitarianism, popular democracy, and the free association of producers.[32] It was precisely the centrality of the *zadruga* to Serbian national culture that led him to see the project of national liberation and social revolution as so closely bound together.[33]

Although, Marković contended, the *zadruga* had been critical to the peasant uprisings of the Serbian revolution, in the years that followed 1815 its popular spirit was stamped out. The subsequent development of the Serbian state was undertaken by a modern political bureaucracy that eroded the radical democratic ethos of the revolution.[34] This process of political modernization was, for Marković, synonymous with the principality's integration into the circuits of global capitalism. During the 1830s and 1840s, the new political class set out to align the country's emerging political institutions with those of the Habsburg Empire, leading to the destruction of the *zadruga*. New property laws and systems of taxation based on European norms of private property fragmented the collective way of life of the countryside.[35] Pressures on the peasantry to participate in the cash economy made them more dependent on trade and undermined traditions of self-sufficiency.[36] The subsequent growth of a wealthy elite of bureaucrats raised demand for luxury goods from Europe, which destroyed local craft industries.[37] Even at this early stage of Serbia's integration into Europe, Marković foresaw the dangers of trade dependency and foreign debt.

The Serbian elite's desire to emulate modern Europe was, for Marković, a sad irony. So eager were they to civilize the Serbian peasantry that they failed to see that European civilization had reached a developmental impasse. The revolutions of 1848 had highlighted the social dislocation at the heart of the modern capitalist world.[38] Meanwhile, the *zadruga* seemed to have shielded Serbs from the illnesses European reformers diagnosed in their own societies: its mutual aid avoided the alienation of modern urban life; its

The Limits of the Nation State

self-sufficiency prevented the crises of overproduction that had beset Western Europe's market economies; its egalitarianism avoided problems like pauperism or prostitution that plagued Europe's major cities.[39] While Marković conceded that Serbian society should adopt the advanced technologies and scientific theories of Western Europe, it could do this without embracing its bureaucratic political structures and capitalist markets. Rather, the natural evolution of the Serbian nation should be to expand the *zadruga* system, reorganizing the state as a series of interconnected communes.[40] By reviving the *zadruga* and introducing the latest scientific theories from Europe, Serbs could pursue an alternative path of development, skipping the stage of capitalism and becoming the most socially progressive state in Europe. The periphery could overtake the core.[41]

To achieve this, however, the Serbian revolution would have to expand throughout the multi-ethnic population of the Balkan Peninsula. And here Marković saw the national character of the Serbian state as an inherent limit on its revolutionary capacity. If the scale of this upheaval was to exceed the borders of a single nation state, then the political community would need to be radically rethought. For Marković, the answer lay in a Balkan federation: "Even if the Serbian state today were to unite the other Serbian lands, what future would such a small state have? The Balkan Peninsula is a mosaic of different peoples. Largest are the Bulgarians; then come Serbs and Greeks almost equally, then Turks, Arnauts [Albanians] and Cincars. Which of these peoples will agree to be 'annexed' to the Serbian monarchy? ... The Serbian people have no way out other than a revolution on the Balkan Peninsula; a revolution, which would end with the destruction of all the states that today prevent these peoples from uniting as free people and equal workers; as an alliance of municipalities – counties – states – as they see fit."[42]

Here Marković pushed beyond his original proposal of a South Slavic union to articulate a more ambitious project that could bring together the diverse ethnic groups of the region. This vision of a Balkan revolution bore traces of the spatial paradigm of circulation. Regional federation was to unfold at a subnational scale, proceeding granularly through the free association of peasant communes, a perspective in line with anarchist theories of the time. Borders in the Balkans were to be eroded and exchange facilitated not by expanding markets but through co-operation, reciprocity, and mutual aid. The states of the region were to be dissolved and the

Balkans remapped at the grassroots. Despite his critique of capitalist modernity, Marković's Balkan federalism was organized around notions of decentralization and exchange that resonated with the spatial dynamics of free market globalization in the middle third of the nineteenth century.

IV

In 1875, at the age of twenty-eight, Marković died after a bout of tuberculosis brought on by his imprisonment by the Serbian state. His early adaptation of European radical ideas to the context of South East Europe, however, would have lasting influence in Serbian politics. Although by the mid-1880s Marković's followers in the People's Radical Party had abandoned his key ideas, a dedicated core of socialists carried his legacy over into the new century, where it shaped the development of Marxist thought.[43] The generation of Serbian social democrats that came of age in the early twentieth century adapted Marković's Balkan federalism for the era of high imperialism. These intellectuals were preoccupied with Serbia's peripheral position in an imperialist world system and the ways it compromised the country's economic development and political independence. A federation of Balkan states was necessary, they insisted, to secure an economy of scale that could underwrite the sovereignty of the small nations of the region. This was a politics of Balkan federalism framed through the new spatial paradigm of concentration that had come to shape capitalist economies in the decades following the depression of the 1870s.

It was in the work of Dimitrije Tucović that this new iteration of Balkan federalism was most thoroughly developed. Tucović was born in 1881 and first became interested in socialist ideas during his high school years in the town of Užice. In addition to the work of an earlier generation of Serbian socialists, most centrally that of Marković, the young Tucović's thought was influenced by the ideas of the German socialist Karl Kautsky, and his newspaper, *Neue Zeit*. When the Serbian Social Democratic Party (SSDP) was founded on 20 July 1903, Tucović became a leading member, organizing workers' clubs, editing party publications, translating the works of French and German socialists, and coordinating contact with social democratic organizations in Bulgaria, Ottoman Macedonia, and the Habsburg Empire.[44]

The SSDP marked a break with earlier iterations of radical politics in Serbia because it took as its role model not the Russian populist or French radical movements but the Marxism of the German Social Democratic Party. Owing to their hegemony within the Second International, German social democrats exercised an inordinate influence on socialist parties in South East Europe.[45] Under this influence, the SSDP jettisoned Marković's earlier anarchist ideals of the peasant commune and embraced the idea of the industrial working class as the active subject of socialist revolution.[46] Perhaps more than his contemporaries, Tucović reflected this commitment to German social democracy. Since his teenage years he had closely followed the theoretical discussions in Kautsky's *Neue Zeit*, and over the winter of 1907–08 he studied in Berlin, where he experienced firsthand the intellectual ferment of the German movement and struck up a personal correspondence with Kautsky.[47]

In his theoretical writings, Tucović strategized the project of Balkan federation as a mediating space within which the small nations of South East Europe would be shielded from the pressures of imperialism and pursue an alternative path of modernization and development. Specifically, he envisioned this project as resolving three sets of problems the region faced. First, a Balkan federation would help to promote local economic development by consolidating the fragmented national economies into a single regional market. Second, it would defend against the depredations of Europe's empires. Finally, it would resolve the region's complex national question. In line with the turn towards state-led projects of national development then being implemented by reformers in industrializing powers like Germany or Japan, Tucović imagined a future Balkan federation as a territorially expansive polity capable of defending national sovereignty and economic development in a competitive world system. Unlike these contemporaneous projects, however, this vision was not to be achieved at a national but rather a supranational scale.

The problem of economic development was a recurring motif in Tucović's writings on Balkan federalism. Only through the political unification of the small states of South East Europe could the region's fragmented markets be integrated and provide an economy of scale for local production. This perspective was indebted to the theories of imperialism then being developed around the Second International by intellectuals like John Hobson, Rudolf Hilferding, and Rosa Luxemburg.[48] These theories sought to explain why the global expansion of capitalist production did not homogenize world economic space, as Marx and Engels had initially predicted, but maintained certain regions in conditions of underdevelopment. This was a vital strategic question for socialists in the agrarian states of South East Europe. The formation of a local proletariat hinged on the industrial development of the region's economies. If these economies could not be presumed to follow an uninterrupted path of industrialization, what became of their prospects for socialist revolution? Although Tucović never provided a convincing answer to this question, he recognized its critical importance. In a 1912 speech, he characterized these uneven dynamics as an "everyday war" between the Balkans and Europe, a war "of our primitiveness with European development, of our craftwork with their industry, of modern traffic with non-modern."[49] The geographic unevenness of globalization had stalled the normative process of capitalist development, giving rise to what Tucović characterized as a conflict of geographic zones: the Balkans versus Europe.

Tucović conceived of the Balkans as a single economic whole whose interdependent parts had been disrupted by "artificially drawn borders."[50] Writing in the immediate aftermath of the Balkan Wars, he pointed to the fate of Ottoman Macedonia as an example of the economic irrationality that the territorial fragmentation of this "one and indivisible" region had brought about.[51] While the Ottoman Empire had presided over this space and fostered the realization of its economic growth, its defeat in the wars of 1912–13 had led to the "destruction of a whole" whose violent and destabilizing consequences could only be resolved "in a *new whole of a higher form.*"[52] The Hegelian language that Tucović used suggested that he understood this process of regional consolidation as a dialectical evolution, in which the fragmentation of an earlier territorial unity was a necessary but transitional moment in its more complete integration at a higher scale. The underlying point, however, was that the Balkans were a spatial totality, one that had been artificially divided by local nationalisms and foreign imperialism. The task of social democrats was to construct a supranational state whose scale corresponded to the underlying economic unity of the region's geography.

Only a Balkan federation could offer Serbia and the other small states of South East Europe a path of economic development. To this end, Tucović and other theorists in the Serbian and Bulgarian social democratic movements demanded a Balkan customs union

The Limits of the Nation State 39

that could, like the *zollverein* of the German states, lay the basis for future political unification of the region.[53] Such a customs union, Tucović argued, would allow Serbia to "transfer the weight of its trade from foreign markets to local" and would, in turn, promote the economic flourishing of the region as a whole. Permitting himself a flight of high modernist fancy, Tucović imagined what this alternative economic policy might achieve: "Establishing rational forestry, regulation of the rivers, irrigating the dry districts, draining the swamps, expanding agricultural cooperatives, multiplying the number of schools, raising the moral and intellectual (level of the) peasant, the state will create the elementary conditions for the modern exploitation of natural wealth."[54] That Tucović's fantasy turned on a program of state-led development highlights the influence of the new spatial paradigm of concentration that animated the era.

Tucović also argued for Balkan federalism as a geopolitical strategy to defend the small nations of South East Europe from the imperial interference of European powers. The first decades of the twentieth century witnessed a series of political and military convulsions brought about by the erosion of Ottoman power. The intrusions of Habsburg and Russian troops in Ottoman Macedonia following the 1903 Ilinden Uprising, the Habsburg Empire's annexation of Bosnia and Herzegovina in 1908, the 1911 invasion of Tripolitania by Italy, and the Balkan Wars of 1912–13 all highlighted the growing risk of military violence in the era of high imperialism. Tucović was especially provoked by the annexation of Bosnia and Herzegovina, which, he thought, foreshadowed the broader "colonization" of South East Europe. Writing in the aftermath of the annexation, he argued that the subsequent economic exploitation of Bosnia and Herzegovina evoked clear parallels with Europe's imperial conquests in Asia and Africa: "Ought we really to appeal to Europe? To the Europe whose humanitarianism towards enslaved peoples has been demonstrated by the latest events in China, India, Persia, Morocco, etc.? ... A hundred years ago, the French revolution carried the ideas of freedom and human rights to the peoples of the East; fifty years ago Western Europe proclaimed the principle of national freedom; today, the entire European bourgeoisie is feeding the awakened peoples of the East with bullets, people she herself revolutionized with her own goods, her own technology, and her own political ideas."[55]

The annexation had brought Bosnia and Herzegovina into the unfortunate community of "enslaved" nations, a community that

Figure 1.1 | The Balkans, 1910. Participants of the First Balkan Social Democratic Conference.

included British-controlled India, Russian-dominated Persia, and French-occupied Morocco. By evoking the recent past of Asia and Africa, Tucović sought an image of South East Europe's immediate future. This comparative procedure demonstrates how the global spatial integration of the late nineteenth century reshaped perceptions of world space, allowing equivalences to be drawn across vast distances.[56] These equivalences, in turn, made possible the expression of new solidarities between the peoples of South East Europe and those of Asia and Africa. By inscribing the Balkans into the geography of the world imperialist system, Tucović pioneered a set of political affiliations that was to have a long life in Yugoslav socialism in the twentieth century.

Opposition to foreign conquest also served as a rallying point for Tucović to promote ideas of political solidarity among the different peoples of the Balkans. While the region's population might have been divided by nationality, language, or religion, they shared a common condition of subjugation to European empires. Desperate to secure the diplomatic and military support needed to pursue their territorial expansion, the ruling elites of South East Europe had become proxies of their European backers, fragmenting the region into rival spheres of great power influence.[57] This humiliating situation of quasi-sovereignty could only be resolved, Tucović insisted, through the political unification of the Balkan states into a common federation that could assert the region's collective sovereignty.[58] The local bourgeoisies, who had become mere adjuncts of their foreign backers, could not be relied on to achieve this goal; it could only be realized by the region's social democratic movements. In other words, because social democracy was the only political movement genuinely independent of international financial and military networks, it was the sole movement capable of action at a genuinely regional scale.

A final reason for which Tucović prioritized the formation of a Balkan federation was that only such a supranational state could resolve South East Europe's complex national question. The national question was a vexed one among the theoreticians of the Second International, especially as it pertained to the geopolitics of South East Europe. Ardent internationalists, like Rosa Luxemburg and Leon Trotsky, opposed any concession to the politics of nationalism, which they saw as antithetical to working class unity. Meanwhile, in the Habsburg Empire, Austro-Marxists like Karl Renner and Otto

42   Mediating Spaces

Bauer proposed to reconcile aspirations for national autonomy with the deeper economic integration of the empire by deterritorializing nationality.[59] Both of these views clashed with the perspective of socialists from South East Europe, who insisted on the legitimacy of small nations' demands for territorial sovereignty.[60] This perspective was strengthened in 1908, when Kautsky himself argued that the role of social democracy in South East Europe was to lead the struggle for national independence and regional unification.[61] While Kautsky had little insight to offer Serbian or Bulgarian socialists, who drew from their own local traditions of federalist thought, his interventions legitimated the Balkan federalist idea within the Second International.[62]

Tucović undertook his most in-depth analysis of the national question in his 1914 work, *Srbija i Arbanija* (*Serbia and Albania*). The book used a study of the Albanian national struggle as the stepping stone for a broader analysis of the national question in South East Europe. The immediate context for the book was the outbreak of interethnic violence in Kosovo and Macedonia following their conquest by Serbian forces in the Balkan Wars. Tucović had witnessed the Serbian army's occupation of these provinces and had been horrified by the massacres and ethnic cleansing of their Albanian populations. *Srbija i Arbanija* was an effort both to defend the Albanian national struggle from its detractors in the Serbian public and to advance the argument for Balkan unification as the only viable resolution to the region's national question. The violence of 1912–13, Tucović argued, was a consequence of the Serbian ruling elite's strategy of territorial expansion. To secure their economic independence from the Habsburg Empire, this elite had sought to expand their state's borders into Macedonia, the emerging heartland of Ottoman capitalist development, and through Kosovo in order to carve out a path to the Adriatic.[63] These aspirations for territorial expansion, however, clashed with the emerging national consciousness of the local Albanian populations. The violence of Serbian forces against these populations had deepened interethnic distrust and, in their desperation, the Albanian national leadership had turned to Italy and the Habsburg Empire for aid. Far from securing Serbia's interests against the ambitions of European imperialism, therefore, its occupation had only given these powers a deeper foothold in the region.[64]

In contrast to what he termed the Serbian bourgeoisie's "policy of conquest," Tucović set out to show that the only means for securing

The Limits of the Nation State

Serbia's national sovereignty lay in "the political and economic community of all the people of the Balkans, not excluding the Albanians, on the basis of full democracy and equality."[65] This was the only policy that could resolve the overlapping claims to multi-ethnic territories like Kosovo or Macedonia.[66] Territorial partitions along ethnic lines would undermine both the viability of nation statehood and the economic development of the region as a whole.[67] The regions over which the Balkan states had gone to war should not be further fragmented but integrated as autonomous entities within a future Balkan federation. Only this policy could facilitate the cultural and commercial flourishing of their populations and neutralize nationalist rivalries in the region.

Tucović's dream of regional unification would remain unrealized. Less than a year after his magnum opus was published, the young socialist again found himself in the midst of battle. In the aftermath of the Sarajevo assassination, his party had worked hard to forestall the rush to war.[68] In the conflagration that ensued, a quarter of the Serbian population lost their lives, and the ranks of the nascent social democratic movement were decimated. On 20 November 1914, Tucović was killed in the Battle of Kolubara. His death marked the closure of the early history of Serbian socialism. When the movement was reborn in the aftermath of the war it spoke a different language, one informed by the ideas and vocabularies of the Russian Revolution and set within the wider borders of the first Yugoslav state. The early intellectual developments of Serbian socialism, however, ensured that ideas of regional unification would remain of critical importance in this new political landscape. Indeed, the problem of how to nest the nation within supranational projects and the effort to reimagine the spatial contours of those projects and map their cultural geographies would continue to animate the thought of Yugoslav socialists throughout the twentieth century.

2

Balkanizing Europe
The Early Comintern and the Yugoslav Avant-Gardes, 1918–26

It is disgusting to chase Europe. I want us to be the first Balkan dam to European degeneracy. Because to wish for the Europeanization of the Balkans nowadays, during Europe's twilight, at a time when the Balkanization of Europe is at hand, means running after one's own tail. Along with the Russian Revolution, the cultural emancipation of the Balkans from Europe is an issue of the utmost significance for us today.

Ljubomir Micić, *Anti-Evropa*, 1926

I

On 1 December 1918, the Serbian Prince Regent, Alexander Karađorđević, declared the formation of the Kingdom of Serbs, Croats, and Slovenes: the first Yugoslavia. The new state faced enormous challenges. The destruction of the war had brought about economic collapse, leaving hundreds of thousands without homes or livelihood. Disease had ravaged much of the population. In the north of the country, thousands of deserters from the Habsburg army joined with armed bands of peasants to expropriate their landlords.[1] In the far south, ethnic minorities in Macedonia and Kosovo had risen up in arms against their inclusion in the new country.[2] Peasant uprisings, mutinies, and insurrections meant that huge swathes of the state's new territories lay in a political vacuum, out of the reach of Belgrade's proclaimed authority. Into this maelstrom, hundreds of former prisoners of war returned from revolutionary Russia, bringing with them the visions, ideas, and skills of the international communist movement.[3] The chaotic situation in the new kingdom strongly favoured the rise of the Socialist Workers Party of Yugoslavia (communist), which had been formed in April 1919. The party quickly became an active presence in workplaces, campuses, and military units and by November 1920, it boasted 65,000 members and was the fourth largest electoral force in the country.[4]

The upheavals brought about by World War I and the Russian Revolution radically rearranged the spatial contours of the wider region of South East Europe. The collapse of the multinational empires that had ruled over large parts of the region led to a process of territorial fragmentation and nationalist reconsolidation in the years that followed the war.[5] At the same time, this region became a site for rival projects of geopolitical mapping, as Western powers sought to contain the spread of Soviet influence into Europe.[6] This geopolitical competition gave rise to two rival political-cultural geographies: the first, a restorationist map that cast Europe as a site of civilization and order under threat from a fanatical and rebellious Asia; the second, a revolutionary map that sketched Europe as a site of imperial decline and bourgeois decadence and Asia as a source of renewed political energies and hopes. These rival geographies framed the transformations of political radicalism in the Kingdom of Serbs, Croats, and Slovenes in the immediate postwar years and reworked the earlier legacy of Balkan federalism.

In December 1920, responding to the rising threat of the communist movement, the Yugoslav Constituent Assembly passed a controversial decree that banned the party and its affiliate organizations. To justify this extraordinary measure, which inaugurated an authoritarian turn that would continue to characterize the Yugoslav state throughout the interwar period, the assembly evoked their country's place within a restorationist map of Europe. In April 1921, Minister of the Interior Milorad Drašković defended the repressive new laws with reference to the threat communism posed to the continent as a whole: "Communism or Bolshevism is a great social movement, the greatest history has known up to now. Greatest by the surface which it covers and by the number of people it has infected. Against this movement two fronts have come into existence: the European and the Asian. Europe has adopted an unfriendly and defensive attitude and has begun to fight it. Asia is looking at it as if it were a discovery, a new social light, and has opened its doors to it. We have, gentlemen, placed our country on the side of Europe."[7] In harmony with the West's geopolitical remapping of Eastern Europe as a cordon sanitaire, Drašković evoked a language of ideological contagion to justify his government's political crackdown. Europe had to quarantine itself from the infection of the communist East, and the new Yugoslav state was the first line of defence. Where once Serbian nationalists had evoked their role as the defenders of Christian Europe from the Islamic world, Drašković now called on Yugoslavs to defend capitalist Europe from communist Asia.

From its headquarters in Moscow, the newly formed Comintern also envisioned the remapping of South East Europe not as a barrier but as a beachhead. Ruled over by fragile governments, riven through with national conflicts, and crippled by dependence on Western markets, the small nations of the region seemed to be a weak link in European capitalism's chain of defence. As hopes for proletarian revolution in the West faded and the Comintern turned its attention to anticolonial struggles in Asia, communists in South East Europe sought to reinscribe themselves on the new map of world revolution. Speaking at the Comintern's 1920 Congress of the Peoples of the East, for instance, the Bulgarian communist Nikolai Shablin assured the gathered representatives that "we, the Balkan peoples, are also oppressed and enslaved just like you by the world bandits of Britain and France. Your struggle means our liberation as well."[8]

Conceiving South East Europe as a bridge between revolutionary Asia and restorationist Europe gave the region a distinct geographical coherence that, in turn, called for a revolutionary strategy tailored to local conditions. Drawing on earlier social democratic ideas of Balkan federalism, the Comintern advised its affiliates to coordinate their activity at a regional scale.[9] In January 1920, representatives from the Yugoslav, Bulgarian, Greek, and Romanian parties met in Sofia to form the Balkan Communist Federation (BCF). The new organization was to strengthen political ties in the region with an eye to the creation of a future supranational state.[10] Initially based in the Bulgarian capital of Sofia, where it was tolerated by the radical government of Aleksandar Stamboliiski, the overthrow of his regime in June 1923 forced the BCF to relocate to Vienna, where it began publishing the multilingual newspaper, *La fédération balkanique*.[11]

Although ideas of Balkan federalism animated the day-to-day work of communists in the Kingdom of Serbs, Croats, and Slovenes, the geographic contours of this regional project were clearest in radical leftist

Figure 2.1 | The Balkans, 1920.

culture, particularly the work of the revolutionary avant-gardes. This was a sharp departure from the pre-World War I period, when social- ist ideas of regional unity were limited to the political economic realm. In the early 1920s, the revolutionary avant-gardes transposed Balkan federalism from a political economic to a political aesthetic register, using new modes of cultural experimentation to reimagine the space of the Balkans. In their work, the Balkans were evoked as a geopoetic figure: a symbolic geography upon which ideas of anti-imperialism, socialist revolution, and literary radicalism converged.

There were three reasons for this conceptual transposition. First, Balkan federalism was a utopian project, chiefly an effort of the imagination. While proponents of Yugoslavism could lean on ethnic logics of community, Balkan supranationalism required a speculative leap. How, after all, was a strategy of political economic development going to be conceived as a project for the revolutionary transformation of everyday life? How were communists to envision a new Balkan man and woman, a new Balkan community? Such questions of revolutionary world-building were better answered by the utopian impulses of the avant-gardes than the day-to-day politi- cal organizing of activists.

Second, ideas of Balkan federalism found such pronounced expres- sion in the realm of cultural production because they resonated with the revolutionary avant-gardes' critiques of Western European cul- tural hegemony. In interwar Yugoslavia, avant-garde intellectuals across the political spectrum were preoccupied with their place in the global hierarchy of cultural prestige. While they participated in the artistic and literary networks that spanned the continent, many were simultaneously critical of their perceived subordination to Western Europe.[12] For these intellectuals, the antagonistic geopolitical imagi- nary that underpinned socialist ideas of Balkan federalism helped to map their own aesthetic rebellion against European hegemony. This was especially the case for intellectuals on the cultural Left, who contested Yugoslavia's place in a restorationist Europe and instead sought to reorient towards the revolutionary East.

Finally, the cultural transposition of Balkan federalist ideas was a result of the sudden repression of the burgeoning communist move- ment by the Yugoslav state in December 1920. Within months of this decision the party, its trade unions, and peasant organizations were outlawed, communist-aligned publications were banned, and many of the party's leading members were imprisoned.[13] In this

The Early Comintern and the Yugoslav Avant-Gardes   49

repressive climate, one of the few avenues left open to communist intellectuals was that of culture. While the party's political newspapers were driven underground, cultural organs, especially those concerned with literature and art, were generally given greater leeway by the government. Unsurprisingly, then, many intellectuals on the Far Left turned their attention to questions of culture in the years that followed.[14]

This chapter traces the contours of the mediating space of the Balkans as it was articulated in the work of three figures of the Yugoslav revolutionary avant-gardes: the journal *Plamen* (*The Flame*), edited by Miroslav Krleža and his comrade August Cesarec (1893–1941); the zenitist movement, led by the Croatian Serb Ljubomir Micić (1895–1971); and the work of the Slovene constructivist poet Srečko Kosovel (1904–1926). It pays close attention to the ways in which these intellectuals crafted the symbolic space of the Balkans to mediate between globally diffused ideologies and local revolutionary traditions. As Steven Lee has observed, the Bolshevik revolution's alignment of socialism, anticolonialism, and aesthetic experimentation presented a worldview through which "marginalized minorities could suddenly envision themselves at the forefront of both modernism and revolution."[15] In 1920s Yugoslavia, this worldview found expression in reimagining the supranational space of the Balkans as a site of revolution.

II

Miroslav Krleža and August Cesarec were perhaps the most influential communist intellectuals of interwar Yugoslavia. In addition to working together on *Plamen*, *Književna republika* (*Literary Republic*), and *Danas* (*Today*), journals which were essential to the local transmission of revolutionary political and aesthetic ideas, they were articulate defenders of the Far Left in the repressive climate of the 1920s. Krleža, in particular, was widely considered a leading light of Croatian literature, with his dramas staged in the national theater and his poetry receiving broad critical acclaim. Although his opposition to the Stalinization of the Comintern would eventually lead him to break with the communist party over the 1930s, he was credited for introducing a younger generation of Yugoslavs to revolutionary politics.[16] Krleža and Cesarec first met in 1905 while attending gymnasium in Zagreb, where they joined the Yugoslav youth movement. In 1908

Krleža left to attend cadet school, and was later enrolled in the Military Academy in Budapest. During these years of military discipline, his political activism gave way to a love for literature: he devoured Baudelaire, Tolstoi, Ibsen, and Strindberg, as well as the Hungarian poets Sándor Petőfi and Endre Ady and the Serbian poets Aleksa Šantić and Vojislav Ilić.[17] He also became a student of Schopenhauer and Nietzsche, the latter's radical iconoclasm paving the way for his later appreciation of Marx and Lenin.[18] Buoyed by fantasies of Yugoslav unity, when the Second Balkan War broke out he was quick to offer his services to the Serbian military. However, upon surveying the battlefields of Macedonia and witnessing the militarism, violence, and chauvinism – the same "politics of conquest" that Dimitrije Tucović would condemn in *Srbija i Arbanija* (*Serbia and Albania*) – Krleža's nationalism began to sour.[19]

Returning to Zagreb, Krleža threw himself into literature. His first collection of poetry had just been published to great acclaim when World War I erupted. The war was a spiritual crisis for Krleža, tearing apart the confidence he once had in the cultural superiority of Europe: "this was all of us," he later bemoaned, "blind poetic devotees of an imaginary Europe, which snatched us up in the storm of 1914 and plunged us into its frenzied cavalcades never to return."[20] "Europe" no longer appeared as a symbol of social progress or cultural achievement; it was the roar of shells and the stench of gas. The experience of the war would inspire him to undertake a radical negation of the ideal of Europe in Croatian culture.

While the teenage Krleža became more politically disillusioned, his friend Cesarec's commitments only hardened. He remained a dedicated activist in the Yugoslav youth movement, going so far as to join the illegal underground. His involvement came to a head in 1912, when he received a three-year jail term for his participation in the attempted assassination of ban Slavko Cuvaj.[21] In prison he read the work of Tucović and other Serbian and Bulgarian social democrats, eventually embracing both their socialism and Balkan federalism.[22] The war further radicalized him. When the communist activist, Vladimir Ćopić, returned from the Soviet Union in 1918 to form the first party cell in Croatia, both Cesarec and Krleža quickly joined.[23]

Even before the new kingdom had been established, the two writers had begun work on a journal that would position Yugoslavia within the expanding horizons of the Soviet revolution. The first issue of *Plamen* was released on 1 January 1919 and the journal continued a fortnightly schedule of publication until it was banned in August of the same year.[24] It had an electrifying effect on the Yugoslav intellectual Left, fusing the radical aesthetics of expressionism with the revolutionary politics of communism. In so doing it helped to translate the ideas of Bolshevism into a local vernacular. The journal was also one of the first avant-garde publications to transpose the politics of Balkan federalism into an aesthetic register. In their contributions to *Plamen*, Krleža and Cesarec evoked the poetic contours of the Balkans in order to foreground a history of imperial dominance and to disarticulate the region from a wider European space. This negation of Europe was, for the two young writers, the precondition for the cultural emancipation of the small nations of the Balkans.

The effort to purge Croatian culture of an idealized Europe was announced in the very first issue of *Plamen*, in Krleža's manifesto-like "Hrvatska književna laž" (The Croatian Literary Lie). The article was an irreverent piece directed against the leading lights of contemporary Croatian literature, who Krleža attacked as merely "aping" European trends and perpetuating Croatia's cultural stagnation in the "most swamp-like of swamps."[25] For him, the representatives of the so-called Croatian "renaissance" of the fin de siècle were little more than "Austrian generals in white dolamas and Hungarian aristocrats in Illyrian tunics"; that is, Croatia's historical oppressors dressed in the mawkish costumes of a rural folk dance.[26] The image captured Krleža's anticolonial critique of the Croatian literary establishment, which, even as it attempted to lay claim to some kind of authentic national tradition, did so using the literary forms and cultural models of its European masters.

Rejecting such idealized portrayals of the nation, Krleža instead sought to show how the very history of Austrian and Hungarian rule had become engrained in the consciousness of the Croatian intelligentsia: "To feel oneself disappear beneath the foot of the Black-Yellow Emperor, that is what it means to be a Croat."[27] It was not that the Habsburgs had wiped out an earlier, more authentic, more dignified Croatian culture, but that Croatian culture itself had been forged under the boots of imperial rule, and from this history it could not be parsed. Indeed, the various efforts of Croatian literati testified to the continued domination of European cultural values, which were inappropriate and inapplicable to contemporary Croatian reality. Against the idyllic village landscapes of his contemporaries, Krleža insisted on a literature that would remain true to the abject reality of life on Europe's periphery. The task of the writer was not to escape from the barbaric and backward Balkan existence but to immerse oneself in it, to confront it in all its horror and decay, and to faithfully reproduce it through new literary forms.

Krleža depicted the masses as abject beings. In this sense, he was as opposed to the patriotic peasant of the national romantics as he was to the socialist ideal of the heroic worker. In Krleža's early writings the people are hideous, barbaric, and abject, unresponsive to the ideals of nationalism: "What does all of this matter to that gigantic, blind animal which is called The People, and which lies motionless in its primary sleep on our waters and mountains just as it has lain for centuries ... What does this luxurious literature matter to these monsters of people? One day, will not this colonial, barbaric and rabid monster, with a thirst for life, squeeze all of its diseased ulcers to expel the pus? It will squeeze them, lose its breath from the pain of squeezing them, and those who think that lectures about national revolutionary health and heroism will be a salve to this decadent wound, will be mistaken."[28] This revolting image of the monstrous people would come to dominate Krleža's writings throughout the interwar period and owed far more to his reading of Nietzsche than to his commitment to Marx or Lenin.

But even within this schema, the writer's communist convictions shine through. Krleža's abject people bear far greater resemblance to Nietzsche's concept of the Dionysian than they do to the contemptible herd. Indeed, Krleža identified the herd with the bourgeois intellectuals whose efforts to co-opt and marshal the energies of the oppressed Balkan masses into civilized European culture would come to naught. The people, on the other hand, represented the unpredictable and destructive forces that would bring about Nietzsche's transvaluation of values: "The People are not given to the reviving of phrases. The People does not mean an empty editorial, nor a militant song, nor a literary career. Today The People can mean only one thing: the shipwreck of all the old values. Today The People means the experience and knowledge that the boat, which will discover the New, needs to be much more solidly built than all those that have previously sunk. The will to build new boats, that is what The People means today!"[29] The people as the "shipwreck of all the old values" linked Krleža's left-Nietzschean goal of an "activist negation" of the existing world to a populist conception of the general will; the people were at once a violent nihilistic energy – barbaric, unpredictable, and monstrous – and also the conditions of possibility for something new, the ground upon which a new civilization had to be built.[30]

The violent force of the Balkan peasantry could not be corralled by Western or Central European cultural models but required something more sturdy, a boat that would not sink in the Dionysian storm. To that end, in the final sections of the essay Krleža identified a "Yugoslav cultural line" which began with the bogumil heretics of the Middle Ages and continued through the fifteenth-century pan-Slavic missionary Juraj Križanić and the nineteenth-century nationalist poet Silvije Strahimir Kranjčević.[31] The choice to locate the origins of this cultural lineage in the bogumils highlighted Krleža's pan-Balkan vision. The bogumils were a dualist Christian sect that spread throughout South East Europe in the tenth and eleventh centuries and resisted the rule of both Byzantium and Rome. In Krleža's work they symbolized a regional resistance to foreign domination. In the modern era this impulse was embodied by the communists. Their advent promised to unite the Balkans, allowing the region to emerge as a force that could "build an arch of salvation over ... Byzantium and Rome ... Europe and Asia ... rich and poor."[32]

Like the fin de siècle social democrats of Serbia, Krleža and Cesarec evoked the Balkans as a space through which to negotiate their small nation's position within global horizons. Following 1917, these horizons were configured through the project of international communism. In the poetic editorial "International Aeterna" for instance, the authors celebrated the new spirit of communist internationalism, clearly situating themselves not in Croatia or Yugoslavia but the Balkans: "We greet this fiery dawn, which is born in your hearts, we from the Balkan darkness cheerfully welcome you: *zdravo!*"[33] This same orientation, through which South East Europe came to mediate the national and the global, was also deployed in Cesarec's "Annamu na Balkanu" (Annam to the Balkans). In this short poem the author staged an imaginary exchange between the Balkans and Indochina, "the two easternmost peninsulas of Mother Asia and Daughter Europe."[34] The poem combined orientalist images – bamboo huts, rice fields, peacock tails, turbans, azure seas, and geishas – with a sense of anticolonial solidarity between the two regions:

54 Mediating Spaces

Through centuries we have been a sweet morsel to the jaws of beasts stronger than ourselves.

Buddha and Confucius and Christ have been forgotten; bayonets have fallen over us like the masts of a pirate ship, in our bodies the victors have stabbed their iron banners and all have shot their lightening into us; we have been oarsmen on pirate ships, in chains – and we are still![35]

Evoking the space of Indochina allowed Cesarec to establish an equivalence between these two geographic zones, bringing to the fore their shared history of foreign rule and exploitation to construct an image of the Balkans as a colonial subject of Europe. Essential to this reimagining was a new experience of global space that could structure affiliations and solidarity between South East Europe and South East Asia. In this anticolonial worldview, the most salient spatial scale was not the national but rather the regional; a Balkan space whose contours became more pronounced the more one pulled back to adopt a global perspective.

On the pages of *Plamen*, Krleža and Cesarec sketched a political geography that divided Europe into a northwest imperial core and a southeast periphery. While their youthful goal of Yugoslav unity had been achieved by the formation of the new kingdom, the project of national liberation remained unrealized, with the country's cultural elite still subservient to European hegemony. National liberation, they maintained, had to be folded into a wider project of regional emancipation, which was possible only as part of the radical efforts to remap global space following the Russian Revolution.

III

The revolutionary remapping of regional space was a central theme in the Zagreb-based journal *Zenit*. *Zenit* was the brainchild of Ljubomir Micić and his wife Anuška Micić (aka Nina-Naj), which they produced in close collaboration with Micić's brother Branislav Micić (aka Branko Ve Poljanski), the French-German poet Yvan Goll, the Serbian film critic Boško Tokin, and the Prague-based Dadaist Dragan Aleksić. The monthly magazine quickly became a node in the international network of avant-garde journals in the 1920s, carrying work by artists, writers, and theorists from around the world. Like *Plamen*, it also translated revolutionary political and cultural ideas from around Europe into a Yugoslav context. While international in scope, *Zenit*'s central focus was to interrogate the Balkans' distinct experience of modernity and to challenge its subordination to European hegemony. To this end, Micić and his comrades developed a language of aesthetic primitivism that reimagined the Balkans as a site of barbaric cultural renewal and anti-Western political revolt.[36]

The first issue of *Zenit* was released in Zagreb in February 1921, and it continued to be published regularly in the Croatian town until Micić relocated to Belgrade in 1924. Although it fetishized the revolutionary rhetoric and political symbolism of the Bolshevik revolution and was inspired by the aesthetic experimentation then emerging from the Soviet Union, *Zenit*'s main collaborators were not part of the communist movement. This is a curious fact as *Zenit*, more than any other publication of the interwar avant-gardes, most energetically engaged the revolutionary Balkan federalism promoted by the Comintern.

Just like Krleža, the writers of *Zenit* set out to destroy what they saw as their compatriots' naïve and humiliating idealization of Europe. Bemoaning Yugoslav audiences' devotion to European trends, Micić concluded that "[t]his undoubtedly stems (as does everything else) from the fact that our country and all of its people without exception ... stand in an inferior position towards Europe (a slavish dependence)."[37] Ve Poljanski went further, bitterly summarizing the Balkans' crippling sense of inferiority in the slogan: "Where the whole of Europe goes, there the slobbering Balkans shall follow."[38] Both brothers saw the Balkans as tailing behind Europe, willingly being led by a civilization it naively felt to be superior. Such an attitude, they maintained, was a pathetic idealization that had perverted their region's vital cultural heritage.[39] In this sense, there are important parallels between the primitivist aesthetic project of *Zenit* and the earlier political theories of Svetozar Marković. Just as Marković inverted the developmental map of Europe, demonstrating that the traditional peasant commune could become the kernel of a modern, communist society, so too did zenitism embrace the apparent backwardness of the Balkans as a vehicle of its cultural modernization.

Against the outdated cliché of Europe as the home of civilization, culture, and progress, *Zenit* called for the Balkans to break with Europe and look to the rising revolts of the East:

> The Balkans is a BRIDGE between East and West.
> It must be free at its most eastern points to allow flow and
> passage through us into the West, and closed at its most western
> points against the West.
> Let us be the guard against the West!
> To you – those to come – this Zenitist conception!
> A new generation of poets – artists – youth –
> of people let them carry revolt in their hearts and the idea:
> East against West![40]

Playing on the well-worn metaphor of the Balkans as a bridge between East and West, Micić sought to alter the flows between its two poles.[41] No fluid space to pass back and forth, the Balkans were to act less as a bridge than a weir that could facilitate a unilateral flow from the dynamic and revolutionary East to the exhausted and reactionary West. Furthermore, consider how this imagined geography completely reversed that of Milorad Drašković, cited above, which depicted Yugoslavia as the easternmost point of Western civilization. For its political and cultural elites, Yugoslavia was Europe's bulwark against Asia. For Micić, however, the Balkans were the guard protecting the East from the West. Indeed, more than a mere "guard against the West," Micić reimagined the Balkans as an insurrectionary force leading an international revolt against Europe:

> Close your doors West – North – Central Europe –
> *The Barbarians are coming!*
> Close them close them but
> > we shall still enter.
> We are the children of arson and fire – we carry *Man*'s soul.
> And our soul is *combustion*.
> Combustion of the soul in the creation of *sublimity*
> > ZENITHISM
> We are the children of the Sun and the Mountains; we carry
> > *Man*'s spirit.
> And our spirit is the life of the cosmic *unity* held together by *Love*.
> We are the children of the *Southeast barbaro-genius*.[42]

Revolutionary politics and primitivist aesthetics are woven together here. Like Krleža's depiction of the people as a diseased and ulcerated monster, Micić's language of barbarism transposes the political-

The Early Comintern and the Yugoslav Avant-Gardes   57

economic categories of backwardness and underdevelopment into an aesthetic register. For Micić, primitivism was not a condition to be overcome – it was the foundation for a spiritual and cultural revival whose scope was both regional and global. Precisely because it had not been incorporated into an exhausted, corrupt, and decaying Europe, the Balkans survived as a powerful force that could contribute to a new, revolutionary world civilization.[43]

Of course, *Zenit*'s efforts to portray the Balkans as a primitive space beyond Europe were largely performative. In fact, the movement's aesthetic primitivism was a profoundly European impulse and was in dialogue with similar trends in European modernism at the time. Since at least the 1890s, European artists intent on pushing beyond dominant aesthetic models sought inspiration from non-European cultures they deemed "primitive" or uncivilized. In the process they often underwrote the cultural and racial hierarchies of European colonialism.[44] As Timothy Brennan has noted, however, aesthetic primitivism could also take on an explicitly anticolonial character.[45] Yugoslav zenitism formed part of this trend and often reflected its ambiguities. At times, for example, *Zenit*'s efforts to use primitivism to project affiliations with non-European cultures reinforced racist tropes. Yvan Goll, for instance, called for the destruction of European civilization, which had "estranged us from primeval nature," and proposed instead a return to "the Barbarisms of Mongolians, Balkanites, Negros and Indians."[46] The racial underpinnings of this vision should be clear enough. Goll was proposing a new art that drew from the reservoirs of "primordial" racial types. What is fascinating though, is that he presents the peoples of the Balkans as such a race. In other words, despite a very recent history of intense ethnic conflict among the nation states of the Balkans, Goll could none the less posit the idea of a common Balkan community that belied these shallower divisions, albeit one grounded in a racial metaphysics. Geography, here, was translated as race.[47]

The primitivist celebration of the Balkans as a vanguard against Europe at times folded back in on itself, giving rise to *Zenit*'s messianic belief in their capacity to save Europe from itself. This was not conceived as a revival of European civilization but, rather, a claim that Europe's salvation required the destruction of its cultural hegemony. It was this belief in the redemptive destruction of Europe that lay behind Micić's idea of the "balkanization of Europe."[48] Just as Krleža imbued his monstrous people with the promise to realize

Nietzsche's transvaluation of values, the "balkanization of Europe" was a project to sweep away the old, torpid, and lifeless culture of Europe by unleashing the young, vital, and barbaric energies of the Balkans.

Zenit's balkanization of Europe was envisioned as one moment in a global process of transformation that would abolish cultural hierarchies and decentre Europe from the stage of world history. Throughout their tracts, zenitists remapped world space in such a way as to disrupt and reconfigure the asymmetries of the existing world order. In his *Manifest zenitizma* (*Manifesto of Zenitism*) of 1921 for instance, Micić plotted new constellations of world space through an imaginary flight of his new man figure, the "barbaro-genius":

> There – on Šar Mountain, on the Urals – stands
> THE NAKED MAN BARBARO-GENIUS
> Fly above the Šar Mountain, above the Urals and the Himalayas –
> Mont-Blanc – Popocatépetl – above Kilimanjaro!
> We are now floating high high above the bodily spheres of
> the Globe.
> Break, bound chains! Fall, suburbs of big and plague-ridden
> Western European cities! Shatter, window panes of gilded courts,
> High towers of National Stockmarkets and Banks![49]

Here world space is flattened, and Europe dislodged from its place atop a hierarchy of cultural prestige. Micić's barbaro-genius traverses a world reconfigured horizontally, leaping across its highest peaks in a journey that takes in Europe, Asia, Central America, and Africa. Europe does not disappear from the world map, rather, the cultural hegemony that had elevated it above the other civilizations of the world is to be undone. The destruction of imperial, bourgeois Europe will create the conditions for the rebirth of a revolutionary European culture open to the world.

In the new world order called for by the zenitists, the Balkans would stand as an independent geopoetic entity, finally freed of its subservience to Europe. Envisioning a future Balkan community necessarily meant wrestling with the problem of the region's linguistic diversity. As members of a small nation historically on the margins of more assertive imperial cultures, zenitists inherited a tradition that ascribed profound importance to the writer as a preserver of national language. This tradition, however, was in tension with the supranationalism of

The Early Comintern and the Yugoslav Avant-Gardes 59

their Balkan project, which necessarily undermined the hegemony of a single national language. Although at times the movement adopted the symbols of Serbian or Yugoslav nationalism, it also mobilized the experimental techniques of the avant-gardes to disrupt linguistic nationalism. Along with other offshoots of Dadaism, *Zenit* invented absurdist or onomatopoeic words that undermined standardized language.[50] It experimented with Esperanto to transcend linguistic differences and foster global affiliations.[51] It attacked the philological nation through its policy of non-translation, publishing texts in Serbo-Croatian, Slovene, Hungarian, German, Czech, French, English, Flemish, Russian, Bulgarian, Italian, and Spanish, as well as Esperanto. This radical polyglossia served Zenitism's broader political-aesthetic project of imagining the supranational space of the Balkans as a geopoetic community.

Of all the avant-garde movements to emerge in the Kingdom of Serbs, Croats, and Slovenes in the years immediately following World War I, *Zenit* most confidently envisioned cultural modernization through the consolidation of regional space. More than any other movement, they sought to give cultural expression to the project of Balkan federalism, deploying a primitivist aesthetics to recode the perceived backwardness of the Balkans as a source of barbaric vitality. The movement provided an important reservoir of concepts for reimagining the space of South East Europe, its consistency as a geopoetic community, and its relation to both Europe and Asia through the language of revolutionary politics and avant-garde poetics. This reservoir would be an important resource for the young Slovene poet, Srečko Kosovel.

IV

If the intellectuals around the Croatian journals *Plamen* and *Zenit* took for granted their belonging to a wider Balkan space, these geographical assumptions were much more contested in the northernmost territory of Yugoslavia: Slovenia. Whereas Zagreb-based writers like Krleža, Cesarec, or Micić shared a common language with those in the former Ottoman lands to the south, tying them into a shared imagined community, Slovenes spoke a different language and had few historical ties with the former Ottoman regions. For this reason, a Balkan identity had far less cultural purchase in Slovenia. For those communist intellectuals who sought to reorganize

Slovenia's political and cultural coordinates towards the south east, this intellectual procedure required much more nuance than the bombastic primitivism of *Zenit*. The communist publicist Vladimir Martelanc, for instance, rejected the idea that Slovenia was part of the Balkans, but nonetheless insisted that "[t]he progressive elements of the Slovene youth must ... search for a path to an understanding of the Balkans ... because [their] future struggles are connected to the liberation of the oppressed people and exploited classes of the Balkans."[52] Similarly, communist poet Ivo Grahor, a key intermediary for the transmission of Russian constructivism into Slovenia, claimed that he spoke for the majority of his fellow Slovenes when he said that he "look[ed] with confidence to the East."[53] In the early 1920s, then, many Slovene intellectuals on the Far Left sought closer affiliations with the Balkans, even if they eschewed the more radical rhetoric of *Zenit*.

Srečko Kosovel went the furthest in his efforts to dislocate Slovenia from Europe and reimagine it within the space of the Balkans. Although he did not echo *Zenit*'s aggressive calls for the "balkanization of Europe," a key theme in his poetic and theoretical work from this period was the reorientation of Slovene culture towards the East.[54] Kosovel was born in the village of Sežana in March 1904 and grew up in the rocky Karst region of what was then the Austrian Littoral. From an early age he immersed himself in Slovene and European culture, reading widely and attending cultural events in the nearby city of Trieste. In 1916, as Karst became the site of intense fighting between Italian and Habsburg forces, Kosovel's parents sent him to Ljubljana. It was here, in the years following World War I, that he became involved in revolutionary politics, joining the youth wing of the communist party and editing its semi-legal magazine, *Mladina* (*Youth*).[55] At the same time he also began his prolific literary career, pioneering radical forms of poetic experimentation that drew from futurism, zenitism, and Soviet constructivism.

Kosovel's effort to reorient Slovene culture towards the East was inadvertently aided by the Italian annexation of the Austrian littoral after World War I. This left approximately 300,000 Slovene speakers inside Italian borders and under threat of violent assimilation campaigns.[56] As Glenda Sluga has observed, Italian nationalist attacks on Slovene and Croatian minorities in the annexed territories "relegated Slavic culture to the margins of a Bolshevik and Balkan East."[57] Italian nationalism, then, reinforced a restorationist map of Europe, linking Slovenes with the threat of revolutionary Asia. Kosovel's hometown fell within the annexed territories and the experience of the Italian occupation shaped his political and aesthetic sensibilities.[58] By relegating Slovenes to a Slavic East, Italian nationalist discourse helped to undermine assumptions of European belonging and loosened the spatial coordinates that embedded Slovenia within Europe. The loosening of these ties served Kosovel's efforts to reconfigure the wider cultural geographies within which Slovenia was nested.[59]

While Kosovel was active in the day-to-day organization of the movement, he believed his poetry was his most valuable contribution to the communist cause.[60] Although he was politically closer to Krleža and Cesarec, it was zenitism that had the most significant impact on his early poetic outlook.[61] Kosovel saw in this chaotic movement a model for a new art that foregrounded dynamism and vitality, an art that "aroused activity."[62] In April 1925, he and other young communists organized an evening of zenitist performances, at which Ve Poljanski gave a rousing lecture on the new movement's ideas.[63] The appeal of *Zenit* for Kosovel lay not just in its exciting, anarchic energies, nor in the anticapitalist direction of its critique, but that it offered a new poetic geography through which to erode Slovenia's ties with Europe and to reorient the country towards a dynamic, revolutionary East.

Kosovel's early poetry already demonstrates a disillusionment with European civilization. "Ekstaza smrti" (The Ecstasy of Death), for instance, renders the continent an apocalyptic landscape of pale corpses and rivers of blood. Kosovel's imagery captures Europe at the ecstatic moment of its death, a point on the cusp of decadence and demise.[64] Although the poem's themes echo the negation of Europe that Krleža and Micić staged in their work, its language illustrates the greater ambivalence of European belonging in Slovene culture. Kosovel's declaration of the death of Europe is not a programmatic slogan but a lament for a civilization in ruins. Nor is his poetic geography as unequivocal as those of his southern role models. Far from seeing Europe's death as a liberation, Kosovel's poem presumes Slovenia to share Europe's fate: "Then the sun's gleaming rays will shine / on us, European corpses," the poem concludes.

Elsewhere, however, in Kosovel's more revolutionary poems such as "Ljubljana spi" (Ljubljana Is Asleep), Slovenia's proximity to Europe is far less clear:

In red chaos a new humanity
Is coming. Ljubljana is asleep.
Europe's dying in a red light.
All the phone lines have been cut.
O, but this one's without a cord.
A blind horse.
[Your eyes as if from
Italian paintings.]
White towers rise
From the brown walls.
A deluge.
Europe has one foot in the grave.
We come with a hurricane.
With poison gasses.
[Your lips are like berries.]
Ljubljana is asleep.
The tram conductor is asleep.
In the Europa Café
They're reading *Slovenski narod*.
The clicking of billiard balls.[65]

While the theme of Europe's collapse is replayed here, the imagery evokes not the apocalyptic epic of "Ekstaza smrti" but rather a scene of political insurrection. References to poison gases and severed phone lines evoke the violence of World War I and its revolutionary aftermath, suggesting scenes of conflict and urban rebellion. Echoing the insurrectionary language of Micić and the zenitists, Kosovel identifies himself with the chaotic forces of a new humanity invading a dying Europe.

The negation of Europe is even staged in the ideographic structure of the poem with the insertion of the bracketed stanzas:

[Your eyes as if from
Italian paintings.]
[Your lips are like berries.]

The use of brackets and the shift from a third to second person disrupts the forward momentum of the poem and reads as if cut and pasted from a sappy love letter. The highly aesthetic, even clichéd metaphors break entirely with the violent imagery and modernist

The Early Comintern and the Yugoslav Avant-Gardes   63

language that animates the rest of the poem. These stanzas are to be read as poetic manifestations of the Europe that is dying, the old art to which the revolutionary avant-gardes are setting flame. Indeed, the reference to Italian paintings suggests that Kosovel is playing on the political geography of Italian imperialism, which posited a divide between a cultured European West and a barbaric Slavic East.[66] The revolt against aestheticism here is thus rendered a revolt against Europe whose flowery language, fragile metaphors, and inconsequential themes are entirely out of sync with the violent and revolutionary postwar world.

What is especially noteworthy in this poem is the subtle geographical shift that Kosovel effects with his revolutionary tone. Where does Ljubljana sit in this conflict between Europe and a new humanity? The image of severed phone lines, so evocative of scenes of urban insurrection, suggests an untethering of sleepy Ljubljana from its European space. More troubling still is the suggestion that the phones to Europe had never actually been connected, raising the possibility that nobody in Europe was listening. This image may be Kosovel's bitter gesture to the Treaty of Rapallo that granted the Slovene littoral to Italy.

The final stanzas of the poem appear to overlay a political-generational conflict over the geographical division. The references to Europa Café, a coffee house in Ljubljana that in Kosovel's time was frequented by the Slovene elite, and *Slovenski narod* (*Slovene Nation*), the liberal newspaper of the day, satirize the old political establishment that belongs to a dying Europe. These are the sleepy middle classes of Slovenia who, Kosovel warns, are about to find themselves engulfed in the red chaos from the revolutionary East. The final stark image of colliding billiard balls, Richard Jackson notes, "prefigure[s] the sounds of gun and cannon" that would herald Europe's destruction.[67] Here the forces of a revolutionary, youthful new humanity clash with the old elite of a lethargic, disconnected Europe.

Although in some of his more programmatic poems Kosovel at times raises the slogan of Balkan federation, the symbolic geography of the Balkans is far less pronounced in his writings than it was on the pages of *Plamen* or *Zenit*.[68] More typically, his efforts to introduce a Balkan geopoetics into Slovene literary culture can be traced through his appropriation of the images and language of zenitism. In "Sifilitični kapetan" (The Syphilitic Captain), for instance, he contrasts the bodies of rugged barbarian troops with their sick leader in ways that restage the zenitist drama of an epic struggle between a vital Balkans and a diseased Europe.[69] "Sivo" (Gray) likewise evokes the Balkans as a space of dynamism and activity in a world of otherwise gray stone streets.[70] Such suggestions of regional space are a long way from the revolutionary proclamations of Balkan insurgency, but they represent a genuine effort to evoke the region as a source of revolutionary political and cultural vitality.

Kosovel's effort to reorient Slovene culture away from Europe and towards the East helped to sustain the anticolonial solidarities that he projected with Asia in his work. Indeed, in contrast to the clumsy orientalist images or racialized fantasies that characterized some of the texts in *Plamen* and *Zenit*, Kosovel's work takes Asia seriously as an intellectual interlocutor. He was deeply influenced by the work of the Bangladeshi poet and philosopher Rabindranath Tagore and references to Tagore's work appear throughout the Slovene's poetry. As Ana Jelnikar has convincingly shown, Kosovel's interest in Tagore stemmed less from a project of reviving an aesthetically exhausted Europe than from a sense of anticolonial solidarity. His adaptations of Tagore's symbolism asserted parallels between the situation of colonized South Asia and South East Europe in ways that undermined traditional Slovene identification with Europe.[71]

V

By the mid-1920s in the Kingdom of Serbs, Croats, and Slovenes, the political situation had stabilized. The new authorities had imposed their rule throughout the country, the peasant rebellions in the north had been quelled, the workers' movement subdued, and the uprisings of national minorities repressed. Although the national question remained unsolved and potentially subversive, it had, for the time being, been successfully contained within the debates of the national parliament. The relative equilibrium of the political situation brought an icy wind to the leftist avant-gardes, chilling their revolutionary aspirations and poetic experimentation, and driving them into political hibernation. The banning of *Plamen* in August 1919 foreshadowed the repression of the communist movement more broadly. In the years that followed, Krleža used his substantial celebrity to try to rally public sympathy for his persecuted comrades.[72] Meanwhile, Cesarec, whose relative lack of celebrity

The Early Comintern and the Yugoslav Avant-Gardes 65

and closer involvement with the political underground made him a target of the regime, spent time abroad and endured several prison sentences.[73] When the two once again began work on a new Marxist journal, *Književna republika*, they acknowledged that it was a much more sober and restrained publication.[74]

The vivid Balkan flame of *Zenit* had also burnt out by the mid-1920s. Although the journal's lack of clear political links with the communist movement had spared it from the first blows of government repression, in 1926 it was officially banned on the charge of spreading Marxist propaganda.[75] Following the ban, Micić fled to Paris, where he attempted to renew his Balkan primitivist project. However, the atmosphere of political disillusionment left its impact on his work and over the following decade, Micić's revolutionary Balkanism tapered off into a narrow Serbian nationalism. Following his return to Belgrade in 1936, he published an obscure far-right journal, *Serbijanstvo* (*Serbianness*), before vanishing into irrelevance.

But it was Kosovel who best summed up the atmosphere of disillusion and depression among the Yugoslav Left in his poem "Deveta dežela" (The Ninth Country):

Those who were overturning the world
have by now sobered up
and those who did not do any overturning,
remain as vulgar as they were before.

And it is so dull, dull and tedious.
The idea of revolutions has died out.
The procession goes on (a man nailed to the cross!)
and behind it a line of abbots.[76]

The description of the grey and mundane ("sleepy") Ljubljana streets confirmed the poet-activist's own depression, tied to the ebbing of the revolutionary tides. To be sure, the idea of revolution had not died out in Yugoslavia completely; it would return with a vengeance, both as a literary theme and as a real political event. But Kosovel would not live to see it. On 26 May 1926, he died from meningitis in his family home in what had since become Mussolini's Italy. Under the suspicious gaze of fascist carabinieri, his comrades Bratko Kreft and Ivo Grahor wrapped his coffin in the Slovene tricolour before lowering it into the soil.[77]

3

Literary Capital in an Age of Global Crisis
The Political Economy of Translation on Europe's Periphery, 1928–34

Confused on our own ground, without contact with our own ground, this newest literature of ours, perfected in laboratory conditions from which it cannot remove itself, spreads only its political stature. Its greatest success is that with the help of its foreign translations, it has revealed us to be not only an economic colony of foreign powers, but also a cultural colony.

Miloš Crnjanski, "The Panic Surrounding Our Book," 1932

I

On 20 June 1928, Puniša Račić, the representative of the Serbian nationalist People's Radical Party, rose to speak in the national assembly. Vying for an audience over the crescendo of heckling from opposition members, he spewed curses and attacks on the liberals, the Croatians, and the Slovenes. Finally, driven to frenzy, Račić stormed to the front of the hall, withdrew a pistol, and brandished it ominously in the air. The president of the assembly, taken aback by the sudden escalation of hostilities, declared an end to the session and made himself scarce. In the next moment Račić sent a round of bullets into the gathered representatives, hitting five opposition activists including the charismatic leader of the Croatian Peasant Party, Stjepan Radić. Six weeks later Radić was dead.[1]

The shooting hastened the breakdown of the Kingdom of Serbs, Croats, and Slovenes. In the days that followed, riots and mass demonstrations broke out in Zagreb, trade unions called a general

The Political Economy of Translation on Europe's Periphery   67

strike, and workers and opposition supporters clashed with police.[2] For King Aleksandar Karađorđević and his closest advisors, the crisis was further proof of the weaknesses of the country's constitution, which had been unable to resolve the rivalry between nationalist and supranationalist visions of Yugoslavism.[3] Desperate to hold his fractious kingdom together, on 6 January 1929, Karađorđević overturned the constitution entirely. The government proceeded to crack down on opposition groups, arresting hundreds of activists, establishing special courts for political criminals, and further empowering censors to ban any material they felt threatened the security of the state.[4] For the following five years the Kingdom was run as a dictatorship, with governments hand-picked by the crown and opposition curbed or outlawed.[5]

The announcement of the January 6 dictatorship dovetailed with a strategic shift within the Comintern that was to have fateful consequences for the Yugoslav Communist Party (KPJ).[6] In the summer of 1928, the Comintern's leadership announced the turn to a more uncompromising, ultra-left strategy. What has come to be known as the Comintern's "third period" was based on Soviet leaders' assumption that the global capitalist system was entering a moment of instability that would create favourable opportunities for revolutionary action. Communist parties were to sever ties with moderate, social democratic forces and adopt a more radical and confrontational strategy.[7] This strategic perspective primed Yugoslav communists to respond to the royal dictatorship with an ill-advised audacity. In February 1929, the party launched an armed uprising.[8] The policy was a disaster and provoked a wave of police raids, arrests, torture, and executions that decimated the party's membership.[9] With the flight of leading cadre to Vienna, Prague, Paris, or Moscow, the already weakened communist movement dissolved into a series of isolated, conspiratorial, and largely inactive cells.

It was in this state of disorganization that Yugoslav communists faced the fallout of the great depression. In October 1929, the collapse of the New York stock exchange sent shockwaves through the world economy. It decimated the hopes of liberal forces who, since 1919, had planned to reconstruct a stable international order on the foundations of market capitalism. As the major lynchpins of this system – the US and Britain – threw up tariffs and unpegged their currencies from gold, withdrawing behind national or imperial borders, the tide of global integration receded. The crisis would offer a window of opportunity for insurgent forces on both the fascist Right and communist Left to project new configurations of national territorial politics and alternative visions of world order.[10]

The great depression exacerbated the geographical unevenness of European capitalism and reinforced South East Europe's peripheral position within the world system. The region's predominantly agrarian economies were hit especially hard by the decline of global food prices and the closure of Western markets. Rapidly deteriorating terms of trade reversed earlier efforts to introduce more modern technologies into local industries.[11] More devastating still was the region's heavy reliance on Western credit, which left both governments and businesses exposed to the spasms of global financial markets. The 1931 collapse of the Austrian Creditanstalt decimated Yugoslavia's economy, making insolvent almost half of its banks.[12] Such relations of dependence became a growing concern among the region's intellectuals. In 1929, for instance, the Romanian economist Mihail Manoilescu warned of the unequal balance of trade between the industrialized economies of Western Europe and those of agrarian South East Europe, which he characterized as a mode of foreign exploitation.[13] The great depression compounded the relations of dependence and vulnerability that marked out the uneven geography of European capitalism.

The simultaneity of these crises had a profound impact on the development of Yugoslav socialism. If the great depression prompted radical intellectuals to more forcefully interrogate the problem of their country's development within the constraints of the global system, the repression of the January 6 regime forced them to direct these questions into the safer realm of culture. During these years of dictatorship and depression, debates around literature and art became especially charged. Ideological differences between intellectuals on the Left and the Right, but also within an increasingly fractured Left, came to be articulated through often vitriolic polemics concerning strategies of cultural development.[14]

This chapter tracks the spatial dynamics of the global economic collapse as they reshaped the cultural geographies of socialists on the European periphery. It attends to a series of polemics that centered on the social literature movement, a literary current that dominated Yugoslav socialism during the period of the Karađorđević dictatorship. Examining a key event in the history of interwar Yugoslav literature – the so-called "conflict" on the literary Left – it proposes a new reading of these polemics.[15] Departing from existing accounts

The Political Economy of Translation on Europe's Periphery 69

that have viewed this conflict as part of a wider international debate concerning the appropriate balance between artistic autonomy and political engagement, I instead argue that it grew out of rival strategies of cultural development and the respective scales at which they were to be pursued. On one side of this debate, social literature's advocates advanced an internationalist strategy that deterritorialized the problem of cultural development and abandoned any strategy of spatial mediation. On the other, the movement's opponents on both the Right and the Left insisted on territorial strategies that remained sensitive to the frictions between local cultural development and the homogenizing tendencies of globalization. The chapter examines two modernist critics of the social literature movement: the Serbian nationalist Miloš Crnjanski (1893–1977) and his literary strategy of national territorialism, and the Croatian communist Miroslav Krleža, who continued to develop the avant-garde's earlier strategy of spatial mediation.

By excavating the rival spatialities that informed the conflict on the Yugoslav literary Left, the chapter makes two broader arguments. First, it demonstrates how the great depression shaped cultural production on the European periphery by infusing literary discourses with wider concerns about sovereignty, modernization, and development. The shock of the global crisis, in other words, deepened the convergence of geopoetic and geopolitical logics that had begun to characterize Yugoslav socialism in the early 1920s. The politics of translation was a critical site at which this convergence took place, facilitating the importation of political-economic concepts into literary discourse and condensing wider anxieties about the corrosive threat of global literary markets on cultural development. Second, the chapter reveals that concerns regarding the Stalinization of the Comintern aggravated core-periphery tensions within an emerging socialist world literary system. As dissident intellectuals in Yugoslavia fretted over the increasing subordination of the world communist movement to the Soviet Union's priorities, many conflated Moscow's power grab with its promotion of the proletarian culture movement. Yugoslav frustrations with a Soviet-oriented proletarian literature were at times indistinguishable from anxieties regarding the deterritorializing and homogenizing effects of capitalist globalization. In fact, the interwar effort to construct a socialist, decommodified model of world literature replicated the global asymmetries of cultural prestige to which writers on the European periphery were especially sensitive.

II

The January 6 dictatorship had a contradictory impact on the KPJ. At the level of the party's organization, it decimated the movement, disrupting its networks and sending the bulk of its cadre into exile or prison. At the level of prestige, however, the persecution of the party gave it an aura of intrigue, adventure, and moral fortitude that helped it build a new constituency. Forced underground and into a life of secrecy, the communist movement, weak though it was, came to hold a mysterious appeal to a generation who came of age during the dictatorship. Graduating from universities and entering the stagnant labour market, this "generation before closed doors," as the Slovene communist Ivo Brnčič christened them, were soon forced into unemployment or emigration.[16] They would play a crucial role in the history of Yugoslav communism, supplying the cadre that would rebuild the party over the 1930s and lead it into the antifascist struggle of World War II.[17]

Many of this generation first fashioned their political ideas through literature, one of the few avenues of intellectual freedom left open by the regime. For many young communists, literature was a natural surrogate for politics, and their first political influences tended not to be Marx or Lenin but rather Stendhal, Tolstoi, or Gorkii.[18] The years of dictatorship and depression saw an explosion of left-wing literary activity in Yugoslavia that came to be known as the "social literature movement." Organized through a disparate network of journals, reading circles, and publishing houses, this movement played a key role in shaping the political and aesthetic sensibilities of a new generation of activists who sought in literature an outlet for their stymied political passions.[19]

Social literature was a striking departure from the aesthetics that guided the Yugoslav avant-gardes of the 1920s. The repression of the communist movement and the ebbing of the revolutionary tides over the first postwar decade had fostered a certain sobriety in leftist culture. By the end of the 1920s, the revolutionary romanticism that had animated the early work of Krleža, Cesarec, the zenitists, and Kosovel was out of tune with the conditions of political repression and economic collapse. Although hardships deepened, the absence of mass social struggle led to disillusion and apathy. The aesthetics of social literature reflected this atmosphere of pessimism, abandoning the radical poetic experimentation

The Political Economy of Translation on Europe's Periphery   71

and revolutionary bombast of the avant-gardes and promoting a constrained realism oriented towards didacticism and the gritty exploration of everyday life.

Yugoslav social literature was part of a worldwide movement of proletarian literary cultures that flourished during the years of the great depression.[20] While the movement promoted literary realism, it drew from an eclectic set of styles including French naturalism, German new objectivity, and Soviet *proletkult*.[21] Although in the Soviet Union and Germany during this period communist intellectuals argued passionately about the appropriate mode of literary realism, with the place of naturalism provoking particular controversy, elsewhere in the world these debates would not take place until later in the decade.[22] The proletarian literary journals of the early 1930s included works of naturalism and reportage alongside those of a more classical realist style, and even texts whose psychologism strayed into modernism. What mattered more in the curation of a proletarian literary canon was a certain class consciousness or political attitude (*partiinost*) that was seen to be necessary to elucidate the contradictions of global capitalist modernity.[23]

Interwar proletarian literature was an effort to construct a revolutionary alternative to what Pascale Casanova has theorized as the world literary system: the field of competition and rivalry in which the metropoles of the West (Paris, London, New York) control the entry of writers from the global periphery into world literary markets.[24] Against this system's valorization of literary autonomy, proletarian critics insisted on writing as a form of class struggle. Against the modernism championed by Western publishers, proletarian writers defended realism as the most objective literary style. Against the prestigious old-world capitals of Paris or London, they instead championed Moscow as the hub of a new, more modern world literature. As Soviet theorists began to play a more active role in the movement following the 1930 Kharkov Congress, proletarian literature was brought into the orbit of what Rossen Djagalov terms "the Soviet Republic of Letters."[25] Not only did the Soviet Union provide the infrastructure for the movement but, as the world's first workers' state, it represented the most advanced stage of proletarian culture. This vanguard status conferred on Moscow an international prestige. By the early 1930s, Soviet critics were sanctioning the aesthetic norms of the movement and curating the texts that entered its international networks of circulation. While never a mere Soviet appendage, the proletarian literary international nevertheless privileged the Soviet Union within its geography of cultural prestige. These asymmetries became especially clear in Yugoslavia during the conflict on the literary Left.

The first major organ of the Yugoslav social literature movement was the journal *Nova literatura* (*New Literature*), founded by the art critic Oto Bihalji-Merin and his brother, Pavle, in December 1928. Bihalji-Merin had become a communist while studying in Berlin during the 1920s, where he closely followed the debates of German and Soviet writers. Upon his return to Yugoslavia, he founded *Nova literatura* to help draw Yugoslav readers into these international discussions.[26] The journal quickly established itself as an important intellectual venue, not least as its editorial board boasted such illustrious names as Henri Barbusse, Johannes Becher, Albert Einstein, Sergei Eisenstein, Maksim Gorkii, George Grosz, Egon Erwin Kisch, Erwin Piscator, Upton Sinclair, and Aleksandr Serafimovich. This international recognition, which Bihalji-Merin had secured through his contacts on the German Left, ensured that the journal survived the first year of the Karađorđević dictatorship before the government finally censored it in January 1930.

Although short-lived, *Nova literatura* made a powerful impression on the Yugoslav Left and inspired similar journals that sprouted up across the country in the early 1930s. In 1930, the Croatian social democrat Božidar Adžija began publishing *Socijalna misao* (*Social Thought*) in Zagreb. The following year *Stožer* (*The Pole*) appeared in Belgrade and *Literatura* (*Literature*) was founded by Stevan Galogaža in Zagreb. A year later, in Ljubljana, the communist theater director Bratko Kreft began editing the Slovene magazine *Književnost* (*Literature*).[27] This movement brought together the older voices of the Yugoslav Far Left, intellectuals such as Jovan Popović, August Cesarec, and Veselin Masleša, with a younger generation of writers including Milovan Đilas, Radovan Zogović, Otokar Keršovani, Ivo Brnčić, Mile Klopčič, the Bosnians Avdo Humo and Eli Finci, and the Macedonian poet Kočo Racine. In addition to Yugoslav writers, these journals relied heavily on translations of foreign texts. Critical essays by Soviet theorists such as Lenin, Georgi Plekhanov, and Leopold Averbakh set out the aesthetic criteria for the movement, while letters from abroad or review essays informed readers about proletarian literary cultures around the world. The movement also published prose and poetry by canonized proletarian writers. While the bulk of these writers came from Europe (Henri Barbusse, André Baillon, Ludwig Renn), North America (Upton Sinclair, Jack London, Michael Gold), and the Soviet Union (Maksim Gorkii, Alexandr Neverov), the movement also translated the work of writers from further afield, such as the Jamaican poet Claude MacKay and the Japanese writer Sunao Tokunaga.[28]

Eager to shake off their historical dependence on the West, Yugoslav intellectuals drawn to social literature believed that their country's cultural development could best be pursued through participation in the proletarian literary international. For left-wing writers and publishers in Yugoslavia, this international movement was a resource for overcoming what they saw as their country's cultural backwardness. Through a campaign of translation and publication, adherents of social literature imported the most advanced literary techniques and themes from the industrialized worlds of Western Europe, North America, and, of course, the Soviet Union. Modernizing the literary consciousness of their readers, these writers and publishers believed, would compensate for their country's lagging economic development. Proletarian literature and its international networks promised a path out of the European periphery's agrarian stagnation and towards global industrial modernity. Bihalji-Merin made this argument explicit in his first editorial for *Nova literatura* when he proclaimed that "[t]he book is the general good of all people: across the borders of a single language it carries thought and ideas through time and space. It teaches us how to handle the mechanisms of development."[29]

As a project of cultural development, social literature privileged a language of temporality that radically reconfigured the cultural geographies of Yugoslav socialism. The movement abandoned the geopolitical antagonism between Europe and the Balkans that had animated both fin de siècle social democracy and the revolutionary avant-gardes of the early 1920s. Instead, it emphasized the integration and homogenization of global space by capitalist time. Capitalist expansion, in this view, had divided the world into two great transnational camps – bourgeoisie and proletariat – each with their cultural program. This vision relied on a totalizing, linear temporality that rendered world space flat and fluid, a smooth surface over which deterritorialized aesthetic forms and literary themes could be transmitted across vast distances. In so doing, advocates of social literature abandoned the avant-garde's earlier strategy of spatial mediation. If cultural development was to be pursued through a socialist mode of globalization, there was no need to mediate the nation's integration into global modernity. Positioning Yugoslavia in the world ceased to be a problem of political or cultural cartography and instead became a concern with locating its place on a global timeline of development.

Bratko Kreft's 1933 short story, "Tempo ... Tempo," illustrates well how this temporal consciousness reformatted a new vision of global space. The story concerns Tone, a Slovene miner who commits suicide after he is fired from his job at the Ugljen coal company. The company has fallen on hard times and has been forced to lay off fifty workers a day to stay afloat. In the final passages, Kreft emphasizes how Tone's fate is woven into the spatiotemporal rhythms of the international economy:

> In Begunje three children and a pregnant woman cry over the corpse of a suicide, who came before the master's doorstep and thought that it would be possible to stop time if he put a bullet in his head ...
> Nothing.
> The sun shines.
> The earth rotates.
> The president sleeps and if tomorrow he is in a good will, he will pay director Tone's widow 300 dinars ... The severance for her husband so that nobody can say that the trading company Ugljen was not a solid enterprise.
> By evening a new fifty will be on the road.
> All moving in a row.
> Tempo.
> Tempo.
> In India bloody battles.
> English coal.
> Crisis in industry.
> Tempo ... tempo ... tempo ...
> And in the morgue in Begunje lies the dead man. Only he stands still, unmoving.[30]

Kreft's closing lines trace the contours of a global capitalism bringing together colonial India, rural Slovenia, and industrial England, uniting each within a singular time. The refrain of "tempo ... tempo ..."

that punctuates the story diminishes the geographical distances between these parts of the world, emphasizing the degree to which the integration of global markets had enveloped spaces as far afield as the Balkans, South Asia, and the British Isles, and harmonized them within a single temporal regime.

The temporality that informed social literature's understanding of cultural development was loosely based on the Comintern's teleological understanding of historical materialism. Plotted on this timeline, semi-feudal Yugoslavia lagged behind the industrial capitalist economies of Western Europe and North America, which in turn had been overtaken by the Soviet Union, well on its way to the construction of socialism. These temporal horizons framed the movement's fascination with what they saw as the two most modern societies of the age: the US and the Soviet Union. That the US and the Soviet Union should occupy such similar positions on social literature's temporal horizon is less surprising when we consider Harry Harootunian's observation that capitalist and communist ideologies in the twentieth century shared a similar temporal structure, one oriented towards "a fantasy destiny of the future perfect towards which the present was being asked to direct its energies."[31] Both communist and capitalist ideologies of the 1930s, that is, were structured by a linear temporality that posited industrial modernity as its telos. For Bihalji-Merin, the modern world was shaped by the push and pull of these two rival poles: "Wall Street contra Kremlin," as he pithily summarized it.[32]

The US and Soviet Union became sites through which the intellectuals of the social literature movement explored fantasies of modernization, although each evoked a very different sentiment. The March 1929 edition of *Nova literatura*, for instance, featured proletarian literature in the US and included translations of Upton Sinclair, Theodor Dreiser, Floyd Dell, Michael Gold, and Jack London. The issue was illustrated with photographs of New York's bustling downtown streets and reproductions of Louis Lozowick's lithographs and sketches of bridges, skyscrapers, subways, and crowded squares.[33] While these images highlighted the allure and excitement of the US as a site of industrial modernity, they also pointed to its deep contradictions. The selected translations foregrounded the social injustice of rampant capitalism, the racism of segregation, and the fallout of the great depression on rural and working-class people. If the US's industrial modernity fascinated social literature's readers, it was not as a model for emulation.

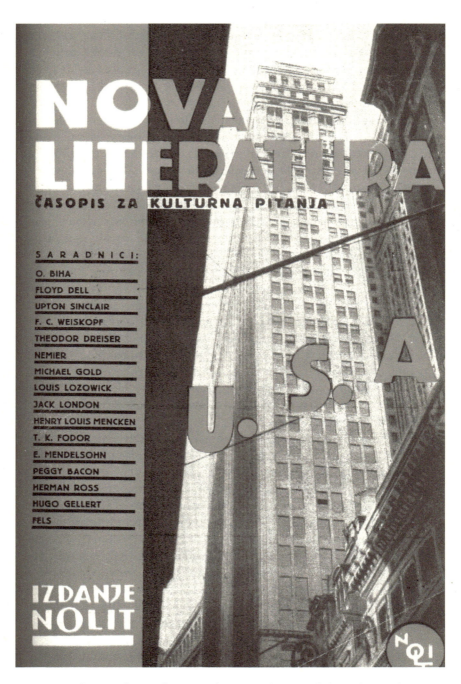

Figure 3.1 | Issue of *Nova literatura* from March 1929, dedicated to proletarian literature in the US.

Figure 3.2 | Issue of *Nova literatura* from April–May 1929, dedicated to contemporary German fiction.

Figure 3.3 | Issue of *Nova literatura* from September 1929, dedicated to contemporary Soviet culture.

The Political Economy of Translation on Europe's Periphery   79

No such ambiguity coloured the movement's representations of the Soviet Union, the capital of proletarian world literature. The fantasy of industrialization propelling Yugoslav society into the modern world was central to the appeal of Soviet communism. A 1932 edition of *Stožer* dedicated to Soviet literature included articles by Lenin, Gorkii, and Averbakh alongside photographs of construction sites and factories.[34] Such images encouraged readers to associate Soviet literary theory with a grandiose industrial modernity. A year later, the same journal published fragments of Louis Aragon's Soviet travel writings, which focused on the rapid industrialization of the Ural Mountains.[35] Women and their place in society was an especially important topic for social literature, as the state of gender relations served as a barometer of progress and modernity. While local works such as Milka Žicina's *Kajin put* (*Kaja's Path*) drew attention to the devastating effects of patriarchy and rural poverty on Yugoslav women, Soviet literature was celebrated for its depictions of the new woman of socialism.[36] In a review of Mikhail Sholokhov's *Red Virgin Soil*, for instance, Miloš Pantić commended the novel's progressive depiction of women, which, he argued, helped Yugoslav readers to "discern perspectives nearer to the future."[37] Precisely because the Soviet Union had reached a more advanced stage of history, translations and reviews of its literature functioned as kernels of a future time whose appearance in the semi-feudal conditions of the periphery would modernize the consciousness of readers. This temporality belied the rigid historical materialism that social literature often professed. Literature, it seemed, was not simply an epiphenomenon of the mode of production but could, in fact, run in advance of history, transmitting the experience of an industrial future.

Indeed, translation from more advanced cultures served as a central strategy in social literature's campaign of cultural development. While translations regularly appeared in the movement's journals, the major thrust of this strategy was undertaken by Bihalji-Merin's publishing house, NOLIT. Throughout the 1930s, NOLIT published dozens of translations of texts by proletarian authors such as André Baillon, Heinrich Mann, Stijn Streuvels, Sinclair Lewis, Upton Sinclair, Jack London, Erich Maria Remarque, Ludwig Renn, Egon Erwin Kisch, Agnes Smedley, and Ernst Toller, and Soviet writers like Isaak Babel, Lidiia Seifullina, and Boris Pilniak. Although these texts conformed to a realist aesthetic, they exhibited diverse styles, from the naturalism of Sinclair to the reportage of Kisch and the romanticism of Pilniak. Rather than their adherence to a single doctrine of realism, what appealed to Yugoslav editors in these texts were their social themes of poverty, class struggle, colonial oppression, or antimilitarism. For socialist intellectuals, these texts were imbued with the tensions of the contemporary world and their translation was intended to help familiarize Yugoslav readers with a modernity that seemed to be unfolding elsewhere.

Borrowing from Casanova's glossary, we might describe social literature's campaign of translation as a "tactic of translation-accumulation."[38] Social literature used translation to build up a canon of contemporary literature in Serbo-Croatian that could serve as a basis for the further development of Yugoslav culture. Through this primitive accumulation of literary capital, Yugoslav writers could theoretically transcend their peripheral position and join the ranks of more advanced, or at least more contemporary, literatures. Bihalji-Merin made this point in 1932, when he argued for the importance of international exchange in promoting Yugoslavia's cultural development: "Industry is being raised in our country, for example. But is it a 'home-grown' mode of production, something that has organically come from our local relations and 'the characteristics of our race,' or is it a form of craftwork that has penetrated our environment from outside and which we develop according to foreign models and, in many cases, with foreign capital?"[39] Translation, this metaphor suggested, was a kind of technology transfer through which more modern literary models could be imported into Yugoslav culture. Just as the country relied on the capital of more developed economies to undertake industrialization, so too would translations from more advanced literatures promote its cultural development. That Bihalji-Merin should reach so easily for an economic metaphor in this discussion is exemplary of the ways in which Yugoslav anxieties of cultural and economic development bled into one another during the years of the great depression.

Social literature's strategy of cultural development undermined the Balkan idea that the revolutionary avant-gardes of the 1920s had carried over from the fin de siècle social democrats. In its place, this younger generation promoted a vision of the world as increasingly integrated by the temporal dynamics of capitalist modernity. This assumption led them to advocate a deterritorialized proletarian aesthetics that would be universalizable across global capitalism's uneven geographies. Within such a spatiotemporal framework, there

The Political Economy of Translation on Europe's Periphery 81

was no need to conceive of spaces that might shield or interface between the national and the global. In fact, cultural globalization was the point, as it corresponded to the universality of the proletarian experience.

The emphasis that social literature's intellectuals placed on translation further eroded the supranational geography of the Balkans as a salient cultural concern. As translation presumed a common target language, the community of readers imagined by social literature was one defined largely by linguistic homogeneity: i.e., as those literate in Serbo-Croatian. This framework excluded the possibility of reimagining a multilinguistic Balkan community.[40] If cultural development was to be conducted through translation from more advanced cultures into local languages, Europe's southeast peninsula fragmented into several different communities of readers. The Balkans, it appeared, no longer had a relevant role to play in a socialist strategy of cultural development.

III

Set against the disruptions provoked by the great depression, social literature's assumption of global integration was strangely anachronistic. As we have seen, the economic crisis dislocated the tendencies towards tighter integration and precipitated the breakdown of a renewed liberal international order. This was, in other words, a moment in which the spatial unevenness of global capitalism was made explicit to even the most detached observer. It also prompted intellectuals in both the centre and the periphery of the world system to look for alternative models of development. The solutions proposed, by insurgents and hegemons alike, amounted to a reassertion of territorialism; states were to delink from an increasingly unstable global system and turn their attention to regulating and developing economic space as delimited by national or imperial borders.[41]

The reassertion of territorial paradigms also took place in the sphere of cultural production. In Yugoslavia, intellectuals on both the Right and the Left sought to address the problem of cultural development in ways that took account of the glaring geographical unevenness of global capitalist modernity. The strategies these intellectuals proposed were most clearly expressed in the polemics they pursued with the social literature movement. During the early 1930s, the movement came under sustained attack from critics who insisted that literary production be anchored within local territories conceived at either a national or supranational scale. On the Right, Miloš Crnjanski argued for an openly nationalist program of cultural protectionism that would more tightly bind, police, and develop Serbian culture within its territorial borders. On the Left, Miroslav Krleža argued for an aesthetics rooted in the unique social and political landscape of the European periphery, a space that transcended the narrow borders of the nation but stopped well short of the global scale of social literature. Both Crnjanski and Krleža's critiques took aim at the strategy of translation-accumulation, which they charged with dissolving the particularities of local literary space in the name of proletarian internationalism. Instead, they sought to aggressively reterritorialize the problem of cultural development, albeit at different spatial scales.

Miloš Crnjanski's initial volley against the social literature movement was launched in March 1932 in the Belgrade daily *Vreme* (*Time*) in a piece provocatively entitled "Mi postajemo kolonija strane knjige" ("We Are Becoming a Colony of Foreign Books").[42] A celebrity of Serbian literature, Crnjanski was a leading modernist who had come to prominence in the Belgrade literary scene in the immediate post-World War I years. Although he had at first been part of the anarchic avant-garde, over the course of the 1920s he was quickly co-opted by the Serbian cultural establishment. During the 1930s he began to move towards a right-wing and at times pseudofascist politics, serving in the diplomatic corps in Berlin and Rome and becoming a sympathizer of Italian fascism.[43] Although at the time he penned his controversial column he had yet to fully develop these sympathies, this polemic was an important moment in his rightward trajectory.[44]

In his column, Crnjanski bemoaned the crisis in Serbian literature. A declining audience for Serbian works, plus an influx of "cheap translations" of foreign books, he argued, threatened to destroy the country's cultural development. Worse still, the craze for foreign books was undermining the national consciousness: "The mentality of the next generations, not to speak of the current, is being created on the basis of foreign books in a foreign atmosphere," he warned. At stake, then, was not just the durability of Serbian culture but the Serb himself. If literature was one of the key means through which a distinctive national subjectivity was developed, the "intrusion" (*naturanje*) of "spiritually foreign" books threatened

The Political Economy of Translation on Europe's Periphery   83

the very existence of the Serbian nation. What had not been realized by several centuries of imperial rule by the Habsburg and Ottoman empires was now being achieved through the anonymous forces of the global market. "We are," he ominously concluded, "slowly becoming a colony for the sale of foreign books."[45] And he laid the blame for much of this condition on the social literature movement.

The solution, Crnjanski maintained, was for the state to restrict the import, production, and sale both of foreign texts and of their Serbo-Croatian translations. This was a revival of a national-territorial model of development: the state was to cultivate local production, defending Serbian writers from the pressures of global literary markets. To be sure, Crnjanski did not call for a total ban on the sale of foreign books. While he was a nationalist, he did not seek cultural isolation from the rest of the world. In fact, in his early career he had translated an anthology of Chinese lyrics and penned an introduction to a translation of Oscar Wilde's *Picture of Dorian Grey*.[46] His demand, he clarified, was not to build "a Chinese wall to protect us from foreign literature" but rather to target the "speculation that goes on at the expense of our writers and the development of our literature."[47] What precisely Crnjanski meant by "speculation" in literature is unclear – if not baffling – but rhetorically it served to conflate the cause of the great depression with the crisis he perceived in Serbian literature.

Crnjanski's language quickly took on a more conspiratorial and chauvinist tone. In a subsequent column, he took aim directly at the social literature movement as the chief threat to Serbian culture. It was communists, he claimed, in league with publishers and literary speculators in Zagreb and Ljubljana, that flooded Serbia with their cheap translations. Croatian and Slovene publishers had opened the floodgates, he argued, because their national literatures were too weak to withstand the influence of foreign cultures. Crnjanski here wove together a dark conspiracy in which communists and the non-Serbian nations of Yugoslavia appeared as a kind of fifth column, traitors to the cause of the country's cultural development. Likely tailoring his argument to better align with the Karađorđević regime's brutal anticommunist campaign, Crnjanski was careful to add that social literature's translations had become a vehicle through which communist propaganda was smuggled into the country. A policy of cultural protectionism, therefore, was as much a matter of defending national security as it was national culture.

84 Mediating Spaces

For Crnjanski, it was not just social literature's reliance on foreign translations that threatened the development of Serbian culture, but its aesthetic doctrine. Precisely because the movement sought to deterritorialize culture and insisted on the immutability of aesthetics across national borders, it led to a "lifeless" literature that demoralized its readers:

> Without talent or even written works, this social and Marxist literature thinks that the time for our literary terror has already matured; that our literature has no more vitality. This is a difficult moment for our local book, this moment where the market trend for foreign books, the books of another, has well and truly arrived. Beneath its flood, in an atmosphere of panic, the foreign book can now conquer by its own superior selling power. Meanwhile, the "social" literature of the future, because of its journalistic, reportage, and constrained side does not have what it takes to demask and clarify, and thus to revitalize our literature ...
>
> Confused on our own ground, without contact with our own ground, this newest literature of ours, perfected in laboratory conditions from which it cannot remove itself, spreads only its political stature. Its greatest success is that with the help of its foreign translations, it has revealed us to be *not only an economic colony of foreign powers, but also a cultural colony.*[48]

As it was uprooted from a national territory, Crnjanski argued, social literature could not produce an aesthetics sufficiently robust to offer Serbian literature a means for revitalization, growth, or development. In this way, Crnjanski aggressively reterritorialized the problem of cultural production, insisting that aesthetics should be developed organically from "local ground." This argument rehearsed romantic theories that understood culture to be the manifestation of national being. All literature, in this view, was national literature. Social literature's internationalism, it followed, was merely a cover through which the movement smuggled in German, American, and Soviet aesthetic sensibilities that would erode Serbian national consciousness.

Crnjanski rejected the supposed autonomy of literature that underpinned the hegemony of Western Europe within the world literary system. Instead, he insisted on a romantic understanding of literature as the spiritual expression of a people inhabiting a distinct

The Political Economy of Translation on Europe's Periphery   85

territory. Literature was to serve the nation, and in turn, the state was to serve literature through its policy of protectionism. Crnjanski saw the world literary field as a site of competition and conflict, in which only the strongest national cultures could compete against the homogenizing pressures of global markets. This competition, however, was not a battle for *recognition* by authorities in Paris or London (still less Moscow!), but rather a struggle for *survival* in a world of rival nations. This was, for Crnjanski, a literary geopolitics for an era of renewed global competition. Small nations on the periphery of Europe, held back by centuries of foreign rule, were engaged in a fight to preserve their distinct cultures from the literary exports of more advanced, more powerful nations.

Crnjanski's nationalism rendered global space in a way that sharply contrasted with the internationalism of social literature. Where the latter celebrated the porousness of borders and the global, if uneven, spread of a universalizing modernity, Crnjanski instead understood world space as fragmented among national territories. For him, as much as for his Romanian contemporary, Manoilescu, the world was divided between economically and culturally advanced nations and the smaller and weaker nations they sought to dominate and envelop. Cultural exchange was not an unmitigated benefit for all parties but rather a field of competition and struggle for survival. This theory reasserted the primacy of national space in literary production. Cultural development, it followed, had to proceed through a national community's unique aesthetic sensibilities and the territorialization and fortification of cultural borders. As with the revolutionary avant-gardes of the 1920s, Crnjanski here transposed the vocabulary of geopolitics into a cultural register. This rhetorical move was anchored in the broader revival of national territorial paradigms in response to the global disruptions of the great depression.

IV

Social literature faced a second, very different critique from one of the giants of the Yugoslav literary Left, the Croatian modernist Miroslav Krleža. Against the professed internationalism of proletarian literature, Krleža insisted on the need for a culture that grew from local conditions. This argument reterritorialized the problem of aesthetics but, unlike Crnjanski's, did not see literary space as coterminous with national borders. Rather, building on and refining

86 Mediating Spaces

the earlier avant-gardes' strategy of geopoetic mediation, he sought to embed a program of national cultural development within a supranational framework delimited by the landscape of Europe's agrarian periphery.[49] At once opposed to social literature's "aping" of foreign trends and Crnjanski's parochial nationalism, Krleža instead rescaled the problem of cultural development to better map onto the uneven geography of European capitalism. In so doing, he traced the contours of a landscape that cut across linguistic or ethnic borders and offered alternative possibilities for regional affiliation. While this strategy bore obvious traces of the Balkanism of the revolutionary avant-gardes, it received a more rhetorically sober and restrained treatment in this era of depression and dictatorship.

Krleža's arguments for a regional aesthetics were outlined in a polemical exchange with the social literature movement following the publication of his 1933 essay, "Podravskim motivima," ("Foreword to *The Drava Valley Motifs*"). The essay was an introduction to *Podravi motivi* (*The Drava Valley Motifs*), a series of drawings by the Croatian artist Krsto Hegedušić (1901–1975). A member of the leftist Zemlja (Earth) art movement, Hegedušić was close to the KPJ, but his work engaged social and political themes outside of the increasingly narrow realist aesthetics of proletarian culture. In the early 1930s he helped found a peasant art collective in the village of Hlebine, whose participants pioneered their own style of naïve peasant art.[50] Hegedušić's style drew from Croatian folk art as well as the work of George Grosz and Pieter Bruegel, who he had studied closely while based in Paris in the 1920s. The drawings of *Podravi motivi* were set in the agricultural region of northern Croatia and rendered this landscape a site of the grotesque, populated by deformed peasant bodies, muddy roads, and rundown villages.

Krleža's introduction to *Podravi motivi* expounded the author's idiosyncratic aesthetics and sparked the first of the conflicts on the literary Left in Yugoslavia. These conflicts, which broke out several times over the course of the 1930s, nominally turned on the question of the autonomy of literature from political ideology, but they also raised broader concerns over modernist and realist aesthetics and the increasing centralization of political and intellectual authority in the KPJ during the years of Stalinization.[51] The polemics pitted the post-World War I generation of avant-garde leftists, including Krleža and his allies in the surrealist movement, against a younger generation of more austere realists affiliated with the social literature

The Political Economy of Translation on Europe's Periphery   87

movement, such as Milovan Đilas, Radovan Zogović, and Ognjen Prica. The sizeable scholarship on this conflict has overlooked the ways in which these polemics were informed by the wider anxieties around cultural development that preoccupied Yugoslav intellectuals during these years. For this reason, it has also failed to acknowledge the degree to which Krleža's interventions sought to reterritorialize the problem of cultural development at a supranational scale by evoking the landscape of the European periphery.

Krleža's main dispute with the social literature movement was sparked by the movement's doctrinaire efforts to impose its political-aesthetic program on socialist writers.[52] Many intellectuals adopted the Soviet *proletkult*'s belief in cultural revolution as a mode of class war, and saw it as their role to weed out "formalist" or "decadent" heresies within Yugoslav literature.[53] Writers who failed to adhere to realism or who dealt with titillating issues of sexuality were derided as "bourgeois" and often accused of "*larpurlartizam*" (a derogative slavicization of "*l'art pour l'art*"). Although Krleža was the most public face of the Yugoslav literary Left, his modernist sensibilities increasingly put him at odds with realist doctrine. By 1933, he identified it with an intellectual conformism that had taken hold of the international communist movement under Stalin's leadership. Such conformism, he argued, crippled cultural development, as it stamped out the primal experience that lay at the heart of artistic creativity. In this way Krleža, like his French contemporary, André Breton, represented an earlier generation of artistic radicals who saw Stalin's Comintern, with its ideological orthodoxy and centralized hierarchy, as a betrayal of the Russian Revolution's emancipatory promise.[54]

Krleža's critique rested on his theory that human creativity lay in the unconscious recesses of the subject. Like the surrealists, he emphasized the irrationality and uncanniness that inspired great works of art. His understanding of the unconscious, however, went further than the Freudian paradigm and pushed beyond the psychological realm into "the guts ... the bowels and ... the buried bodily paroxysms" of the human organism.[55] Such an understanding of man's unconscious drives called on the artist to look deeper than repressed thoughts and desires, the material that surrealists explored through dream work or free association, and to instead try to capture the spark of raw physiological sensation: "Manifestations of beauty are emotional agitations, which are born out of elementary, human, sensory traumas, bodily

Figure 3.4 | Miroslav Krleža in the late 1930s.

unrests and emotional potential amidst dark and colossal creation, which digests, slaughters, and devours its own self, which digs itself into the ground, rises and builds itself despite gravity, breathes like the ebb and flow of tides and pregnant like a womb, it crawls across centuries experiencing the pains and pleasures through the existence of animated and animalistic elements, which in recent times have

The Political Economy of Translation on Europe's Periphery   89

been christened by wretched bipeds with the epithet – 'human.'"[56] By reducing art to an epiphenomenon of vital processes – consumption, digestion, growth, decay, pain, and pleasure – Krleža's aesthetic philosophy broke with any teleological understanding of progress or enlightenment. Beneath all culture, he argued, lay a primal creature driven by irrational, often violent desires. Grounding artistic inspiration in this theory of the subject led Krleža to reject as misguided any attempt to direct artistic inspiration into predetermined aesthetic programs. Social literature, which imposed a realist doctrine on art, cut itself off from this vitality of immediate experience. As such, it would "inoculate" artistic creativity with a "fatal injection of rationality."[57]

The philosophy of an unbound, irrational creativity grew out of Krleža's early interest in Nietzsche, but it was also informed by his equally ardent – if idiosyncratic – Marxism. Artistic creativity was not simply the effect of primal desires and physiological agitations, but also of the interaction of the subject with the "material and climatic foundations by which they were conditioned."[58] This materialism was as much ecological as it was sociological, and presupposed that different environments would produce different artistic experiences. The art of the rural periphery would differ from that of the urban metropole.[59] Creativity, then, was intimately shaped by the social and historical conditions that pertained to a particular landscape and could not be codified into doctrinaire programs and exported around the world. From Krleža's perspective, social literature's internationalist realism ignored the differences generated by the geographical unevenness of modern capitalism, an unevenness that did not fall neatly along national borders. Haranguing Yugoslav writers to adopt the styles of more advanced literatures did not promote cultural development but further entrenched their dependence on a metropole, whether that be Paris or Moscow. Instead, he argued, revolutionary artists needed to develop a culture that spoke to South East Europe's specific experience of modernity, something that would only come about by tapping into the deep physiological and psychological reactions that the landscape of the periphery provoked in them.

Hegedušić's work, Krleža argued, offered an example of art that used the deep subjective experience of the artist to explore the abject conditions of the European periphery. Although consciously drawing from the work of Western European artists like Grosz and Bruegel, Hegedušić didn't merely ape their style but rather appropriated particular techniques or images and recast them to create

Figure 3.5 | Krsto Hegedušić, "Muži," from the 1933 series *Podravi motivi*.

"something distinctly ours, local and native."[60] This local art, Krleža claimed, was profoundly shaped by the material conditions of life in South East Europe:

> [Hegedušić's] apparent exaggeration of the sickly elements, his unconcealed inclination for the grotesque, the pronounced crudeness of his strokes, his ridicule of shameful elements – this entanglement of doltish, lumpy pumpkin-heads, swollen, sensual lips, engorged arms and deformed movements – all this

The Political Economy of Translation on Europe's Periphery   91

represents a negation of our contemporary feudal absurdity, where Singer's sewing machines coexist with the twelfth century, and where this world of goitrous necks, swollen noses, chubby cheeks and low foreheads still believes in the Evil One, in werewolves, in the church, and in witches. The neurotic reaction to the twitching of these physiognomies, as sorrowful growths of life amidst universal wretchedness, across which the economic imperatives of contemporary Europe stomp like Atillas through our vineyards and ploughed fields.[61]

Krleža was drawn to the abject aesthetics through which Hegedušić represented the peasantry. Far from casting them as noble bearers of national purity, Hegedušić accentuated their poverty and ignorance to construct something barbarous, even monstrous. Krleža was focused not just on the backwardness of the rural population, but on the unevenness of capitalist development that was manifested in the landscape of South East Europe, where the symbols of modern industrial consumption (Singer's sewing machines) sat alongside ancient superstitions and feudal conditions of life.

Instead of realism's emphasis on temporality, Krleža argued for the importance of local space. Certainly, as a Marxist, he operated according to some understanding of history as a progression of stages from feudalism to capitalism and onwards, eventually, to communism. But he rejected the position advocated by his contemporary, Georg Lukács, who promoted realism as the only aesthetic form capable of laying bare the dynamics of historical time.[62] Instead, Krleža was fascinated by the historical exception, the world of the periphery that seemed stranded between history's stages and whose temporal liminality was manifested in the combined, uneven development of the landscape. While this exception only became legible within a linear framework that presumed feudalism to be eclipsed by capitalism, the aesthetic experience of this exception only became accessible by suspending that framework's teleological momentum. Precisely because he or she inhabited it, the artist could not treat the world of the periphery as merely a transition between two more real historical stages; they had a responsibility to explore its unique landscape. Consequently, instead of a diachronic realism which sought to elucidate the forward dynamics of history, Krleža advanced a modernist, synchronic, and phenomenological method that telescoped into the interiority of the periphery, expressing its sense of stasis, stagnation, and lag. Hegedušić's grotesque drawings, he argued, captured precisely this aesthetic experience.

While Krleža's approach recognized the cultural sphere as one of geopolitical contestation, he rejected the narrow framework of Crnjanski's nationalism. Although he had jettisoned the more revolutionary rhetoric of his youthful avant-garde writings, Krleža continued to recognize the limitations of the nation and to pursue strategies of cultural development at a supranational scale. His 1932 novel, *Povratak Filipa Latinowicza* (*The Return of Filip Latinowicz*), for instance, evoked the space of Pannonia – a region that included parts of contemporary Hungary, Yugoslavia, Romania, Czechoslovakia, and Austria and thereby transcended national borders – as a landscape whose geography was mapped by the uneven contours of European capitalist development. Pannonia functioned as a mediating space, a regional landscape in which the author could explore the Croatian experience of capitalist modernity and embed it within a wider confrontation between industrialized Europe and its rural periphery.

The plot of the novel follows Filip Latinowicz's return to the provincial town of his birth after a twenty-five-year career as an artist in Western Europe. Exhausted by the urban space of the western metropolises, Latinowicz seeks respite and revival in the countryside. However, he is shockingly out of place in rural Pannonia, a stagnant space governed by the cyclical rhythms of agricultural labour. By foregrounding the material processes that shaped the Pannonian landscape, Krleža decentres the nation and rescales his literary critique to a more expansive regional space. Rather than offering an allegory of Croatian or Yugoslav nation-building, the novel explores the political, aesthetic, and existential conditions of life on the European periphery.[63] In one infamous passage, as Latinowicz traipses through villages in which "the acrid smell of ammonia from languid manure and stables" fills the air, Krleža evokes the metaphysics of the rural periphery:

All an incomprehensibly immense overflow of something that spreads out in space and is entangled in itself like a satiated boa constrictor; it swallows itself and vomits and turns into stinking pitch. Movement in all directions, a confused circulation of particles without foundation and without any inner meaning;

Figure 3.6 | Pannonia in the 1930s.

our humanity walks and buries itself, and is reborn and springs up, like water, like mud, like food. It kills itself, devours itself, digests itself, secretes itself, swallows itself, moves and travels along the intestines, along roads, along ravines, in waters! At one place it begins to fade, and at another it flourishes like weeds on a dunghill, and all this, however hellish in its essentiality, is fleshy and strong and ineradicable within us. There is no one-way direction or development, since everything is entangled, jungle-like, marshy, Pannonian, hopeless and dark.[64]

Here the Pannonian landscape is governed by the chaotic repetition of rural ecology and agricultural production, of consumption, excretion, rot, and rebirth. The use of scatological imagery – the references to mud and manure and the reappearance of intestines and digestive systems – evoked the base, organic processes of agrarian life.[65]

This grotesque vision confounded models of historical progress. If the social literature movement imported kernels of a more complete, more advanced modernity into the rural periphery to spur its forward movement, Krleža suspended any such teleological momentum. In this passage, Nietzsche's eternal return found its expression not in the lofty musings of German philosophy but in the everyday labour of the Pannonian peasant. This irrational, dark, and chaotic world was inaccessible to social literature, whose didactic realism obscured a deeper metaphysical reality. But it was also lost on a provincial nationalism that artificially limited its horizons to the borders of a single nation state. The material processes that underpinned the grotesque world of the periphery were infused in a regional landscape that cut through contemporary national borders.

If social literature pursued cultural development within the framework of a more egalitarian, proletarian internationalism, Krleža's criticism suggested a more complex strategy. For him, the asymmetries of power and prestige that structured world literary space were inescapable. They were inscribed in the physiology and psychology of the peripheral writer not as national or racial characteristics but as embodied manifestations of centuries of foreign domination, economic exploitation, and uneven capitalist development. Cultural dependence on the West could not be overcome by simply importing a supposedly universalizable realism, nor by mobilizing the state to impose a homogenous national culture, but only through immersion in the existential conditions of the periphery.

Pannonia, in this sense, served Krleža as a mediating space that helped to clarify the path towards a distinctly local culture. To be sure, this was a purely intellectual venture. Krleža was not proposing the creation of institutions or policies that could operate at a Pannonian scale. Rather, Pannonia served as the imagined site through which to critique the asymmetries of world literary space while simultaneously decentering the nation as the primary site of resistance, sovereignty, and development. The fate of the Pannonian writer, for Krleža, was to inhabit a psychological complex in which one's compassion for the peasantry concealed a visceral disgust for their poverty, ignorance, and brutality; in which a deeply felt patriotism belied a cringing sense of inferiority and intellectual dependence; in which a heroic heritage of peasant uprisings and national rebellions had led to an era of dictatorship, poverty, and economic collapse. While such contradictions promised a rich resource for artistic creativity, the works they inspired could not easily be translated into the field of politics. Nor, in effect, could cultural independence be achieved outside of the world literary system. Opposition could only be undertaken as a war of position within it, to speak from the space of the periphery and confront the prestigious metropole with its abject other.

V

The great depression undermined the efforts of international leaders to restore global trade and financial links in the decade after World War I. The crisis ruptured the contours of global capitalist space and exacerbated the geographic unevenness of the world system. The turn to protectionism, the collapse of world money markets and the gold standard, and the resurgence of aggressive projects of national territorial expansion in the 1930s amplified the asymmetries of power, wealth, and prestige across the globe. If, as we've seen, intellectuals in Eastern Europe had historically been sensitive to the processes of their region's integration into the global system, the great depression showed they were equally vulnerable to that system's dislocation. The crisis starkly highlighted the problem of the development of small nations' political power and economic capacity in an increasingly unstable order. In Yugoslavia, where the January 6 dictatorship suppressed open discussion of radical political strategies, anxieties around development were channeled into the field of culture. The intense literary polemics of this period, therefore, need to be read against the backdrop of the global disruptions brought about by the great depression.

The global crisis prompted the search for strategies of survival within new, antagonistic, and unstable geopolitical coordinates. The most common impulse, as in the fallout from the depression of the 1870s, was the reassertion of a national territorial paradigm of state power. This was, after all, the default that major powers – both liberal hegemons like the US and Britain, and nationalist insurgents, like Japan and Germany – would pursue over the course of the 1930s.[66] It was the solution promoted by Manoilescu as the only strategy for the small nations of South East Europe to break from their dependence on the markets of the West. Crnjanski was in perfect harmony with this impulse, transposing these political-economic strategies of protectionism into the register of political-aesthetics to argue for a program of Serbian cultural renewal safeguarded and consolidated by the state. As the pillars of a liberal capitalist order collapsed around him, he perceived the contours of a new world space shaped by rival national units struggling for survival.

On the Yugoslav Left, however, this impulse found few adherents. Although Krleža certainly shared Crnjanski's understanding of world literary space as a field of antagonism between asymmetrical powers, he rejected the narrow horizons of the nation state as both strategically insufficient and culturally parochial. Instead, he revived an earlier strategy of spatial rescaling, mapping a project of cultural development within supranational coordinates. While this project was no longer framed through the bombastic revolutionary rhetoric of his youth, Krleža continued to promote a vision of South East Europe as a mediating space that both enveloped but also exceeded the nation. It was at the scale of the supranational region – at times referred to as the Balkans, at times as Pannonia – that the processes of global integration and peripheralization could be most astutely perceived and their cultural schemas most critically interrogated.

But it was social literature, locked in the orbit of the Soviet Republic of Letters, that captured the imagination of a younger generation of Yugoslav communists. With its exciting depictions of industrial modernity, its revolutionary cosmopolitanism, and its activist commitments, this movement captivated young intellectuals stranded on Europe's agrarian periphery. It enacted its own strategy of cultural development through the primitive accumulation of foreign translations. There was a historical irony to this movement: in a moment characterized by the fragmentation of global capitalist space, the retreat behind national and imperial borders and the severing of international networks, social literature almost nostalgically imagined world space as a smooth surface across which ideas and texts could seamlessly flow. This vision eroded the Balkan geographies that had been so crucial to orienting earlier generations of Yugoslav socialism and, in fact, did away with any sense of a wider supranational space within which Yugoslavia might be nested. With the flattening and homogenizing of global space, social literature lost a language through which to speak about the uneven geographies of capitalism and the specific historical experience of the European periphery. While the Comintern and KPJ continued to promote a strategy of Balkan federalism, on the Yugoslav literary Left, the contours of such a mediating space were erased by a proletarian aesthetics. The deterritorialization this aesthetics fostered would clear the ideological path for Yugoslav communism's rapprochement with a vision of European belonging during the years of the Popular Front.

4

The Popular Front, World Literature, and a Rapprochement with Europe, 1934–38

It cannot be denied that the Middle Ages are making a comeback. How far have we gone from them? Like the surface of a plowed field, so Europe – the heart and brain of the world – was tidied up and dressed up, combed and made up, just as peasants comb and make up the soil when they want to cheat the tax inspector. And we – we fooled the world. Under a thin layer of culture, the seeds of superstition, rudeness and barbarism continue to live. Now weeds have broken through and are growing. Western Europe may be overwhelmed by the Middle Ages. To a large extent, it has already been "balkanized."

Martin Andersen Nexø, speech at the Paris Congress for the Defense of Culture, 1935

I

In May 1933, the Dalmatian city of Dubrovnik became the focus of writers and intellectuals around Europe. The city was host to the congress of PEN International, an event that local organizers and the regime had hoped would put Yugoslavia on the world literary map. On the opening night, the congress staged a performance of Ivan Gundulić's seventeenth-century drama, *Dubravka*, to showcase Yugoslavia's cultural achievements. A review of the performance by the treasurer of the Croatian PEN society, Josip Horvath, indicated the anxiety the organizers felt regarding their reception before a European public:

The production of Gundulić's *Dubravka* ... was meant to show to the foreign writers that our cultural life was not exactly in its rudimentary stage, and that despite our unfavorable geopolitical

World Literature and Rapprochement with Europe   99

position we had managed to develop an authentic culture of our own and contribute significantly to the cultural life of Europe ... All foreign spectators were informed about the significance of Gundulić's work and his well-deserved place in world literature, by means of a brochure published for the occasion in French, English and German ... The fact that *Dubravka* was written and performed several decades before French classical plays and Molière, that it is a contemporary of Shakespeare and that its language in form and idiom was already definitive while the German literary language was only nascent, all that was acknowledged with great respect by intellectuals from abroad.[1]

The cringing sense of self-awareness in this passage, the comparisons with Shakespeare and Molière, the desire of the organizers to prove to their foreign audience just how "European" a cultural heritage they boasted, all pointed to the organizers' attempt to secure the recognition of metropolitan elites and be inscribed on the map of world literature. In the event, the congress *would* capture the attention of Europe's intellectuals, but not for the reasons its organizers intended.

The Dubrovnik congress was the first international confrontation between fascist and antifascist intellectuals following Hitler's shocking rise to power in January 1933. Controversy erupted on the very first afternoon, when the PEN international leadership permitted an unofficial, antifascist delegation of exiled German writers to address the congress. After a heated exchange, the official German delegates stormed out. The following day the leader of the antifascist delegation, socialist playwright Ernst Toller, publicly denounced those Germans who collaborated with Hitler's regime. The congress, after all, took place as Nazi activists in Germany set fire to books deemed antithetical to the German spirit.[2] Amidst such displays of barbarism, Toller argued, literature could not pretend to be a "neutral ground."

Toller's call for engagement resonated powerfully with the members of Yugoslavia's social literature movement. Following the conference, the German author traveled throughout Yugoslavia giving public readings of his work and speaking on the rising dangers of fascism. He was greeted with jubilation by young leftists, and on at least one occasion was reportedly carried through the streets on the shoulders of communist youth.[3] After four years of political repression and state censorship, Toller's intervention at Dubrovnik and his subsequent tour through the country breathed new life into the literary Left. It also signaled a growing awareness on the part of moderate writers that the looming threat of fascism demanded from them a more politically committed mode of public engagement. As the Communist Party of Yugoslavia (KPJ) shifted towards the more open policy of the Popular Front in the years that followed, this broad antifascist sentiment cohered in an organized cultural front.

The period of the Popular Front marked a sharp shift in the political and cultural geography of Yugoslav socialism. Politically, the KPJ broke with its ultra-left policies of the third period and sought out alliances with more moderate political forces. This moderation carried over into the party's assessment of the national question and led to a new policy in favour of a supranational Yugoslav federation.[4] On the cultural front, writers and literary theorists abandoned social literature in favour of what they termed "new realism." This led them to embrace the legacy of nineteenth-century realism, to lay claim to national traditions, and to foster a sense of European belonging. The KPJ's new policies aligned with the broader geopolitical shifts prompted by the international communist movement's turn to the Popular Front strategy. The Comintern's efforts to ally with social democratic and liberal forces across Europe was paralleled by a move away from the iconoclastic attitudes of proletarian literature and an embrace of a shared European cultural inheritance.[5] Silhouetted against Nazi bonfires, the progressive, democratic, and humanist dimension of this European inheritance stood out more clearly, and during the second half of the 1930s, Comintern intellectuals called for a defence of European civilization from fascist barbarism.

This chapter reconstructs the intellectual contours of this rapprochement with Europe among the Yugoslav literary Left during the years of the Popular Front. It situates this geopoetic shift in the broader geopolitical reconfigurations that took place in Europe following the rise of the Nazi regime. As South East Europe was drawn into the political, economic, and cultural orbit of the Third Reich, Yugoslavs on the radical Left appealed to a vision of a united, antifascist Europe. Breaking with the proletarian internationalism that animated the social literature movement, leftist writers began to embrace distinct national traditions and to present the antifascist Left as the inheritors and defenders of their respective nations' cultural heritage. As they set out to ground revolutionary culture more forcefully in the nation, they simultaneously nested these national cultures within a wider European geography. This move marked a radical negation of earlier aesthetic traditions that had emphasized the geopolitical antagonism between the Balkans and Europe, and instead posited a shared sense of European belonging. The "barbaro-genius" of the Balkans had become the defender of Europe's cherished cultural heritage.

II

In 1938, Leni Riefenstahl's film *Olympia* hit German screens. Ostensibly a documentary about the 1936 Berlin Olympic games, its primary purpose was to celebrate the new, purified body of national socialism. The camera lingers on the bodies of athletes and their feats of strength or agility, establishing a direct link between the Third Reich and the idealized heritage of classical antiquity. While Riefenstahl's film has long been acknowledged as an expression of Nazi neo-classicism, what is less commonly observed is the distinct way in which it re-envisioned the space of Europe in its opening sequences.[6] As it tracks the path of the torch from Mount Olympus to Berlin, Reifenstahl's camera pulls back to reveal a map of South East and Central Europe: from Athens over the Rhodope Mountains into Sofia, the camera pans westward to the cityscape of Belgrade on the banks of the Danube, which it follows north to Budapest, continuing through Vienna and Prague before arriving at its destination in Berlin. Along the route the names and flags of the respective nation states are superimposed over the map: Greece, Bulgaria, Yugoslavia, Hungary, Austria, Czechoslovakia, Germany. This sequence reconfigured the coordinates of European civilization, no longer plotted through its prestigious Western capitals – Paris, London, Rome, Amsterdam – but those of South East and Central Europe.

The map of Europe that Riefenstahl presented in this opening sequence traced the contours of the informal empire that the Third Reich constructed in the 1930s. Since the Paris Peace Conference, the space of Central and South East Europe had been the focus of French diplomacy, which sought to foster an alliance of Czechoslovakia, Romania, and Yugoslavia as both a cordon sanitaire against the spread of Bolshevism and a means to contain a future resurgent Germany.[7] The impact of deglobalization during the great depression, however, dissolved this geopolitical barrier. As France followed Britain and the US in their withdrawal behind tariff walls, the small export economies of Europe's east were cut off from the Western markets that were critical to their recovery and future growth. For a faction of German capitalists and state officials, this retreat of the liberal powers from Eastern Europe created an opportunity to rebuild Germany's economic and political influence at a continental scale. With the coming to power of Nazism, these efforts went into full force. Anchored in a series of bilateral trade deals, expanding networks of cultural exchange, and development projects designed to better align the region's economies with the needs of German industry, the Nazi government sought to consolidate the space of Eastern Europe within a broader Reichsmark bloc.[8] By 1938 the French-sponsored petite entente had been fragmented and its parts reorganized to correspond to German geopolitical priorities.[9]

The Third Reich's efforts to integrate the space of Eastern Europe within a broader German zone of influence was also realized at the level of culture. Although Popular Front intellectuals on the Left caricatured fascists as anticultural barbarians, during the 1930s German and Italian officials actively pursued a renewal of European culture. The Nazi-fascist project of European cultural renewal expressly rejected the cosmopolitanism associated with postwar international organizations like the League of Nations, and instead envisioned a future European order of "purified" national cultures.[10] Proponents of this new order presented it as a means of defending the interests of Europe's small nations from the powerful commercial pressures of Western mass culture. While this project was often a thinly-veiled effort to project German and Italian soft power, it nevertheless resonated with the concerns of nationalist or conservative intellectuals in many of Europe's smaller nations.[11] One need only think back to Miloš Crnjanski's polemics against the "flood" of mass-produced translations of foreign texts, explored in the preceding chapter, to see how this fascist vision of a new cultural order could appeal to nationalist intellectuals on Europe's periphery.

The rise of Hitler and his imperial ambitions in Eastern Europe prompted a radical realignment of the spatial coordinates of world communism. Since Stalin's rise to power at the end of the 1920s, the Comintern had largely retreated from efforts to promote revolution throughout Eurasia. The combined impact of the failure of revolution in the West, the catastrophic collapse of the united front policy in China, and Stalin's program of socialism in one country, led Soviet leaders to focus their efforts on internal consolidation both within the Soviet Union and in the world communist movement. The rise of Hitler, his regime's rapid decimation of the German Left, and the obvious threat he posed to the Soviet Union forced the leadership in Moscow to reenter the game of geopolitics to seek a means for containing German militarism. The most obvious candidate for an alliance was France, whose political elite shared Soviet anxieties about German expansion.[12]

The form that this new alliance-building took came to be known as the Popular Front. Although it would be too simplistic to reduce the Popular Front to a mere veil for Soviet geopolitics, Moscow's priorities were the deciding factor in this strategic reversal. The Popular Front model evolved initially in France, where communists responded to the fascist riots of early 1936 by forming a broad-based antifascist alliance with the reformist socialists and the liberal Radical Party. The French model was quickly identified by the Comintern's new general secretary, the Bulgarian Georgi Dimitrov, as a viable tactic for communists around Europe.[13] This, of course, marked an abrupt volte-face from the sectarianism of the third period and led to a new era of communists adopting a more conciliatory attitude to capitalist states and working alongside more moderate political forces. The tactic, however, was ultimately viable because it aligned with and, indeed, helped provide ideological justification for, the Soviet leadership's pursuit of a collective security pact with the French government. The Franco-Soviet Mutual Assistance Pact of May 1935 locked that alliance in place, framing the Soviet Union's rapprochement with the West over the next four years.[14]

In Yugoslavia, the new Popular Front policy prompted a change in how communists approached the national question and how the nation was to be configured within broader political and cultural geographies. Most immediately, the break with the third period opened the way for a reevaluation of the politics of Yugoslavism. Since May 1926, the KPJ had criticized the Yugoslav state as a project of greater Serbian hegemony, calling for its dissolution and the reconstitution of its distinct national communities within a broader Balkan federation.[15] From March 1935 the KPJ jettisoned this critique, and instead proposed its own vision of the country reorganized along federal lines. Rejecting the centralizing Yugoslavism that had been pursued by the Karađorđević dictatorship since 1929, they instead called for a state that would be the home of multiple nations. Yugoslavia was now to be conceived as a mediating space, a supranational project in which the constituent nations would enjoy extensive cultural and political autonomy. This more measured response to the Yugoslav idea was intended to foster an alliance with moderate political forces that had been uncomfortable with the party's earlier call for the total dissolution of the state. The policy also reflected a growing unease with the degree to which the party's anti-Yugoslavism aligned with the irredentist ambitions of far-right organizations like the Internal Macedonian Revolutionary Organization or the Croatian Ustasha. As communists came to view these groups as the handmaidens of German and Italian imperialism, they sought to more clearly delineate their own criticism of the Yugoslav state from that of the fascist Right.[16]

The Popular Front period also led to a growing sense of European belonging among Yugoslav communists. In part this was a consequence of the more moderate political outlook. The embrace of Yugoslavism led the party to de-emphasize the Balkan federalism that had been a central part of its earlier, ultra-left policy. As this Balkan idea receded in communist policy, so too did the antagonistic geopolitical imaginary it sustained with Europe. During this period, Yugoslav communists increasingly emphasized their part in a continent-wide struggle to defend Europe from the threat of fascism. This new political geography was underpinned by the European scale of the party's activity. Since the proclamation of the royal dictatorship in January 1929, much of the cadre had fled into exile, creating a Europe-wide network of Yugoslav communists in cities like Vienna, Prague, and Paris.[17] Yugoslav participation in the Spanish Civil War and the passage of hundreds of activists across the alps to reach Spain also helped to plot the party's activity within a European geography.[18] As Yugoslav communists increasingly understood themselves to be manoeuvering within European horizons, an earlier anticolonial Balkanism gave way to an antifascist Europeanism.

III

The European scale of the Comintern's antifascist campaign was especially pronounced in the realm of cultural production. Just as German and Italian officials sought to coordinate a new authoritarian, nationalist, and anti-Semitic cultural order in Europe, so too did Popular Front intellectuals call for the defence of a collective European culture from the threat of fascist barbarism. The PEN

World Literature and Rapprochement with Europe   105

congress of 1933 had hinted at the resonance such a broad antifascist cultural front might have in the heightened political climate. The Comintern's subsequent shift to the Popular Front strategy opened the space to forge a meaningful alliance with antifascist intellectuals across a broad ideological spectrum. This new spirit of cultural co-operation was manifested at the International Writers' Congress for the Defense of Culture held in Paris in June 1935. The meeting brought together around two hundred writers from fourteen countries, including some of the leading lights of world literature of the day: André Gide, André Malraux, Henri Barbusse, Louis Aragon, Romain Rolland, Julien Benda, E.M. Forster, Aldous Huxley, Ernst Toller, Heinrich Mann, Anna Seghers, Bertolt Brecht, Ilia Ehrenburg, Boris Pasternak, Robert Musil, Max Brod, and Lion Feuchtwanger.[19] Given such a lineup, it is unsurprising that the three-thousand-seat hall at the Palais de la Mutualité was filled to capacity.

The Paris meeting revealed the narrowly European horizons within which the antifascist cultural front of the mid-1930s operated. The organizers left little doubt that the culture they sought to defend was that of Europe's great nations. The walls of the venue were hung with portraits of the masters of European literature: Shakespeare, Tolstoi, Molière, Gogol, Cervantes, Heine, Pushkin, and Balzac.[20] Representatives from France, Germany, Britain, and the Soviet Union dominated the platform. Their speeches traced a distinctly European cultural geography, with many speakers evoking a heritage they traced from Ancient Greece to the Renaissance and Enlightenment and on to the French Revolution. For the Danish writer Martin Andersen Nexø, the soil of Europe – "that heart and brain of the world" – was at risk of being overwhelmed by a fascism that harked back to the darkness of the Middle Ages. From the seemingly cultivated soil of Europe's fields, he warned, the weeds of "superstition, rudeness, and barbarism" were beginning to sprout. Nexø gave a name to this threat: balkanization.[21] Although he was not to know it, his choice of term revealed the gulf between the antifascist Left of the Popular Front years and the revolutionary avant-gardes of the 1920s. If the latter had evoked the Balkans as a space of vital, revolutionary resistance to European hegemony, in the mid-1930s the Balkans became synonymous with a violent archaism that haunted enlightened and civilized Europe.

The participation of prominent communist writers in the congress indicated a marked shift in the literary geopolitics of the world communist movement. Whereas communist writers of the late 1920s had pursued an internationalist proletarian alternative to the hegemonic literary system of bourgeois Europe, Popular Front writers instead laid claim to this very system, casting communism as a defender of a European legacy of democratic humanism.[22] Communist writers had already been exhorted by Comintern and Soviet leaders to adopt a more open and conciliatory attitude to Europe's cultural heritage. In August 1934, a year before the Paris meeting, the First Soviet Writers' Congress had revised official cultural policy, condemning the sectarianism of the *proletkult* movement and adopting the more open policy of socialist realism. This revision did away with the class war paradigm of culture that had informed the *proletkult* and instead promoted a reappraisal of national-popular cultural traditions, a renewed respect for the classical literary tradition of Europe, and greater collaboration between communist and non-communist writers.[23] The policy complimented the emerging doctrine of the Popular Front, as the Soviet official Karl Radek observed when he exhorted communist writers to learn from those progressive bourgeois writers of the West who had joined the ranks of the antifascist movement.[24]

Far from smashing the bourgeois cultural order, communists were now to embrace its more progressive elements. Speaking at the Moscow Writer's House in 1935, Georgi Dimitrov called on writers to draw inspiration from the literary heritage of the European bourgeoisie in its early, revolutionary stage: "At one time the revolutionary bourgeoisie fought lustily for the advancement of their class, using all means, fine literature included. What made a laughing stock of the remnants of knighthood? *Don Quixote* by Cervantes. *Don Quixote* was a powerful weapon in the hands of the bourgeoisie against feudalism, against the aristocracy. The revolutionary proletariat has need of at least one little Cervantes who would give them such a weapon for their struggle."[25] As a key text in the formation of the European novel, *Don Quixote* was a central plank of what a mere five years before would have been unflatteringly dismissed by *proletkult* activists as "bourgeois literature." For Dimitrov, however, this text was part of a progressive historical tradition, a heritage from which the proletariat could draw political inspiration and aesthetic models in its struggle against fascism. During the period of the Popular Front, in other words, communist and anti-fascist writers were called upon to take their points of reference from the bourgeois classics of the European literary canon.

World Literature and Rapprochement with Europe   107

Nobody in the Comintern's cultural establishment did more to theorize and promote this revised attitude to the cultural heritage of Europe than the Hungarian Marxist and literary theorist Georg Lukács (1885–1971). Since his exile from Hungary following the repression of the 1919 soviet government, Lukács had been intellectually active in Central European communist circles, moving first to Vienna, then Berlin, before settling in Moscow in the 1930s. It was here, while working at the Marx and Engels Institute, that he most forcefully advanced his argument for the appropriation of the European realist canon. Lukács was especially critical of the shallow realism that had characterized proletarian literature, and instead insisted that progressive writers return to the more robust, humanist realism of the early nineteenth century. This literature, represented by figures like Scott, Balzac, Goethe, and Tolstoi, was able to capture human reality as an artistic totality that offered an immediate experience of the development of history. It was able to do this because, in contrast to naturalism and its proletarian literary offshoots, it emphasized narration and characterization over description and psychologization.[26] This capacity to confidently reflect the development of historical reality, Lukács argued, was a product of the emancipatory and revolutionary spirit of the early bourgeois era. It had receded, however, following the 1848 revolutions, when the European bourgeoisie increasingly found itself challenged by the worldview of a rising proletariat.[27]

Lukács took these arguments up in his 1939 work, *The Historical Novel*, a series of essays composed over 1936–37 and published in leading Soviet journals over 1937–38.[28] In this work, he sought to offer a direction to antifascist culture by advocating the European historical novel as a suitable model for the revival and development of progressive, revolutionary, and democratic humanist literature. The historical novel, Lukács argued, had its origins in the explosion of historical consciousness that emerged across Europe in the wake of the French Revolution and Napoleonic Wars. This consciousness was exemplified in the literature of Walter Scott who, despite his efforts to retreat from the social conflicts of industrializing Britain into a heroic, traditional past, none the less articulated a modern historical consciousness.[29] Despite Scott's reactionary politics, Lukács argued, his work expressed an understanding of history that centred on the dramatic changes to popular life brought about by large-scale social conflicts. Historical time was neither a cyclical repetition nor a stage on which the great men of an era played, but rather a process that unfolded through the contestation and conflict that brought about the rise and fall of social orders. This historical consciousness, Lukács argued, allowed Scott to infuse the individualistic form of the novel with a popular character that could manifest the wider social forces at play in a given nation at a certain period of its development.[30]

The emphasis that Lukács placed on the national popular character of Scott's work was of particular significance to the new paradigm of culture that came to dominate the Popular Front era. Forced to account for the obvious popularity of fascist ideology among huge swathes of the European population, some Comintern theorists turned to the framework of the national question. Fascists, they argued, had hijacked the popular political traditions of different national communities to pass themselves off as their historic realization.[31] In a speech at the Seventh Congress of the Comintern in 1935, Dimitrov urged communist intellectuals to challenge this fascist "ransacking" of national culture: "Communists who suppose that [the fascist ransacking of national culture] has nothing to do with the cause of the working class, who do nothing to enlighten the masses on the past of their people in a historically correct fashion, in a genuinely Marxist-Leninist spirit, who do nothing *to link up the present struggle with the people's revolutionary traditions and past* – voluntarily hand over to the fascist falsifiers all that is valuable in the historical past of the nation, so that the fascists may fool the masses."[32]

Communists, in other words, were to compete with fascists as the inheritors and interpreters of national popular traditions. They were to explore and stage the popular revolutionary traditions of individual nations the better to channel national sentiment into an international antifascist struggle. This cultural paradigm spread quickly, and it leant to communist parties a certain national individuality and broader popular appeal that the iconoclasm and ultra-leftism of the third period had undermined. In France, communists evoked the legacy of Jacobin republicanism; in Britain they laid claim to the history of Chartism; in Czechoslovakia they celebrated the egalitarian struggles of the Hussites.[33] Here was the Popular Front's reply to the Nazi-fascist vision of a new European cultural order; in place of a coalition of ethnically purified national fortresses, they offered a vision of a European community of nations, a supranational project that preserved and elevated the democratic humanist impulses of its composite cultures.

The cultural reappraisal of the Popular Front era fostered a new geopoetic project articulated at the continental scale of Europe. In an effort to present themselves as inheritors of their national traditions, communist intellectuals increasingly articulated these claims in terms that aligned their respective cultures with a universal humanist legacy coded as distinctly European. This reappraisal marked a shift from the proletarian literary movement in two ways. First, it reversed the deterritorializing impulse of proletarian literature and instead reterritorialized cultures within distinct national-historical landscapes. Communist writers and their literary fellow travelers sought to embed their work in local traditions in ways that evoked a distinctly national cultural geography. Second, it reconfigured the horizons within which communist writers operated from the global to the European. This was, however, a Europe of nation states: national communities were to be brought into tighter and more harmonious alignment through their unification within a shared European cultural zone. Europe, then, named a mediating space within which the historically progressive strands of the continent's national cultures could be reinforced and cultivated the better to resist the rising tide of fascism.

IV

The transmission of this new cultural strategy to Yugoslavia led to a rupture with the aesthetics of social literature and the turn to what became known as "new realism." Over the second half of the 1930s, leftist writers and critics across the kingdom sought to recover their distinct local traditions and to rework these within a democratic, humanist, and European framework. New realist writers took inspiration from historical struggles for national liberation, while critics scoured their national literary histories with new eyes, eager to craft a more inclusive canon of progressive literature. The proletariat was no longer to be conceived as the globally dispersed protagonist in the distinctly modern drama of the international class war, but rather the contemporary iteration of a collective subject known as "the people," whose historical drama was played out on national and European stages. At the same time, the historical model along which new realist critics plotted these national literatures took as its norm the history of France, Britain, Germany, and Russia. Writers began to seek out the Serbian Balzac, the Croatian Tolstoi, the Slovene

Goethe, and through this process the Yugoslav literary Left came to advocate what could be described as a rapprochement with Europe. The comparative nature of this project, of course, often found the national cultures of Yugoslavia wanting, thereby reinforcing asymmetries of prestige at a European scale.

The reception of Lukács's ideas was central to the turn to new realism in Yugoslavia. From 1936 onwards, the Hungarian Marxist's literary theories began to find fertile ground, especially among a group of young communists in Belgrade that included Milovan Đilas (1911–1995), Radovan Zogović (1907–1986), and Đorđe Jovanović (1909–1943).[34] These intellectuals had come from different literary and political backgrounds: Đilas and Zogović had been ardent followers of social literature, while Jovanović began his career in the Belgrade surrealist movement. But by the mid-1930s all were active in the underground work of the KPJ and saw their literary interventions as closely bound up with the political tasks of building an antifascist Popular Front.[35]

In Yugoslavia, laying claim to a European cultural inheritance meant first putting to rest the earlier Balkanist ideas of the revolutionary avant-gardes and their anticolonial critique of Europe. To this end, Đilas, Zogović, and Jovanović recast this earlier avant-garde tendency as a protofascist aesthetics. Just as Nexø had warned that fascism threatened to "balkanize" Europe, by which he meant its destruction through the revival of reactionary and violent archaisms, so too did new realists point to the Yugoslav avant-gardes' aggressive aesthetic primitivism as evidence of its underlying fascist sympathies. To be sure, they were not without compelling evidence. As we've already seen, two scions of the revolutionary avant-gardes, Ljubomir Micić and Miloš Crnjanski, had by the mid-1930s gravitated towards the fascist Right. Moreover, several right-wing intellectuals had evoked the avant-gardes' antagonistic geopolitical imaginary, identifying with a primitive, vital, and irrational Balkans against what they perceived as an effete, decadent, and overly intellectualized Europe. A stark example of this far-right adaptation of the Balkan idea was a 1938 work by the Serbian writer Vladimir Velmar-Janković, *Pogled s Kalemegdana – ogled o beogradskom čoveku* (*The View from Kalemegdan – Reflections on Belgrade Man*).[36] The piece was a modernist reflection on Serbian national culture staged through the view of a kind of Belgrade flaneur, a figure that recalled the primitive vitality of Micić's "barbaro-genius."

Janković, who was a member of the pseudo-fascist Jugoslavenska akcija (Yugoslav Action) movement, argued that the barbaro-genius's vitality was rooted in a distinctly Serbian, Balkan, and Eastern way of being that he contrasted with the soullessness of European man. In a way that echoed the irrationalist discourses of interwar far-right movements elsewhere in Europe, Janković sought to repurpose elements of an earlier revolutionary primitivist aesthetics for use in a fascist mythologization of the Balkans.[37]

The new realists in Belgrade were quick to point out the continuities between the radical aesthetics of the early avant-gardes and the language and symbolism of Yugoslav fascism. In a damning critique of Janković's essay, Đorđe Jovanović attacked what he saw as its essentializing and reactionary depiction of both Europe and the national cultures of Yugoslavia: "As with all those local balkanizing and yugoslavizing sages of the postwar years ... so too with Mr. Janković do we come across the fear of this 'old,' 'eaten away,' 'decadent' Europe, which with its poison gas, wants to corrode our 'young and raw' national – whether Slavic, Balkan or Oriental – organism. This clumsy Belgrade deformation of Spengler's variation on the fall of the West is unwieldy, intrusively sticks out like some kind of foppish curl on the otherwise meticulously crafted coif ... of our lonely and inspired Kalemegdan wanderer."[38] Tracing a line of descent from Micić's zenitism to the fascism of Janković and other Serbian nationalist intellectuals of the late 1930s, Jovanović implicated the early avant-gardes with the rising tide of fascism. The aesthetic Balkanism of the early 1920s, for him, was not an anticolonial geopoetics, an effort to secure regional autonomy from Europe's cultural dominance, but rather a reactionary rejection of Europe's legacy of progress, democracy, and humanism. What was called for, Jovanović insisted, was a Left that understood its role as a defender of these European values. Rejecting the iconoclasm of both the avant-gardes and the social literature movement, he called for an antifascist cultural front that could defend "those achievements ... which carry the character of the bourgeoisie in the period of its revolutionary ascendance."[39] As the rightful heir to this progressive legacy, the proletariat had an obligation to defend it from the ravages of fascism. By explicitly identifying avant-garde Balkanism with fascist mysticism, Jovanović implicitly aligned the antifascist struggle in Yugoslavia with a defence of European belonging.

The emphasis on Yugoslavia's belonging to a broader European cultural geography informed the new realists' reappraisal of national popular traditions. Adherents of the movement called on writers and critics to look to the classical canon of European literature as a point of reference for their respective nations' cultural development. In a programmatic article from 1936, for instance, Milovan Đilas advised writers to familiarize themselves with and seek artistic inspiration from the national histories and literary traditions of the Yugoslav peoples, suggesting as possible topics the Slovene-Croat peasant rebellion of 1573, the poets of the Illyrian movement, the Serbian national revolutionaries of 1804, the Montenegrin bishop-king and epic poet Petar Petrović Njegoš, the nineteenth-century Croatian national revolutionaries Ante Starčević and Eugen Kvaternik, the Slovene novelist Ivan Cankar, and the Serbian poet Jovan Jovanović Zmaj. Indeed, even folk poetry, which Đilas understood as a genuine expression of the people's aspirations and anxieties and therefore "a deep outflow of popular hatred towards the exploiters and love for freedom," should be mined for themes by Popular Front writers.[40] However, although he prioritized local themes and materials, he also emphasized the need to take up the lessons and experiences of more advanced cultures elsewhere in Europe: "We must," he insisted, "create our own expressions, tones and colours, our own literature, using the experience of new and old Europe and of our past."[41] New realism's project of national literary development, that is, was to be plotted within a broader European constellation that would provide points of reference, models of emulation, and a normative measure through which to calibrate their small nations' cultural progress.

Because new realists adopted a historical framework of literary development whose normative periodization was modeled on the canons of Europe's dominant literary cultures, its adherents tended to couch their call for a revival of national-popular traditions as integration into a wider European cultural zone. This was especially clear in Radovan Zogović's 1937 study of the Serbian epic poem. In this work, Zogović drew attention to the way in which this feudal genre was transformed during the period of Ottoman rule to become a vehicle for popular aspirations for national liberation.[42] The argument here was illustrative of new realism's efforts to reframe national traditions for use in the antifascist struggle. However, Zogović maintained that the genre had died out, living on only as a historical artifact; the onset of modernization and the integration of the Balkans into a global capitalist system dissolved the conditions that had given meaning to the epic form. With greater proximity to

Europe's major centres, this local, Balkan poetry had receded, giving way to European cultural influences.[43] It was within these European horizons, Zogović argued, that contemporary revolutionary writers from the Balkans were now to operate.

If the indigenous poetic genres of the Balkans had died out, then the development of progressive literature would come through a close study of the classics of European realism. In line with the new process of canon formation advocated by Lukács and other Popular Front intellectuals in Europe and the Soviet Union, Zogović directed young writers to model themselves on a particularly conventional, one might even say *conservative*, selection of writers from the literatures of France, Germany, Russia, and Britain. In particular, he cited favourably the work of Balzac and Tolstoi.[44] While the attendant call for a greater excavation of local cultures and traditions averted a shallow mimicry of the European canon, Zogović's pronouncements on the end of the Serbian epic and his orientation towards the classics of European realism amounted to a call for the Europeanization of Yugoslavia's national literatures. The further development of Serbian literature, that is, would formally converge with that of a wider European literature.

New realist theorists, like Zogović, Đilas, and Jovanović, helped to inaugurate a conceptual shift from the worldview of social literature in two major ways. First, they reconfigured the spatial scale of activity of Yugoslav revolutionary literature from the global to the European. Second, they reconceived the temporal rhythms of cultural development, moving away from notions of acceleration, rupture, and leaps into the future and towards a logic of cultivation that pursued a more measured recuperation of the past. Europe came to be understood as a cultural ecosystem within which the early shoots of Yugoslav progressive literature would find fertile soil. The history of the great literatures of Europe – in particular, French, German, Russian, and British – could be used to identify those "living" or "healthy" trends in the developing national literatures of Yugoslavia. Planting those cultures within a wider European cultural geography, new realists contended, was essential if they were to develop in a progressive direction. The Comintern's reconciliation with the world literary system during the years of the Popular Front was, in Yugoslavia, articulated as an integration into Europe.

In this sense, the cultural geography of Europe served a particular strategy of spatial mediation. As deployed by Yugoslav new realists,

Europe was envisioned as at once a community of nations organized into an antifascist alliance and an imagined cultural inheritance that was synonymous with the world literary system. If the revolutionary avant-gardes had evoked the Balkans as a means to defend the cultures of the region against the threat of European cultural dominance, the new realists' claim to European belonging served to facilitate their integration into that very order. By embracing Europe, new realists sought to negotiate the asymmetries of cultural prestige from a privileged position within the global hierarchy. This did not, of course, erase the gradations of prestige that characterized Europe's cultural order; Yugoslav new realists continued to perceive their national literatures as lagging behind those of more established cultures. But by extending the borders of Europe to encompass the small nations of its periphery, they acknowledged that their literary development would continue at a European scale. Two examples of leftist cultural production will serve to illustrate this process: the Slovene playwright Bratko Kreft's (1905–1996) *Velika puntarija* (*The Great Rebellion*, 1937), and the Croatian writer August Cesarec's *Sin domovine* (*Son of the Homeland*, 1940).

V

Born in 1905 in the regional capital of Maribor, Bratko Kreft had by the age of twenty become a major figure of the revolutionary avant-garde in Slovenia, active alongside Srečko Kosovel, Ivo Grahor, and Ludvik Mrzel. His political career had begun as early as 1923, while he was still living in Maribor and where he published in the town's daily *Tabor* (*Camp*) as well as in the pages of the socialist newspaper *Socialist*.[45] After studying theater in Vienna in the mid-1920s, during which time he worked at the editorial offices of the Comintern's *La fédération balkanique*, Kreft returned to Slovenia in 1927 and founded the amateur proletarian theatre company, Delavski oder (Workers' stage).[46] The group's first performance was a modern adaptation of Molière's *Les Fourberies de Scapin* (*Scapin's Deceit*) and its production reflected both the agitational and globalizing vision of the social literature movement. The young director, inspired by the ideas of Erwin Piscator and Bertolt Brecht, adapted the play to the modern era, setting it in the bustling streets of contemporary New York and featuring a formerly enslaved man from the American South and a member of the Apache nation.[47] Despite his known

World Literature and Rapprochement with Europe 115

affiliation with communist publications, in 1930, at the height of the Karađorđević dictatorship's persecution of political dissidents, Kreft was hired as a director of the Slovene National Theater. At the age of twenty-five, he became a prominent figure in the ranks of Slovene bourgeois culture and, as the 1930s progressed, moved further away from experimentation and towards more conventional forms, increasingly turning to the genre of historical drama.[48]

Velika puntarija dramatized the Slovene-Croatian peasant uprising of 1573, a formative event in the historical consciousness of Slovene nationalism. Kreft's account set the uprising within a broader historical matrix of diverse social struggles, including the Protestant Reformation and Habsburg Counter-Reformation, and the attendant conflicts between an Austrian state, Magyar aristocracy, and Slavic peasantry. Unsurprisingly, the drama was a sympathetic portrayal of the peasants' struggle against a cruel and cynical ruling elite, and didn't shy away from depicting the violence that had been used to repress the uprising. It was also notable for its use of a folk song by the leftist poet Mile Klopčič, a nod to the Popular Front effort to incorporate popular culture. Kreft published the work in 1937, and it had been intended to open the National Theater's 1938–39 season. However, after prominent figures in the Slovene political and economic establishment warned that its themes of social conflict might provoke unrest among the population, it was pulled from the schedule. Perhaps more appropriately, the play's first performance was staged in November 1938 by a peasant amateur theater in the rural province of Styria.

The peasant rebellion of 1573 had been of great interest to leftist intellectuals in Yugoslavia during the years of the Popular Front.[49] The most culturally significant work to explore the event was Miroslav Krleža's *Balade Petrice Kerempuha* (*The Ballads of Petrica Kerempuh*) from 1936. The cycle of poems, which were written in the Kajkavian dialect, captured the carnivalesque, chaotic, and violent atmosphere of peasant life in the 1500s.[50] Although the work's modernist sensibilities, in particular its use of a highly-stylized, historic dialect infused with Latin, Hungarian, and German to explore dense and abstract philosophical themes, frustrated many on the left, it none the less reflected something of the Popular Front effort to recuperate national popular traditions. In his typically provocative way, however, Krleža's cycle managed to enrage the nationalist Right, who criticized its use of the Kajkavian dialect.[51] The work was so controversial that it had to be published in Ljubljana, an arrangement facilitated by none other than Krleža's good friend, Kreft.[52] Kreft, then, was immersed in contemporary debates among the Croatian and Slovene Left regarding the appropriate treatment of the 1573 rebellion.

Before delving further into Kreft's drama, it is worth taking a few moments to offer a brief historical account of the Slovene-Croatian peasant rebellion of 1573. The epicentre for the uprising was the land of the Hungarian nobleman Ferenc Tahy de Tahvár et Tarkő, who had not only instituted a crippling taxation on his serfs but was also accused of sexually abusing their wives and daughters. In 1572 an uprising across his sizeable estates instituted a peasant common-wealth, which threatened to spread throughout the Slovene- and Croatian-speaking lands and forced Tahy to flee. Although the upris-ing was quelled by an intervention from Vienna and promises of resolving the peasants' disputes, the return of Tahy to his estate and the Croatian diet's attack on the peasants sparked a renewed rebel-lion. Over January and February of 1573, a peasant army of 12,000 controlled a territory that spanned the northwest border region of the Croatian territories, the region of Lower Styria, and parts of Carniola. The movement was crushed when the local uskoks, who had only decades before immigrated to the region, sided with the lords.[53] The ensuing repression was brutal, with peasants tortured, hung, impaled, and drowned, in an effort to stamp out any future rebellions. Ambroz (Matija) Gubec, who was a leader of the revolt, was executed in an extended public spectacle in which he was cel-ebrated as the "king of the serfs" and had a hot iron crown forced on his head before he was tortured and finally quartered.[54] While hardly a work of grand-guignolesque sensationalism, *Velika puntar-ija* did not shy from referencing the horrors perpetrated against the leaders of the uprising.

Anxious that the political dimension of his play not be over-looked, Kreft introduced the drama with a lengthy historical study of the uprising, situating it within the wider history of the dissolu-tion of the feudal system in Europe. The rebellion, Kreft informed his readers, took place amidst a growing competition between the feudal order and the agents of the new capitalist system.[55] This com-petition spanned four centuries, beginning with the French jacquerie of 1358 and ending with the French revolution, which cemented the power of the bourgeoisie and inaugurated a new, modern era

World Literature and Rapprochement with Europe 117

of capitalism and revolutionary democracy. Kreft analyzed several of the key events that took place over these four centuries of conflict, including the English peasant revolts of 1358 and 1450, the 1514 peasant revolution in the Kingdom of Hungary led by the crusader György Dózsa, the peasant wars of Germany and the leadership of Thomas Müntzer, the Cossack revolts led by Stenka Raza (1668–71) and Yemelian Pugachev (1773–74), and the peasant rebellions of Romanians in Transylvania in 1784.[56] Reconstructing a well-established Marxist historiography, he identified these four centuries of political and social conflict as the extended crumbling of the feudal system and the spread of a new commodity-oriented economy throughout the European continent. As this transition was under way, it disrupted traditional relations between serfs and lords, sparking mass peasant uprisings like that staged in his drama.[57]

The historical preamble detailing the peasant revolts of early modern Europe provided the reader with a backdrop upon which they could locate the events of 1573. Indeed, Kreft went further. The point of the drama was not simply to tell the story of an isolated historical event, but to offer a vision of Slovene history that was woven into a much longer and more epic European past and which continued to inform popular struggles in the present. As Kreft claimed in his conclusion: "The Slovene nation (*narod*) grew from a peasant people (*ljudstva*) and the peasant revolts are our very heroic past. Long before the French Revolution, the masses of Slovene peasants were subconsciously struggling for the same democratic rights as the French bourgeois revolutionaries ... Whoever says that our people does not have its own history in its distant past is blind and a liar. With pride we can refer to this, our history – the Slovene peasant revolts. Furthermore, the heroism in [these revolts], is higher and grander than all the medieval chivalry that existed in our lands."[58]

This passage, which outlined the political impetus for Kreft's drama, exemplified the cultural strategy of the Popular Front. Of particular importance is the fact that for Kreft, this was a question of offering a history of the people, not a single social class. The Slovene nation (*narod*) had grown from a peasant people (*ljudstvo*), the former denoting a sense of national community or folk, the latter implying a sense of the masses. Kreft was here identifying Slovene national history with a legacy of the struggles of subaltern classes; national identity grew out of the struggles of the popular classes in their conflict with the feudal order. Furthermore, in staging

118 Mediating Spaces

the struggle of a Slavic peasant population against a German and Hungarian aristocracy, he also cast the uprising as a prelude to the modern struggle of Slovene national liberation from the Habsburg Empire. Although the anticolonial thrust of this critique was somewhat out of step with the more moderate, European politics of the Popular Front era, it did allude to a growing anxiety regarding little Slovenia's place in a European map redrawn by an ascendant Nazi Germany and its allies.

Kreft's early career nicely signposts the reconfigurations of the mediating spaces of Yugoslav socialism over the interwar period. In 1925 we find him working as an editor on the Comintern's Balkan newspaper *La fédération balkanique* and, with his comrade Srečko Kosovel, singing the glories of a future Balkan federation premised on a break with European domination. In 1928 he is directing a production of Molière set in present-day New York, in line with the global, modernizing vision of social literature. And in 1937 he is delving backwards, recreating a distinctly national, Slovene past now conceived as part of a wider European cultural heritage. As the Comintern in the era of the Popular Front sought alliances with democratic, liberal, and even conservative forces across Europe in a joint struggle against fascism, the anticolonialism that had informed the revolutionary avant-gardes' aesthetic Balkanism withered away. In its place, the literary Left of Yugoslavia came to see themselves within the cultural space of a Europe now coded as humanist, enlightened, and democratic.

VI

The European scale of Popular Front culture in Yugoslavia was also reflected in another historical drama, *Sin domovine*, by the Croatian communist writer, August Cesarec. As we saw in chapter two, Cesarec had been a founding figure of Croatian communism. Alongside Miroslav Krleža, he had edited the first Marxist cultural journal in the Kingdom of Serbs, Croats, and Slovenes and been a leading figure of the early literary Left. During the 1920s, he was active in local projects of the Comintern's International Red Aid organization, defending the legal rights of political prisoners in the kingdom.[59] Following the declaration of the January 6 dictatorship, the pressure of state persecution and censorship forced him to withdraw from the political field. However, unlike his longtime comrade

World Literature and Rapprochement with Europe   119

Krleža, Cesarec moved closer to the KPJ during the years of dictatorship and depression. While he eschewed more open political work, he embraced the social literature movement as one of the few avenues open for left-wing intellectuals.[60] It wasn't until 1934, when he clandestinely left Yugoslavia to travel to the Soviet Union, that he was once again free to engage more openly in political debates. After living in Moscow for several years, where he researched a book on contemporary life in the first socialist state, he then traveled to Spain in the summer of 1937 to report on the struggle of the Republican forces, before eventually settling in Paris.[61] In the summer of 1938 he finally returned to Zagreb and began to pen what would become his last major work.

Cesarec's biography during these years of travel marked out key sites on the Comintern's European map during the period of the Popular Front. He attended the historic Seventh Congress in Moscow, when Dimitrov announced the new strategy. He found himself on the battlefields of Spain, the frontlines of the struggle against fascism. He witnessed the French Popular Front in power from the cafés of Paris. Throughout this period, he remained connected to broader cultural debates on the communist Left, tracking the major aesthetic shifts as they were announced by figures like Lukács. These ideological shifts were registered in *Sin domovine*. The play dramatized the political career of Eugen Kvaternik, the nineteenth-century Croatian nationalist revolutionary. By the time Cesarec sat down to write his drama, Kvaternik had become synonymous with an uncompromising vision of Croatian independence. Alongside Ante Starčević, he had founded the Party of Rights in 1861 to campaign for the unification of the Croatian crownlands and the country's autonomy and eventual independence. Persecuted by the Habsburg state, he had spent much of his life in exile – in Russia, France, and Italy – before eventually leading an ill-fated uprising in the military frontiers of the Croatian interior in 1871. His opposition to more moderate "trialist" solutions to the Habsburg Empire's national question and his uncompromising insistence on Croatian independence had, by the early twentieth century, made him synonymous with an anti-Yugoslav strain of Croatian nationalism. When the Party of Rights was outlawed during the period of the January 6 dictatorship, for instance, many of its activists joined the underground fascist Ustasha movement in exile.[62] Kvaternik was, then, considered by many at the time to be very much a figure of the nationalist Right.

Sin domovine was Cesarec's effort to challenge the far-right appropriation of Kvaternik's legacy and to reclaim him for a democratic, nationalist heritage. Like many Croatian and Yugoslav nationalists in the early twentieth century, the young Cesarec had been fascinated by Kvaternik and took inspiration from his uncompromising and revolutionary politics. But as we saw in chapter two, by the outbreak of World War I, he had begun to move away from nationalism and embrace revolutionary socialist and Balkan federalist ideas. In the second half of the 1930s, however, Cesarec returned to his youthful fascination. As early as 1934–35, he pored over material on Kvaternik's life in the archives and libraries of Moscow.[63] During his stay in Paris and his subsequent travels through Italy, he also found himself dwelling on the figure of Kvaternik and his own exile to France and Italy.[64] After his return to Zagreb, alongside work on the drama, he also published a series of historical studies of Kvaternik and the Party of Rights movement, critiquing their appropriation by the Far Right and attempting to integrate them into a historical materialist account of the early Croatian nationalist movement.[65] Just as Kreft sought to offer a populist, leftist account of the Slovene-Croatian peasant rebellions of the 1570s, Cesarec hoped to claim the most radical and uncompromising figures of Croatian nationalism as part of a progressive history of popular struggle.

The central thread that ran through Cesarec's work from the late 1930s, including *Sin domovine*, was that Kvaternik represented a progressive, if tragically flawed, moment in the struggle for national liberation. This reading cut against contemporary efforts by far-right intellectuals to use Kvaternik's legacy to justify racialist and authoritarian-statist visions of Croatian nationalism in an attempt to more closely align him with fascist Italy and Nazi Germany.[66] Instead, Cesarec drew attention to Kvaternik's liberal democratic and republican sensibilities. In *Sin domovine*, for example, several scenes bring to the fore Kvaternik's foreign policy and his repeated efforts to forge an alliance with Napoleon III and the leaders of the Italian Risorgimento. Cesarec's hero strikes up a friendship with Jerome Bonaparte, announcing that "Croatia will happily open its borders to the French army if it comes to her aid in her fight for freedom!"[67] He longs for Garibaldi to land troops in Dalmatia and lead an uprising against the Habsburgs.[68] He fantasizes about a French intervention against Austria that would open the way to simultaneous national revolutions in Croatia and Poland.[69] These visions of Croatian liberation stressed Kvaternik's belonging to an earlier age of revolutionary, democratic nationalisms associated with the uprisings of 1848 and contrasted him with the organic, integral nationalisms for which the Far Right of the 1930s hoped to claim him.

Kvaternik's foreign policy served to free his legacy from its appropriation by Croatian fascism, but it was also his most politically tragic quality. The hero of Cesarec's drama remains committed to a world shaped by the ideals of 1848, seemingly unaware or unwilling to acknowledge that the world has changed, the revolutionary moment has passed. Kvaternik's faith in Napoleon III for example, is naively misplaced. The emperor no longer represents the revolutionary ideals of his uncle but sits atop an imperial regime beset by decadence and corruption. In private, we see Jerome condemn his nephew's cowardice, his efforts to impose a monarchy in Mexico while refusing to come to the aid of Polish insurgents.[70] While Kvaternik plots an uprising in Croatia aimed to attract the support of the French, one of his followers recounts a warning from an Italian socialist that they should not put their faith in Napoleon III "who has enslaved and deceived even his own people, so will certainly deceive all other nations as well."[71] Elsewhere, Cesarec made clear that the lesson of Kvaternik's tragic fate was that "a dictatorship that stifles the rights and freedoms of its own people, no matter how great its slogans are about nationality and the right of national self-determination, cannot bring freedom to any other people."[72] This tragic reading of Kvaternik was, no doubt, a pointed attack on those far-right nationalists that looked to Nazi Germany or fascist Italy as the future guarantors of Croatian independence.

A major consequence of Cesarec's decision to foreground Kvaternik's foreign policy was that it effectively staged his political career at a European scale. In *Sin domovine*, what sets Kvaternik apart from the rest of the post-1848 generation of Croatian nationalists is his refusal to limit his scope of struggle to the borders of the empire. A key narrative tension in the drama concerns the hero's conflicts with his rivals within the Croatian political class, in particular those around Bishop Strossmayer, who pursue a strategy of autonomy within the Habsburg Empire. Critical of Kvaternik's utopianism, they insist that the only solution to the Croatian national question will be found within the borders of the empire itself. Kvaternik, by contrast, remains committed to a strategy in which

Croatian independence will be synchronized with a wider remapping of Europe. "[T]he Napoleons are interested in our fate and our faith in them is deeply justified," he tells his confidants. "When the map of Europe is drawn again, it is certain that they will have the scissors in their hands and we Croats will not be deprived!"[73] In effect, then, Cesarec's hero rescales a project of Croatian national liberation to a European plane.

In its evocation of a European geography, *Sin domovine* certainly resonated with the geopolitical horizons of the Comintern during the years of the Popular Front. But it also aligned with Cesarec's own itinerant biography over this period. Just as the political career of Kvaternik plotted the Croatian national struggle of the nineteenth century within the coordinates of a broader European space, so too did Cesarec's plot the major sites of Popular Front Europe: Moscow, Madrid, Paris. Such an itinerary was not unusual for Yugoslav communists of this era, many of whom were forced to flee the country by the January 6 dictatorship and were subsequently displaced from Berlin, Vienna, or Prague by the disturbing geopolitical realignments of the late 1930s. In this sense, the European horizons of the Comintern were reinforced by the geography of exile that many Yugoslav communists traversed. These European horizons were, however, a significant break from the geopoetics that had animated Cesarec's earlier work. As with Kreft, this one-time advocate for an anticolonial Balkan federation that fostered affiliations with Asia, had by the outbreak of World War II come to insist on Croatia's place within Europe.

VII

On the 6 April 1941, the Axis powers of Germany, Italy, Hungary, and Bulgaria occupied Yugoslavia. Within ten days, the Yugoslav army and state institutions had collapsed in the face of the onslaught. The occupying powers set out to dismember the country, annexing some parts and placing others under direct military authority. On 10 April, the Far Right Ustasha party, led by Ante Pavelić, was placed at the head of the Independent State of Croatia, a fascist puppet state that was given control over large swathes of territory that had been Croatia, Bosnia and Herzegovina, and parts of western Serbia. In response, KPJ activists and intellectuals went underground and began to prepare for a prolonged struggle against the occupation.

Cesarec was among a handful of well-known party intellectuals who took refuge in safe houses in Zagreb in the early days of the war. On 15 April, though, worried for the safety of his wife, who was both Jewish and a well-known communist herself, he came out of hiding and was swiftly arrested and interned in the Kerestinec prison camp, where he joined the swelling ranks of communist, Jewish, and Serb political prisoners. As armed opposition to the Ustasha and their Axis allies began to erupt over the summer, the situation of these prisoners became especially precarious. On 9 July, in response to the killing of a police agent by partisan fighters, several of the most prominent leftist intellectuals held in Kerestinec were executed.[74] When news of this atrocity reached the KPJ's leadership, they quickly devised a plan to liberate the remaining prisoners. In the early hours of the morning on 14 July, the communist inmates in Kerestinec sparked an uprising, overpowering the guards and joining a group of armed comrades outside the prison walls. In this daring act 111 prisoners, including Cesarec, were freed and fled to join the partisans. En route, however, Cesarec's column was ambushed, captured, and returned to Zagreb. Condemned to death for his role in the escape, Cesarec was among several prisoners who were executed in the forest on the outskirts of the city. A faithful communist until the last, on the eve of his execution he scrawled on the wall of his cell his last written words: "Long live Soviet Croatia!"[75]

News of this atrocity shook the Yugoslav Left. Cesarec had been an idol of many of the young KPJ cadre who had been formed politically under the influence of the social literature movement. For Milovan Đilas, the Kerestinec execution was the moment that the full scope of the war was made clear: "The aim was to strike terror and to dispel any thought of leniency ... An unfathomable, unbridgeable chasm suddenly opened within me: this was not merely a struggle for survival, but unto death."[76] Cesarec's murder symbolized the ruthlessness of the struggle between the forces of fascism and those of the antifascist resistance. The "unbridgeable chasm" that Kerestinec had opened up forced intellectuals to pick a side in that struggle and, in the months that followed, hundreds fled the towns to join the partisan movement.

The cultural policies devised during the Popular Front continued to inform the KPJ during the years of partisan struggle, and often helped provide advantages that enabled the party to overcome opponents better resourced and better armed. The leftist appropriation of national and folk traditions, for instance, served the movement well in broadening their base of support.[77] As young partisan fighters marched off to confront the occupying forces, they imagined themselves part of a longer history of popular struggle that stretched back centuries. Importantly, however, during the years of the war the spatial horizons within which these national cultures had been nested were recast. The continent-wide dislocations produced by the war, the necessities of guerilla struggle and the new alliances it fostered eroded the contours of a European mediating space. Increasingly, Yugoslav communists looked to new forms of supranational affiliation that might better correspond to these new conditions of struggle.

5

The Slavic Vanguard of the Balkan Revolution
Race and Region in Yugoslav Stalinism, 1941–48

> These years of struggle have enacted a new morality, have changed the
> face of man and of humanity. Time has moved us with a mighty lever
> from the dark and discarded Balkans to that place in the world where
> history is made. From Trieste to Vladivostok – that is now the axis of
> the world.
>
> Dušan Pirjevec, "Most," 1946

I

The invasion began on 6 April 1941. Early in the morning, a fleet
of the Luftwaffe buried Belgrade under a rain of bombs and strafing
attacks. The destruction of the capital marked the opening of the
broader occupation of the Kingdom of Yugoslavia. Over the months
that followed, the western Balkans was completely remapped, par-
titioned among Germany and its allies of Italy, Hungary, Bulgaria,
and the fascist Independent State of Croatia. The partition of Yugoslavia was one act of the broader geopolitical reconfiguration that
Hitler and his allies sought. Eurasia was to be entirely remapped
in line with new ideologies of racial hierarchy, borders were to be
redrawn to serve the priorities of German, Japanese, and Italian
empire building, and the old order was to be overturned to clear the
way for a new coalition of nationalist regimes. The global dimensions of this conflict were not lost on Yugoslavia's communists. The
spring of 1941 reportedly found their leader, Josip Broz Tito, reading Edgar Snow's *Red Star over China*. This sympathetic account of
Mao Zedong's guerilla struggle in the Chinese countryside presum-
ably helped to inform Tito's decision to direct the Communist Party

of Yugoslavia (KPJ) into its own partisan war in the forested mountains of the interior.[1] From the summer of 1941 through to their seizure of power in the spring of 1945, the KPJ led a mass struggle against Axis forces throughout Yugoslavia, from the Julian Alps to the Vardar Valley.

The Allied victors of World War II had their own plans for a new global order and for reconfiguring Eastern Europe's place within it. While each agreed to build and participate in the major institutions of the postwar international system, the Soviet Union and the US and Britain nonetheless maintained their respective spheres of influence. As set out at the Yalta conference of February 1945, Eastern Europe was to be integrated into a wider Soviet geopolitical zone, its borders were redrawn to alleviate Moscow's security concerns, its economies were rerouted eastwards, and projects of affiliation and exchange were promoted to draw the region into a Soviet cultural orbit.[2] Yugoslavia's communists were prominent actors in this reconfiguration, becoming widely perceived as Moscow's most staunch allies in the region.

During the war, Yugoslav communism was transformed from an underground opposition movement and countercultural trend into a confident project of state power.[3] The foundational moment came in November 1942, with the formation of the Anti-fascist Council for the National Liberation of Yugoslavia (AVNOJ), a communist-led government that established control over large swathes of the country's mountainous interior. Having experimented with governance in the liberated territories they controlled during the war, after the spring of 1945 the KPJ became the leading force of the People's Front government, the sole ruling power in the new Yugoslav state. On 29 November 1945, this government declared the formation of the Federal People's Republic of Yugoslavia. The new country's internal borders were extensively redrawn: Yugoslavia became a federation of six national republics – Serbia, Croatia, Bosnia and Herzegovina, Montenegro, Slovenia, and Macedonia – each with their distinct governments, cultures, and histories.[4] This was Yugoslavism as a mediating space, a broader supranational formation within which its constituent parts could pursue their respective paths of national development while enjoying a degree of collective security and economic consolidation. The union was held together by the organizational might of the KPJ, whose networks ran deep into Yugoslav society and who commanded the loyalty of the Peoples' Army.[5] Under their leadership Yugoslavia was to be radically reorganized in line with the Soviet model.

Throughout their wartime struggle and well into the first years in power, Yugoslavia's communists were animated by two projects of supranational affiliation, each with their own distinct, if partially overlapping, geographies. On the one hand, the new Slavic movement sought to cultivate ties of solidarity among the peoples of Slavdom, a civilizational zone that was seen to stretch from the Adriatic to the Pacific. On the other, renewed plans of Balkan federalism proposed a more modest consolidation of the region into a supranational polity. The constitution of these mediating spaces – Slavdom and the Balkans – became a pressing concern over the course of the 1940s, as they came to play a more central role in the KPJ's political strategy. During the war, ideas of Slavic and Balkan affiliation served as crucial reference points for partisans who sought to evoke the international coalition of forces of which they were a part, the better to raise morale in the face of overwhelming odds. After 1945, the new communist leadership took advantage of the networks and platforms that these spaces offered in order to project and cultivate their international prestige in Eastern Europe and the Balkans.[6] It was, ultimately, Stalin's suspicion of this prestige, which he saw as a potential challenge to his own influence, that precipitated his expulsion of the KPJ from the newly founded Cominform in the summer of 1948.[7] The Tito-Stalin split, the first open schism between two communist states, was the result of Soviet and Yugoslav contestations over the configuration of power and prestige in the supranational projects of postwar communism.

Projects of Slavic unity and Balkan federalism, however, were in implicit tension with one another, as each relied on different, indeed contradictory, logics of community. Slavism evoked a racial paradigm that prioritized affiliations rooted in ancestral lineages. Slavs were to form a single community because they shared a common blood, a common ancestry, a common spirit. Balkan federalism, however, explicitly sought to transcend racial or ethnic logics of community. Radical ideas of Balkan unification, as we have seen in previous chapters, were rooted in a politico-strategic logic of community that saw regional integration as a necessary response to the geographically uneven contours of capitalist development. The peoples of the Balkans shared a sense of being in common because they inhabited a region shaped by the same political-economic conjunctures. Not only did languages of ethnicity or race not aid this project of regional federation, they posed an obstacle to it. This was especially the case with Slavism, which raised anxieties of "slavicization" among Yugoslavia's neighbours in Greece and Albania, and threatened to exacerbate interethnic suspicions in border regions like Macedonia and Kosovo.[8] Throughout the 1940s, Yugoslav communists were often compelled to adjudicate between and, if possible, reconcile these rival mediating spaces.

This chapter explores the history of ideas of Slavism and Balkan federalism as they animated Yugoslav socialist thought from the invasion of Yugoslavia in the spring of 1941 to the Tito-Stalin split of the summer of 1948. It explores how these mediating spaces were initially formulated and deployed by Yugoslav intellectuals in support of the partisan struggle against Axis occupation, and then traces the ways in which they were recalibrated to serve the goals of postwar state building. If, during the interwar period, the KPJ was able to exert little influence over the wider left-wing cultural field, during the 1940s they were able to play a much larger role in directing and shaping the work of leftist and antifascist writers and artists. This decade, then, witnessed a closer alignment of political ideology and cultural production, especially with regards to the construction of the movement's mediating spaces. As these Slavic and Balkan geographies began to be embedded in emerging international institutions and expanding networks of cultural exchange, this work of cultural mapping became more concrete, moving beyond the realm of the imagination and increasingly falling under the purview of ideological commissioners and cultural officials.[9]

Pursuing this intellectual history, the chapter makes four broader contributions. First, it sheds light on the little-known history of Soviet-sponsored Slavism and the significant role it played in shaping Yugoslav socialist thought during the formative period of the 1940s. Second, it demonstrates how notions of Yugoslav federalism were given salience through a wider paradigm of Slavic affiliation that appealed to racialized notions of community. Third, it moves beyond discussions of these projects as political or economic alliances to explore their literary articulations in order to better understand the role of cultural production in crafting supranational affinities. Finally, it pays close attention to the implicit tensions,

Race and Region in Yugoslav Stalinism 129

which, although largely unacknowledged by Yugoslav intellectuals at the time, were registered in the different logics of community and geographies of kinship that underpinned these two projects. In so doing, the chapter excavates the conceptual substrata that conditioned these rival projects and poses broader questions about the ways in which imagined communities are conditioned by political ideologies.[10]

II

The new Slavic movement emerged in the Soviet Union over the summer of 1941 following the outbreak of Operation Barbarossa – the Nazi invasion of the Soviet Union that began on 22 June. In the atmosphere of panic that engulfed the country as the Soviet military was forced back across the western borderlands, Yemelian Yaroslavskii set out what would become the movement's major ideas. Yaroslavskii, a historian and former editor of the antireligious newspaper *Bezbozhnik* (*The Godless*), framed Germany's invasion through the language of race war, a struggle of Germandom against Slavdom. Reviving nineteenth-century ideas of pan-Slavism, he pointed to the antifascist resistance of the Slavic nations of Eastern Europe and called on Soviet Russia to live up to its historical mission to protect Slavdom. Within weeks, the Slavic idea became a major theme of Soviet war propaganda.[11] On 10–11 August 1941, Moscow hosted a radio broadcast of an All-Slav gathering that brought together intellectuals, politicians, and military leaders from the Slavic nations to call on their peoples to defend the motherland.

The August broadcast was the first of several highly publicized "All Slavic" meetings held during the war. These gatherings were intended to promote a united front against Hitler: speakers condemned the Nazi aggression against the Soviet Union, drew attention to Hitler's genocidal intent towards the Slavic race, and made appeals to the shared "freedom-loving spirit" that animated the Slavic peoples. While these meetings were dominated by Soviet cultural figures such as Aleksei Tolstoi, Oleksandr Korneichuk, and Dimitri Shostakovich, each also featured speakers from the different Slavic nations of Eastern Europe – Poland, Czechoslovakia, Yugoslavia, and Bulgaria.[12] The meetings were organized by the All-Slav Committee, a Moscow-based organization that was chaired by the Soviet general Alexandr Gundorov and was under the purview of the Soviet Information Bureau.[13] In addition to its international gatherings, the committee also formed a series of subcommittees to work on outreach among Slavic women, youth, and scholars.[14] The movement had a global reach, making contact with and helping to organize diaspora groups in North America, Australia, New Zealand, and Latin America with an eye to rallying support for the Soviet Union's struggle against Germany.[15] In addition to its radio broadcasts, the main medium of this new Slavic movement was the monthly magazine, *Slaviane* (*Slavs*), published in Moscow from the summer of 1942.[16]

In a region characterized by often ardent anticommunist sentiment, appeals to Slavic unity in the face of the existential threat of German fascism provided a framework for promoting solidarity with the Soviet cause that circumvented the thorny question of political ideology.[17] In its meetings and publications, the movement emphasized the role of Soviet Russia as a defender of the Slavic peoples. Indeed, this claim often spilled over into almost messianic rhetoric regarding Russia's historical mission to liberate and protect the Slavic peoples.[18] The defence of Soviet Russia, then, was presented as an existential priority for the Slavs of Eastern Europe. Militarily this position implied that, even if they were grossly outnumbered and outgunned, the small Slavic nations should do all they could to disrupt the Nazi war effort, to sabotage their supply lines or bog down their forces in costly counterinsurgency campaigns; anything to weaken the Germans' ability to attack the Slavic motherland.[19]

As the war drew to a close and the Soviet Union emerged as the hegemonic power over Eastern Europe, the movement was recalibrated to serve a new set of priorities. For the Soviet leadership and its allies among the communist parties of the region, the paradigm of Slavic unity served to legitimize the Soviet Union's geopolitical influence in Eastern Europe and the Balkans without reference to communist ideology. While the spokespeople of Soviet Slavism were emphatic that their movement had nothing in common with the reactionary pan-Slavism that had served as a tool of tsarist power, they nonetheless accorded Soviet Russia a leading role in the Slavic community. In a new world order dominated by the three allied powers, Russia was presented as a defender of the interests of the small Slavic nations on the world stage.[20] Meanwhile, Slavic solidarity served as a vehicle for Soviet policy preferences in the new national front governments of the Slavic nations.[21] This is not to say that Slavism had no organic base of support. In fact, by preserving a sense of existential struggle between Slavdom and Germandom, the movement provided a justification for postwar nation-building policies such as the Czechoslovak expulsion of the Sudeten Germans, the Polish annexation of East Prussia, or Yugoslav efforts to incorporate Trieste, Gorica, and Carinthia.[22]

The new Slavic movement found incredibly fertile soil among Yugoslav communists both during the war and in the immediate postwar years. In large part, its appeal lay in the fact that the ideological horizons of Slavism offered a framework for justifying the partisans' policy of Yugoslav federalism. It will be recalled that the KPJ had only reconciled itself to Yugoslavism in the mid-1930s, with the turn to the Popular Front strategy and its efforts to forge a coalition with more moderate forces. The party was, however, eager to distance its vision of Yugoslav unity from the assimilationist Yugoslavism of the interwar regime, which they dismissed as a greater Serbianism. To this end, they argued for the need to forge a new, federal Yugoslavia in which each constituent nationality would preserve its distinct cultural and historical identity.[23] But if Yugoslavia was to be conceived as a supranational project, what justified this specific configuration of nations? Why was this federation to include Slovenia but not Albania or Greece, whose incorporation might have helped resolve wider regional tensions over territories like Kosovo or Macedonia? These narrowed geographical horizons appear all the more surprising when set against the audacity and confidence of the partisan struggle, which seemed to promise a bold era of revolutionary world-building. By reinforcing a shared sense of Slavic community, albeit one rooted in ideas of race, Slavism helped to provide ideological scaffolding for the KPJ's Yugoslavism. A federal Yugoslavia was to be one step in a wider system of Slavic affiliations.

But ideas of Slavic unity stood in tension with a second project of supranational unification that resurfaced during the years of and following World War II: Balkan federalism. Although, as we've seen, the Balkans had ceased to be a significant cultural-geographical reference point for Yugoslav socialists since the late 1920s, formally, the KPJ remained committed to the long-term goal of Balkan unification.[24] With the coming to power of communist parties in Yugoslavia, Albania, and Bulgaria, and the possibility of a partisan victory in the Greek Civil War, the moment seemed especially propitious for

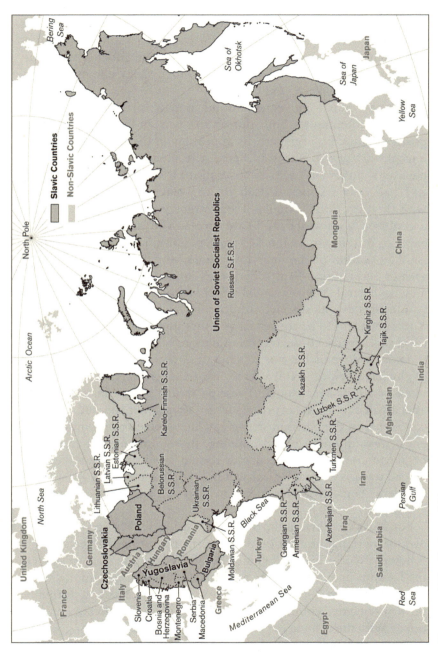

Figure 5.1 | The Slavic world in 1946.

Race and Region in Yugoslav Stalinism   133

realizing the project of a Balkan Communist Federation. Already, in November 1944, Yugoslav and Bulgarian leaders had met to discuss a possible union of the two countries. These discussions moved quickly towards a concrete plan for a South Slavic federation that would eventually expand to include the non-Slavic nations of Albania and, possibly, Greece.[25] Meanwhile, Yugoslav-Albanian relations, which had been fortified through joint partisan operations during the war, flourished in the postwar period, with the two countries signing a treaty of friendship in the summer of 1946 that was envisioned as a step towards their eventual unification.[26] The Yugoslav government's commitment to regional federation was also reflected in the support it offered the Democratic Army of Greece, allowing its forces to operate on their territory and providing military and humanitarian aid.[27] A leftist victory in Greece offered a genuine possibility for a united, communist Balkans.

As projects of supranational affiliation, Slavism and Balkan federalism were organized around their own distinct and implicitly contradictory logics of community, geographies of kinship, and models of growth. Slavism justified its program of supranational affiliation as a community of consanguinity; that is, it appealed to a common ancestry that was supposed to be historically antecedent and ontologically prior to modern nations.[28] This racial logic of community underpinned the geography of kinship that the movement mapped, which traced the historical migrations of Slavic tribes and the contemporary mosaic of nation states into which they had evolved.[29] Conceived in this way, the domain of Slavdom evoked a historical landscape that stretched from the Elbe and Adriatic in the West across the expanse of Siberia to the Pacific in the East. Communist Slavism framed the political and cultural association of Slavs through a mode of concentric nesting organized around increasingly broader scales of affiliation from the regional up to the national and eventually the supranational space of Slavdom. This matryoshka-doll model promised both to sustain the autonomy of its national parts and ensconce them within wider supranational formations that would guarantee geopolitical security, facilitate economic co-operation, and foster cultural exchange.[30]

Balkan federalism was a profoundly different project. Its logic of community derived not from relations of consanguinity but rather a historical-geographic paradigm of affinity. Balkan solidarity, that is, was undergirded by a shared sense of the entangled history of struggles that had been conditioned by the region's place at the frontiers of rival empires. This was a more voluntarist logic of community, one that appealed to a politico-strategic rationale rather than racial lineage. Its geography of kinship was mapped out by the uneven historical development of European capitalism, which demarcated the space of South East Europe as a site of economic backwardness and geopolitical contest. Regional space, in this sense, was envisioned not as an empty, passive surface across which the migration and settlement of ancestral tribes played out, but rather an active force propelling the process of supranational affiliation. The sense of community that informed Balkan federalism also led to an aggregative model of growth in which a future union was to be formed through the piecemeal addition of constituent national elements: first Yugoslavia and Bulgaria, then Albania and, provided the leftist insurgency was victorious, Greece. Although these two projects were, in their conceptual foundations, in sharp tension with one another, this was rarely acknowledged by Yugoslav intellectuals, who often evoked both Slavic and Balkan geographies during the 1940s. The tension can, however, be evidenced in the rhetorical strategies that many of these intellectuals deployed to bring the two mediating spaces into closer conceptual alignment.

III

During their four-year struggle against the Axis occupiers and their local collaborators, Yugoslav partisans made frequent appeals to both Slavic and Balkan projects of supranational affiliation. These played a critical, if underexamined, role in the partisan war effort. For most of the war, Yugoslavia's partisans were vastly outnumbered and outgunned by Axis forces. Indeed, in the early years of the war, the KPJ emphasized that their liberation would depend on the victory of the Red Army and, to that end, they foregrounded the diversionary role their struggle would play, forcing the Germans to tie down troops in South East Europe and weakening their assault on the Soviet Union.[31] Confronted with incredibly asymmetrical conditions of warfare, projects of supranational affiliation became strategically vital for the partisan cause. Maintaining morale meant consistently reminding their supporters that they were not fighting a lone battle but were part of a larger movement of resistance. To this end, intellectuals affiliated with the partisan struggle promoted both Slavic and Balkan visions of community.

Race and Region in Yugoslav Stalinism   135

Given that many Yugoslav partisans understood their struggle as ancillary to that of the Soviet Union, it is perhaps unsurprising that affiliation with Russia was a key affective element of wartime Slavism. Official statements, pamphlets, and newspapers produced during the guerilla war were peppered with references to Russia as a protector or saviour of the Slavic peoples. In a pamphlet designed to be circulated through the ranks of the Bulgarian army, Serbian partisans scolded their brothers for their government's collaboration with Nazi Germany: "Your place is not against but on the side of the Slavs and our great Mother Russia," they insisted.[32] An article in the Croatian antifascist paper, *Vjesnik* (*Herald*), emphasized the supposed influence of Russian partisans on Yugoslavs' own guerilla struggle, noting that "in difficult moments, beneath a hail of grenades and tanks, our young partisans think of their great brother in the East."[33] Was Russia, then, a brother or a mother? A statement published in *Bilten* (*Bulletin*), the KPJ's organ in Bosnia and Herzegovina, tried to split the difference, proclaiming to its readers: "Long live the fraternal Slavic mother, Soviet Russia!"[34] This language, which appeared throughout partisan propaganda, framed wartime solidarity with the Soviet Union as family loyalty, helping to justify the sacrifices such solidarity would certainly demand.

Soviet Russia's role as an ideological focal point in the struggles of the Slavic peoples was more subtly explored in the wartime writings of the Slovene-American writer, Louis Adamič (1898–1951). One of the ways in which the new movement of the 1940s differed from nineteenth-century pan-Slavism was its global horizons, in particular its efforts at outreach among the diasporas of the Americas, Oceania, and Western Europe. In the US this outreach was coordinated through organizations such as the American Slav Congress and the United Committee of South Slavic Americans, which sought through their links with diaspora groups to build support for the Allied cause and to push US public sentiment towards positions more favourable to the Soviet Union. Adamič, who had made a name for himself in the 1930s as a proletarian writer, became one of the leading figures of the leftist Slavic diaspora during the war, using his significant public platform to promote the cause of the Yugoslav partisans among the US public.

To this end, in 1943 Adamič published *My Native Land*, a major work designed to familiarize US readers with the Yugoslav situation. The book wove together the author's recollections of his previous journey to Yugoslavia, biographies of key Yugoslav political, diplomatic, and cultural figures, reports of the most recent military episodes in the country, and a lengthy history of the Yugoslav peoples. It set out to demonstrate that not only were the partisans the only force offering genuine resistance to the Axis powers in the region, but also that they were the only movement providing a viable political vision that might stabilize the country after the war. As his biographer, John Enyeart, has argued, Adamič's wartime writings foregrounded the multinational character of the partisans' Yugoslavism to better appeal to the antiracism of progressive readers in the US.[35] The text mused openly on the need for South East Europe to be reorganized as a supranational federation, perhaps as part of a wider Eastern European confederation, that would promote cultural pluralism and racial tolerance. The joint struggle of the region's peoples against Axis occupation, Adamič argued, was laying the foundation for this kind of multinational state.[36]

Although Adamič's text emphasized the need for a regional federation that transcended ethnic or racial ties, a position likely reinforced by his contact with leftists within the Greek-American diaspora, his account of Yugoslav history was saturated with the ideas of the new Slavic movement.[37] The middle third of *My Native Land* was dedicated to recounting the history of the Yugoslav peoples. Starting with their origins among the ancient Slavic communities of western Russia, Adamič tracked the migration of tribes into South East Europe, where the mountainous territory and the cross-currents of empire had over time led these tribes to lose their "potential oneness," their sense of belonging to a single "big race," and to start along divergent paths of national development.[38] The arc of history, however, seemed to bend towards unification, and over the course of the nineteenth century, Slovenes, Croats, Serbs, and Bulgarians had all begun to aspire to common statehood. Perhaps the "potential oneness" that the early Slavic migrants had carried with them from ancient Russia had not been entirely forgotten but had merely lain dormant. In the modern era, Adamič's historical account suggested, this sense of Slavic belonging was being revived, not as an alternative to contemporary national communities but to compliment them and reinforce them. It was this underlying sense of Slavic belonging that gave the project of a supranational Yugoslavia its ideological coherence. It also accounted for the "national-emotional impulses" that led the Slavic peoples of Eastern Europe to "lean" on Russia.

Race and Region in Yugoslav Stalinism 137

This sentiment was a kind of revival of a primordial oneness that all Slavs had once felt in their ancestral lands and, for Adamič, it ensured that the Soviet Union was going to have a powerful influence in the region after the war.[39]

Wartime Slavism's appeal among Yugoslav socialists, however, was not solely based on affiliation with Russia. Indeed, it would probably have remained a marginal gesture had it not also spoken to a more immediate, more local set of priorities. Key among these was that Slavism offered an ideological framework that gave coherence to the KPJ's Yugoslav vision. During the war, the partisan leadership framed their project of Yugoslav federalism within the wider paradigm of Slavic affiliation. In their propaganda, they often presented this vision through a model of concentric nesting organized around increasingly broader scales of affiliation. Set within this paradigm, a Yugoslav federation could be presented as a stepping-stone between the individual nation and the wider domain of Slavdom. The most obvious expression of this paradigm appeared in the proclamations of solidarity with which Yugoslav partisans often concluded their propaganda statements. A 1942 pamphlet published by the KPJ in Montenegro, for example, closed with the following set of declarations:

Long live the national-liberation struggle of the people of Montenegro and Boka! ...
Long live the brotherhood and unity of all the peoples of Yugoslavia in the struggle against the fascist occupier!
Long live Soviet Russia and its English [sic] and American Allies!
Long live the solidarity of the Slavic peoples in the struggle against the fascist enemies of Slavdom![40]

Each of these proclamations marked a step within this concentric system of affiliations: from the national-provincial level of Montenegro and the Bay of Kotor to the multinational community of Yugoslavia and, through the struggle of Soviet Russia, to the outer ring of Slavdom. This model gave ideological coherence to the KPJ's vision of a federated Yugoslavia as a step within a system of progressively expansive Slavic associations.

The concentric model of Slavic affiliation was expressed clearly in the work of the most prominent writer to join the partisans. Vladimir Nazor (1876–1949) had been raised on the Dalmatian island of Brač and became a vibrant voice of Croatian poetry in the first decades of the twentieth century. His early work was infused with pan-Slavic themes, drawing on the symbolism and myths of Slavic paganism and celebrating the ideal of a united Yugoslavia. At the same time, however, Nazor was a Croatian patriot and clearly saw a distinction between the different nationalities that would make up a future South Slavic state.[41] His Slavism, that is, was a supranational one and his work nested these overlapping affinities within a concentric system of cultural geographies: from poems in his native Čakavian dialect that evoked the coastal province of Dalmatia, to his celebrations of Croatian nationalism that he saw as being realized within a multinational Yugoslav state, up to his efforts to draw inspiration from a pre-Christian mythology that was the common heritage of all Slavic peoples.

In the winter of 1942–43, Nazor, together with the young leftist poet, Ivan Goran Kovačić, made the momentous decision to escape fascist-controlled Zagreb and join the partisans in the mountains of Bosnia. Nazor's decision was a huge propaganda victory for the partisans. As an intellectual of the early Yugoslav movement and a Croatian nationalist, his support for the antifascist cause helped to counter accusations of the movement's supposed Greater Serbian ambitions.[42] And as a writer who had not previously been associated with the Far Left, Nazor's defection to the partisan camp reflected their growing base of support. The partisans were keen to make hay from this propaganda victory. In April 1943, they had Nazor compose a "Message to the Dalmatians," a patriotic call to arms addressed to the people of his native province. The text documents well the way in which Nazor sought to nest the multiple Slavic geographies that animated his work. While most of the brief message appealed to Dalmatia's history of resistance to foreign rule, referencing the Narentines and the uskoks as forefathers of the contemporary antifascist struggle, Nazor also called on his audience to adopt broader horizons: "Let us also help Slavdom, promote Croatianess (*Hrvatstvo*) and let us Dalmatians be workers in the new construction of the destiny of humanity!"[43] This appeal placed Dalmatia within a broader Croatian nation which was, in turn, part of the racial community that encompassed all Slavic peoples. Set within these nested geographies, a supranational Yugoslavia was merely one layer of a system whose small central rings delimited the Adriatic coast and whose outer rings stretched across the Eurasian expanses of Slavdom.

Nazor's appeal to Slavdom was not a mere rhetorical flourish but a recurrent theme in his wartime writings. In his diary, the poet frequently cast the Yugoslav struggle as a defence of Slavdom. After hearing reports of partisan battles in Dalmatia, he noted that his "faith has become concretized. I believe in the future of Slavdom and in the more just social order that it will bring to the world – I believe in Stalin!"[44] Elsewhere he celebrated the partisan struggle for "awakening" greater feelings of "Slavdom and Croatianess" (*Slavenstva i Hrvatstva*).[45] But perhaps the most stark reference to Slavdom appeared in his 1943 song, "Uz Maršala Tita" ("With Marshal Tito"), which quickly became an anthem among partisan forces. A song of fortitude and heroism, the second verse defiantly proclaims:

We are an ancient race, but we are not Goths
We are part of Ancient Slavdom.
Whoever says otherwise, slanders and lies,
and will feel our fist.

Rod prastari svi smo, a Goti mi nismo,
Slavenstva smo drevnoga čest.
Ko drukčije kaže, kleveće i laže,
našu će osjetit pest.

The verse took up the racial ideology of the Ustasha regime, which postulated that Croats were not part of the inferior race of Slavs but an estranged tribe of Goths, and therefore Aryans. This ideological step was, of course, key to justifying the regime's alliance with Nazi Germany.[46] What is noteworthy is that rather than dismiss the racial discourse of the Ustasha entirely, Nazor asserted his own racial genealogy, one that identified contemporary Yugoslavs with "ancient Slavdom." This assertion of a historically and ontologically prior Slavic community placed contemporary Croatia and Yugoslavia within a geographically broader and temporally deeper set of affiliations, allowing Nazor to reconcile his ardent Croatian nationalism with his commitments to the new Yugoslavia for which the partisans were fighting. It also allowed him to cast the partisans' alliance with the Soviet Union as an expression of racial solidarity rather than ideological affinity.

While Slavism might have served to cultivate support for the partisan cause among South Slavic populations in the Yugoslav heartlands, it did little to promote solidarity and co-operation with populations in the multi-ethnic regions of Kosovo or Macedonia. Among Albanian or Greek minorities in these regions, the rhetoric of Slavism risked stoking fears of a repetition of the ethnic cleansing of the Balkan Wars or the repressive cultural assimilation of the interwar regimes. Albanian, Yugoslav, and Greek partisans, therefore, were forced to rely on one another's connections with the local population and to co-operate on joint campaigns.[47] Over time, this fostered a genuine sense of regional solidarity among partisan forces that revived ideals of Balkan federalism.

The figure most associated with this Balkan vision was the Montenegrin communist, Svetozar Vukmanović Tempo (1912–2000). Tempo had become involved in communist circles at university in Belgrade in the late 1930s and was brought into the inner circle of the party following the Axis invasion. Serving first in the KPJ's underground press before taking up a military role among partisan forces in Bosnia, in February 1943 he was sent by the supreme staff to organize partisan divisions in Macedonia and Kosovo. Tempo was a shrewd analyst of the region's national question and was aware that any efforts to cohere the resistance would need to reckon with the legacy of Yugoslav and Greek domination over the region and the resentment this had created among the Albanian and Slavic Macedonian populations. To this end, he promoted Macedonian nationalism, aiming to undermine Bulgarian efforts to assimilate the local population into a Greater Bulgaria and to associate Macedonian independence with the cause of Yugoslav federalism. He also began to establish closer ties with Greek and Albanian partisans.[48] In the summer of 1943 this co-operation reached a high point, when Tempo proposed the formation of a joint Balkan command composed of the leadership of each of the resistance armies in South East Europe. While these plans were agreed to by the Greeks and Albanians, Tito ultimately quashed the project.[49] Nevertheless, Tempo continued to pursue grassroots co-operation between Yugoslav, Albanian, and Greek forces in Macedonia and Kosovo.

Military co-operation in this multi-ethnic region necessarily posed the problem of the postwar organization of South East Europe. To Tempo's mind, the only viable solution for the region's national question was to be found in a Balkan federation. Indeed, it is clear from his memoirs that he initially envisaged the Balkan command as a kernel of this future union.[50] The prospect of such a federation allowed partisan forces to resolve or, at least defer, several problems that might have posed an obstacle to their wartime co-operation. Most obviously, it bracketed the question of where national borders would be drawn in this historically contested territory.[51] In a future federation, Tempo insisted to his Greek and Albanian comrades, "borders will be overcome (*prevazidene*)."[52] The capitulation of Italy in September 1943 gave Tempo the brief opportunity to realize this vision of Balkan unity. In the aftermath of the Italian withdrawal from western Macedonia, Albanian and Yugoslav partisans seized control of several towns and set about forming a new government. Partisan rule was to manifest the equality of the Albanian and Macedonian nations, with both flags flown on public buildings, both languages granted equal authority, and new Albanian and Macedonian partisan units raised. Tempo himself visited the newly liberated town of Debar, where he addressed a crowd from the balcony of the town hall. Holding an Albanian flag in one hand and a Macedonian flag in the other, he emphasized that the partisans were the inheritors of both nations' long struggle for national liberation, which was now to be realized in a brotherly union.[53]

But appeals to the shared histories of the region also bore a more tragic dimension. In one of his wartime recollections, Tempo recounted a sabotage mission that took his partisan unit into Greek Macedonia. Upon entering a local village, the Yugoslav partisans were welcomed by the villagers who kissed their red flags and shed tears of joy. Having assumed the village to be occupied by Slavic Macedonians, Tempo and his men were surprised to learn that they were, in fact, ethnic Greeks, who had been forcibly settled in the area after their expulsion from Turkey in 1922: "Our joy from the sympathy that the population of that region expressed towards us was clouded by the knowledge that it had once been Macedonians that had lived here and who had since been displaced. But these Greeks who settled here had also been displaced from their homes in Asia Minor. All of this was a consequence of the meddling of the great powers in the relations of the Balkan countries!"[54] Tempo was, here, crafting a sense of affiliation rooted in a shared history of suffering, of mutual displacement, dispossession, and bloodshed. This isolated village in the mountainous north of Greece was not cut off from world history but had, rather, been tragically shaped by larger forces. Balkan federation was necessary, therefore, not only to resolve the national question but also to redeem this history of suffering. Moreover, this being in common was to be rooted in an ardent anti-imperialism directed against great power interference in the region.

While Yugoslav partisans appealed to both Slavic and Balkan ideas of affiliation during the war, the relative appeal of these two geographies was not evenly weighted. The balance sheet shows an overwhelming preference for Slavism rather than Balkan federalism. There are several reasons for this preference. First, as we've already discussed, Slavism provided a framework for justifying the partisan vision of a federalized Yugoslavia, which would become part of a more expansive system of Slavic political and cultural affiliation. Second, Slavism could rely on a reservoir of concepts and vocabularies that had been accumulated over more than a century of pan-Slavic activism. For a figure like Nazor, for instance, the Soviet-sponsored Slavism of the war years merely revived his own earlier pan-Slavic commitments. Balkan federalism lacked a similarly rich cultural legacy. Third, Slavism was promoted by the Soviet Union as a key leitmotif of its wartime propaganda in a way that Balkan federalism was not. There were no "All-Balkan" congresses, no Balkan equivalent of the *Slaviane* magazine, no international outreach efforts among Balkan diasporas. The international institutional support that Slavism enjoyed gave it greater purchase on the cultural imaginary of Yugoslav partisans.

Tempo's reference to the Balkan peoples' entangled histories of suffering highlights a further difference between these two projects that also helps to explain Slavism's greater appeal. While both Slavism and Balkanism envisioned a future moment in which a history of suffering would be redeemed by a revolutionary event, Slavism had one concrete advantage. With its strong affective investments in Soviet Russia, its adherents could identify with a concrete historical force, the Red Army, as the endogenous source of Slavic liberation. Balkanism had no such reference point. Furthermore, the idea of Balkan unity struggled against a widespread trope of the Balkans as immersed in an endless cycle of violence and intercommunal bloodshed.[55] While Tempo could point to individual partisan victories as evidence of a kind of salvatory moment that might rupture this cyclical history of suffering, these moments could never amount to as monumental an event as Stalingrad, whose world historical scale promised a turning point in the war.

IV

On 29 November 1945, the newly elected People's Front, led by the KPJ, declared the formation of the Federal People's Republic of Yugoslavia. In this new era of state building, projects of Slavic and Balkan affiliation became more central to the KPJ's political strategy and were recalibrated to the geopolitical configurations of the postwar order. Infamous as the most ardent disciples of Moscow, the KPJ quickly set out to reorganize society and the economy in line with Stalinist orthodoxies, nationalizing industry, introducing a new regime of propaganda and censorship, and organizing mass mobilization campaigns among the population.[56] This fealty to Moscow, however, was tempered by the fact that Yugoslav communists had come to power on the back of their own local revolutionary struggle. Unlike the people's governments elsewhere in Eastern Europe, therefore, the Yugoslav regime enjoyed a substantial degree of local support that provided a basis of autonomy from the Soviet Union. This autonomy accounts for the leadership's regular attempts to extend its geopolitical influence throughout the region, as it does the more aggressive brinksmanship that Tito demonstrated in these early postwar years, much to Stalin's exasperation.[57]

The friction between Yugoslav deference to and autonomy from the Soviet Union was sustained within the new supranational formations that the Soviet Union and its communist allies had begun to forge in Eastern Europe. These projects provided a geopolitical and geocultural field within which the Yugoslav leadership could project their influence and boost their prestige, taking advantage of the networks and platforms that these mediating spaces offered.[58] In his highly publicized diplomatic visit to Czechoslovakia, for instance, Tito represented Yugoslavia as a symbol of Slavic unity.[59] In the name of Balkan solidarity, Yugoslav diplomats defended Albanian territorial integrity and provided aid to the Democratic Army of Greece.[60] Yugoslavia's prestige within these supranational formations was reflected in the fact that Belgrade was selected as both the headquarters of the World Slavic Committee and the seat of a future Balkan federation. Unsurprisingly, then, projects of Slavic and Balkan unity achieved a renewed importance for the socialist regime, which increasingly called upon its intellectuals to invest these mediating spaces with ideological meaning, to sketch their geographies, and to popularize them among the wider population.

The crowning achievement of Yugoslavia's efforts to project its influence within the postwar Slavic movement was the World Slavic Congress hosted by Belgrade in December 1946. Over four days, around 300 representatives from the Slavic countries and Slavic social or cultural associations from around the world gathered at the University of Belgrade to hear speeches commemorating the victory of the Slavic peoples over German fascism and celebrating Slavdom's contributions to world culture.[61] Alongside the official proceedings, cultural events were held throughout the city, including film screenings and museum exhibitions, designed to showcase the culture of the different Slavic nations. Meanwhile, the Yugoslav government organized a mass rally, attended by 200,000 supporters, to greet the congress participants.[62] The congress cemented both Yugoslavia's prominence within this emerging supranational formation and the importance of Slavism as a legitimating ideology for the new regime.

The importance of the Slavic movement was also registered in the breadth of cultural exchanges, translations, and journal articles designed to cultivate a sense of Slavic affinity among the Yugoslav public. This was a stated priority of the newly formed Union of Yugoslav Writers, whose board regularly emphasized the need to "deepen cultural connections of our peoples with all the Slavic peoples and other progressive forces in the world."[63] To achieve this, the union invited foreign writers on high profile visits to Yugoslavia. Minutes of the union's meetings suggest that these invitations were apportioned according to the relative weight of the respective country within this new cultural geography. In 1947, for instance, the union intended to invite five writers from the Soviet Union, three each from Czechoslovakia, Poland, and Bulgaria, while France was to send two and Hungary and Albania one writer each.[64] The priority accorded Slavic countries was replicated in the translations of foreign texts over this period: the vast bulk of these were from Soviet literature, mostly Russian and Ukrainian, but Polish, Czech, Slovak, and Bulgarian writers were also translated.[65] Indeed, translation was considered a vital means of fostering a new Slavic consciousness among Yugoslav readers. In 1947, for instance, Miodrag Popović bemoaned the fact that so few young poets in Yugoslavia looked to the literatures of those "brotherly nations of the Soviet Union, Bulgaria, the Czechs, and Poles," whose writers "create literature that is of a kindred spirit (*po duhu srodnu*) and close to our peoples."[66]

Figure 5.2 | Postage stamps issued to commemorate the World Slavic Congress, held in Belgrade in December 1946. The stamps depict major Slavic capitals: Sofia (½ dinar), Prague (1 dinar), Warsaw (1½ dinars), Belgrade (2½ dinars), and Moscow (5 dinars).

As much as the Yugoslav leadership saw Slavic affiliation as a means of increasing their own prestige in Eastern Europe, these modes of cultural exchange served to consolidate the space of Slavdom in ways that reinforced the region as a sphere of Soviet influence. This operated by promoting a geography of kinship that oriented the Slavic nations towards Russia, deemphasizing cultural or religious ties that might have drawn certain national communities towards the West, and foregrounding a language of racial community that positioned Russia as an ancestral centre of gravity. This new spatial dynamic was captured by the notorious Slovene partisan commander and literary theorist, Dušan Pirjevec: "In these years of struggle, which have enacted a new morality, the face of man and of society has changed. Time has moved us with a mighty lever from the dark and discarded Balkans to that place in the world where history is made. From Trieste to Vladivostok – that is now the axis of the world."[67] Pirjevec's vision illustrated two elements of the spatial dynamics of the new Slavic movement. First, it loosely sketched the geography of this mediating space, which stretched from the Adriatic across the Eurasian steppe to the Pacific. This was by far the most expansive supranational space yet within which Yugoslav socialists imagined themselves, well exceeding the Balkan or European geographies of the interwar period. Second, it infused this imagined space with a messianic meaning: the Red Army's victory marked a historical realignment that would centre global humanity on the axis of Slavdom. By orienting themselves towards a victorious Soviet Russia, the Slavic peoples of South East Europe would be drawn out of their provincial Balkan backwaters and placed at the centre of world events.

Affiliation with Russia was crucial for this redemptive vision of world history. There were a number of reasons for this view: Russia was the largest and most powerful Slavic state, one of the three Allied powers that had reordered the postwar world; there was a degree of intellectual path dependency as the new Slavic movement often leant on earlier pan-Slavic traditions that had similarly accorded Russia a privileged place; and finally, wartime Slavism grew out of and was intellectually harmonized with Stalin's turn towards a greater Russian nationalism from 1939 onwards.[68] Consequently, Russia loomed large as a point of reference for Yugoslav writers who set out to sketch this new geography of Slavic kinship. This was true even for those authors who sought to explore the horizontal ties between smaller Slavic nations but who were often compelled to do so with point of reference to Russia. Take, for instance, Igo Gruden's poem celebrating Yugoslav-Bulgarian solidarity:

We are brothers, and now we are one domain!
From the shores of the Adriatic and Triglav
to the sun's rays on the Black Sea.

In the Spring that came from Russia,
the flags of free brotherly nations
have sprouted from the healthy seeds in our hearts.[69]

Despite the obvious point that co-operation between South Slavic radicals in the nineteenth century predated the Russian Revolution and was, in fact, often premised on an anti-imperial opposition to the Russian Empire, Gruden's poem plotted Yugoslav-Bulgarian solidarity within a new era of Slavic affiliation inaugurated by Russia. Revolutionary Russia, that is, served as the prime mover of Slavic unity in ways that aggrandized the country's position within this supranational configuration.

That participation in a Slavic community led by Russia would draw the small Slavic peoples of Eastern Europe into world history was a common theme in Yugoslav literature at this time. This notion was central to Miško Kranjec's first postwar novel, *Pesem gora* (*Song of the Mountains*, 1946), which followed the protagonist, Maks's, journey from demoralized loner wandering the Slovene mountains to a dedicated partisan fighter. In his student days, we learn, Maks had been a "Slavic enthusiast," and believed the liberation of Slovenia would be achieved by a redemptive Russian Empire. He is painfully disabused of his pan-Slavic illusions during World War I when, first, Russia fails to liberate the Habsburg Slavs and, second, his childhood sweetheart, Lenka, runs off with a wounded Russian officer. These twin betrayals lead him into his reclusive life amidst the mountains. Only with the outbreak of World War II, and after witnessing German atrocities against the local villagers, does Maks decide to rejoin the world, helping local partisans navigate the Slovene wilderness and eventually playing a key role in the liberation. Amidst the partisans he reconnects with Lenka, who has returned to Slovenia following the death of her Russian husband and her two children in the war. The return of Lenka comes to symbolize the revival of Maks's earlier Slavic ideals of a homeland spanning "from Triglav to the Urals."[70] However, now his hopes are invested not in the Russia of the tsars but of the soviets. For Maks, the victory of "this other Russia, this real Russia," not only realizes the "redemption of his race" (*odrešenje svojega rodu*), but also facilitates the entry of the Slovene people into world history.[71]

148   Mediating Spaces

V

Although Slavism continued to enjoy greater appeal than Balkan federalism, the postwar period did see a more balanced treatment of these ideas among Yugoslav cultural workers. The fact that the Yugoslav leadership had been given freer rein by Moscow to promote their influence in South East Europe meant that ideas of Balkan unification began to receive much more serious attention than they did during the war. This was evidenced most obviously in the immediate postwar years, when there was a flourish of publications reassessing the legacy of Balkan federalism. In 1946, Tucović's *Srbija i Arbanija* was republished, with a critical introduction by Milovan Đilas explaining the book's relevance.[72] A year earlier, the Macedonian literary critic Dimitar Mitrev had celebrated the twenty-first anniversary of the death of the Bulgarian socialist revolutionary, Dimo Hadžidimov. Mitrev's essay foregrounded Hadžidimov's Balkan-wide perspective and his insistence that Macedonia could only be free as part of a Balkan federation.[73] The centennial of Svetozar Marković's birth, in the autumn of 1946, provided the opportunity for Yugoslav writers to reassess his historical legacy, drawing particular attention to the Balkan horizons of his thought. While these texts occasionally highlighted Marković's connections to Russia and sometimes framed him as a distinctly South Slavic thinker, they nevertheless presented him not as a forefather of the contemporary Yugoslav state, but rather as a progenitor of a Balkan federation yet to come.[74]

But Yugoslav ideas of Balkan unity received their most focused expression with regard to two contexts: first, the growing connections between Yugoslavia and the People's Republic of Albania, and second, surrounding Yugoslav engagement with the Greek Civil War. Yugoslav-Albanian relations were a key site for promoting broader ideas of Balkan affiliation. As the sole non-Slavic communist state in the Balkans, Albania, and the question of its place in a future regional union, highlighted the tension between Slavic and Balkan geographies that played out in Yugoslav socialism at this time. During World War II, relations between the Yugoslav and Albanian communist parties were especially strong, with the Central Committee of the KPJ even sending representatives to help form the Albanian party and advise its antifascist guerilla campaign.[75] These ties continued to flourish in the immediate postwar years. At the

Paris Peace Conference, Yugoslav leaders emphatically defended Albania from territorial claims by the Greek government.[76] In July 1946, the two countries signed the Treaty of Friendship and Mutual Aid, which laid out a framework for closer economic integration.[77] Albanian-language press in Yugoslavia celebrated these agreements as indications of the "blood brotherhood" (*vellaznim gjaku*) of the two countries, and as a cornerstone of peace in the Balkans.[78] When massive flooding devasted parts of Albania in October 1946, the Yugoslav party launched a mass fundraising effort, eventually sending 57 million dinars in aid to its southern neighbour.[79] Albanian and Yugoslav youth also participated in joint labour brigades, building roads and railways that linked the two countries and that offered chances for fraternization.[80] Meanwhile, efforts were made to foster cultural exchanges, with delegates of writers' unions visiting one another.[81] These affiliations were informed by the expectation that the two countries would soon be unified, either through Albania joining the Yugoslav federation as a seventh republic or through the formation of a wider Balkan federation.

Despite the flourishing of these concrete ties, Albanian culture was poorly represented in Yugoslav literary journals, a paucity that contrasted markedly with the treatment of literatures from Slavic nations. While major journals occasionally carried reviews of or works of poetry or prose by Albanian writers, these were exceptions to the general neglect of Albanian culture.[82] Yugoslav cultural officials were clearly aware of the need to address these weak cultural ties. In January 1947, for instance, the KPJ's Ideological Commission castigated the Croatian party for the dearth of proposed translations from other Balkan nations in its annual publishing plan. "It is necessary," the commission instructed, "to publish something – anything – from Albanian literature. Obligatory."[83] In the absence of quality translations, some journals published essays designed to better familiarize their readers with Albanian culture.[84] In 1948, for example, Marjan Jurković published a full-page spread in *Književne novine* (*Literary Newspaper*) recounting his recent visit to Albania. The essay featured thorough descriptions of contemporary Albanian art and literature and reflected on the growing cultural ties between the two countries. Jurković was especially proud to see a copy of Tucović's *Srbija i Arbanija* in the national library, which he believed demonstrated Albania's commitment to a future Balkan federation.[85]

150   Mediating Spaces

While it was often drowned out by the amplified Slavism of the period, the theme of Albanian-Yugoslav affiliation animated the work of some Yugoslav writers in ways that traced the contours of a specifically Balkan geography. The Montenegrin poet, Radovan Zogović, is perhaps the best example of this tendency. Zogović had grown up in Kosovo in the 1920s and had been radicalized by the Yugoslav government's repression of the Albanian population. One of his first celebrated collections, *Došljaci* (*The Newcomers*, 1937), explored this repression through the figure of Ali Binak, an embittered Albanian nobleman who documents the horrors perpetrated against his people by the new regime.[86] Two years later, Zogović penned *Skadar na Bojani* (*Shkodra on the Bojana*), a cycle of impassioned poems protesting the Italian occupation of Albania.[87] These poems were animated by Zogović's belief that Albanians, Montenegrins, and Serbs shared a historical destiny in their entangled struggles against foreign domination.[88] His work found wider audiences in the immediate postwar years as his message of Yugoslav-Albanian solidarity held greater resonance in an age of growing Balkan affiliation. In 1948, for instance, the Slovene journal *Novi Svet* (*New World*) translated selections of *Skadar na Bojani*.[89] The same year, the poet Dušan Kostić penned an account of his recent visit to Kosovo in which he dwelled on the figure of Ali Binak, and what his place might be in a newly "liberated" Kosovo.[90] Meanwhile, during his visit to Albania, Marjan Jurković noted with pride that, amidst the explosion of translations of Yugoslav literature into Albanian, Zogović's work was the most published. Such was his popularity, apparently, that demand for his poetry outpaced publishing capacity, with the result that several of his writings circulated among Albanian readers in handwritten copies.[91]

The youth labour campaigns offered a productive lens for exploring Yugoslav-Albanian solidarity. In addition to bringing together youth from each of the Yugoslav republics, these campaigns also included volunteers from around Eastern Europe and the Balkans, and sometimes further afield. For some writers, these volunteers served as a synecdoche for a project of regional solidarity. In his 1946 poem "Zheleznicata" (The Railroad), the Macedonian poet Venko Markovski used the paths of the different volunteers to trace the geography of socialist Yugoslavia and its links to a wider regional space. In the poem, Yugoslavia becomes a rallying point for revolutionary forces in the Balkans, as Greek partisans with their "old, iron feet" and Albanians "who cannot be constrained by fences," come rushing to join their Yugoslav comrades "like an avalanche."[92] In one of her youth brigade poems, the young Serbian poet Mira Alečković imagined the semi-mythic figure of Rade Borović, the fourteenth-century Serbian architect, looking down on the young builders of socialism and being inspired by their efforts.[93] Although according to folklore Borović was reported to have built a number of sites throughout the western Balkans, the poem refers solely to his work in the town of Shkodra, once part of the medieval Serbian kingdom but, in 1947, the northernmost city of Albania. This geographic reference blurred contemporary national borders, evoking a shared Balkan geography revived by the youthful spirit of the revolution.[94]

The second site through which Yugoslav writers explored themes of regional solidarity was that of the Greek Civil War. Although Yugoslav partisans had developed a thorough critique of the Greek Communist Party's strategy during World War II, the Yugoslav leadership wasted little time in providing support to the Democratic Army of Greece when they took up arms in 1946. This support was motivated by both the new regime's bid for regional hegemony in South East Europe and ethnic solidarity with the Slavic Macedonian minority of northern Greece.[95] Anxious to avoid accusations of either communist expansionism or ethnic irredentism, the leadership fell back on a language of anti-imperial solidarity, highlighting the role of the US and Britain in fueling the conflict and situating it in a longer history of imperial interference in the Balkans. In contrast to the destabilization and conflict that Western imperialism had produced in Greece, Yugoslav writers pointed to the peace and stability that the new socialist states of the Balkans had secured through their co-operation.[96]

Yugoslav Macedonian writers were especially attuned to the civil war in Greece, not least because Slavic Macedonians in northern Greece constituted a key element of the leftist insurgency.[97] They were also keenly aware that the plight of the Macedonian national community, which crossed the borders of Yugoslavia, Greece, and Bulgaria, necessarily raised the question of Balkan unity in ways that exceeded the racial framework of Slavism. In his short story "Nepokoreni" ("The Unconquered"), Jane Sapozhnikov explored the war through the character of Sime, a Slavic Macedonian from Kastoria, on trial for his support of the Democratic Army. Sime's family history plots the longer history of Macedonian oppression:

his grandfather had been hung by Ottoman authorities and his father murdered by Greek nationalists in the Balkan Wars. Sime sees the redemption of this sorrowful history in the struggle for a democratic Greece and, at his trial, he denounces the judges and the new government for their wartime collaboration, which he contrasts with his own struggle within the ranks of the Greek partisan army. Furious, the judges sentence him to death, but he is liberated by partisans and rejoins the struggle.[98]

A similar approach was evident in Blazhe Koneski's 1947 poem "Na granitsa" ("On a Border"). The eponymous border seems to be that running through Lake Prespa, dividing Yugoslav from Greek Macedonia. Koneski uses this geographic reference to contrast the fate of the two countries: while the sun shines on the Yugoslav fields, in Greece a cloud has fallen, villages are burned, and bodies are trampled. These images evoked the violence leveled against Slavic Macedonian populations in northern Greece by government forces in the immediate postwar years. But across these villages Koneski's narrator can see a people's army rising, made up of Greeks and Macedonians uniting to overthrow tyranny.[99] What is significant in both Sapozhnikov's story and Koneski's poem is that, although the central theme concerns Macedonians' national oppression, their liberation is not sought in a struggle for independence or secession from Greece, but rather in the alliance of Greeks and Slavs. The underlying vision is not of national consolidation but supranational co-operation. In this way, Slavic Macedonian characters are used as a thematic bridge between socialist Yugoslavia and revolutionary forces in Greece to promote themes of Balkan affiliation.

But the Yugoslav writer that most thoroughly explored the Greek Civil War was not Macedonian but a Jewish Serb. Oskar Davičo (1909–1989) had come to revolutionary politics as a member of the Belgrade surrealist movement before joining the KPJ in the late 1930s. During the war, he was captured in Dalmatia and transferred to an internment camp in Italy. After 1945 he became a valuable and trusted asset of the new communist government, and enjoyed a celebrated career as a prominent poet and journalist. In the winter of 1946–47, Davičo was selected to accompany a UN investigative commission to Greece as a representative of the Yugoslav press. The commission was charged with investigating the Greek government's accusations of interference in the civil war by Greece's Balkan neighbours.[100] This task led it through the towns of northern Greece, interviewing witnesses and eventually seeking a meeting with the head of the guerilla forces, General Markos Vafeiadis. Daviěo's account of the journey was published later that year as *Među Markosovim partizanima* (*Among Markos's Partisans*) and was widely celebrated in the Yugoslav press. In 1948 it received the prestigious award from the Committee of Culture and Art, and was translated and published in Slovene, Bulgarian, Hungarian, Norwegian, and Arabic.[101]

Među Markosovim partizanima was a work of reportage that blended war correspondence and slices of life with the tropes of spy fiction. In the first half of the work, Daviěo is forced to parse events on the ground from the sensationalism of the Western press and the intrigues of the US and British delegates. Shady figures with rumoured connections to Western intelligence agencies flit in and out of the story; bumbling UN officials are hoodwinked by silver-tongued British diplomats; Greek witnesses, ostensibly called on to present evidence of partisan atrocities, recant under the forensic enquiries of the Soviet delegate. Despite the protests of the British and American delegates, the lead commissioners agree to a meeting with General Markos, but their efforts to rendezvous with his unit are constantly thwarted by Greek offensives. Frustrated, the group breaks up: the Western delegates and reporters return to Thessaloniki while the delegates of the communist powers (Soviet Union, Poland, Bulgaria, Yugoslavia, and Albania) continue their mission to meet General Markos and proceed deep into partisan-held territory. The split in the delegation marks a turning point in the text. Once in liberated territory, the subplots of intrigue and murder fall away, and the work becomes a more straightforward piece of embedded war reportage. Daviěo celebrates the courage of the Greek partisans, bemoans the devastation the Greek government and its British supporters have inflicted on the rural population, and uses biographical sketches of the people he meets to explore the contemporary history of Greece.

Although he didn't belabour the point, Daviěo's account of the Greek struggle often drew reference to his own participation in the antifascist struggle of World War II in ways that established parallels between the Yugoslav and Greek experience. These parallels emerge when the commission leaves the urban environment of Thessaloniki and moves into the mountainous hinterlands of Aegean Macedonia. Throughout the text, descriptions of the Macedonian landscape are used to suggest affiliations between Greek and Yugoslav struggles and, by extension, the peoples themselves.[102] Daviěo also presents the

154 Mediating Spaces

conflict in Greece as a continuation of World War II, thereby drawing parallels between the Greek partisan struggle and the Yugoslavs' own increasingly mythologized wartime history.[103] This framework helped translate the Greek experience to a Yugoslav audience and promote solidarity with their cause.

While such efforts to foster Greek-Yugoslav affiliation are often subtle, at times Davičo becomes more didactic, setting up scenes that speak to political projects of Balkan unity. When the residents of a village welcome the UN delegation with a celebration in the streets, Davičo notes that they sing the lines of a popular partisan song that quotes the Greek national hero and early proponent of Balkan unity, Rhigas Feraios:

The Serbian and the Greek people,
Together with the Albanian and Bulgarian,
Will find their full freedom,
In the unity of Balkan republics.[104]

As formulaic as this verse sounds (one wonders how catchy it would have been when sung!) the citation of Rhigas in this context is revealing. If communist Slavism could draw on the wellsprings of over a century of pan-Slavic cultural activism to sustain its claims for racial community, this citation of Rhigas suggests that proponents of Balkan federalism could also evoke a deeper intellectual legacy, one that stretched back to the region's Enlightenment.[105]

While the question of Balkan unity is never far from the surface, Davičo's text is not without its own nod to Slavism. Indeed, one way of reading *Među Markosovim partizanima* is as an effort to reconcile the Slavic and Balkan geographies whose tensions were playing themselves out in Yugoslav socialism during these early postwar years. At times, Davičo's descriptions turn on surprisingly racialized language. Remarking on the differences between the ethnic Greek and ethnic Slavic Macedonians, for instance, he writes: "The new comrades were Greek women. They were shorter and also much darker than the Macedonians. They had big and bright eyes. But Andromache [Davičo's guide, a Slavic Macedonian woman] was still brighter than everyone and more beautiful, with that fiery-bold and open look. She had delicate skin, white and smooth as polished stone, and wavy black hair in which she had just put the red flower of a wild rose."[106]

This description is a striking example of the tension that played out between Slavic and Balkan geographies. The contrast that Davičo imagines between Greek and Slavic physiognomies cuts against the text's themes of Balkan unity. Against the political and social commonalities Davičo keeps returning to, such references to racial difference remind Yugoslav readers of the distinction between the short, dark Greeks and tall, fair Slavs. Furthermore, while the Greek characters in this scene remain unremarkable, the Slavic partisan, Andromache, is framed as a vision of revolutionary boldness and passion, made all the more obvious by the wild red rose in her hair. Between the nondescript Greeks and the Slavic vision of revolutionary desire, it isn't hard to conclude who Davičo thought played the greater role in animating the partisan struggle.

Davičo's text tried to reconcile the tension between Slavic and Balkan geographies through a narrative framework that postulated Slavs – and Yugoslavs in particular – as the vanguard of revolutionary struggle in South East Europe. This script drew on the racial paradigm that imbued Slavdom with essentialized features: anti-authoritarianism, a love for freedom, an instinct for democracy, revolutionary courage, and passion. These traits supposedly made the Slavic peoples a vanguard in the global struggle for socialism. In Yugoslavia this framework seemed to have been borne out: the partisans had emerged as the most confident revolutionary force during the war, provided leadership to the Albanian antifascist struggle, and saw evidence for the correctness of their position reflected in the Greek Left's failure to seize power after 1945. Federal Yugoslavia was also a model for a future Balkan union, again leading the way for the non-Slavic peoples of the region. This script that ascribed to Slavs a role as the revolutionary vanguard ran through Davičo's account of the civil war. Throughout the text he emphasized the leading role Slavic Macedonians played in the partisan struggle, quoting ethnic Greeks to corroborate this assessment.[107] He also presented Slavic Macedonians as a bridge linking Greece's revolutionary forces to the vanguard state of Yugoslavia to the north.[108]

VI

The model of Yugoslavia as the vanguard of Balkan liberation was not Davičo's invention but proliferated through several postwar texts. Its origins, however, lay back in the war, when a number of partisan leaders sought to bring the Slavic and Balkan horizons of their struggle into closer alignment. The clearest example is perhaps a speech that Milovan Đilas gave to partisan forces in Bosnia on the anniversary of the October Revolution in 1943. The war, Đilas proclaimed, was a transformational event that had set alight a Slavic consciousness among Eastern Europeans who now "connected their fate with the cradle of Slavdom – the Soviet Union."[109] This consciousness had been critical to the Yugoslavs' own success, inspiring them to great feats of sacrifice and heroism. The result was that Yugoslavia was no longer "some small unknown country" but a "homeland of heroes" whose reputation was gaining worldwide significance. "Our struggle," he continued, "has become a centre around which all the Balkan peoples gather, a flame that shines a light on the enslaved nations that surround us."[110] The superior revolutionary qualities of the Slavic nations were also reflected in the pathway that Đilas envisioned for the postwar unification of South East Europe. This was to proceed first through the fusion of Yugoslavia and Bulgaria. Such a consolidation of the space of South Slavdom would, he projected, "exert a power of attraction to the other peoples of the Balkans tortured by imperialism – the Albanians and the Greeks."[111]

The idea of Yugoslavia as the Slavic vanguard of a Balkan revolution became an important ideological leitmotif over the 1940s as the partisans' strategy began to bear fruit. In the postwar period, it provided an ideological framework within which to sustain the tension between Belgrade's fealty to and autonomy from Moscow. On the one hand, Slavism ensured a posture of deference to the Soviet Union as the "cradle of Slavdom"; on the other, Balkan federalism held out the promise of a future supranational structure within which Yugoslav autonomy could be more securely consolidated. In effect, Yugoslav communists leveraged the broader appeal and institutional support that Slavism enjoyed to project their influence and prestige at a regional scale.

Cultural producers allied with the partisan struggle and the postwar socialist state played an essential role in this process. The KPJ's prestige on the international stage could only be converted into domestic political capital if the Yugoslav public were ideologically invested in the wider supranational configurations within which the new state was plotted. This required writers and artists who could trace the imagined geographies of and foster affective investment in the party's geopolitical projects. As the KPJ centralized and concentrated political power through its own networks over the 1940s, it was able to exert greater influence and oversight on the field of official culture. Cultural producers, then, came to play a key role in crafting the ideological framework through which Yugoslavia's communist leadership sought a balance between maintaining fealty to and pursuing autonomy from Moscow.

Such a strategy could not withstand Stalin's paranoia for long. In the aftermath of the Tito-Stalin split, the mediating spaces of both Slavism and Balkan federalism would dissolve. Yugoslav socialism's search for its place in a wider supranational formation, however, would not weaken; in fact, it would take on more ambitious, more geographically expansive horizons as the country's leadership turned its attention to the newly liberated countries of the Third World.

6

Cultural One-Worldism and the Geographies of Non-Alignment, 1948–68

> Out of a desire to emphasize our exceptional position and the isolation
> of our country, some foreign journalists have taken to writing that
> the world is divided into East, West, and Yugoslavia. Although witty,
> it is not exactly an accurate phrase. Through the millennia the world
> has been divided into only two parts: a camp of progress and freedom
> and a camp of darkness and slavery. We have the honour of living in a
> country whose exceptional position arises from its extraordinary efforts
> to defend its independence and peace in the world. Such an exception
> is not isolation!
>
> Joža Horvat, "Mir," 1950

I

On 28 June 1948, the Federal People's Republic of Yugoslavia was expelled from the Cominform. Frustrated with the Yugoslav leadership's confrontational stance with the West over Trieste and its continuing support for Greek communists in the country's civil war, by the summer of 1948 Stalin had settled on a policy of toppling the Yugoslav leadership.[1] Ultimately, his plans of removing Tito's faction and replacing it with a more obedient clique failed, and the Yugoslavs survived the confrontation. However, the split with the Soviet Union profoundly disrupted the ideological horizons of Yugoslavia's socialist leadership and scrambled the country's geopolitical coordinates. The supranational projects of Slavic or Balkan affiliation within which Yugoslav socialists had sought to plot their revolution over the 1940s dissolved overnight. Disengaging from Stalinist orthodoxies, over the 1950s the Yugoslav leadership set out to craft

One-Worldism and the Geographies of Non-Alignment   159

their own path to socialism, grounded in the principles of workers' self-management, cultural liberalization, and non-alignment in foreign affairs.[2] The reforms of the 1950s radically recast the vision of socialist revolution and reconfigured Yugoslavia's position across multiple scales of the postwar international order.

The schism with the Soviets forced Yugoslavia from the borders of the socialist world and into the geopolitical uncertainties of the emerging Cold War. Cut off from Soviet support and increasingly threatened with invasion from the Eastern bloc, over the early 1950s Tito's government gradually opened to the West and sought deeper integration into the liberal international order. Although neither in Belgrade nor Washington were leaders quick to publicly acknowledge their new-found convergence of interests, the US's early efforts to sustain the small country's independence through food aid, military support, and favourable trade deals set Yugoslavia on a path of incorporation into the trade and financial networks of the West.[3] By the late 1950s, the country was routed into Western European export and capital markets and increasingly reliant on international loans. While Yugoslav leaders continued to pursue a project of socialist modernization and maintained a degree of autonomy from both sides of the Cold War, the country's debt-driven economy was deeply embedded in the financial networks of postwar capitalism.[4]

At a national scale, the aftermath of the Tito-Stalin split reconfigured the country's political-economic space, with profound consequences for the future coherence of the federation. These transformations grew from the new ideology of self-management socialism that Yugoslav theorists like Edvard Kardelj, Milovan Đilas, and Boris Kidrič formulated from 1949–53. In place of the centralized model of Stalinism, self-management socialism instead pursued the decentralization of administrative powers, the expansion of participatory forums in the economy, and the strengthening of the autonomy of social collectives from the state.[5] Over the 1950s and 1960s, this emphasis on decentralization promoted the political devolution of the country, transferring greater authority from federal institutions to those of the national republics and local municipalities.[6] While such policies were justified domestically on the grounds of breaking with the Stalinist legacy and introducing a more participatory model of socialism, its growing reliance on market mechanisms accelerated the country's integration into and increased its sensitivity to the dynamics of the global capitalist economy.[7]

160   Mediating Spaces

But it was at a regional scale that the break with Moscow had its most immediate and profound consequences. As we saw in the last chapter, Yugoslavia's entry into the Soviet-led socialist world had been configured through the mediating spatial projects of Slavism and Balkan federalism. Indeed, it was Tito's eagerness to leverage his influence within a future regional federation that earned him the distrust of Stalin.[8] After 1948 these projects quickly collapsed, and Yugoslavia's proximities to its Slavic and Balkan neighbours suddenly appeared to be vulnerabilities, as Albania and Bulgaria became potential launch pads for a Soviet invasion. Any plans for the formation of a Balkan federation or for pursuing further Slavic affiliation were abandoned. The impetus to seek security and project influence within a wider supranational entity, however, continued to inspire Yugoslavia's socialist leadership. By the mid-1950s, these aspirations had been redirected towards an alliance with a handful of states in Asia and Africa and gave rise to what would become the Non-Aligned Movement.[9]

The first steps towards the formation of this international alliance were taken in the halls of the UN, as Yugoslav representatives increasingly found themselves working in coalition with colleagues from Asia, Africa, and Latin America.[10] This early international co-operation provided the foundations for a more durable alliance and in July 1956, Tito met with the Indian Prime Minister Jawaharlal Nehru, and the President of Egypt, Gamal Abdel Nasser, on the Adriatic island of Brioni to discuss non-aligned co-operation. Five years later, in September 1961, Belgrade hosted the first summit of non-aligned countries, affirming Yugoslavia's influence (or its aspirations for such influence) in the postcolonial world.[11] The Non-Aligned Movement sought to secure the sovereignty and economic development of peripheral nations by promoting ideas of non-intervention, peaceful coexistence, and respect for national self-determination. While it eschewed an explicitly socialist ideology, the movement's vocal support for anticolonial and anti-apartheid struggles, the prominent involvement of Cuba, and its pursuit of a more redistributive global economic system, often aroused suspicion among Western cold warriors.[12] From the mid-1950s to the 1980s, Yugoslavia's alliance with the Third World would be a key pillar of the country's path to socialism.[13] As their regional horizons dissolved in the wake of the Tito-Stalin split, Yugoslav socialists scaled up their supranational aspirations and began to replot their small

One-Worldism and the Geographies of Non-Alignment   161

federation within the coordinates of a new mediating space, one that brought it into closer affiliation with Asia and Africa.

To interpret Yugoslav non-alignment as a project of spatial mediation requires refining the conceptual apparatus this book has deployed up until now. Specifically, we need to address two likely protests. The first would contest the extent to which non-alignment can be conceived as a mode of mediation. Non-alignment, this criticism might continue, is better understood as a strategy of global, rather than supranational, politics. There is strong evidence for this argument. After all, the strategists of non-alignment organized at a global scale, coordinating their activity through the institutions of the UN and presenting themselves as the most ardent defenders of its internationalist principles.[14] Their goal was not the creation of a new geopolitical bloc to rival those of the US and Soviets, but the reform of the international system as a whole.

Nevertheless, the efforts to coordinate the activity of non-aligned states frequently gave rise to makeshift supranational platforms that were rendered most visible by the irregular international conferences of non-aligned heads of state.[15] These platforms, while provisional, offered the representatives of postcolonial states the capacity to project power and influence in two directions: upwards, towards the international institutions and great powers that structured the global system; and downwards, into their national political landscapes. The leading strategists of non-alignment argued that the historical task of realizing a more equitable international order fell on the shoulders of the small, peripheral, and postcolonial states. Only those states whose existence was rooted in the struggle against foreign rule had the necessary historical perspective to realize the internationalist principles the UN embodied. Non-alignment was a means for coordinating these states' activity, cohering their interests, and amplifying their influence in international institutions where they might pressure the great powers.

Simultaneously, the supranational platforms of non-alignment could also serve postcolonial leaders as a stage from which to project influence into their domestic politics. Eager to circumvent challenges at home, some non-aligned leaders, including Tito, sought to scale up processes of political legitimation through their involvement in the non-aligned movement.[16] Participation in the movement allowed these leaders to share in the prestige that accrued from its international standing and to use the legitimacy this international recognition gave them to reinforce their regimes at home.[17] In this sense, non-alignment can be usefully conceived as a strategy of geopolitical mediation, an effort to structure a field of activity between the national and the global that at once accorded peripheral states greater room to manoeuver and new opportunities for political influence.

But if non-alignment can be understood as a strategy of geopolitical mediation, is it helpful to conceive of this in spatial terms? Can we really speak of the *space* of non-alignment? Such a proposition would certainly be in tension with Vijay Prashad's pithy observation that "[t]he Third World was not a place. It was a project."[18] Prashad's point – that the proximate geographical borders of the Third World are less significant than its discursive mobilization and the political subjectivities it sustained – is well taken. In fact, it is an especially salient observation for the case of Yugoslavia, where proponents of non-alignment, especially during the 1950s and 1960s, were hesitant to use any geographical shorthand to describe the movement. This hesitancy is unsurprising given that each of the available terms – "Afro-Asia," "Asia, Africa, and Latin America," or even the "Third World" – all marked Yugoslavia as an anomalous participant. While Yugoslav leaders had become especially adept at taking advantage of their country's geopolitical liminality, straddling both the Cold War's East-West axis and the developmental axis of the global North and South, that liminality became a liability if geographical borders were taken to map geopolitical allegiances literally. As such, Yugoslav leaders tended to disavow geographic language when theorizing the strategy of non-alignment.[19]

Nevertheless, despite their disavowals, socialist Yugoslavia's turn to Asia and Africa in the 1950s evoked what we might call an emergent geography of non-alignment. This was especially noticeable in the cultural production from this period, which closely tracked the country's diplomatic efforts. Because non-alignment was premised on rectifying the asymmetries of the existing global system, it necessitated an effort on the part of Yugoslav writers to proactively foreground coverage of the postcolonial states of Asia, Africa, and Latin America. Newspapers celebrated Yugoslavia's new geopolitical alliances, relayed pictures of Tito's diplomatic visits to these countries, and published reports of their histories and cultures.[20] Taken together, these trends had the effect of sketching the contours of a non-aligned geography that framed the country's geopolitical turn and the new relations of solidarity it sustained.[21]

One-Worldism and the Geographies of Non-Alignment 163

This geography was, however, amorphous, fuzzy around the edges. As such, it demanded a new cultural paradigm that could capture its nuanced terrain.

This chapter recovers the ephemeral geography of non-alignment by reconstructing the modes of cultural internationalism that Yugoslav socialists developed over the 1950s and 1960s. It argues that during this period, intellectuals formulated a paradigm of cultural one-worldism that offered fertile new ways of mapping Yugoslav affiliations with Asia, Africa, and Latin America. This project was facilitated by the rehabilitation of interwar anti-Stalinist intellectuals who rooted this paradigm of cultural one-worldism in the figure of a longue durée humanity. This chapter makes three broader contributions. First, it offers a cultural history of non-alignment as this project was formulated by Yugoslav socialists over the 1950s. While histories of non-alignment have often characterized the movement as a revolutionary challenge to the West, this chapter joins a growing scholarship that tells a more modest story of compromise and accommodation.[22] By demonstrating the ways in which cultural reforms in the early 1950s aligned concerns for artistic and national autonomy, it shows how a cultural paradigm of one-worldism framed both Yugoslav socialists' reorientation to Asia and Africa and their reconciliation with the liberal internationalist order.

Second, the chapter reconstructs an early moment in the exchanges and interconnections between the Second and Third worlds. While the recent explosion of scholarship on this topic has tended to focus on politics and economics, I echo Theodora Dragostinova's argument that attention to the cultural dimension of these ties offers "a unique perspective in comprehending how conflicting worldviews clashed, conversed, and accommodated each other in a global context."[23] As earlier chapters have demonstrated, the mediating spaces that animated Yugoslav socialist thought throughout the twentieth century were as much aesthetic as they were political. Fostering affiliations between different cultural, religious, and linguistic communities required cultural forms that could give meaning to these supranational projects, sketch their geographical contours, and create the conceptual and affective conditions for a political identity that spanned vast distances. This work was even more crucial for the early formulations of non-alignment, which exhorted Yugoslavs to identify with peoples in Asia, Africa, and Latin America with whom they had little to no history of being in common. Conceived

164   Mediating Spaces

as a narrowly pragmatic foreign policy, non-alignment was unlikely
to inspire the bonds of solidarity the Yugoslav leadership hoped to
foster. Cultural projects were required to make these solidarities a
felt reality.

Finally, by interpretating the Non-Aligned Movement as a mediating space, the chapter understands the Yugoslav leadership's turn to
the postcolonial world in the 1950s not simply as a pragmatic policy
forced by the 1948 split, but as a logical outgrowth of the intellectual history of Yugoslav socialism.[24] In other words, the Yugoslav
vision of the Non-Aligned Movement built on earlier traditions that
sought to craft spatial assemblages that could sustain affiliations
between the peoples of South East Europe, Asia, and Africa. The
anti-imperialist commitments that had once been projected within
the horizons of a future Balkan federation were rescaled to the more
geographically ambitious project of non-alignment.

II

During the 1950s intellectuals in Yugoslavia crafted a mode of cultural internationalism that this chapter characterizes as cultural
one-worldism. "One-worldism" was a concept that had its roots in
World War II, when it was popularized by English-speaking intellectuals to name a postwar ideal of global governance based on international cosmopolitanism and co-operation. This ideal animated several
international institutions of the postwar liberal order, but arguably
found its clearest expression in the early work of UNESCO. From
1945 to 1950, one-worldism captured the imagination of intellectuals and officials around UNESCO, fostering a renewed appreciation
for the cultural diversity that was to underpin a new consciousness
of world community.[25] This presupposed that humanity was being
propelled towards greater unity and mutual understanding, and that
governing institutions should be constructed at a global scale to
correspond to this worldwide integration. Although Glenda Sluga
has identified the imperial origins of some of its key concepts, in its
more radical articulations one-worldism challenged the legitimacy
of empire and envisioned an international order based on the right
of national self-determination and racial equality.[26] Conceived as
a cultural paradigm, one-worldism sought, in the words of Julian
Huxley, "the orchestration of cultural diversity within an advancing
world civilization."[27] This framework was capable of reconciling the

countervailing tendencies of global integration and the principles of national self-determination and sovereign equality. It also offered a valuable schema for envisioning a more inclusive and egalitarian world culture in an era of decolonization.

One-worldism fostered a new consciousness of world space that had important implications for how Yugoslav socialists of the 1950s formulated ideas of supranationalism. Most immediately, it reconceptualized the global as a problem of scalar politics. By making real the prospect of international governance, one-worldism framed the global as a sphere of regulation and reform. Inspired by allied co-operation during the war, seeking to leverage the allied powers' verbal commitments to the principle of sovereign equality of states, and spurred on by a growing awareness that the new destructive capacities of atomic warfare posed problems of planetary scope, advocates of one-worldism began to take seriously the reconfiguration of power relations at a global scale.[28] This consciousness of the global as a sphere of regulation and reform was a crucial precondition for the strategy of non-alignment. It was, after all, primarily through the institutions of the UN that the Non-Alignment Movement sought to alleviate the tensions of the Cold War and craft a world order more amenable to the interests of small or peripheral states.[29]

However, by positing an all-inclusive framework of world community, the paradigm of one-worldism necessarily thinned the contours of any geography that might have traced the more circumscribed boundaries of the non-aligned alliance. Furthermore, the distinct spatiality of the Non-Aligned Movement, namely, its lack of territorial consolidation or even geographic contiguity, made it difficult to represent as a coherent space. This meant that the Non-Aligned Movement wasn't characterized by the same impulse to delineate a distinct cultural geography in the way that earlier projects of Balkan federalism, Popular Front Europeanism, or wartime Slavism were. At the same time, because one-worldism became the mode of cultural internationalism through which Yugoslav audiences were to be introduced to their newfound allies in the postcolonial world, intellectuals and cultural producers often gave greater attention to the cultures of Asia, Africa, and Latin America. The priority accorded to these parts of the world meant that one-worldism helped to foster certain tentative geographies of what would, over the 1960s, become crystallized as the "Third World."

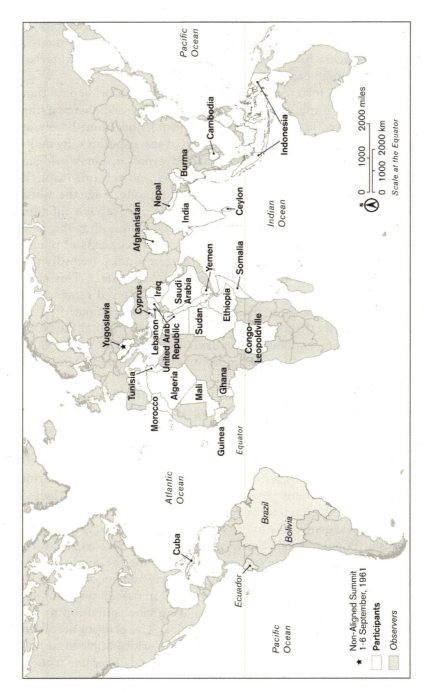

Figure 6.1 | States that sent representatives to the first Meeting of Non-Aligned Heads of State, 1961.

One-worldism also eschewed the question of political ideology, evoking instead a vision of a shared humanity that transcended political divisions. Such a paradigm aligned well with the geopolitical goals of the Yugoslav leadership, who sought a means to reconcile their gradual opening-up to the West with a newfound interest in the political potential of the postcolonial world.[30] Indeed, Yugoslav representatives explicitly resisted any efforts to associate the Non-Aligned Movement with a political ideology.[31] The non-ideological character of Yugoslav one-worldism was also shaped by the radical liberalization of the cultural field that took place in the country following the split of 1948. The need to reform the Stalinist system of cultural production led theorists to advance a new concern with the artist's autonomy from the state. This more open policy broke with the constraining aesthetic principles of socialist realism and instead promoted a new openness to innovation and experimentation that came to be known as "socialist modernism."[32] As Bojana Videkanić has observed, socialist modernism complemented Yugoslavia's unique geopolitical configurations, at once integrating the country into the Western-oriented networks of international modernism and drawing them into close dialogue with emerging cultural movements in the postcolonial world.[33] This project of reorganizing socialist culture around the preservation of artistic autonomy drew from, and in the process rehabilitated, a local tradition of anti-Stalinist Marxism that had been developed by avant-garde theorists like Miroslav Krleža and Marko Ristić in the interwar years.[34]

Marko Ristić (1902–1984) was Yugoslavia's preeminent cultural diplomat during the 1950s and the key intellectual link between the anti-Stalinist Marxism of the interwar period and the one-worldism of the 1950s. As the leading figure of the interwar surrealist movement in Belgrade, he had become a bête noire of the communists for his criticism of the Stalinization of the communist party. During the war he had remained in occupied Belgrade, refusing to join the partisan movement and thereby confirming the communists' disdain. In the aftermath of the 1948 split, however, Yugoslav officials saw in this critic of Stalinism an intellectual asset in their efforts to formulate a new cultural line purged of Soviet influence. Within a few years of the split, Ristić was promoted to the position of president of the newly formed Commission for Foreign Cultural Relations, where he liaised with representatives from international organizations such as UNESCO and the European Society of Culture.[35] During the 1950s, he used this position to theorize a new cultural internationalism that complemented the country's geopolitical realignment.[36]

Ristić's cultural one-worldism was premised on the rapid pace of global integration that characterized the postwar order. Owing, he argued, to the expansion of world trade, technological development, scientific progress, and growing international co-operation, otherwise disparate societies had become part of a single, integrated totality.[37] This unprecedented global interconnectedness inaugurated a new stage in human culture, making possible the collective preservation and higher development of humanity.[38] Likely inspired by the one-world utopias that animated UNESCO in its early years, Ristić saw this emerging world culture as a synthesis, "multi-formed, differentiated, because it is constantly being created with the contributions of different, differentiated national cultures."[39] The formation of a contemporary world culture was to occur dialectically, through the simultaneous preservation and transcendence of cultural differences.

Although early articulations of one-worldism often carried traces of colonial ideas of cultural hierarchy, Ristić's development of this paradigm led him to advocate for an anticolonial defence of the political and cultural self-determination of small nations. Drawing on the new priority that Yugoslav cultural policy accorded to creative autonomy, he emphasized that the cultural independence of small nations unleashed the creativity that would allow humanity's diversity to flourish. Yugoslavia had a leading role to play in these efforts. First, its struggle for an independent path to socialism defended the principle of national self-determination and thereby undermined great power politics. Second, as a supranational federation it modelled the possibilities of a world culture built on the integration of autonomous national elements.[40] Given the way that Yugoslavia had "correctly" resolved its national question, Ristić argued, the country could serve as a blueprint for a future political and cultural remapping of the world. These early efforts to formulate the philosophy behind Yugoslav cultural internationalism laid the conceptual foundations upon which socialist intellectuals would build over the course of the 1950s.

As the rest of the chapter will argue, the paradigm of cultural one-worldism that Yugoslav intellectuals crafted during this period was organized around three related ideas: first, a decolonial historical teleology that envisioned the remapping of world space as a mosaic of national cultural territories; second, a concern with the

One-Worldism and the Geographies of Non-Alignment   169

preservation of global cultural diversity; and finally, a new sensitivity for the deep time of human history. Not only did these ideas represent a sharp break from earlier visions of world revolution, they also marked a meaningful move away from the Marxism that had dominated Yugoslav socialism, in one interpretation or another, since the fin de siècle. This capacious paradigm helped to give form to an emergent geography of non-alignment that would, by the late 1960s, become more clearly conceived as the Third World.

III

The first element of Yugoslav cultural one-worldism was an understanding of world history that posited decolonization and national sovereignty as its telos. This idea grew out of the central importance Yugoslav socialists placed on the principle of national self-determination, which was a guiding thread of their policy of non-alignment. Culturally, this principle was often conceptually aligned with the newfound value of creative autonomy. In a major speech that he delivered to the Congress of the Yugoslav Union of Writers in Ljubljana in 1952, Miroslav Krleža explicitly rooted artistic autonomy in an understanding of national sovereignty. Arguing for a break with the totalitarian policies of Stalinism, Krleža instead sought a new program that prioritized the creation of an autonomous, self-conscious citizenry.[41] This autonomy, however, was premised on the freedom of the nation, whose sovereignty secured the freedom of its people from foreign domination. A genuinely independent socialist culture, in Krleža's view, was to cultivate an awareness of the individual's belonging to a distinct national community, to foster "an enriched memory of our own history."[42] This policy aligned romantic assumptions about the creative autonomy of the individual with the Wilsonian principle of the self-determination of the nation, drawing on the two concepts' shared intellectual genealogy.[43]

National sovereignty was a key component of Yugoslav cultural one-worldism. Writing a year before Krleža's watershed speech, the former surrealist, Oskar Davičo, argued that the proliferation of sovereign nation states after World War II was the realization of a "centuries-long dream of human freedom." This dream had initially sprung from the ideals of eighteenth-century liberalism before being extended into the social sphere by the Russian Revolution. However, the betrayal of that project by Stalinism and its imperial conquests,

Davičo insisted, had made it obvious that human freedom could only be fully realized through the security of national sovereignty: "The proletarian, human dream of happiness, man's dream of freedom, equality and brotherhood is today called the independence of nations. In order for man to become an active subject (*da bi čovek bio dejstvujući čovek*) he must, alongside a place in production, also have a specific place on the land. Without this there is the risk of an exodus into the 'higher region' of abstraction, which is just as real a danger as banishment to Siberia."[44] Territorialized national self-determination was an essential guarantor of human freedom, overcoming the limits of both classical liberalism, which could only approach man as an abstraction, and Stalinism, which led to man's ultimate negation. To become truly free, Davičo argued, man needed his own national *territory*, his "specific place on the land." This argument presaged that which Krleža would present a year later in Ljubljana and harked back to the Fichtean claim that the liberty of the nation guaranteed that of the individual.[45] This argument resonated loudly with demands for the self-determination and the equality of sovereign states then being advanced by anticolonial activists within international institutions at the time.[46]

Decolonization was central to this vision of world history, and Yugoslav socialists understood the end of European empires as inaugurating a new, dynamic moment of human liberation. Reporting on the historic meeting of African and Asian heads of state at the Bandung Conference, for instance, the Serbian journalist, Predrag Milojević, spoke in clear terms of the peoples of Asia and Africa transforming "from the object of imperialism to the subject of world politics."[47] As these nations liberated themselves from colonial rule and began to articulate their own sovereignty on the international stage, they ushered in a new phase of world history. Milojević's rhetorical sleight of hand here was significant, presaging, as it did, the Third-Worldist ideologies of the 1960s that would decentre the industrial working class and insist on the postcolonial world as the new vanguard of historical progress.[48]

In thinking about the contemporary moment of decolonization and their relationship to the countries of Asia and Africa, Yugoslav intellectuals frequently postulated a shared history of foreign oppression.[49] Although they recognized that their own country had not been "colonized" in the same way as their newfound allies, many saw parallels between the experience of colonialism and their own subjugation to the Habsburg and Ottoman empires.[50] In his 1952 speech to the Ljubljana Congress, for example, Krleža asserted precisely this parallel between Yugoslavia and the colonized world. Recounting the events that led to the present historical conjuncture, he centred on the traumatic consequences of European colonialism for the small nations of the world: "The superiority of the Western European spirit followed the criminal victories of individual imperialisms like a shadow, and this magnificent construction of Western European civilization was built on the bones of defeated and downtrodden nations, among which we were unfortunately a part ... The greatness of Byzantium and Constantinople, of Aachen and Venice, the Lateran, Vienna and Budapest was founded on our defeats and thus we belong in that category of civilizations that were unable to develop because foreign powers contested our right to moral and material survival."[51]

With the rising tide of national liberation movements across Asia and Africa, Europe's empires were on the verge of being swept away and, in the process, the ground was being prepared for a cultural renaissance among the small and marginalized nations of the world. This process would remap world space, dissolving imperial borders and rearranging their territories into new national and regional configurations. The shared vision was of a world community made up of a patchwork of national cultures. For the country's socialist intellectuals, Yugoslavia, which had withstood centuries of occupation by Europe's empires and the aggressions of fascism and Stalinism, had a critical role to play in this historical process.

IV

The second characteristic of Yugoslav one-worldism was an emphasis on the preservation of national and regional diversity that led to an effort to promote greater familiarity with the cultures of Asia, Africa, and Latin America. This concern was a corollary of the central place that the principle of national self-determination had come to occupy in Yugoslav ideology. It was not only the *political* independence of small or historically oppressed nations that had to be defended from colonial empires and Cold War superpowers; so too did their *cultural* independence. Such a principle challenged the global hierarchies that accorded the West the status of cultural vanguard, and instead rendered the planet into a mosaic of different national and regional cultures that each expressed a common human creativity. In this view, the contours of world space appeared at once radically heterogeneous and tightly integrated. At the same time, Yugoslav efforts to rebalance the asymmetries of cultural prestige led them to foreground the contributions of Asia, Africa, and Latin America in ways that shaped a tentative geography of non-alignment.

A key goal of Yugoslav cultural internationalism during the early 1950s was to familiarize the public with this mosaic of national cultures. In his interventions during this period, Ristić was adamant that Yugoslav cultural workers needed to more actively promote the "mutual awareness, engagement, and interpretation of the cultures of individual peoples and countries of all the continents, all the parts of our planet."[52] From the first half of the 1950s, prominent cultural journals like *Književne novine* or *Republika* regularly carried reports about cultural movements from around the world, with a particular emphasis on those of Asia and Africa. These included, for instance, articles on Japanese woodcuts and kabuki theatre, reviews of the Guinean dance troupe of Keita Fodeba, reports on modern Burmese literature, photographic series on craftwork in the Gold Coast or classical Indian sculpture, discussions of contemporary Arabic art movements, and interviews with theatre directors from India, Indonesia, and China.[53] Meanwhile, prominent academic or cultural figures such as the theorist and student of Indian literature Svetozar Petrović, or the documentary filmmaker Stevan Labudović, set out to promote greater understanding of the contemporary cultures and anticolonial struggles of the Third World.[54]

As in the interwar period and the early postwar years, a key task of this cultural internationalism was translation. In the earliest years of reforms, China was the main object of these efforts, no doubt as the now-communist country was initially seen to offer a possible counterweight to the Soviet Union. Yugoslavs were active in translating writings from or about China's revolution, including speeches from Mao, reports on cultural policies, and works by writers such as Lu Xun and Lao She.[55] As the decade progressed, however, the geographic horizons of Yugoslav publishers and translators expanded rapidly. From 1954, editions of Francophone and Anglophone poetry from Africa and the Caribbean began to appear, including Amos Tutuola's *The Palm Wine Drunkard* (1954), two anthologies of contemporary poetry, and an abridged edition of the German ethnologist Leo Frobenius's collection of African fables.[56] Manuscripts

One-Worldism and the Geographies of Non-Alignment   173

and anthologies of contemporary fiction from India, Japan, and Turkey, among others, were published, while regular translations of contemporary poetry, folklore, and spiritual texts from Central America, West Africa, Ethiopia, India, and the Middle East appeared in leading cultural journals.[57]

Importantly, these translations eschewed explicitly ideological motivations. This stood in contrast to the interwar social literature movement or the Stalinist cultural politics of the immediate postwar years, which carefully curated translations based on their ideological appropriateness. To be sure, some explicitly political writings from anticolonial leaders, such as Nehru's *The Discovery of India* (1952 in Serbo-Croatian, 1956 in Slovene) and Nasser's *Philosophy of Revolution* (1956), also found their way to the Yugoslav public.[58] But most of the translations produced for Yugoslav audiences were designed not to communicate a specifically socialist ideology or geopolitical alliance, but rather a vision of and respect for global cultural diversity. These efforts to familiarize Yugoslav readers with the cultures of Asia, Africa, and Latin America were central to the cultural internationalism of the early reform years.

Travelogues also served as an important avenue for promoting this one-world paradigm. From the mid-1950s onwards, Yugoslavs witnessed the publication of a steady stream of travel writing from diplomats or journalists who had visited the Third World. Beginning in 1954 with Aleš Bebler's *Putovanje po sunčanim zemljama* (*Journey through the Sunny Lands*) and Radoljub Čolaković's *Utisci iz Indije* (*Impressions from India*), the Third World travelogue introduced readers to the history and cultures of the non-European world while reflecting on the contemporary political moment of decolonization.[59] These texts often differed in their generic styles. While Bebler and Čolaković's works were memoirs of their diplomatic tours, works by journalists such as Živko Milić's *Koraci po vatri* (*Steps across Fire*), Mahmud Konjhodžić's *Video sam Egipat* (*I Saw Egypt*), Fadil Hadžić's *Budha me lijepo primio* (*The Buddha Received Me Well*), and Josip Kirigin's *Palma Misira* (*The Palms of Misr*) and *Tišine pod Himalajama* (*Silence beneath the Himalayas*), were more engaging travel writing, often combining elements of cultural tourism and even light adventure plots with an orientalist gaze.[60] As Yugoslav intellectuals became more familiar with the Third World, travelogues began to offer richer and more nuanced depictions of these cultures. Texts like Zuko Džumhur's *Pisma iz Azije* (*Letters from Asia*) and *Pisma iz Afrike i Evrope* (*Letters from Africa and Europe*), and Čedomir Minderović's modernist *Tragovi Indije* (*Traces of India*), blended more introspective accounts of their authors' journeys in Asia and Africa with political or philosophical reflections on the moment of decolonization.[61]

Politically, these travelogues often demonstrated a profound ambiguity regarding Yugoslavia's relation to the non-European world. On the one hand, some operated within an orientalist framework that fetishized the distance separating the Yugoslav author from the Third World. On the other hand, even the most frivolous and titillating of these texts still exuded a deep sense of solidarity with the cause of anticolonialism and national independence.[62] An excellent example of this ambiguity was an article penned by Kirigin, who accompanied Tito's delegation to Ethiopia in 1956. Although the text was preoccupied with almost ethnographic descriptions of traditional dances and village life, and at times evoked a primitivist fascination with the "life" and "energy" of African culture, Kirigin also reflected on his sense of shame as a European: "Among everyone here I feel that I am a son of the European continent. In the depths something is hard and upsetting, a kind of rock pressing into the back. And something icy flows through the heart. But nevertheless that is not me. I'm not, nor could I be, because these Europeans who came here ... And all at once, in a dance which became noisier and noisier, the energy, which had been worn out a little earlier, was renewed and I felt that I, a white man (*bijelac*), was not like those that came carrying the same whiteness (*bijelinu*), with smiles on their faces but something else in their hearts. I do not have any ties with them."[63]

Kirigin's article evidenced the complex political terrain that Yugoslavs negotiated in their approaches to the Third World (and to Africa especially). As we've seen, during their geopolitical reorientation Yugoslav socialists drew parallels between their struggles for national liberation and contemporary anticolonial struggles. Likewise, figures like Krleža had long criticized those Western European discourses that marked the peoples of South East Europe as barbaric, wild, or primitive in ways that echoed the racializing discourses of colonial powers in Asia and Africa.[64] At the same time, however, in those parts of the world where colonial discourses had congealed around racialized notions of "whiteness" and "blackness," as in Africa, Yugoslavs understood that they risked falling on the wrong side of this racial binary. This anxiety was clearly at the forefront of Kirigin's mind when he announced to his Ethiopian hosts: "I am white, but I'm not a 'white man'" (*bijeli sam, ali nisam bijelac*). If his reports are to be believed, the Ethiopians he met did not seem as wedded to this racial binary as Kirigin assumed. They were perfectly able to distinguish Yugoslavia from the colonial powers of Europe. Indeed, the diplomatic visit to which Kirigin was attached was part of a brief but important alliance between Ethiopia and Yugoslavia that sought to pressure Italy for reparations for war crimes committed against the two states during World War II.[65] In effect, then, both countries could draw equivalences between their experiences of occupation and domination by Western Europe in ways that undercut a simple association of whiteness with a colonizing Europe and blackness with a colonized Africa.[66]

Kirigin's uneasiness is also evident in the style of his writing. Although his reportage evoked the kind of orientalist or primitivist tropes associated with the European colonial gaze, Kirigin was emphatic in his support of the anticolonial cause. This ambiguity, which appeared throughout many of the Third World travelogues of this period, is best understood as an expression of the shifting cultural coordinates that the socialist revolution had brought about within Yugoslav literature. As journalists and popular writers sought to interpret the new theme of decolonization and familiarize readers with the peoples of the Third World, they often fell back on familiar tropes passed on through Western colonial travelogues.[67]

While many of these attempts to open Yugoslav audiences to a more inclusive world culture during the 1950s relegated non-European cultures to a precolonial, premodern past, it would be too simplistic to reduce this to an expression of Yugoslav orientalism. Figures like Ristić were careful to emphasize that the promotion of cultural diversity was not to be confused with the fetishizing of alterity; rather, the goal was to promote the free and autonomous pursuit of each culture's unique development.[68] In making this argument, Ristić was echoing a new set of antiracist critiques then being promoted within UNESCO, which was prompted in part by the growing prominence of French anthropologists such as Claude Lévi-Strauss, Roger Callois, and Michel Leiris within the organization.[69] The priority Yugoslav socialists assigned to the premodern civilizations of Asia, Africa, and the Americas needs to be understood as an effort to identify cultural models that predated European colonialism.[70] The transmission of these models was essential to sustain the cultural diversity upon which the paradigm of one-worldism rested.

V

The interest in the premodern world was also motivated by the third characteristic of the Yugoslav paradigm of cultural one-worldism, namely a shift away from the temporal regime of historical materialism towards the deep time of a longue durée humanity. This paralleled a global trend in the early years of the Cold War, which, as Stefanos Geroulanos has argued, was a moment in which epic narratives of humanity "described human history, globality, and futurity in terms both isomorphic to and influential on the international imagination around the 'end' of empire."[71] These narratives entailed simultaneously expanding the spatial scales and deepening the temporal horizons within which humanity was plotted. This idea was most clearly evidenced in the intellectual activity that took place within UNESCO.[72] Inspired by the one-world utopianism of the postwar moment, intellectuals affiliated with the institution sought to reconstruct a universalizing humanism that extended the timescale of human history.[73] As Yugoslavia became more engaged with UNESCO's work from 1950 onwards, intellectuals and cultural workers in the small socialist country began to deepen their own historical horizons too.[74]

This temporality of a longue durée humanity was perhaps the most significant shift in Yugoslav socialists' cultural attitudes during the 1950s. It represented a break with the historical materialism that was so central to writers of interwar proletarian literature, new realism, and postwar socialist realism. Not only did these realisms place greater emphasis on the modern era of capitalism as the penultimate stage of history, but their focus on themes of class struggle tended to fragment any vision of a common humanity. As discussed in chapter 4, for instance, a theorist like Radovan Zogović could trace the origins of Serbian epic poetry as far back as the Ottoman occupation of the late fourteenth century, but his focus on the changing socioeconomic relations of Balkan society meant that this poetry was not conceived as the heritage of a common humanity. Rather, its historical meaning shifted as it found itself in the new class coordinates of Ottoman feudalism and, later, agrarian capitalism, eventually losing its relevance in the modern era.

One-Worldism and the Geographies of Non-Alignment   177

This historical materialist framework was markedly different from the deep temporal horizons that characterized the cultural one-worldism of the 1950s. For intellectuals of this later movement, history was conceived as the collected and preserved experiences of humanity. In tracing the contours of a world culture, for instance, Ristić insisted on the need for an expansive account of human civilization that reached back before the birth of modern national cultures: "That which is called *national art and literature* is only one part of the foundations of this huge building of general human culture, this building whose dimensions and whose architectonic harmony, complete and harmonious in its diversity, are already beginning to be perceived with particular clarity, delineated against the deep, temporal background of our becoming as a human species."[75]

In Eastern Europe, where literary cultures had emerged through the transmission of what Pascale Casanova termed the "Herder effect," literature was closely tied to the project of nation building.[76] Although the Versailles Treaty, with its reorganization of the region into independent nation states, seemed to promise the liberation of literature from its historic role, this hope proved to be misplaced. The example of a writer like Miloš Crnjanski, as discussed in chapter 3, demonstrates just how closely literature continued to be bound up with the nation in a region where sovereignty seemed to be under constant threat.[77] Here, however, Ristić was relativizing the place of the nation, and asking his audience to consider each national culture as a recent event in the timeline of human evolution. Such a decentering of the nation from the timelines of human history sat well with Ristić's surrealist, cosmopolitan instincts as well as the utopian impulse of postwar one-worldism. At the same time, we should be careful not to read this argument as a dismissal of the nation in total. Such a move would have been inconceivable in Tito's Yugoslavia, where a key plank of the government's legitimacy lay in its defence of the country's distinct national cultures. Ristić's point, rather, was that these national cultures had to be situated within an expanded history of human creativity.

The expression of this new temporal regime can be registered in three shifts in Yugoslav cultural practice during this period. The first was a growing interest in the preservation and study of premodern cultural heritage. Prior to the reform years, the historical horizons of Yugoslav socialists were relatively shallow, with the greatest emphasis placed on recent events such as the antifascist struggle of World

War II, or the national liberation movements of the nineteenth century. During the 1950s, however, these horizons deepened, and there emerged a growing concern with recovering and reappraising earlier cultural moments such as the Dalmatian Renaissance, the enigmatic culture of the Medieval Bogumils, or the Neolithic Vinča civilization.[78] In no small part, this shift was shaped by heritage practices within UNESCO.[79] It is significant, for instance, that the first collaboration between Yugoslavia and UNESCO was an exhibition of Medieval frescoes that toured Western Europe during 1953–54.[80] As an effort to represent Yugoslavia and its revolutionary vision to the West, this exhibition did little to capture the ideological themes of self-management socialism; its value, rather, lay in its portrayal of the Yugoslav socialist state as a caretaker of a fragment of humanity's common heritage. Heritage, that is, served as the first framework through which Yugoslavia's culture began to be actively promoted through UNESCO's networks.

This renewed attention to cultural heritage was not limited to the borders of Yugoslavia but also underpinned the emphasis that socialist intellectuals placed on premodern cultures when writing about the Third World. Indeed, as Ljiljana Kolešnik has noted, heritage served Yugoslav cultural officials as a valuable means to frame their cultural exchange with postcolonial states.[81] In his 1954 travelogue, for instance, the Slovene diplomat Aleš Bebler frequently celebrated the monumental glory of the precolonial civilizations of Central America, the Middle East, and South Asia.[82] He was also impressed by what he saw as the surviving traces of these civilizations in the modern world, noting that "[a]ll of these lands are sprinkled with old temples and pyramids ... old sculptures and frescoes, in these lands the people know the names of former great leaders and the sayings of great sages."[83] Preservation of these precolonial traces was essential to provide the foundations for the autonomous development of national cultures in the era of decolonization and independence. They also evoked the long durée of human creativity that figures like Ristić promoted in their vision of cultural one-worldism.

A similar interest in the ancient civilizations of Asia, Africa, and the Americas motivated the translation of texts designed to familiarize Yugoslav readers with the philosophical and spiritual wealth of these premodern cultures. *Književne novine* regularly published classical works of poetry or philosophy, including fragments from the Bhagavad Gita, Ancient Egyptian love poems, accounts of the

One-Worldism and the Geographies of Non-Alignment   179

creation of man from Sumerian and Aztec mythology, Yang Zhu's writings on death, and Polynesian tales on obtaining immortality.[84] Similarly, the journal of the Croatian Union of Writers, *Republika*, carried translations and expositions of classical Indian texts by the Buddhist scholar Čedomil Veljačić.[85] Introductions to these fragments often emphasized the "eternal human feelings" the texts expressed, weaving these specific cultural artifacts into a deep historical vision of a single, universal humanity.[86] The importance of heritage is also evidenced in the growing interest in archeology and prehistory which began to receive greater attention in Yugoslav publications from this period.[87]

The second expression of this deepened sense of historical time was a reappraisal of aesthetic primitivism and its interwar legacy within Yugoslavia. This legacy and its revival in the socialist modernism of the 1950s provided a framework through which a handful of Yugoslav intellectuals began to uproot the teleological structure of historical materialism and complicate earlier Marxist understandings of cultural progress and social evolution. The effect of these interventions was to create a new appreciation for the ideas, techniques, and artifacts of premodern cultures, and incorporate these within an eclectic modernist canon.

A fascination with "the primitive" animated several avant-garde movements in interwar Yugoslavia.[88] Although many of these movements mimicked the exoticization of African and South Pacific cultures that took place elsewhere in Europe, others pursued a very different aesthetic primitivism rooted in local folk cultures. This intellectual movement was associated with the peasant art of the Croatian Zemlja (Earth) collective and the Hlebine School, both leftist institutions that sought to cultivate an artistic language rooted in peasant traditions. Intellectuals affiliated with this movement foregrounded the "naïve" and "primitive" style of these artists, which, proponents believed, bypassed the Western European influences that dominated the bourgeois cities.[89]

Although the peasant art movement was discouraged in the immediate postwar years by advocates of socialist realism, the cultural reforms of the early 1950s reignited this interwar modernist legacy.[90] The watershed moment for its reappraisal seems to have come in 1953, when the former Hlebine School painter, Ivan Generalić, held an exhibition of his works in Paris. The exhibition not only served to distance Yugoslavia's exciting new cultural openness from what Western audiences understood as the stale propaganda of Soviet culture, but also displayed a unique and contemporary artistic language. Following this triumph on the world stage, Ristić's Commission for Foreign Cultural Relations even set up a council to promote Yugoslav primitivism internationally.[91] In the years that followed, primitive artists such as Mirko Virius, Petar Smajić, Eugen Buktenica, Franjo Mraz, and Emerik Feješ received growing attention in the Yugoslav press.[92] Unlike in Western Europe, where it was bound up with a colonial, orientalizing gaze, the discourse of primitivism in Yugoslavia also had roots in an effort by left-wing intellectuals to infuse modernist aesthetic sensibilities with local folk traditions. Primitivism, therefore, was as much a regionally introspective discourse as it was one of colonial othering.

To the extent that it shaped the emerging paradigm of one-worldism of the period, the reappraisal of primitivist aesthetics was significant for the respect it accorded cultural forms that Marxist theorists had previously considered eclipsed by history. This included the folklore of Balkan peasants as much as it did traditional sculptures of West Africa or ritual masks of Polynesia. While much of the Yugoslav writing on the supposedly "primitive" cultures of Africa and Asia continued to exude the same exoticism and paternalism that characterized an earlier Western European primitivism, these examples were part of an effort to craft a more inclusive, non-Eurocentric understanding of world culture.[93] Primitivism, in other words, complimented and reinforced the idea of a longue durée humanity and reinscribed prehistoric, premodern, or folkloric artifacts within a modernist aesthetic field.

The fluidity of aesthetic forms that the reappraisal of primitivism allowed helped to facilitate the third characteristic of the deepened temporal regime of Yugoslav culture in the 1950s, namely a flattening of historical time. This entailed a suspension of historical periodization and episodic sequencing in ways that blurred the delineations between past and present. It allowed one to conceive the accretions of humanity's extensive cultural history as dispersed across a flat plane, at once comprehensible and attainable to the contemporary observer. Somewhat paradoxically, deepening the horizons of human time did not imply extending the temporal distance and exacerbating the differences between historical cultures but, rather, recasting them as a vast reservoir of cultural forms. This was a further, in some ways more radical, departure from historical

One-Worldism and the Geographies of Non-Alignment 181

materialism, whose proponents understood the past through a system of clearly delineated stages defined by their most salient social conflicts. Within this system, the differentiation of historical stages meant that, while cultural forms might survive across epochs, their social content would necessarily change. French revolutionaries, to take Marx's often cited example, might well have understood themselves through the language and symbolism of the Roman Republic, but the social relations their revolution engendered were historically unprecedented. As such, their efforts "to present this new scene in world history in time-honored disguise and borrowed language" meant that they anachronistically misunderstood the novel historical meaning of their revolution.[94] It was precisely these stages of history that were ironed out in the deep temporal horizons many Yugoslav intellectuals came to inhabit in the 1950s.

Central among these intellectuals was Ristić. For the former surrealist, the significance of this flattened history was not simply that it allowed for the practice of a certain modernist eclecticism, but rather that it helped give expression to a universal human experience that transcended historical periods and geographic borders. In a polemical article from 1955, in which he set out to defend the legacy of European modernism then coming under renewed attack from Serbian realists, Ristić evoked precisely this vision of a flat and deep time.[95] Key to his argument was a rejection of realism's claim to be the most historically progressive and modern artistic method. In response, the surrealist set out to defend the modernity of (supposedly) historically eclipsed, premodern or, indeed, "primitive" aesthetic forms:

> That which in us is alterable, that which can be changed, can never be integrally new, and in the extraordinary works of the past or the distant past, contemporary man recognizes himself, his restlessness, his enrichment, his traumas, his pulse. Because even that which in us is alterable, that which can be changed has its roots in the core of being, not on the surface, and thus can find and therefore searches for its analogies in the pronounced anxieties and enthusiasms of human beings in conditions fundamentally different from those of contemporary people. The paths along which our associations pass and intersect are tangled, twisted, and darkened. Is it strange, for instance, that the associations of a man who, perhaps having

read the contemporary French poet Saint John Perse, should
recognize *himself* in some sentences of the sacred texts of the
Book of the Dead, texts that contain an esoteric doctrine from
Egypt and which were written down on papyrus some four
thousand years before Christ? And in this way, these texts
appear and are enjoyed as *absolutely modern.*[96]

The modernity of a text, Ristić suggested, had little to do with the date
of its composition, but was rather determined by its capacity to speak
to or to be spiritually relevant for modern man. He went on to list a
canon of similarly "modern" artifacts, which included the monumental architecture of the pre-Colombian Americas, the Ajanta frescoes,
masks from New Guinea, idols from Hawaii, sculpture from Camer-
oon, classical Chinese sculpture, French church architecture, Sumerian and Mesopotamian idols, and "the visions of Hieronymus Bosch
and the Caprichos of Goya," to list only a few![97] This canon flaunted
its temporal promiscuity in the face of Ristić's realist interlocutors.
Overthrowing a Eurocentric canon of world literature that privileged
the nineteenth-century realist novel as its apogee, he instead sought
to outline an understanding of culture that drew from the diverse creativity of a common humanity.[98] In the process, Ristić rejected the
interpretation of history as a sequence of progressively unfolding
stages. This, in turn, made possible a radical fluidity of aesthetic ideas
and symbols over cultural space and historical time, allowing for the
appropriation and cross-fertilization of modern, prehistoric, folkloric,
or tribal motifs from around the world.[99]

This flattening of time had a pervasive effect in Yugoslav culture
during the mid-1950s and is especially clear in the graphic design
of flagship cultural journals that prioritized an engagement with
Asia, Africa, and Latin America. When the editors of *Republika*, for
instance, published a translation of Li Gongzuo's "The Governor
of Nanke," they chose to illustrate the work with sketches by the
contemporary Serbian-Jewish artist Zlatko Bourek.[100] The pairing
of this ninth century Chinese short story with Bourek's grotesque
and naïve style of modernism served not to juxtapose but, rather,
synchronize late antiquity China and contemporary Yugoslavia. A
similar, though more dramatic example appeared on the front page
of the February 1955 issue of *Književne novine*, which ran with an
image of a mushroom cloud and the banner headline: "From the
Nucleus of the Atom a Classless Society Will Be Born." The article

Figure 6.2 | *Književne novine*, 15 February 1955. The heading that surrounds the image of the mushroom cloud reads: "From the Nucleus of the Atom … a Classless Society Will Be Born." In the bottom right corner, a photo of the Sanchi Stupas is accompanied by the heading: "Tito-Nehru: Hope in the Progress of the World Demands Accepting Peaceful Coexistence."

celebrated the scientific achievements of humanity and the possibilities (but also dangers) that atomic power heralded. Immediately below, the paper ran with a notice of a meeting between Tito and Nehru: "Tito-Nehru: Hope in the Progress of the World Demands Accepting Peaceful Coexistence." The slogan appeared alongside an image of the Sanchi stupas, intricate examples of first century Buddhist architecture.[101] The placement of these headlines and their accompanying images suggested a non-linear world in which the most modern scientific discoveries and the spiritual heritage of ancient India existed alongside one another. It eschewed a developmental schema, in which religion was historically superseded by science or the ancient East was overtaken by the modern West. Instead, this aesthetic posited a contemporaneity between East and West, ancient and modern, each folded into the deeper history of a common humanity.

VI

The paradigm of cultural one-worldism that Yugoslav socialist intellectuals devised during the 1950s complemented the foreign policy of non-alignment. Both programs served to offset a major contradiction at the heart of Yugoslavia's geopolitical configuration: namely, its position as a socialist state, ideologically committed to the cause of anticolonial liberation yet dependent on its links with the capitalist West. They were able to temporarily resolve this contradiction because they explicitly eschewed efforts to map the world ideologically. This solution came under increasing strain in the 1960s, however, as a younger generation of socialists, radicalized by affiliation with revolutionary struggles in Asia, Africa, and Latin America, began to challenge the Yugoslav leadership's quietude in an era of growing political upheaval. Over the course of the 1960s, confrontations between national liberation movements and Western militaries in Congo, Algeria, and Vietnam undermined the one-world utopias of the 1950s. As Britain, France, and the US demonstrated increasing disregard for the liberal internationalist norms that supposedly underpinned the postwar order, young socialists in Yugoslavia began to question what they saw as their country's Western tilt in the Cold War. Their demands for Yugoslav leaders to demonstrate a more fervent anti-imperialism began to create a generational divide within Yugoslav socialism between an Old Left, largely committed to non-alignment, and a New Left that demanded a more proactive support for Third World liberation. The polarization of geopolitics at a global scale, that is, fed back into Yugoslavia, inspiring more radical visions of the country's socialist revolution.

Over the 1960s, Yugoslavia's engagement with the Third World deepened as the policy of non-alignment fostered greater contact and exchange with countries in Asia, Africa, and Latin America.[102] These new ties were most clearly visible in the growing number of international students who came to study at Yugoslav universities.[103] These students quickly formed their own organizations and began to collaborate with the Yugoslav Union of Students to promote greater engagement with global politics and familiarity with the societies of the Third World.[104] This fraternization shaped the political consciousness of a younger generation of Yugoslav socialists that came of age over the decade, and whose political imagination was captured by liberation struggles in places such as Congo, Algeria, Palestine, and Vietnam. While these young socialists reaffirmed the politics of anti-imperialism and national self-determination that characterized Yugoslavia's non-aligned foreign policy, they also began to demand that the country's leadership pursue a more uncompromising policy of solidarity with the Third World.

These generational tensions snapped in the second half of the 1960s over the issue of the Vietnam War. The US's growing involvement in Vietnam highlighted the contradiction in Yugoslavia's geopolitical configuration, forcing the leadership to walk a fine line between maintaining friendly relations with the West and living up to its commitment to Third World solidarity. This position came under increasing strain domestically with the formation of the anti-war movement in 1965. Although the movement was organized through the officially sanctioned channels of the Union of Students, from the outset the Union's cadre struggled to contain more militant initiatives. Following large antiwar protests in 1965 and 1966, students in Zagreb and Belgrade attacked the US consulate and embassy. In each instance these protests ended in confrontations with the police, exacerbating a growing sense among students that the socialist government was not as committed to its policy of anti-imperialism as it wanted the world to believe. During the Belgrade protests of December 1966, students went so far as to call the police "Johnsonites" (*Džonsonovci*), a not-so-subtle suggestion that they had taken the side of US imperialism.[105]

Yugoslav participation in international student organizations also exacerbated the growing generational division as representatives from the Soviet Union, China, and North Korea criticized Yugoslavia for its refusal to condemn the US and its allies over Vietnam. These dynamics were presented in stark geographic terms when Yugoslav representatives traveled to Ulan Bator to attend the Ninth Congress of the International Union of Students in 1967. As one of the delegates later reported: "In the hall of the parliament in which the congress was held, there was a great map of the world with the title: 'The Peoples and Governments that Help the Liberation Struggle of Vietnam.' Little red circles marked, it seemed to us, all of the countries of the world except our own."[106] Far from the vision of Yugoslavia as a supporter of the Third World, this exhibit scrubbed the country from the map of world revolution. While clearly intended by pro-Soviet and pro-Chinese organizers to tarnish Yugoslavia's standing in the socialist world, the map was nonetheless an uncomfortable reminder of the contradiction at the heart of Yugoslav foreign policy, its cozy relation to the West undermining its rhetorical commitment to Third World liberation.

Pressures at the international scale quickly fed back into the national. Although the conflict between leftist students and Yugoslav officialdom also had its roots in domestic problems such as youth unemployment and student poverty, frustration with the country's foreign policy was an important factor. In 1967 the far-left activist, Vesna Gudelj-Velaga, was elected to the presidency of the Zagreb University Union of Students. Gudelj-Velaga had been active in the antiwar movement and had witnessed the police crackdown on student protesters in front of the US consulate in December 1966. In her campaign, she criticized the Union of Students' "inadequate" engagement with foreign affairs, which she noted had been criticized "even by students in capitalist countries," and insisted that the organization's international solidarity needed to move beyond mere declarations.[107] This growing spirit of criticism was also evidenced at the Eighth Congress of the Union of Students in 1968, during which delegates called on the union to adopt a more independent position from the government, citing its stance on Vietnam as a key reason.[108] As a new generation of socialists in Yugoslavia were radicalized by the geopolitical antagonisms of the 1960s, they became increasingly critical of their own regime. The programs of non-alignment and cultural one-worldism seemed far too timid, too conciliatory, in this more polarized era.

The conflicts over Third World solidarity that sharpened during the course of the 1960s exploded into open rebellion in June 1968, when students across Yugoslavia occupied university buildings in protest at police brutality, political repression, poor living conditions, and unemployment.[109] These protests were an effort to revive Yugoslav socialism, drawing from contemporary Marxist humanist and other New Left intellectual currents. Students raised slogans condemning the "red bourgeoisie" and proclaiming their solidarity with the working class. They put up posters of Marx, Lenin, Tito, and Che Guevara. In their occupied buildings, they organized lectures and study circles on contemporary Marxist theory, hosted public debates, and presented theatrical performances and poetry readings. The carnivalesque atmosphere clearly resembled similar New Left protest movements elsewhere at the time, and Yugoslav students were very aware of the events in Paris the previous month.[110] They were, in other words, part of the global wave of protests of 1968 that spanned the three worlds of the Cold War. And like many of these student-led movements of 1968, the June protests in Yugoslavia had their origins in the movement against the Vietnam War.[111]

The tumultuous events of 1968 in Yugoslavia were a result of the spatial reconfigurations the country underwent following its break with the Soviet Union twenty years earlier. Specifically, its integration into the Western-led liberal international order and its efforts to affiliate with the Third World through the Non-Aligned Movement came under increased pressure. While the contradiction between these two projects could be papered over in the 1950s through the paradigm of one-worldism, the sharpening antagonism between the West and anticolonial movements in the Third World over the 1960s made such compromise unviable. In effect, the students of the Yugoslav New Left demanded a return to the more explicit anti-imperialism that had, in the first three decades of the century, been plotted in the geography of the Balkans and was now in the 1960s being replotted in the more amorphous space of the Third World. While the repression of the student movement of 1968 eliminated the immediate threat of a revolutionary challenge to the regime, it also portended the narrowing of Yugoslav socialism's global horizons and its disavowal of Third World alliances in the decades to come.

7

The Cultural Spaces of Late Socialism
European Integration, Yugoslav Fragmentation,
1974–95

> Perhaps that is when tectonic landslides will occur. The Balkans will
> detach from the Alps and stick to the Mediterranean shores of Africa.
> It will tear us apart: it will finally – physically – tear us in half. Our
> corpses with our culture will be sunk to the bottom of the ocean.
>
> Taras Kermauner, *Letters to a Serbian Friend*, 1988

I

In the early months of 1992, Europe witnessed two events that signaled the diverging trends of the post–Cold War era. On 7 February, representatives from the twelve members of the European Communities met in the Dutch town of Maastricht to sign the Treaty on European Union. The treaty marked an acceleration and deepening of the process of European integration and was met with celebrations that resonated with the liberal triumphalism of the 1990s. Two months later, on the other side of the continent, Bosnian Serb leaders declared their secession from the newly independent state of Bosnia and Herzegovina, inaugurating the bloodiest phase in the breakup of the Socialist Federative Republic of Yugoslavia. European integration and Yugoslav fragmentation: at first glance the synchronicity of these events seems accidental, the first, promising the birth of a future of European unity, free market dynamism, and cultural cosmopolitanism; the second, a regression to the authoritarian nationalism, ethnic cleansing, and territorial fragmentation that recalled the darkest moments of the twentieth century. But what if these two events were more entangled than we have previously thought? What if the conjunction of European integration and Yugoslav disintegration were, in fact, deeply intertwined?

This chapter offers an account of the fragmentation of Yugoslavia as it was registered in the work of socialist intellectuals of the late 1980s and early 1990s. Situating the country's collapse in the history of the global spatial reconfigurations that began in the 1970s with the breakdown of the Bretton Woods order, it argues that global economic and geopolitical processes produced new and competing cultural geographies that undermined the coherence of Yugoslavia and its wider Third World ties. Specifically, the notion of "Central Europe" – which flourished in dissident circles throughout Eastern Europe during the 1980s and came to capture the imagination of intellectuals in Yugoslavia – marked a profound ideological shift. The imagined geography of Central Europe offered Yugoslav socialists and anti-socialists alike a language of cultural belonging through which to level moral claims to participation in the creation of a European community. These intellectuals set out to negate the anti-colonial legacy of Yugoslav socialism, disengaging their small nations from the country's affiliations with the Third World and replotting their coordinates within a new mediating space of Europe. In the process, many came to reject a supranational Yugoslavia as well.

In pursuing this argument, the chapter makes three broad contributions. First, building on the political-economic accounts of revisionist historians of Yugoslavia, it tracks the ways in which cultural discourses processed the local effects of the transformations of global capitalism from the mid-1970s.[1] Specifically, it highlights the role of writers in mediating the spatial configurations that undergirded the new political subjectivities and cultural communities that emerged on the European periphery. Second, it offers a critical account of the conceptual history of Central Europe that emphasizes its harmonization with neoliberal narratives of European integration and its negation of earlier, emancipatory projects.[2] Situating the Central Europe idea within a longer history of mediating spaces in Yugoslavia, the chapter brings into relief the ways in which this cultural geography served to extricate the country from its ideological affiliations with the Third World. In this sense, it recounts an important moment in the decline of co-operation between the Second and Third worlds and the attempt to construct an alternative cultural imaginary centred on Europe.[3]

190 Mediating Spaces

Finally, while existing intellectual histories of the late socialist period have focused on the resurgence of nationalist movements in Yugoslavia, this chapter instead centres those leftist writers who resisted Yugoslavia's fragmentation, raised questions about the European promise, and continued to draw attention to the geographic asymmetries of power and prestige in late capitalist modernity.[4] Furthermore, whereas much scholarship from this period has prioritized the intellectual cultures of Slovenia and Serbia as two poles in the nationalist rivalries of the 1980s, the argument here is pursued through a reading of the work of two Croatian writers, the philosopher Predrag Matvejević (1932–2017), and the novelist Dubravka Ugrešić (1949–2023). In so doing, it highlights a neglected element of the intellectual landscape of Yugoslavia in its final years of existence.

II

The intertwined processes of European integration and Yugoslav fragmentation had their beginnings in the turbulent events that shook the global economic system over the 1970s. This decade was beset by a series of crises that brought the Bretton Woods system, which had ordered the global economy since the end of World War II, to an end. In 1973, the OPEC oil embargo and the Nixon government's suspension of gold-dollar convertibility sent shockwaves through the global economy. The collapse of Bretton Woods and the rapid rise of energy prices inaugurated a new era of economic insecurity.[5] Eager to shield their populations from the inflationary pressures of the OPEC shock, states borrowed heavily from financial markets, newly flush with the revenues of oil-producing nations. The effect was the rapid growth in both size and power of international financial institutions whose control of sovereign debt gave them enormous disciplinary power over states in the capitalist West, socialist East, and developing South.[6] The 1979 decision by the head of the US Federal Reserve, Paul Volcker, to dramatically raise interest rates on the dollar further deepened these disruptive processes. Overnight, governments found their dollar-denominated debts had risen to unsustainable levels, sparking a series of debt crises that further subjected states to the demands of financial institutions.[7] Over the course of the 1980s, the contours of a new global economic system began to cohere around policies of free trade, rapid capital mobility, and domestic economic discipline.[8]

On the Cultural Spaces of Late Socialism   191

This new era of capitalist globalization prompted the recalibration of state power in ways that would have profound consequences for the geographic organization of the system. A key factor in these transformations was what Fritz Bartel has insightfully termed "the politics of breaking promises." As national governments struggled to demonstrate their economic viability to international lenders, they were compelled to abandon the generous social spending programs that had formed the basis of the postwar social contract in both capitalist and socialist states. These pressures necessitated the introduction of radical social and economic reforms that in turn fostered new modes of thinking about the state and the economy premised on the valorization of austerity, self-discipline, and efficiency. Thatcherism in Britain, Reaganomics in the US, and perestroika in the Soviet Union were each programs of reform designed to extricate the state from its prior social commitments.[9] In the developing world, similar reforms were achieved through the structural adjustment programs that international financial institutions now insisted upon as a condition of debt relief in line with what would come to be known as "the Washington consensus." These reforms, which emphasized the deregulation of capital markets and the opening-up of national borders to global trade, facilitated new mobilities and concentrations of wealth and power.[10]

These decades of crisis and restructuring precipitated deep tectonic shifts in the spatial foundations of the global system and gave rise to new political, economic, and cultural geographies. In Yugoslavia, these transformations were most keenly felt at a supranational scale, in the reconfiguration of the mediating spaces that framed the socialist project. Beginning in the late 1970s, three spatial processes began to recast the ideological coordinates of Yugoslav socialism and bring about its final crisis. First, the global sovereign-debt crisis eroded the power of the Third World as a potential geopolitical force and thereby hollowed out the project of the Non-Aligned Movement. Second, the acceleration of the process of integration among the members of the European Economic Community (EEC) forced Yugoslavs to urgently redirect attention to a more geographically delimited European space. Finally, the effort to better calibrate the Yugoslav economy to the new global system exacerbated preexisting tendencies towards economic divergence and political dysfunction within the federation itself, ultimately compromising the project of supranational Yugoslavism. These processes were mutually

reinforcing: the collapse of the Third World accorded greater importance to affiliating with the project of European integration, which
in turn further fueled discord within Yugoslavia over the future
direction of the federation.

The global debt crisis of the 1980s decimated the developing
economies of Africa and Latin America and eroded the potential of
the Third World to effect a more egalitarian transformation of the
global system. Although the 1970s had seemed to promise a new
era of influence for the Third World, manifested most obviously in
the ambitious plans for a New International Economic Order, this
proved to be short-lived.[11] The sudden rise of US interest rates had
a devastating impact on the developing economies, which found
themselves saddled with unsustainable levels of debt.[12] By 1982,
this debt raised the specter of a Third World default and prompted
US officials to reorganize the global financial system to defend the
stability of international lenders. At the centre of this new system
stood the International Monetary Fund (IMF), which now began
to make access to international loans conditional upon liberal economic reforms.[13] During this decade, the widespread application of
structural adjustment programs across the Third World pried open
previously nationalized economies and regional blocs, dismantled
state-led development projects and social services, and led to a massive transfer of wealth from the Third to the First World.[14] IMF
conditionality increasingly became the mechanism for the politics
of breaking promises in developing economies.[15] The dissolution
of the Third World as a geopolitical force eroded the foundations
of the Non-Aligned Movement, that mediating space within which
Yugoslav socialists had sought to project their influence globally
since the 1950s.[16]

As dissident intellectuals and even disgruntled party officials began
to rethink Yugoslavia's relationship to the Third World, many began
to look to a new geography of affiliation: Europe. The dramatic transformations of the global economy over the 1970s accelerated the
push towards European integration. Although plans for the economic
consolidation of Western Europe had been a key pillar of the West's
Cold War strategy since the founding of the EEC in 1958, the crises
of the 1970s gave this project new urgency and salience.[17] When the
fallout from the events of 1973 hit European shores, national governments initially relied on the EEC to implement protectionist policies
that might shield their economies from the global turbulence. By the

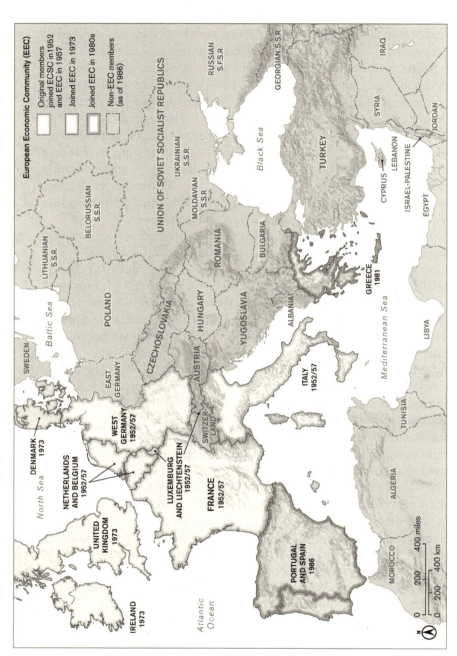

Figure 7.1 | European Economic Community, 1986.

end of the decade, however, the structures of the EEC had evolved to play quite a different role. As Keynesian policies failed to curb rising inflation and international financial markets began to impose fiscal discipline, governments in Western Europe increasingly relied on the framework of the EEC to implement policies designed to recalibrate their states' position in the global economy. The formation of a common exchange rate regime over the 1970s at once allowed Western European governments to delink themselves from an increasingly unstable dollar and push through domestically unpopular austerity reforms demanded by international lenders.[18] European integration, in this sense, was part of the wider politics of breaking promises that took place during these decades of global restructuring.[19]

The economic integration of Europe over the 1970s was accompanied by parallel processes of political and cultural affiliation that further enshrined a European geography in the mind of Yugoslav intellectuals. Détente was a key factor here, with Western European governments' overtures to their eastern neighbours prompting a renewal of interest in the historical and cultural unity of Europe. The formation of the Organization for Security and Co-operation in Europe (OSCE) in 1975 and the subsequent Helsinki Process, which established a series of international agreements that laid the basis for East-West cooperation, had a powerful role in fostering the idea of Europe as a more stable and harmonious site in the Cold War. Some Western observers even came to imagine a time when Europe might transcend its geopolitical divisions and become a unified "zone of human rights, free markets, and political moderation."[20] The horizons of a common European project expanded in the 1980s, when first Greece, and then Spain and Portugal joined the EEC. Indeed, the integration of these southern European states was the outcome of a strategy that the EEC had pursued throughout the 1970s to leverage its economic weight to promote political stabilization in the Mediterranean. Yugoslavia was included within the scope of this strategy, although the country's commitment to non-alignment foreclosed any possibility of formal membership. During the 1970s, the EEC signed a number of trade agreements with Belgrade that drew the country, and especially its northern republics of Croatia and Slovenia, closer into the economic orbit of a rapidly integrating Europe.[21] By the 1980s, the political and economic ambitions of Yugoslav leaders had been narrowed from the global horizons of the Non-Aligned Movement to the more delimited space of Europe.[22]

The process of European integration exacerbated a growing divergence within the economic and political geography of the Yugoslav federation in the late Cold War. The self-management reforms of the early 1950s had opened up a question regarding the appropriate balance of powers between the federal Yugoslav and national republican governments. The struggle over the structures of the self-management system was, in many ways, a struggle over the final settlement of this balance of powers. Proponents of centralization emphasized the need for greater macroeconomic coordination. If the state was to deal effectively with regional economic disparities in the country, it needed the power to tax wealthier republics in the north and redirect that wealth towards the south. Meanwhile, proponents of decentralization argued that their opponents undermined both the principles of workers' self-management and national autonomy, and risked returning to the authoritarian, bureaucratic structures of Stalinism. The 1966 downfall of Aleksandar Ranković, the figurehead of federal centralization, marked the victory of the decentralizers and inaugurated a period of constitutional reforms that lasted until 1974.[23] The constitution of this year, effectively composed by the Slovene theorist Edvard Kardelj, radically decentralized the country's key political and economic institutions, and inadvertently took the first step towards the dissolution of the Yugoslav federation.[24]

The reforms of 1966–74 delinked the economies of the federation and undermined the creation of an integrated Yugoslav economic space.[25] This tendency towards economic divergence was entrenched by the transformations of the global economy during the 1970s. As rising oil revenues boosted the purchase power of the Soviet Union, Middle East, and parts of Africa, the primary commodity-producing economies of Yugoslavia's south sought closer economic ties with those parts of the world.[26] On the other hand, as the EEC implemented protectionist measures in response to economic turbulence, Slovene and Croatian leaders and businesses, worried about being cut off from crucial Western markets, sought tighter alignment with Europe. The chaotic reconfigurations of global capitalist space following the collapse of the Bretton Woods system, then, had a centrifugal effect on Yugoslavia, exacerbating the unevenness of the federation's economic geography and furthering the tendency towards dissolution.[27]

The sovereign debt crisis of the 1980s amplified these centrifugal tendencies and placed greater strain on the Yugoslav political and economic system.[28] The US interest rate hike hit Yugoslavia hard. The effort of the West to court Yugoslavia and ensure its independence from the Eastern bloc had led to a massive influx of international capital into the federation over the 1970s. In 1981 the country owed just under $20 billion in foreign debt, and a year later stood to default. Yugoslavia became one of the first countries in the world to sign up to the IMF's structural adjustment programs. In line with these programs, over the next decade reformers in the federal government sought to radically overhaul the Yugoslav economy by reintegrating markets, restricting foreign borrowing, promoting export sectors, and introducing austerity measures.[29] When the impact of structural adjustment began to undermine the social cohesion of the country, republican governments channeled citizens' discontent into rival nationalist campaigns in opposition to the federal government, eventually precipitating the violent dissolution of the federation in the 1990s.[30]

By the end of the 1980s, the geographical divergence of the Yugoslav federation had given rise to two rival strategies of neoliberal reform.[31] The first of these programs, articulated most vocally by Slovene intellectuals and leaders, called for the further decentralization of Yugoslavia and its transformation into a loose confederation of affiliated states. In line with laissez faire economic principles, proponents of this program argued for the need for lean states and low taxation to foster greater efficiency and innovation. The goal of this program was to streamline Slovenia's economy by freeing it from the federal tax burdens that were used to develop the southern economies. With their eyes set on future membership in the EEC, Slovene leaders increasingly came to perceive federal taxes as a drag on their country's economic dynamism. By the end of the decade, then, Slovene leaders had come to advocate the bare minimum of confederal ties, suggesting that they be limited to only those structures (such as a single currency) that would be required for eventual EEC membership.[32]

The second program of neoliberal reform called for a recentralization and marketization of the Yugoslav economy in line with the IMF's proposals. This program was pursued by the faction of the Serbian socialists led by Slobodan Milošević, whose immediate priority was the constitutional reconsolidation of the Serbian state. To further this effort, he appealed to a Serbian nationalist counterculture and framed his project of recentralization as an effort to address the supposed historical injustice perpetrated against Serbs by the 1974 constitution, which had accorded vast autonomous powers to the provinces of Vojvodina and Kosovo. This openly nationalist appeal worried leaders in neighbouring republics, who suspected Milošević of aspiring to transform Yugoslavia into a greater Serbian state. The role that his leadership played in fostering a reactionary and intolerant Serbian nationalism, however, has distracted historians from the striking degree to which his vision of Yugoslav recentralization was conceived within the spatial framework of European integration. In an interview from 1988, for instance, Milošević argued that the future of Yugoslavia lay in pursuing closer ties with the future EU, noting that "[n]o reasonable person would allow himself to be cast out of the orbit of this powerful economic grouping."[33] At the same time, however, he insisted that inclusion within this economically integrated Europe demanded that "we must first be integrated ourselves."[34] Membership in a future EU required a reunification of the Yugoslav market along free trade lines, abolishing restrictions to labour and capital mobility throughout the federation.

By the end of the 1980s, therefore, Yugoslavia was bifurcated by two rival neoliberal projects that sought to pursue integration into Europe through appeals to nationalism and free markets: on the one hand, a Slovene model called for further decentralization and national autonomy with an eye to the eventual confederalization or even outright dissolution of Yugoslavia; on the other, a Serbian model that sought recentralization and the reconsolidation of a unified Yugoslav market. Both were efforts to come to terms with the impact of the global reconfigurations of the 1970s and to recalibrate the state to a new, more austere, more competitive global environment. This rivalry ultimately eroded the legitimacy of Yugoslavia as a mediating space for its constituent nations, allowing rival visions of political affiliation to take root. As the crisis of the 1980s placed greater strain on the federation, elites and large sections of the public fell back into respective nationalisms. These nationalisms, however, were articulated within the geographic framework and teleological horizons of a European project. In this way, the events of 1992, the synchronicity of which is so jarring to our contemporary sensibilities, were in fact twin consequences of the spatial disruptions of late-twentieth-century capitalism.

III

The new mode of globalization that emerged from the crises of the 1970s disrupted the supranational configurations within which Yugoslavia had been plotted since the 1950s, eroding the salience of the Third World and raising the stakes of the country's belonging to a wider European space. This shift can be registered in the cultural polemics over the concept of Central Europe that broke out in the country during the 1980s. Although the idea of Central Europe stretched back to the late nineteenth and early twentieth centuries, it received renewed attention during the final decade of the Cold War when it was revived by Czechoslovak, Hungarian, and Polish dissidents. For intellectuals like Milan Kundera, György Konrád, and Czesław Miłosz, the concept served to remap the postwar space of Eastern Europe in a way that delegitimized their nations' integration into the Soviet sphere of influence. Animated by a profound cultural nostalgia, the "Central Europe" idea evoked a fantasy of a multicultural pluralism that had supposedly been embodied in the Habsburg Empire and the region's transnational Jewish community, both of which had been destroyed by the violence of the twentieth century.

The concept of Central Europe served a strategy of spatial mediation that dissident intellectuals across Eastern Europe pursued in the final years of the Cold War. Although never conceived as a territorial polity, the imagined space of Central Europe provided a framework within which intellectuals could simultaneously reject affiliations with the Soviet East and align themselves with a common European geography. Articulated at a time in which the process of economic and political integration was gathering pace in the West, this concept helped leverage a moral claim to belonging to a shared European cultural inheritance.[35] The supranational dimension of Central Europe at once allowed its adherents to distance themselves from a parochial nationalism in lieu of a regional cosmopolitanism while at the same time the concept's strict geographical demarcation served to re-border the region, cutting it off from its ties to a wider Eurasian space.[36]

The Central Europe idea played a particularly divisive role within Yugoslavia, where it disrupted earlier spatial assemblages and, eventually, undermined the consistency of the Yugoslav project itself.[37] Just as Eastern European dissidents mobilized the concept to negate their ties with the Soviet East, so too did Yugoslav discourses of Central

On the Cultural Spaces of Late Socialism   199

European belonging frequently negate earlier ideas of Balkan federalism or Third-Worldism. In this sense, the Central Europe idea was
a project of ideological disengagement from the anticolonial commitments and affiliations that earlier iterations of Yugoslav socialism had
sustained. My point here is not to force an overtly geopolitical reading
of Central Europe, as Yvonne Živković warns against, but rather to
better understand this concept, its utility, and its intellectual purchase,
in light of the global spatial reconfigurations of the 1970s and their
impact on the coherence of Yugoslav socialism.[38]

Yugoslav debates on the concept of Central Europe predated its
revival in dissident circles elsewhere in Eastern Europe. From the
outset, however, its reception was marked by a profound ambivalence. As early as 1968, for instance, Miroslav Krleža dismissed
the concept entirely as "a quiet nostalgia for those distant days
when the Spanish dynasty still ruled."[39] Krleža, who died before
the concept really began to take hold, cast a long shadow over
the intellectual and literary life of Yugoslavia, and his critique of
Central Europe certainly contributed to its later ambivalent reception.[40] Even Danilo Kiš, one of the few internationally prominent
Yugoslav writers to adopt the idea, did so very carefully, emphasizing the porous borders of the space, its dark and traumatic legacy,
and its importance as a means of critiquing nationalist division in
the region.[41]

The reasons for Yugoslav ambivalence are not surprising, given
that the map of Central Europe, as sketched by figures like Kundera
or Konrad, closely tracked the historical contours of the Habsburg
Empire. This geography risked throwing up an imagined border
within the Yugoslav federation, one that roughly mapped onto the
growing antagonism between the country's northern and southern
republics. In other words, by placing such emphasis on the civilizational legacy of the Habsburg Empire, the concept of Central
Europe risked undermining the unity of a country whose constituent parts were divided into post-Habsburg and post-Ottoman
zones. Furthermore, to the extent that the concept of Central Europe
aimed to promote the idea of a multicultural region that transcended
national borders, Yugoslav intellectuals did not need to engage in
nostalgia for a lost Habsburg Empire; they already belonged to such
a multinational community.[42] Tellingly, therefore, it was not until the
late 1980s, when the supranational project of Yugoslavism entered
its final crisis, that the discourse of Central Europe was adopted

uncritically by prominent intellectuals, principally in Slovenia. By this point, the concept served as a spatial framework through which to negate Yugoslavia and its attendant Third World ties.[43]

The destructive role of the Central Europe idea in Yugoslav political and cultural discourse in the 1980s is demonstrated with particular clarity in the writings of the Slovene philosopher and literary theorist, Taras Kermauner (1930–2008). Kermauner was raised in a prominent communist family and, although he became alienated from the postwar Titoist regime, maintained a commitment to socialism. During the 1950s he pursued a career in philosophy, studying first in Ljubljana and then in Paris under the mentorship of the Marxist Henri Lefevbre, and became an active member of the left-wing dissident movement around the Marxist humanist journal *Praxis*. Over the 1960s, however, Kermauner adopted a more critical attitude to his earlier Marxist commitments and became a close reader of Gilles Deleuze and Jean Baudrillard, thinkers who offered him an exciting critique of what he had come to see as the totalizing and homogenizing tendencies of Hegelian Marxism. These critiques, in turn, paved the way for his embrace over the 1970s of Christianity and, in particular, of the personalist philosophy of the Catholic socialist, Edvard Kocbek. Drawing on both the tradition of interwar Slovene personalism and postwar French poststructuralism, Kermauner had by the 1980s devised a critique of the Titoist system that aligned with key ideas and arguments of anticommunist intellectuals in both Eastern and Western Europe.

In *Pisma srbskemu prijatelju (Letters to a Serbian Friend)*, a series of polemical essays he penned over 1987–88, Kermauner mobilized the concept of Central Europe to set out his critique of Yugoslavia's socialist system. Through this critique, he analyzed the dangers of rising Serbian nationalism and defended the right of Slovenia to secede from the federation. In pursuing these arguments, he reconfigured the cultural space of Yugoslavia in a way that traced a civilizational border between the democratic Central European heritage of the north of the country and the despotic Balkan or Third World cultures of the south. Kermauner's critique rested on the rejection of Stalinism, which he saw as an effort to sacralize the state, the leader, and the party.[44] In this sense, modern totalitarianisms, both of the Far Left and Far Right, revealed their origins in the spiritual-political structure of Asiatic despotism. These origins made communism incompatible with the political culture of Christian Europe, which,

On the Cultural Spaces of Late Socialism 201

Kermauner insisted, was rooted in respect for political and religious pluralism, the autonomy of the individual and civil society, and the rule of law.[45] And just as Stalinism erased the natural autonomy of the individual and civil society in the name of a homogenizing political totality, so too did a unitarist Yugoslavism erase the national autonomy of the different peoples of the country by promoting political centralization and cultural assimilation. For Kermauner, that is, Milošević's desire to recentralize Serbia was a stalking horse for a more ambitious Stalinist effort to recentralize the entire Yugoslav federation.[46] Under such circumstances, he argued, Slovenes had a political and spiritual duty to secede.

In his attacks on Milošević's Serbian nationalist project, Kermauner deployed an essentialist language of cultural difference that posited a civilizational gulf between the post-Habsburg and post-Ottoman regions of the country or, as he put it, "European Yugoslavia" and "Balkan Yugoslavia." Slovenia and Croatia, he insisted, belonged to a Central European space that possessed a longer and more robust tradition of civil society, political pluralism, and individual liberty than the southern republics, whose political cultures had been shaped under the Asiatic despotism of the Ottomans. Kermauner asserted a political-spiritual continuity from the Ottomans, through the Greater Serbian project of the interwar Karađorđević regime, the Stalinism of the early communist period, and the contemporary revival of Serbian nationalism in the 1980s. Should this Balkan-Asiatic trajectory continue, he insisted, Slovenes had no choice but to secede from the federation or risk being led on "an exodus from Enlightened, Christian Europe to the Third World."[47]

As this image suggests, Kermauner was adamant that Slovenia needed to disengage from the mediating space of the Third World, which had been so central to Yugoslav socialist ideology since the 1950s. If an earlier generation of socialists had seen in the Non-Aligned Movement an anticolonial cosmopolitanism, he argued that the orientation to Asia, Africa, and Latin America reflected the Asiatic roots of Balkan Yugoslavia: "The Federation still operates on the assumption that we are not a European country. We fraternize with Arabs and Africans. We project ourselves to the level of the third and fourth worlds. Religious sympathies at the state level are directed from Orthodoxy to Mohammedanism and the superficial road to atheism."[48] Despite the 1948 break with the Soviets opening the possibility to a more "European" socialism, Kermauner argued, the Titoist regime's subsequent orientation to the Third World had reinforced the oligarchic, patriarchal, and despotic qualities of Balkan Yugoslavia. In so doing, it had alienated Slovenes who could not be expected to "identify with a pro-Asian or pro-African Yugoslavia" given their Central European roots.[49]

Disengaging from Yugoslavia's Third World affiliations was critical, Kermauner insisted, for Slovenia joining a modern Europe. In this, his vision of Central Europe differed from many of his Eastern European contemporaries, whose use of the concept was typically oriented towards the past and pursued a cultural politics of nostalgia, commemoration, or historical introspection.[50] Although Kermauner laid claim to the historical legacy of the Habsburg Empire to justify his remapping of South East Europe, he did so in light of his understanding of global capitalist modernity. While critical of the contemporary Yugoslav federation, Kermauner was in favour of supranational statehood, and insisted that an independent Slovenia should join a European federation. In an age of "intensifying internationalization," he argued, small nations could not close themselves off but had to embrace "openness on all sides."[51] Slovenia was to extricate itself from one mediating space – the Third World – in order to integrate into another – Europe. Kermauner's justification for this spatial reorientation was rooted in a moral discourse informed by an increasingly hegemonic neoliberalism.[52] Although Yugoslavia's socialist leadership fancied themselves players on a global stage, their affiliations with Third World dictatorships had in fact closed them off to the new wave of global integration. Through irresponsible borrowing and profligate spending, the Yugoslav regime and its Third World allies imagined they could isolate themselves from the deepening processes of global economic integration. "Thank god," Kermauner exclaimed, "the creditors submitted the bill to us, as it was only because of this that we started to sober up."[53] To Kermauner's mind, the IMF's structural adjustment program offered Yugoslavia one last chance to disengage from a profligate, ill-disciplined, and parasitical Third World and instead reorient towards a Europe of austerity and self-control.[54] This was an iteration of the politics of breaking promises, a moral economic discourse for remapping the spaces of Europe, the Balkans, and the Third World in a new age of economic discipline.

Kermauner's letters provide a crucial insight into the role of the Central Europe idea in the aggressive polemics that engulfed intellectual life in late socialist Yugoslavia. In these polemics, the critique of the Yugoslav system frequently took on geographic dimensions. Breaking with state socialism implied not just reforming political and economic structures, but also recalibrating the spatial horizons through which intellectuals from these small nations understood their position in the world. In this sense, the Central Europe idea was not just a positive moral claim for inclusion in the European project, but also a disavowal of the supranational project of Yugoslavia and the wider mediating space of the Third World.[55]

The broader spatial contours of these polemics, in turn, meant that intellectuals who set out to defend the Yugoslav socialist project from its nationalist critics frequently had to both engage with the seductive appeal of the Central Europe idea and to reimagine the meaning of the Third World and Yugoslavia's place in it. Two texts from the late 1980s offer examples of the nuanced ways in which socialist intellectuals pursued such a defence: Predrag Matvejević's poetic essay, *Mediteranski brevijar* (*Mediterranean Breviary*, translated into English as *Mediterranean: A Cultural Landscape*, 1987) and Dubravka Ugrešić's postmodern novel, *Forsiranje romana reke* (*Fording the Streams of Consciousness*, 1988). Both Matvejević and Ugrešić were ardent defenders of the Yugoslav project and, in the first democratic elections of 1990, were vocal supporters of the Association for the Yugoslav Democratic Initiative and its final desperate efforts to reimagine the federation along democratic socialist lines. As the country descended into civil war, they became two of the most prominent and internationally recognized critics of the nationalist regimes that took power in the post-Yugoslav republics. Despite their political prominence in the 1990s, however, scholars have tended to read their poetic works from the 1980s largely in isolation from the broader polemics that animated Yugoslav intellectual life. By delving into these two texts, I want to offer a reading of the ways in which seemingly apolitical poetic and fictional works engaged with the politically charged geographies that underpinned the polemics of late socialist Yugoslavia.

IV

Predrag Matvejević was born in 1932 in the Herzegovinian town of Mostar to a Russian émigré father and a Croatian mother. Intellectually, he was a product of the Marxist humanist philosophies that took root in Yugoslav universities during the liberalizing reforms of the 1950s.[56] Studying first in Sarajevo and then Zagreb, he quickly fell in with the circle of philosophers around the journal *Praxis* and became one of the leading Yugoslav interpreters of the work of Jean-Paul Sartre. Through Sartre's philosophy, Matvejević was drawn to the question of the ethics of literary engagement, and much of his early work centred on this concern. Like many of his Marxist humanist contemporaries, Matvejević sought to renew Yugoslav socialism in line with a more radical understanding of human freedom and creativity. This position led him to walk a fine line between critical support for the Titoist regime and measured dissent; he defended what he saw as the important gains and values of socialism but also became increasingly vocal in his criticism of the suppression of free speech and the persecution of the regime's critics.[57]

The vitriolic debates around national identity that erupted among Yugoslav intellectuals in the 1980s deeply disturbed Matvejević, who remained an ardent Yugoslav throughout his life. In his 1982 collection, *Jugoslavenstvo danas* (*Yugoslavism Today*), he marked himself out as one of the most vocal advocates for a Yugoslav cultural consciousness and a critic of the disintegrative tendencies of nationalism. In the essays in this volume, Matvejević foregrounded the processes of capitalist globalization that, he insisted, framed all national cultures within a wider "planetary culture." Cultural globalization, he argued, pulled modern subjects out of a parochial national framework, opening them up to more cosmopolitan cultural exchanges. At the same time, he acknowledged the risk of this global culture becoming merely a homogenizing process of Americanization.[58] Cultural particularity, in other words, needed to be maintained, but in a way that led to an openness towards the world and not a retreat into nationalist provincialism. The cultural community of Yugoslavia served such a project.

Yugoslavism, Matvejević argued, should not be confused with an assimilationist nationalism, but rather served a project of spatial mediation, a structure to foster regional affiliation and consolidate the national cultures of the country with an eye to their survival in a competitive global environment: "The relations among the different Yugoslav cultures are not, in spite of everything, the same as those between Yugoslav and Japanese or Greenlandic culture ... before our exit into world space we must first turn to address one another, alone with ourselves, in our Yugoslav space."[59] Yugoslavism, that is, did not compromise its constituent national cultures but brought them into closer dialogue and co-operation, cohered them with an eye towards their greater collective durability within a planetary culture. However, he argued, the institutional framework within which this kind of co-operation could have taken place had broken down since the reforms of 1966–74. While he celebrated the break with the early model of Stalinist centralization, Matvejević also warned that the decentralization of the federation had led to "the parcelization of cultural space, the influence of republican or regional bureaucracies on their respective cultural initiatives, the emboldening of particularism and provincialism."[60] As in the political economy, where devolution of administrative powers had fostered a kind of autarky and the fragmentation of an integrated Yugoslav market, so too had the decentralization of cultural policy undermined any efforts to foster a shared Yugoslav culture. To reverse this provincialization, he called for a more concerted program of interrepublican cultural co-operation.[61] Institutions needed to be constructed that could operate at a supranational scale to foster those cultural tendencies that grew towards a common Yugoslav consciousness.[62]

Matvejević's efforts to salvage Yugoslav socialism and renew its mission in the late 1980s prompted him to address the bitter polemics that raged regarding the geographic contours of Central Europe and the Balkans. This project infused the text that first led to his breakthrough beyond Yugoslav audiences: *Mediteranski brevijar*.[63] *Mediteranski brevijar* was an effort to rethink Yugoslavia as part of a wider Mediterranean space and, in that sense, offered an alternative mapping to the binary of Central Europe/Balkans. This argument had a longer lineage in Yugoslav socialism, perhaps best represented by the work of the former partisan leader Vicko Krstulović. A native of Split, Krstulović had published his *Jadranska orijentacija* (*The Adriatic Orientation*) in 1967, a moment in which the future organization of Yugoslavia was beginning to be reconceived by party reformers. In it, Krstulović advanced the Adriatic as Yugoslavia's doorway to the world economy and called on the leadership to more actively promote a reorientation of the country's investment towards the coast.[64] Here the Adriatic and the larger space of the Mediterranean served as a framework for reconciling the tension between Yugoslavia's postwar geopolitical position between the capitalist West, socialist East, and developing Third World. It was a prescient vision, pre-empting as it did the West's own efforts to position Yugoslavia within a broader Mediterranean security framework in the 1970s.[65] Although Matvejević's breviary was a far more literary endeavour than Krstulović's policy program, it mobilized the Mediterranean in much the same way, using it as a mediating cultural zone within which Yugoslavia could preserve its autonomy within a wider global system.

Matvejević's Mediterranean shared many qualities with dissident ideas of Central Europe. Most obviously, it evoked a history of multinational pluralism and posited a sense of regional belonging that transcended its constituent national cultures. It also highlighted Jewish contributions to promoting this multicultural, regional identity, although for Matvejević it was the Sephardi and Mizrahi communities that took centre stage, not the Central European Ashkenazi. But despite these similarities, there were sharp differences between these two cultural geographies that reflected Matvejević's ideological disagreements with the Eastern European dissidents.[66] First, Matvejević's concept did not rest on the cultural legacy of a single empire but rather on the physical geography of the landscape; Mediterranean peoples were forged by the currents, winds, and soils; they were not heirs to a privileged cultural tradition. This emphasis on physical geography meant that Mediterranean belonging transcended religious, national, or civilizational borders. Where Central Europe was frequently evoked to demarcate the boundaries between Europe and a Russian or Balkan East, Matvejević rejected such geocultural reifications. For him, the Mediterranean stretched from Gibraltar to Sevastopol, encompassing the Catholic, Orthodox, Jewish, and Muslim traditions that inhabited the space. Lastly, if partisans of Central Europe evoked an elite cultural community of writers, artists, and intellectuals, Matvejević's Mediterranean had a distinctly plebian quality, drawing as much on the knowledge of sailors, fishermen, shepherds, and dockworkers as that of writers or philosophers.[67] This popular democratic quality spoke to Matvejević's fidelity to the radical egalitarianism of the socialist project, a commitment that set him apart from many of his Eastern European contemporaries.

This argument implicitly leveled two critiques at the Central Europe idea. First, the Mediterranean destabilized the binary of Central Europe/Balkans that had polarized Yugoslavia along a north/south axis. To be sure, Matvejević did not conceive of the Mediterranean in opposition to Central Europe, but he did use the concept to complicate and dilute the stark divide that figures like Kermauner posited: "Our culture has developed in a symbiosis with Mediterranean cultures as a 'third component' among such oppositions as east/west, north/south, land/sea, Balkan/European, and others more homegrown ... Like everyone, we ask ourselves what we are, individually and as a whole. The answers – peoples on the edge of the European continent, inhabitants of the Balkans, Slavs on the Adriatic, the first Third World country in Europe, the first European country in the Third World – are not mutually exclusive: the Mediterranean does not determine where we belong."[68] The idea of a Mediterranean cultural landscape, that is, offered Matvejević a means for breaking up the oppositional binaries in the nationalist polemics of Yugoslav intellectuals. Introducing the Mediterranean as a third civilizational zone within Yugoslavia undermined the idea that the country was bifurcated along a simple axis of a European north and Balkan south. In fact, precisely because the Mediterranean was "a place for overcoming oppositions," Matvejević believed it provided a framework for reconceiving the heterogeneity of Yugoslavia, thereby defusing the acrimony that the question of European belonging had provoked.[69] Yugoslavia, he argued, could inhabit multiple worlds.

Second, by positing the Mediterranean as a "third component" of a diverse Yugoslav culture, Matvejević sought to undermine the nationalist use of the Central Europe idea by disrupting monolithic views of national culture. The influence of the Mediterranean, he pointed out, did not fall neatly along national borders. Although Croatia was the most obviously Mediterranean of the Yugoslav republics, this only applied to its westernmost regions, along the Dalmatian coast and Istrian Peninsula. The interior of the country, however, was thoroughly Central European in its cultural history.[70] The tripartite cultural geographies of Yugoslavia – Central European, Balkan, Mediterranean – could not be mapped along national borders, but intersected them. This argument further undermined the efforts to bifurcate Yugoslavia along a Central Europe/Balkan axis. Even Kermauner's Slovenia, Matvejević pointed out, was divided between its coastal, Mediterranean culture in the south, and its northern alpine, Central European regions.[71] Yugoslavia's constituent national cultures, in other words, were no more purely European, purely Balkan, or purely Mediterranean than the supranational federation as a whole. If one accepted such geocultural diversity at a national scale, then it could surely be accepted at a supranational, Yugoslav scale.[72] "Nationality," Matvejević slyly commented, "has often been tenuous along the Mediterranean."[73]

As a mediating space, the Mediterranean allowed Matvejević to map contemporary Yugoslav affiliations with the Third World within a longue-durée cultural geography, thereby preserving something of the spatiotemporal configurations of the Non-Aligned Movement. A central motif of the book was his insistence that the Mediterranean not be understood as a "European" space. In fact, the sea was primary to the continent: "Hellenic emporia were markets and embassies; Roman roads spread power and civilization; Asian soil provided prophets and religions. Europe was conceived on the Mediterranean."[74] This rejection of a Eurocentric Mediterranean took aim at those arguments, like Kermauner's, that read Yugoslavia's ties with Asia and Africa as evidence of the degenerative influence of the Balkans on Yugoslavia's European nations. Such affiliations, Matvejević insisted, were not the result of postwar geopolitical alliances, but extensions of a long history of cross-cultural exchange between Europe, Asia, and Africa on the Mediterranean. In contrast to Kermauner's characterization of the Arab world as one of religious fanaticism or despotic oligarchy, Matvejević recalled the contributions of Arabic and Islamic scholars and travelers to Mediterranean culture. Arabic cartography, he noted, played an enormous role in the mapping of the sea, and he was careful to situate his own breviary in a lineage that stretched from Ptolemy through Ibn Khaldun to Mercator.[75] Elsewhere he offered lengthy etymologies that demonstrated the sheer volume of Arabic and Persian vocabulary that had been taken up by other Mediterranean languages.[76] These etymologies targeted contemporary nationalist calls in Yugoslavia to purify national languages of foreign, especially "eastern" loanwords.[77] Far from reflecting the degenerative influence of the Third World on Yugoslavia, Matvejević showed how these loanwords pointed to the country's historical belonging to a multicultural Mediterranean space.

The chronotope of the Mediterranean also allowed Matvejević to evoke the deep time of the landscape to undermine Eurocentric accounts of the area. The breviary did not present Mediterranean history within a singular continuous narrative but rather offered "brief tableaux, juxtaposed without a linear plot linking one to the other."[78] The book recovered the histories of olive oil, bread, and incense, the rituals and techniques of seafaring or ship-building,

On the Cultural Spaces of Late Socialism   209

even the practice of exiling opponents to barren islands and the superstitions surrounding winds, all of which it wove into a dense, impressionistic account that eschewed an overarching narrative. As with the paradigm of one-worldism that Yugoslav socialists advanced in the 1950s, this Mediterranean chronotope abolished a language of "developed" and "underdeveloped," "advanced" and "backwards," "modern" and "primitive," and instead evoked a flattened temporality within which the histories of multiple cultures and civilizations played out: "Ocean currents are like vast rivers: they are determined and taciturn, indeterminable and uncontrollable. Unlike rivers, however, they are ignorant of their source or mouth; they know only that they are both somewhere at sea. Nor do they know their exact dimensions or how their waters keep separate from others, their only bed being, once more, the sea itself."[79]

Here Matvejević deployed the Mediterranean as a kind of geographic palimpsest; rejecting the question of origins, he instead argued that the overlapping and entangled histories that stretched back to before antiquity ought not to be organized through a progressive narrative that began in the ancient East and concluded in the modern West but rather cohabited in the apparent permanence of the sea. This flattened temporality helped to undermine the long-held Eurocentric accounts of the Mediterranean that needed to be negated if the sea was to serve as a mediating space for a non-aligned Yugoslavia.

Matvejević's breviary has been read as a poetic footnote to the revival of interest in the Mediterranean that followed the momentous realization of European unification in 1992.[80] Far less attention, however, has been paid to the ways in which it spoke to the cultural and political polemics of late-socialist Yugoslavia. This is likely because the text differed both stylistically and thematically from some of the author's more explicitly political writings from this period.[81] However, by situating the text within the polemics of the 1980s, the original ideological valence of his Mediterranean idea can be better understood as an attempt to recalibrate the mediating spaces of Yugoslav socialism in a way that might defuse the antagonism between Central European aspirations and Third World affiliations. That a polemicist of Matvejević's stature should have taken up this question highlights the ideologically charged place these cultural geographies had in the culture of late-socialist Yugoslavia.

In early 1989, Matvejević joined with other prominent intellectuals to found the Association for the Yugoslav Democratic Initiative.

The fledgling political party was formed with an eye to the first free elections to be held in the country, scheduled for the next year. The Association hoped to rally pro-Yugoslav sentiment and save the multinational country from the rising threat of nationalist forces.[82] In the event, however, the election results were ominous, delivering a wave of victories for nationalists and casting grave doubt over the durability of a reformed Yugoslav state. In Croatia, the right-wing Croatian Democratic Union (HDZ), led by the former general and historian, Franjo Tudman, won a resounding victory. The failure of Matvejević's Association to halt the trend to nationalist division and to revive the Yugoslav union not only pointed to the lack of momentum behind the reform project but also the gulf that had opened between the intellectual Left and its traditional constituency in the working-class suburbs and the countryside. As the country began its descent into war, Matvejević's vocal criticism of the new government in Croatia put him in the crosshairs of radical nationalists. In 1991, after threats were made on his life, he relocated to Paris.

V

On 19 May 1991, in a national referendum, the Croatian electorate voted overwhelmingly to dissolve its ties with Yugoslavia, and the next month Tudman declared Croatia's independence. The decision deepened interethnic distrust, which had already spilled over into violence when Serbian minority communities responded to the referendum results with their own calls for secession from Croatia. Over the summer of 1991 these conflicts grew into open war, as the federal army began engagements in Croatia in support of Serbian paramilitary forces. The war poisoned the waters of any shared Yugoslav intellectual public, as writers, artists, philosophers, and filmmakers sought to position themselves in the new ideological environment. While some, seeking positions of influence and power in the nationalist governments, became shameless ideologues, others sought merely to avoid denunciation in the heightened climate of fear and paranoia. As intellectuals of all stripes disavowed their friendships or associations with those in neighbouring republics, or their earlier commitments to Yugoslav socialism, the intellectual sinews of a supranational Yugoslav cultural space were torn apart.

It was against this backdrop of war on the European periphery that Dubravka Ugrešić shot to international prominence as a vocal critic of the new, post-Yugoslav nationalist regimes. A professor of literary theory at the University of Zagreb, Ugrešić was also a celebrated writer in Croatia, having started her career as an author of children's books before moving into more experimental, postmodern fiction in the 1980s. Although she had largely eschewed public political engagements, the growing crisis of the Yugoslav federation in the late 1980s jolted her into activism and she became an early supporter of Matvejević's Association in 1989. It was during the nationalist wars of the 1990s, however, that Ugrešić became a more visible political commentator, penning satirical essays in major Western newspapers that attacked both the new nationalist governments and an ignorant Western punditry. Against parochial nationalisms, she defended the legacy of a supranational, socialist Yugoslavia that, whatever its faults, she believed had offered a more vibrant, less provincial cultural space. As with Matvejević, Ugrešić's opposition to the new nationalist regimes garnered her the ire of a censorious and increasingly intolerant Croatian public and in 1992, following a series of threats and a public smear campaign, she left the country and took up "voluntary exile" in Amsterdam.[83]

Ugrešić's polemical essays from this period were compiled in her 1995 collection, *The Culture of Lies*, originally published in Dutch. These essays dissected the nationalist cultures that had taken root across the former Yugoslavia, particularly in Croatia and Serbia, and interrogated their subordination of literary aesthetics to ethnonationalist politics. In her reading of these essays, Dragana Obradović argues that their central critique lay in their identification of "kitsch" as the aesthetic mode of contemporary nationalist culture. Nationalists of the post-Yugoslav states, according to Ugrešić, unironically embraced a garish, overly sentimental aesthetic. The flourishing of kitsch aesthetic forms during the Yugoslav wars of the 1990s was a consequence of the effort of nationalists to commercialize their respective cultures, a tendency that demonstrated the "discomfiting fit between market forces and nationalist ideology."[84] Nationalism and globalization were in fact parallel processes, harmoniously aligned and mutually reinforcing. Nationalist discourses served to commodify culture in order to peddle cultural wares in global markets. The new nationalist regimes of the post-Yugoslav states were not aggressive, parochial reactions to greater global integration, but rather the very expression of its commodifying processes. Nations, Ugrešić suggested, were logos, advertising brands burned into the backsides of Yugoslavs by their new leaders that they might be better categorized and marketed to a global public.[85] In this reading, the cause of the Yugoslav wars lay not in the social pathologies of the Balkan peoples but rather the impact of capitalist globalization in fostering the provincial nationalisms of the periphery.

Scholars point to the essays compiled in *The Culture of Lies* as marking a radical break in Ugrešić's work. According to this biographical interpretation, the wars of the 1990s shocked the author into jettisoning the playful postmodernism that characterized her fiction of the 1980s and led her to adopt the more politically engaged essay form. Such an interpretation is in keeping with a wider assessment of Yugoslav postmodernism as having actively avoided political or social concerns in favour of narrow experimentation, preventing writers from addressing the growing social dislocation of the country. Through such aesthetic indifference, critics suggest, postmodern writers failed to stem the tide of nationalist extremism that engulfed the country and tore it apart.[86] I want to build on Obradović's challenge to this reading by taking a closer look at the last novel Ugrešić wrote before the outbreak of war in her country, the 1988 postmodern farce, *Forsiranje romana reke*.[87] Specifically, by situating the novel within the polemics of the late-socialist period I want to draw out its political engagement, including her critique of the relation of national and global scales and her interrogation of the mediating spaces of Central Europe and the Third World. Despite its playful style, *Forsiranje romana reke* prefigured many of the more politically explicit critiques Ugrešić would make in her essays from the 1990s. Whereas those essays targeted the cynicism of politics, the asymmetries of globalization, and the resurgence of nationalist ideologies directly, her 1988 novel engaged these themes obliquely, through the lens of writers and their thorny relationships with the global literary market.

Forsiranje romana reke is set at an international literary convention in Zagreb, which it uses to stage the intrigues, petty jealousies, insecurities, and frustrated ambitions of a troupe of writers, critics, and cultural officials. This setting allows Ugrešić to develop a critique of late capitalist globalization through the lens of what Pascale Casanova would later term "the world literary system."[88] The novel, in other words, satirizes the asymmetries of prestige and cultural authority that privileged literatures of the Western metropoles

On the Cultural Spaces of Late Socialism   213

over those of the periphery. Ugrešić's decision to set the novel at an international convention brings these structures to the fore and anticipates her later criticism of cultural commodification. Much of the novel plays with the national or regional stereotypes through which minor writers were made legible to global readers. The dramatis personae includes a Croatian poet who, in obvious imitation of Maiakovskii, gives readings of his militant proletarian poetry to workers in the local sausage factory, the Danish feminist who indignantly cites Virginia Woolf and fumes against the literary patriarchy, the Hungarian and Croatian writers who jealously spar over their respective ethnic claims on an obscure seventeenth-century author, the Soviet delegate who relishes boring his audience with official literary formulations, and the unassuming Czech poet whose secret manuscript is an indictment of the cruelty of the Stalinist system. These exaggerated stereotypes are reinforced by the novel's play with genre, switching from detective or spy fiction to dissident memoir or feminist epistolary and even to the dark satire of the modern Czech novel. Aligning stereotype with genre points to the ways in which politically or geographically marginal writers were then being branded for consumption in international markets.

Ugrešić offers her sharpest critique of globalization, however, through the novel's Blofeld-like character, the verbose French poet, Jean-Paul Flagus. The supposed nephew of Gustave Flaubert, Flagus is a walking embodiment of the world literary canon, whose charm and wit become the core of social life at the conference. Later in the novel, however, it is revealed that Flagus is, in fact, a super-villain who harbours ambitions for world domination. In a scene in which he attempts to court the Croatian organizer of the conference, Prša the poet, Flagus reveals his plans for a system of global literary engineering: "When most people look at a map, they think in terms of geography, politics, demography, geology, ecology. Well, when I look at a map, I think in terms of literature. I divide it into unmarked, unchartered areas and areas that on a more conventional map would be designated as rivers, mountains, cities ... My point is that I am a visionary. We live in an age of information, my boy, and the literary map I envision has its own reality. It won't be long now before anything not specifically entered into an information network will cease to exist. And that includes whole countries, cultures, languages. Our 'spiritual map' is in for a sea change, wouldn't you say?"[89]

Through Flagus's megalomaniacal vision, Ugrešić parodies the asymmetries of the world literary system by exaggerating its spatial organization into major and minor writers, metropoles and peripheries. His ambitions for world dominance are conceived as a project of remapping that will determine not just the success of a particular writer, but the very survival of small nations or minor literatures. Flagus's stated goal is cultural homogenization for the purpose of totalitarian control. In place of the originality of the literary masterwork, which escapes control owing to the unpredictability and spontaneity of its composition, he envisions an army of critics, theorists, and comparativists producing a globalized literature as uniform in its branding as Coca Cola. While Flagus's plans for world literary domination are obviously fantastic and read as a spoof of Cold War spy fiction, they also foreshadow Ugrešić's later concern with commodification and globalization.

Throughout the novel, Ugrešić aligns the scales of the minor writer and the small nation, both of which, she insists, are small and pitiable, dwarfed by the global structures that dominate them.[90] The minor writers of the novel and the small nations of her later essays are subject to the demand to make themselves legible to world markets through their commodification, a process that leads to their own corruption and fosters a dark and violent impulse. *Forsiranje romana reke* sets up this line of critique through the figure of Prša the poet. Prša is a middle-tier cultural official whose service for the regime has advanced his literary career. Perhaps because of this, he is deeply insecure and swings between bouts of absurd self-importance and vicious vindictiveness, fantasizing over the deaths of his rivals and critics. In pursuing his plans for global literary engineering, Flagus enlists Prša, offering him a position as an "Agent of the Totalitarian Control of Literature." Seduced by the promise that such a position would allow him to settle accounts with his critics, Prša sanctifies his ambitions with the veneer of patriotism: "if somebody at this latitude and longitude failed to take matters into his own hands, it would turn into one of those uncharted areas on Flagus's literary map."[91] Just as Ugrešić would later establish the alignment of nationalism and globalization, the novel suggests that the only path for the recognition of minor literatures within the world literary field is through the nefarious processes of the global market. This harmonization of the national and global scales takes place through the medium of dark personal ambitions: Prša's desire for career advancement and Flagus's schemes for world literary domination.

The way in which Ugrešić aligns the national and global scales here marks an important departure from their previous configuration among Yugoslav socialists. If earlier intellectuals assumed a tension between the national and global that compelled them to forge spaces of mediation, Ugrešić's work posits a harmony between these scales; her concern in the novel is not the ways in which globalization compromised the sovereignty or economic development of the nation, but rather the repressive cultural authority it seemed to foster at the level of the nation state. This reformulation of the relation between the national and global scales, however, does not lead Ugrešić to dispense with the problem of mediating spaces. Indeed, *Forsiranje romana reke* is clearly in dialogue with the broader cultural remappings that animated Yugoslav intellectual life of the 1980s. As we've seen, key to these polemics was the new cultural geography of Central Europe, which was increasingly evoked in opposition to the country's Third World affiliations.

Forsiranje romana reke offers a critique of Central Europe that drew on Ugrešić's wider concern with the commodified cultural forms through which minor literatures were integrated into global markets. The idea is satirized in the character of Ranko Leš, a poet who in several scenes lectures his fellow writers about the importance of Central Europe: "'Europe is in!' he declares pompously. '*Mitteleuropa*! And we're smack in the *mittel*. Austria-Hungary is on the march! On the march to trend-dom! It's all in the nose. You've got to have a good nose for these things or you can wave bye-bye to the choo-choo of history.'"[92] Leš's cynical deployment of Central Europe here reduces the concept to a mere marketing strategy, a gibe at the mythopoetic power so many Eastern European intellectuals of the 1980s ascribed to it. Here Central Europe does not evoke Konrad's lost world of multicultural tolerance, or Kiš's traumas of the twentieth century, or the austere civilizational legacy that Kundera saw as the last preserve of European high culture, but rather a brand, cynically evoked to further a minor writer's professional ambitions. Central Europe plays much the same role as Ugrešić would later identify with the nation: that is, it serves as a fashionable means of packaging the minor literatures of Eastern Europe to make them intelligible for Western consumers.[93]

216   Mediating Spaces

While Ugrešić ruthlessly skewered her contemporaries' fixation on the horizons of Central Europe, she adopted a more complicated and ambiguous attitude to the space of the Third World. In the central plot of *Forsiranje romana reke*, Yugoslavia's Third World affiliations are noticeably absent. With the exception of the American, Marc, all of the delegates to the Zagreb conference hail from Europe. However, this fictional plot is bookended by autobiographical chapters that recount Ugrešić's composition of the novel, and here the text offers deeper evidence of the author's engagement with the Third World. The action in these chapters is also set at various international literary gatherings – a writing workshop at the University of Iowa, a symposium in Havana – but these settings provide for a more globally inclusive set of characters. During her stay in Iowa, for instance, Ugrešić notes that most of her fellow workshop participants are from the Third World, and she is moved to learn that her dorm room had in previous years been occupied by writers from Asia, the Middle East, and Africa. In contrast to the petty rivalries and jealousies of the novel's characters, Ugrešić uses these affiliations to suggest a sense of community, describing writers as "like one big family."[94] Similarly, the decision to conclude the novel in Cuba charts the expansive global exchanges that Yugoslav writers enjoyed thanks to the Non-Aligned Movement.

While these settings plotted the coordinates of the Third World to which socialist Yugoslavia still belonged and hinted at the feelings of solidarity it sustained, the novel also evidences the hollowing out of this mediating space and the fraying of its affiliations. The Third World is evoked as a much more muted and fragile set of ties than the celebrations of anticolonial struggles in the 1950s and 1960s. Ugrešić's friendships with her Asian and African colleagues are disconnected from a wider sense of Third World belonging; they are all part of a global community of writers unmoored from any cultural or political space. Furthermore, at several moments the novel highlights the limitations of these ties. Upon her return to Zagreb from the US, for instance, Ugrešić remarks on how small and provincial her native city feels, describing the psychological downscaling she undergoes as a kind of spiritual deflation as she is forced to adjust from the expansive horizons of a world literary community. In a brief vignette, Ugrešić suggests that this experience of deflation was not hers alone: "I spent half my salary on postcards with *Greetings from Zagreb* on them. Soon I got a postcard from a writer in Ghana

On the Cultural Spaces of Late Socialism 217

with *Greetings from Accra* on it."[95] The scene points to the failure of this global community of writers to manifest itself as a durable formation. Outside of the exceptional moments of international gatherings, Ugrešić's ties with the Third World can only be manifest through the exchange of kitsch images of the very national capitals she now finds so narrow and constricting. The failure of Third-Worldism is registered as a begrudging retreat to the smaller scale of the nation.

It is only at the supranational scale of the Yugoslav federation that Ugrešić identifies a cultural space able to disrupt the alignment of globalization and nationalism. The importance of Yugoslavia as such a mediating space was later developed in an essay entitled "Parrots and Priests" that Ugrešić presented to an international conference organized in the US by the editors of *Partisan Review* in April 1992.[96] Here she set out the plight of the Yugoslav writer who, in the midst of nationalist fragmentation and war, found their horizons of belonging dissolving. In its analysis of the contemporary crisis and disorientation of the Yugoslav writer, the talk offered an insight into Ugrešić's understanding of Yugoslavia as a mediating cultural space:

> The contemporary Yugoslav writer created in the freedom afforded him by his position as an outsider. He wrote conscious of his insignificance within his own culture, without pretentions of any significance abroad. He wrote in Europe, but on its edge; he wrote in the European East but on its Western edge. The Yugoslav writer lived an underprivileged social life but a privileged literary one. Because it was only in a wild, non-commercial, disorganized and unarticulated culture that astonishing un-provincial gestures could occur, such as the abundant translation of books which could not have been translated in other, commercially oriented cultures. It was only in that confused, half-literate and at the same time highly literate culture, that our own books could be printed in lavish bindings. Only in an extravagant, crazy country between communism and capitalism ... could books be printed whose costs could not be covered by sales, the expense of whose production exceeded their price. From an entirely literary point of view, the Yugoslav writer lived like a rich pauper.[97]

Ugrešić's defence of Yugoslavia in this talk lay in its capacity to bypass the commercialization of literary production that would otherwise have restricted the freedom of the writer. By creating a regionally integrated literary market, one that was generously subsidized by a socialist state, Yugoslavia shielded local writers from the commodifying pressure of the world literary system. Precisely because the alignment of global markets and small nationalisms reinforced a kitsch provincialism, it was only at this intermediary scale that "un-provincial," cosmopolitan creativity could thrive. The autonomy that Ugrešić sought to preserve in this Yugoslav mediating space was not that of the nation, but the writer. Autonomous literary creativity was not achieved by greater openness to global markets, precisely because these markets forced minor writers to conform to national or regional ("Central Europe") brands that stamped out their originality. Rather, autonomy was only to be secured in a cultural space constituted somewhere between the national and the global. Only such a mediating space could disrupt the homogenizing effects that the alignment of nationalism and globalization had brought about.

VI

As this book has set out to demonstrate, from the late nineteenth century to the end of the twentieth, Yugoslav socialists sought to construct supranational spaces through which they could mediate their small nations' integration and position in the global capitalist system. Each set of transformations at the global scale, we have seen, necessitated a reconceptualizing and reimagining of these mediating spaces in order to secure political sovereignty, economic development, and cultural modernization in the new global environment. In the 1990s, the most durable and effective of these mediating spaces, the Socialist Federative Republic of Yugoslavia, fragmented in the midst of violent civil wars, effectively marking the closure of the history of Yugoslav socialism that this book has traced. The collapse of Yugoslavia was a moment in the wider history of the spatial reconfigurations of global capitalism that began in the 1970s. Specifically, the acceleration and deepening of the processes of European integration, and the crisis of the Third World, disrupted the ideological and geographical constellations within which the Yugoslav socialist project had been plotted since the 1950s. The political

On the Cultural Spaces of Late Socialism 219

and cultural significance of these mediating spaces were registered in the highly charged polemics of the 1980s. As socialist Yugoslavia and the Third World of which it was a part were shattered by the global debt crisis, their capacity to shield their constituent nations from the turbulent dynamics of capitalist globalization was undermined. For many intellectuals in the northern republics of Yugoslavia, Europe became an alternative mediating space, one that could better secure their economic development without compromising their political and cultural autonomy. In turn, the anticolonial affiliations with Asia and Africa that had so long animated the Yugoslav socialist imagination were quickly jettisoned in favour of an aspirational European identity, one that redrew lines between Europe and the Balkans.

Owing to the ways in which the supranational Yugoslav project was entangled in these wider geographies, leftist intellectuals that sought to defend the federation from its critics had to engage questions about both Europe and the Third World. Matvejević answered these questions by proposing a third geographic paradigm: the Mediterranean. Resituating Yugoslavia at the nexus of three cultural zones – Central European, Balkan, and Mediterranean – he sought to defuse growing ideological polarization and to reconcile European aspirations with Yugoslavia's Third World affiliations. Ugrešić, although offering little in the way of a positive project and preferring a mode of criticism that recalled the polemical style of Krleža, still understood the need to engage these mediating spaces. In both her fiction from the 1980s and her political essays from the 1990s, she lambasted the pompous discourse of Central Europe and the disdain with which its proponents looked on their déclassé cousins from Yugoslavia. Her defence of Yugoslavia as a cultural space that disrupted the unhealthy alignment of capitalist globalization and nationalist commodification came too late, at a point at which that space was already "dissolving like an ice cube in water."[98] Meanwhile, Yugoslavia's Third World vision was a promise that failed to be realized.

Yet something of the Third World legacy of Yugoslav socialism survived in Ugrešić's later work, and it remains a living symbolic and affective reservoir throughout much of the post-Yugoslav space. In the final years of her life, both Ugrešić's fiction and her essays adopted a more critical stance towards the EU, taking aim specifically at what she saw as a sanctimonious discourse of liberal humanitarianism that veiled an increasingly hardened and discriminatory border regime. This rejection of a liberal "fortress Europe" helped give form to a politics of solidarity between refugees from the postsocialist and postcolonial worlds who now inhabit the marginal spaces of Europe's metropoles.[99] Here, perhaps, is a last glimpse of the radical political visions that animated Yugoslav socialism throughout the long twentieth century and that sought to foster ties between the peoples of South East Europe and the non-European world.

Conclusion

> To know is not so much to run up against the real as it is to validate the possible by rendering it necessary. From then on, the genesis of the possible is as important as the demonstration of the necessary. The fragility of one does not deprive it of a dignity that the other gains by its stability. The illusion could have been a truth. The truth will perhaps reveal itself one day to be illusion.
>
> Georges Canguilhem, "Cell Theory," 1945

I

On 17 February 2008, the Assembly of Kosovo unilaterally declared the province's secession from Serbia. The territorial separation had been a long time coming. Kosovo had been ground zero for the collapse of Yugoslavia in the 1980s, when the majority-Albanian population rose up against rule from Belgrade. Slobodan Milošević had launched his bid for power in opposition to the unrest, promising to roll back the autonomy that the province had secured in the 1974 constitutional reforms. During the years of his rule, the Belgrade government imposed a brutal police regime in Kosovo, eventually provoking an armed insurgency by a group of former Maoists known as the Kosovo Liberation Army. The ongoing violence opened the door to Western intervention in the region and in the spring of 1999, NATO launched air strikes against Serbia. The attacks led to the informal separation of Kosovo and inaugurated almost a decade of foreign rule of the province by UN and EU officials. The Assembly of Kosovo's declaration of independence in February 2008, although contested by Serbia, received broad international recognition. The separation marked the final moment in the territorial fragmentation of Yugoslavia.

When the Kosovo assembly declared its independence, I was living in Belgrade and working as an English teacher. Although the writing had been on the wall for some time, the declaration provoked widespread protests throughout Serbia. Even before the announcement, the streets of the capital had been marked with graffiti reading "Kosovo = Serbia" or "Kosovo is the heart of Serbia." In the weeks that followed, mass demonstrations took to the streets of the major cities condemning the decision and denouncing those countries that recognized Kosovo's independence. A handful of these protests led to attacks on the symbols of Western power: the US embassy was torched, as was a downtown McDonald's restaurant.[1] The protests were about more than Belgrade's control over a poor, rural province in the south; Kosovo had become a symbol of Serbia's weakness in the post-Cold War order.

A few weeks after the protests had subsided, a colleague asked me for a favour. Her students were preparing a debate on Serbia's future following the independence of Kosovo. As a native speaker, would I be willing to give them tips on their spoken English? I was very happy to oblige. Two teams faced off against one another: Russophiles and Europhiles. The Russophiles went first. In light of the West's betrayal of Serbia over Kosovo, they argued, the country should pursue closer ties with Russia, which continued to support Belgrade's territorial claims. Only by leaning on the power of their Orthodox brothers could Serbia's interests be protected in the new Western-dominated global order. Then it was the Europhiles' turn. Kosovo was a provincial backwater, they insisted, a drag on Serbia's economy. The West had done Serbia a favour by unburdening it of this medieval baggage. Now the country was free to rejoin the path of European integration and democratization.

Both sides in the debate defended their cases passionately. But when each had concluded, the despondence of the audience was palpable. "Does anyone have anything they'd like to contribute?" my colleague asked her students. "Which side did you find more convincing?" An awkward silence followed. By so starkly posing the options before Serbia, the debate had brought home just how powerless the small country was, how dependent on its more powerful neighbours. For the middle-class professionals enrolled in the course, it was a depressing reminder of their narrow career prospects and the stunted future that awaited their children. My colleague, who suddenly seemed as dispirited as her students, was unable to raise the mood. Finally, after several minutes of painful silence, a gawky man with a thick accent mused out loud: "I think maybe we should make a federation with Venezuela." The room burst into laughter.

The student's joke was a soft gibe at the legacy of supranational thought that this book has recovered. The proposal that Serbia forge a union with a far-off socialist country in South America was, on its surface, a geographical absurdity. What possible reason would these two states have for pursuing such a merger, short of the most opportunistic and short-term convergence of interests? At the heart of the joke was the geopolitical hubris that had led twentieth-century Yugoslav socialists to pursue such ambitious projects as a Balkan federation or the Non-Aligned Movement. It was the juxtaposition between these socialists' grandiose ambitions and the now marginal status of their nations on the global stage that seemed so comical. There was more than a touch of gallows humour here, an implicit acknowledgement that Yugoslav socialism had failed to remap world space according to its own utopian visions. In the sober days of the 2000s, in the aftermath of the Cold War and the violent breakup of Yugoslavia, these students could look back on the revolutionary promises of the twentieth century with a degree of sardonic disdain.

II

I recount the story of the unrealized Serbo-Venezuelan federation by way of posing two problems this book has raised but, as yet, left unanswered. The first concerns how we are to account for the defeat of supranationalism in the long twentieth century. After all, the students in that Belgrade classroom were not wrong. As this book has made clear, the history of Yugoslav socialism's mediating spaces is ultimately a history of failure, of the fragility of the supranational and the stubborn durability of the national as the primary scale of political action in the era of capitalist globalization. This problem is not restricted to the case of Yugoslavia. Writing of a recent surge of interest in the history of federalism in the postcolonial world, Samuel Moyn observes that "[n]eo-federalist historians rarely take it upon themselves to solve what ought to be the central puzzle: Why did the nation-state model win out, when the alternatives were supposedly so compelling?"[2] The history of Yugoslav socialism offers some answers to this question.

In his wonderful literary history of the Yugoslav idea, Andrew Wachtel suggests that a key factor in the collapse of the Socialist Federative Republic of Yugoslavia was the lack of a common supranational culture. In the absence of a cultural fabric, the ties that bound the Yugoslav nations together frayed, leaving the state vulnerable to the destructive energies of rival nationalist forces.[3] Wachtel was building on the warnings of Predrag Matvejević, who in the 1980s had argued that the decentralization of Yugoslavia had eroded the basis of a common cultural space.[4] As this book has demonstrated, however, Yugoslav supranationalism had a vibrant cultural life. Yugoslavism, Balkan federalism, Slavism, non-alignment, and European integration were each accompanied by concerted efforts on the part of intellectuals to provide cultural texture to these projects, typically by sketching the geographies upon which their respective identities, affinities, and antagonisms could be sustained.

If we cannot blame the paucity of cultural production, to what, then, are we to chalk up the failure of Yugoslav socialists' supranational projects? The answer, I believe, lies in the structure of mediating spaces themselves. Three mutually reinforcing qualities contributed to their fragility. First, mediating spaces fortified the national as the primary scale of sovereign initiative. As this book has argued, supranationalism emerged as a field structured by the tensions between global processes of economic integration and geopolitical competition and nationally scaled sovereignties. Projects of supranational consolidation, that is, were not efforts to transcend or abolish the nation, but to better negotiate its position in the global system. Mediating spaces, therefore, reinforced rather than eroded the centrality of the nation to political life.[5]

Second, the supranational projects of Yugoslav socialism were highly sensitive to the dynamic interplay of globally and nationally scaled processes. To the extent that mediating spaces interfaced between the national and the global, they were premised on a relatively stable configuration of these two scales. When that configuration changed, so too did the salience of the supranational project. Changes in the patterns of those dynamics meant that previous supranational projects were often found to be misaligned and had to be abandoned, repurposed, or recalibrated to serve a new strategy of spatial mediation.

Third, because Yugoslav socialists' strategies of supranationalism were typically reactions to changed circumstances in the global environment, the mediating spaces they devised were often characterized

Conclusion

by a degree of impermanence. The frequent spatial reorientations that this book has detailed – from the Balkans to Europe to Slavdom to Asia and Africa and back to Europe – made the supranational geographies of Yugoslav socialism appear ephemeral. This sense of transience was often reinforced by their distinct spatialities. Although the territorialism of a Yugoslav, Balkan, or European federation lent these projects a degree of concreteness, the more abstract spaces of Slavic affinity and the Non-Aligned Movement meant that these geographies were less clearly delineated. Amidst this geographical flux, the nation remained a relatively constant site of identity and community, making it an anchor in moments of crisis. The transient nature of Yugoslav socialism's supranational projects, therefore, undermined their durability, while their tendency to reinforce the nation as the scale of sovereign initiative limited their purchase on the political subjectivities of the population.[6]

III

If the mediating spaces of Yugoslav socialism were so structurally compromised, then we are faced with a second concluding problem: What, ultimately, is the value of studying them? What insight may be gleaned about politics or culture in the age of globalization from such a history of failures? Tracking the intellectual history of Yugoslav socialism provides a valuable case study through which to enrich our understanding of the dynamics of the supranational as a geopolitical and geopoetic field. There are several observations that this book has made.

The first is that supranationalism was bound up with the experience of global capitalist modernity. The mediating spaces of Yugoslav socialism were products of an epoch of globalization that produced profoundly uneven geographies of power, wealth, and prestige. In the small nations of the European periphery, this experience of geographic unevenness fostered a search for modes of political unification, economic consolidation, or cultural affiliation that exceeded the narrow bounds of the nation. The supranational projects that political thinkers from these small nations devised could be deployed to a number of strategic ends: to strengthen small states' defences in a world of imperial predation, to integrate disparate local markets into a larger economic zone, to consolidate regional actors to better project their geopolitical influence, or to resolve complex national questions.

The mediating spaces that grew out of these supranational political and cultural strategies could be articulated across multiple registers of spatiality: from concrete territorial polities such as the Socialist Federative Republic of Yugoslavia or the European Communities, to looser projects of geopolitical alliance or cultural affiliation such as the Non-Aligned Movement or postwar Slavism, to the imagined spaces of the Balkans, Europe, Slavdom, or the Third World. These projects differed markedly in their geographic contours, their teleological horizons, and their conceptual cohesion. Determining the political borders of a Yugoslav federation was, quite obviously, a very different action than tracing the symbolic geography of the Balkans. What warrants their common classification is that each was conceived and articulated within a conceptual field that was structured by the frictions of the national and global.

Furthermore, the boundaries between these diverse spatialities were quite porous. The political efforts to form a Balkan federation in the 1920s inspired an avant-garde geopoetics of the Balkans as an imagined space of aesthetic rebellion. During World War II, the cultural geographies of Slavic kinship reinforced the territorial project of Yugoslav federal state-building. In the crisis of the 1980s, the imagined space of the Third World became a whetstone against which intellectuals could sharpen their arguments for European integration. This porousness was, in part, a result of historical contingency: the repression of the communist movement in the 1920s in Yugoslavia prompted revolutionary intellectuals to shift their attention to the realm of culture. But it was also a consequence of the speculative nature of many of these projects, which made the realm of cultural production a more fertile site for imagining alternative supranational configurations. The transposition of strategies of spatial mediation from a political-economic to a political-aesthetic field led to a closer imbrication of politics and culture; geopolitical projects for the creation of supranational polities increasingly became entangled with symbolically charged cultural geographies. Grouping these multiple spatialities into a common frame of analysis, this book has sought to better understand the cross-pollination of political and cultural geographies that animated the supranational imaginary of Yugoslav socialism.

The supranational was not a flat scale but a field of activity that could be structured by gradations of verticality. This argument is most clearly demonstrated by the example of Yugoslav federalism.

Conclusion 227

Throughout the history of Yugoslav socialism's mediating spaces, the politics of Yugoslavism was a consistent preoccupation, conceived at times as variously working in harmony, counterpoint, or dissonance with other supranational projects. While Serbian social democrats of the fin de siècle often dismissed Yugoslavism as a distraction from what they saw as the more urgent goal of Balkan federalism, the creation of a Yugoslav state after World War I changed the Left's calculations. Yugoslavia was no longer one imagined future among others, but a real territorial polity whose borders, institutions, and identities had to be taken into account for socialist strategy. Initially, the communist party conceived of Yugoslavism in unitarist terms, at first embracing it in the name of national unification and then unceremoniously condemning it as a project of greater Serbian hegemony. But in the years of the Popular Front, communists reconceived Yugoslavism as a mode of supranational federalism.

This federalism became a bedrock of Yugoslav socialism throughout the struggles of World War II and into the decades of postwar state building. Reinvigorated by the Tito-Stalin split of 1948, Yugoslavia became more explicitly conceived as a mediating space. Breaking with the centralized bureaucratic model of Stalinism, over the following decades Yugoslav reformers devolved political administration and economic and cultural policies to the constituent national republics. In the process, Yugoslavism was actively denuded of its historically accrued ethnic or national connotations.[7] As we have seen, however, decentralization reinforced the divergence of the country's economic geography, leaving it ill-equipped to respond to the vicissitudes of the global economy in the turbulent 1970s. The sovereign debt crisis that beset the federation over the 1980s aggravated social conflicts and fueled tensions between the different republics, leading to its violent disintegration.

Throughout this history, the Yugoslav federation was conceived and reconceived within wider supranational geographies: as part of Balkan or European federations, within projects of Slavic or Third World affiliation, or as a member of a Central European or Mediterranean cultural zone. The mediating space of Yugoslavia, that is, itself became an object of spatial mediation, envisioned as nested within more geographically expansive projects. Different supranational projects configured this Yugoslav federation in different ways: while the projects of Slavism and non-alignment both served to brace a federal Yugoslavia, the rapid consolidation of the

228   Mediating Spaces

European Communities undermined its coherence. What emerges from this history is a clearer understanding of the ways supranational politics can be configured within diverse gradations of verticality.

While this book has primarily focused on those modes of supranational politics that pursued what we might term emancipatory ends, it would be remiss not to note that they could also be turned to projects of domination. Supranationalism, for instance, could facilitate the hegemony of a single state over its constituent allies. This was obviously the case with the new Slavic movement, which, despite the protestations of its adherents, projected Soviet power and influence across Eastern Europe. At other times, supranational federalism could be promoted by outside powers with an eye to undermining the independence of the federal units. In the immediate postwar years, for instance, Stalin pushed his Bulgarian allies to form a Balkan federation with Yugoslavia precisely to dilute Tito's growing influence in the region.[8] Echoes of this same strategy could be observed in the post-2014 efforts of the Russian leadership to promote the federalization of Ukraine, with the proposed federal units in the east serving as stalking horses for Russian interests.[9] The EU represents a third mode of hegemonic supranational politics, one in which the transfer of sovereign power to intra-European bodies has strengthened technocratic modes of governance and eroded the space for meaningful mass democratic contestation.[10] Mediating spaces, then, have often served a politics of domination as much as they have emancipation.

IV

Since the collapse of socialist Yugoslavia in the 1990s, its former constituent states have all pursued paths of integration into the EU. Their success has been varied. On 1 May 2004, Slovenia was the first of the former Yugoslav states to join, followed by Croatia almost a decade later in July 2013. As of this writing, the remaining five states, including Kosovo, are on the path to EU candidacy. However, the lackluster response of the students in that English class in Belgrade in February 2008 gives one reason to suspect that much of the shine of European integration may be wearing off in the region.[11]

Indeed, today the EU is in crisis. From the Brexit vote of 2016, the sovereign debt crisis of Greece, the rise of Eurosceptic politics, and the widening gulf between its core and periphery, the project faces

Conclusion 229

mounting challenges. While the expansion and institutionalization of this mediating space over the past thirty years may give the impression of solidity, we should recall that the Yugoslav federation seemed similarly stable well into its fourth decade. The current crisis of Europe is an opportunity to reflect on alternative organizations of the continent's political, economic, and cultural space. We find ourselves in a moment desperate for imagining new political projects, economic strategies, and cultural visions that can chart a way out of the present impasse.

In this effort, the history of Yugoslav socialism, with its rich understanding of South East Europe's distinct experience of global modernity and the emancipatory, egalitarian, and internationalist projects that it crafted, offer a valuable intellectual reservoir of concepts and practices. That these projects failed is undeniable. But as Georges Canguilhem eloquently notes, a history of failures is simultaneously a history of possibility, an account of alternatives that could have been and could still be: "The illusion could have been a truth. The truth will perhaps reveal itself one day to be illusion."[12] More than anywhere else in the long twentieth century, socialists in Yugoslavia fostered a vibrant supranational imaginary that led them to reflect on the practical and philosophical problems of spatial mediation, to devise paradigms that could configure the balance between national autonomy and supranational consolidation, to craft cultural frameworks that could ascribe political salience to these imagined geographies, and to provide ideological formulations that could articulate modes of being in common across ethnically, linguistically, and confessionally heterogenous populations. If a supranational politics has continued relevance today, the history of Yugoslav socialism will be critical for thinking through its problematics.

Notes

ACKNOWLEDGMENTS

1 Alain Badiou, *Ethics: An Essay on the Understanding of Evil*, trans. Peter Hallward (London: Verso, 2001), 47.

INTRODUCTION

1 Krleža is likely referring to Chedorlaomer/Kedorlaomer, who is mentioned in the Book of Genesis as a king of Elam.
2 Miroslav Krleža, "Hodorlahomor the Great," trans. Drenka Willen, in *The Cricket beneath the Waterfall and Other Stories*, ed. Branko Lenski (New York: Vanguard Press, 1972), 245.
3 Miroslav Krleža, *Davni dani: Zapisi 1914–1921*, in *Sabrana djela*, vols. 11–12 (Zagreb: Zora, 1956), 39. Unless otherwise noted, all translations into English are my own – JR.
4 Cited in Stanko Lasić, *Krleža: kronologija života i rada* (Zagreb: Grafički zavod Hrvatske, 1982), 103.
5 Krleža, *Davni dani*, 156.
6 Ibid., 537–8.
7 This concept is indebted to Rebecca Karl's observation on the way in which "Asia" served early Chinese nationalists as a "mediating conceptual and historical structure – a space – that helped link 'China' and the world." Karl, *Staging the World: Chinese Nationalism at the Turn of the Twentieth Century* (Durham, NC: Duke University Press, 2002), 153. Diana Mishkova points to a similar use of the Balkans in the work of Romanian historian Nicolae Iorga, who, she notes, deployed the region as a "mediating zone" to "bridge national history and universal history."

232   Notes to pages 6–7

Mishkova, *Beyond Balkanism: The Scholarly Politics of Region Making* (London: Routledge, 2019), 61.

8 There is a large literature on federalist ideas in Central, East, and Southeast Europe. See, for instance, Rudolf Schlesinger, *Federalism in Central and Eastern Europe* (London: Kegan Paul, Trench, Trubner, 1945); Vojtech Mastny, "The Historical Experience of Federalism in East Central Europe," *East European Politics and Societies* 14, no. 1 (Winter 2000): 64–96; Holly Case, "The Strange Politics of Federative Ideas in East-Central Europe," *Journal of Modern History* 85, no. 4 (December 2013): 833–66; Victor Neumann, "Federalism and Nationalism in the Austro-Hungarian Monarchy: Aurel C. Popovici's Theory," *East European Politics and Societies* 16, no. 3 (2002): 864–97; Eva Boka, "From National Toleration to National Liberation (Three Initiators of Cooperation in Central Europe)," *East European Politics and Societies* 13, no. 3 (1999): 435–74; Samuel J. Wilson, "Lost Opportunities: Lajos Kossuth, the Balkan Nationalities, and the Danubian Confederation," *Hungarian Studies* 8, no. 2 (1993): 171–93; György Szabad, "Lajos Kossuth's Role in the Conceptualization of a Danubian Federation," in *Geopolitics in the Danube Region: Hungarian Reconciliation Efforts, 1848–1997*, ed. Ignac Romsics and Bela Kiraly (Budapest: Central European University Press, 1999), 61–98; L.S. Stavrianos, *Balkan Federation: A History of the Movement toward Balkan Unity in Modern Times* (Northampton, MA: Smith College, 1944); Mark von Hagen, "Federalisms and Pan-Movements: Re-Imagining Empire," in *Russian Empire: Space, People, Power, 1700–1930*, ed. Jane Burbank, Mark Von Hagen, and Anatolyi Remnev (Bloomington: Indiana University Press, 2007), 494–510; Houri Berberian, *Roving Revolutionaries: Armenians and the Connected Revolutions in the Russian, Iranian, and Ottoman Worlds* (Berkeley: University of California Press, 2019), 121–42. For a detailed overview of this tradition of thought, see Balázs Trencsényi et al., *A History of Modern Political Thought in East Central Europe: Volume 1: Negotiating Modernity in the "Long Nineteenth Century"* (Oxford: Oxford University Press, 2016), 512–43.

9 A rich body of literature from geography and history has identified the first age of capitalist globalization as inaugurating a new epoch in the history of the production of space. See David Harvey, *The Limits to Capital* (London: Verso, 2018); Neil Smith, *Uneven Development: Nature, Capital, and the Production of Space* (Athens: University of Georgia Press, 2008); Karl, *Staging the World*; Sebastian Conrad, *Globalisation and the Nation in Imperial Germany*, trans. Sorcha O'Hagan (Cambridge:

Cambridge University Press, 2010); Manu Goswami, *Producing India: From Colonial Economy to National Space* (Chicago, IL: University of Chicago Press, 2004); Michael Goebel, *Overlapping Geographies of Belonging: Migrations, Regions and Nations in the Western South Atlantic* (Washington, DC: American Historical Association, 2013); Berberian, *Roving Revolutionaries*, 41–3; Stephen Kern, *The Culture of Time and Space, 1880–1918* (Cambridge, MA: Harvard University Press, 2003); Jürgen Osterhammel, *The Transformation of the World: A Global History of the Nineteenth Century*, trans. Patrick Camiller (Princeton, NJ: Princeton University Press, 2014), 77–116.

10 An exception to this tendency is Holly Case, who situates the proliferation of federalist visions in a broader international public sphere over the course of the nineteenth century. Case, *The Age of Questions* (Princeton, NJ: Princeton University Press, 2018), 135–52.

11 Similar efforts to frame supranationalism in a global context include Cemil Aydin, *The Politics of Anti-Westernism in Asia: Visions of World Order in Pan-Islamic and Pan-Asian Thought* (New York: Columbia University Press, 2007); Nicole CuUnjieng Aboitiz, *Asian Place, Filipino Nation: A Global Intellectual History of the Philippine Revolution, 1887–1912* (New York: Columbia University Press, 2020); Adom Getachew, *Worldmaking after Empire: The Rise and Fall of Self-Determination* (New York: Columbia University Press, 2019); Clare Newstead, "Scaling Caribbean (In)Dependence," *Geoforum* 36 (2005): 45–58.

12 Victor Roudometof, *Nationalism, Globalization, and Orthodoxy: The Social Origins of Ethnic Conflict in the Balkans* (Westport, CT: Greenwood Press, 2001), 29–45.

13 John Connelly has convincingly argued that this sense of existential precarity became a "regional syndrome" across the nations of Eastern Europe in *From Peoples into Nations: A History of Eastern Europe* (Princeton, NJ: Princeton University Press, 2020), 22–8. On the concept of quasi-states, see Robert Jackson, *Quasi-States: Sovereignty, International Relations and the Third World* (Cambridge: Cambridge University Press, 1990), 5. Vladislav Lilić's forthcoming dissertation promises a rich study of the notion of quasi-sovereignty in South East Europe during the nineteenth century. Lilić, "Laboratory of Statehood: Empire, Law, and International Order in Ottoman Europe, c. 1830–1912" (PhD diss., Vanderbilt University, est. 2024).

14 Ivan T. Berend, *History Derailed: Central and Eastern Europe in the Long Nineteenth Century* (Berkeley: University of California Press, 2003),

234 Notes to pages 7–9

134–80; John Lampe and Marvin Jackson, *Balkan Economic History, 1550–1950: From Imperial Borderlands to Developing Nations* (Bloomington: Indiana University Press, 1982), 297–308.

15 Albeit only following the Balkan Wars of 1912–13. Maria Todorova, *Imagining the Balkans* (Oxford: Oxford University Press, 1997), 121–2.

16 Charles Maier, "Consigning the Twentieth Century to History: Alternative Narratives for the Modern Era," *The American Historical Review* 105, no. 3 (June 2000): 814; John A. Agnew and Luca Muscarà, *Making Political Geography* (Lanham, MD: Rowman and Littlefield, 2012), 61–72; Conrad, *Globalisation and the Nation in Imperial Germany*, 61–2.

17 Osterhammel, *The Transformation of the World*, 108.

18 Berend, *History Derailed*, 156–8, 174; Lampe and Jackson, *Balkan Economic History*, 297–308; Trencsényi et al., *A History of Modern Political Thought in East Central Europe*, 533–4; Klaus Richter, "The Catastrophe of the Present and That of the Future: Expectations for European States from the Great War to the Great Depression," *Contemporary European History* (2023), doi:10.1017/S096077732200100X.

19 Wilson, "Lost Opportunities"; Szabad, "Lajos Kossuth's Role"; Mastny, "The Historical Experience of Federalism in East Central Europe."

20 Stavrianos, *Balkan Federation*, 196–223.

21 Hans Kohn, *Pan-Slavism: Its History and Ideology* (New York: Vintage Books, 1960); Zdeněk V. David, "Frič, Herzen and Bakunin: The Clash of Two Political Cultures," *East European Politics and Societies* 12, no. 1 (Winter 1998): 1–30; von Hagen, "Federalisms and Pan-Movements."

22 Mastny, "The Historical Experience of Federalism in East Central Europe," 72. For an overview of the federalist and supranationalist projects in Eastern Europe during this period, see Trencsényi et al., *A History of Modern Political Thought in East Central Europe*, 512–43.

23 This history would, for instance, encompass federalist projects in West Africa and the Caribbean as well as pan-Islamist, pan-Asianist, or Black internationalist efforts to reconfigure global space in line with alternative world orders. See Frederick Cooper, *Citizenship between Empire and Nation: Remaking France and French Africa, 1945–1960* (Princeton, NJ: Princeton University Press, 2014); Newstead, "Scaling Caribbean (In) Dependence"; Aydin, *The Politics of Anti-Westernism in Asia*; Getachew, *Worldmaking after Empire*.

24 Neil Smith, "Contours of a Spatialized Politics: Homeless Vehicles and the Production of Geographical Scale," *Social Text* 33 (1992): 54–81; Anssi Paasi, *Territories, Boundaries and Consciousness: The Changing*

Geographies of the Finnish-Russian Border (Chichester, GB: John Wiley and Sons, 1996); John Agnew, "The Dramaturgy of Horizons: Geographical Scale in the 'Reconstruction of Italy' by the New Italian Political Parties, 1992–1995," *Political Geography* 16, no. 2 (February 1997): 99–121; Helga Leitner, "Reconfiguring the Spatiality of Power: The Construction of a Supranational Migration Framework for the European Union," *Political Geography* 16, no. 2 (February 1997): 123–43; Andrew Herod, "Labor's Spatial Praxis and the Geography of Contract Bargaining in the US East Coast Longshore Industry, 1953–1989," *Political Geography* 16, no. 2 (February 1997): 145–69; Byron Miller, "Political Action and the Geography of Defense Investment: Geographical Scale and the Representation of the Massachusetts Miracle," *Political Geography* 16, no. 2 (February 1997): 171–85; Kevin R. Cox, "Spaces of Dependence, Spaces of Engagement and the Politics of Scale, or: Looking for Local Politics," *Political Geography* 17, no. 1 (January 1998): 1–23; Sallie Marston, "The Social Construction of Scale," *Progress in Human Geography* 24, no. 2 (June 2000): 219–42; Neil Brenner, "The Limits to Scale? Methodological Reflections on Scalar Structuration," *Progress in Human Geography* 24, no. 4 (December 2001): 591–614; Neil Brenner, *New State Spaces: Urban Governance and the Rescaling of Statehood* (Oxford: Oxford University Press, 2004); Adam Moore, "Rethinking Scale as a Geographical Category: From Analysis to Practice," *Progress in Human Geography* 32, no. 2 (April 2008): 203–25; Danny MacKinnon, "Reconstructing Scale: Towards a New Scalar Politics," *Progress in Human Geography* 35, no. 1 (February 2011): 21–36.

25 MacKinnon, "Reconstructing Scale," 24.

26 Ibid., 25.

27 In this sense, the book responds to Howitt's insistence that spatial scale is best understood "by building up an understanding of complex and dynamic relationships and processes in context." Richard Howitt, "Scale," in *A Companion to Political Geography*, ed. John Agnew, Katharyne Mitchell, and Gerard Toal (Malden, MA: Blackwell Publishing, 2003).

28 The bulk of literature on spatial scales has been preoccupied with studying the transformations brought about by the second wave of globalization starting in the 1970s. See, for instance, Brenner, *New State Spaces*.

29 Neil Smith, "Remaking Scale: Competition and Cooperation in Prenational and Postnational Europe," in *Competitive European Peripheries*, ed. Heikki Eskelinen and Folke Snickars (Berlin: Springer,

236   Notes to pages 10–12

1995), 59–74; Brenner, *New State Spaces*; Leitner, "Reconfiguring the Spatiality of Power"; Quinn Slobodian, *Globalists: The End of Empire and the Birth of Neoliberalism* (Cambridge, MA: Harvard University Press, 2018), 91–120; Philip Cunliffe et al., *Taking Control: Sovereignty and Democracy after Brexit* (Cambridge: Polity Press, 2023).

30 This research is indebted to Clare Newstead's study of West Indian federalism: Newstead, "Scaling Caribbean (In)Dependence," 49. It also draws from Adom Getachew's account of the anti-colonial "worldmaking" of black internationalists in the twentieth century. Getachew, *Worldmaking after Empire*, 107–10.

31 As Manu Goswami has argued, avoiding such a teleological distinction is important for reconstructing the historical futures that animated radical thought in the twentieth century. Goswami, "Imaginary Futures and Colonial Internationalisms," *American Historical Review* 117, no. 5 (December 2012): 1463.

32 Larry Wolff, *Inventing Eastern Europe: The Map of Civilization on the Mind of the Enlightenment* (Stanford, CA: Stanford University Press, 1994); Milica Bakić-Hayden, "Nesting Orientalisms: The Case of Former Yugoslavia," *Slavic Review* 54, no. 4 (Winter 1995): 917–31; Todorova, *Imagining the Balkans*.

33 Byron Miller has demonstrated how spatial scale can serve to obscure the divergence between cultural and political geographies. See Miller, "Political Action and the Geography of Defense Investment," 172–4.

34 Raymond Williams, *Keywords: A Vocabulary of Culture and Society* (New York: Oxford University Press, 1983), 204–7.

35 Few works have set out to examine Yugoslav socialism through a strictly intellectual historical framework. However, works that have studied the formation of socialist politics in Yugoslavia have tended to prioritize themes relating to the national question. See, for instance, Ivan Avakumović, *History of the Communist Party of Yugoslavia*, vol. 1 (Aberdeen, GB: Aberdeen University Press, 1964); Aleksa Đilas, *The Contested Country: Yugoslav Unity and Communist Revolution, 1919–1953* (Cambridge, MA: Harvard University Press, 1991); Mladen Iveković, *Hrvatska lijeva inteligencija 1918–1945* (Zagreb: Naprijed, 1970); Gordana Vlajčić, *Revolucija i nacije: evolucija stavova vodstva KPJ i Kominterne 1919–1929. godine* (Zagreb: Centar za kulturnu djetlatnost SSO, 1978); Dennison Rusinow, *The Yugoslav Experiment* (Berkeley: University of California Press, 1977); Janko Pleterski, *Nacija Jugoslavija revolucija* (Beograd: Komunist, 1985). In recent years this has begun to change, as scholars have looked beyond the national question and in the

process placed Yugoslav socialism within more expansive geographic horizons. These works have, however, tended to remain within the post-World War II era: Miroslav Perišić, *Od Staljina ka Sartru: formiranje jugoslovenske inteligencije na evropskim univerzitetima 1945–1958* (Beograd: Zavod za udžbenike, 2012); Bojana Videkanić, *Nonaligned Modernism: Socialist Post-colonial Aesthetics in Yugoslavia, 1945–1985* (Montreal and Kingston: McGill-Queen's University Press, 2020); Zvonimir Stopić, *Revolucionari, revizionisti, dogmatičari, pseta i ludaci: Kina i Jugoslavija od 1948. do 1971* (Zagreb: Srednja Evropa, 2022). An account of the global dimensions of Yugoslav socialist thought over the scope of the long twentieth century is currently lacking.

36 David Harvey, *The Condition of Postmodernity: An Enquiry into the Origins of Cultural Change* (Malden, MA: Blackwell, 1990), 264.

37 E.P. Thomson, *The Age of Empire, 1875–1914* (New York: Vintage, 1989); C.A. Bayly, *The Birth of the Modern World, 1780–1914: Global Connections and Comparison* (Malden, MA: Blackwell, 2004); Sugata Bose, *A Hundred Horizons: The Indian Ocean in the Age of Global Empire* (Cambridge, MA: Harvard University Press, 2006); Vanessa Ogle, *The Global Transformation of Time, 1870–1950* (Cambridge, MA: Harvard University Press, 2015); Osterhammel, *The Transformation of the World*; Conrad, *Globalisation and the Nation in Imperial Germany*; Goswami, *Producing India*.

38 On this "global turn" in intellectual history, see Samuel Moyn and Andrew Sartori, eds, *Global Intellectual History* (New York: Columbia University Press, 2013).

39 Kris Alexanderson, *Subversive Seas: Anti-colonial Networks across the Twentieth-Century Dutch Empire* (Cambridge: Cambridge University Press, 2019); Benedict Anderson, *The Age of Globalization: Anarchists and the Anti-colonial Imagination* (London: Verso, 2013); Houri Berberian, *Roving Revolutionaries*; CuUnjieng Aboitiz, *Asian Place, Filipino Nation*; Getachew, *Worldmaking after Empire*; Michael Goebel, *Anti-imperial Metropolis: Interwar Paris and the Seeds of Third World Nationalism* (Cambridge: Cambridge University Press, 2017); Ilham Khuri-Makdisi, *The Eastern Mediterranean and the Making of Global Radicalism, 1860–1914* (Berkeley: University of California Press, 2010); Kris Manjapra, *M.N. Roy: Marxism and Colonial Cosmopolitanism* (London: Routledge, 2010); Maia Ramnath, *Haj to Utopia: How the Ghadar Movement Charted Global Radicalism and Attempted to Overthrow the British Empire* (Berkeley: University of California Press, 2011).

238 Notes to pages 13–17

40 Karl, *Staging the World*; CuUnjieng Aboitiz, *Asian Place, Filipino Nation*. As evidence of the growing sense of global synchronicity during this period, see Aydin, *The Politics of Anti-Westernism in Asia*, 71–2.

41 Smith, *Uneven Development*, 121.

42 Ibid., 119–23, 132–74. On the notion of geographic differentiation, see also Neil Brenner, "Critical Sociospatial Theory and the Geographies of Uneven Spatial Development," in *The SAGE Handbook of Economic Geography*, ed. Andrew Leyshon, Roger Lee, Linda Mcdowell, and Peter Sunley (Los Angeles: SAGE, 2011), 135–148; Goswami, *Producing India*, 39–42.

43 Brenner, "Critical Sociospatial Theory and the Geographies of Uneven Spatial Development," 142–5.

44 Maier, "Consigning the Twentieth Century to History," 818.

45 Osterhammel, *The Transformation of the World*, 108.

46 Karl, *Staging the World*, 6–17; Conrad, *Globalisation and the Nation in Imperial Germany*, 27–76; Goswami, *Producing India*, 40–72.

47 Deborah R. Coen, *Climate in Motion: Science, Empire, and the Problem of Scale* (Chicago, IL: University of Chicago Press, 2018), 17.

48 Case, *The Age of Questions*, 135.

49 Ibid., 137.

50 Henri Lefebvre, *The Production of Space*, trans. Donald Nicholson-Smith (Oxford: Blackwell, 1991), 39. For a discussion of Lefebvre's levels of spatial analysis and their various interpretations, see Łukasz Stanek, *Henri Lefebvre on Space: Architecture, Urban Research, and the Production of Theory* (Minneapolis: University of Minnesota Press, 2011), 128–9. For a study that applies this framework to Eastern Europe, see Yvonne Živković, *Literary Politics of Mitteleuropa: Reconfiguring Spatial Memory in Austrian and Yugoslav Literature after 1945* (Rochester, NY: Camden House, 2021), 12–13.

51 CuUnjieng Aboitiz, *Asian Place, Filipino Nation*, 27.

52 David Damrosch, *What Is World Literature?* (Princeton, NJ: Princeton University Press, 2003), 3–4. On the place of world literature in *The Communist Manifesto*, see Martin Puchner, *Poetry of the Revolution: Marx, Manifestos, and the Avant-Gardes* (Princeton, NJ: Princeton University Press, 2006), 47–66.

53 Karl Marx and Friedrich Engels, *The Communist Manifesto: A Modern Edition* (London: Verso, 2012), 39.

54 Fredric Jameson, "Third World Literature in the Era of Multinational Capitalism," *Social Text* 15 (Autumn 1986): 65–88; Franco Moretti, *Atlas of the European Novel, 1800–1900* (London: Verso, 1998); Franco

Moretti, "Conjectures on World Literature," *New Left Review* 54, no. 1 (January 2000): 54–68; Pascale Casanova, *The World Republic of Letters*, trans. M.B. DeBevoise (Cambridge, MA: Harvard University Press, 2004); Amir Mufti, *Forget English! Orientalisms and World Literatures* (Cambridge, MA: Harvard University Press, 2016).

55 Mufti, *Forget English!*, 19–32; Casanova, *The World Republic of Letters*, 87–90.

56 Casanova, *The World Republic of Letters*, 126–7.

57 Ibid., 85–7.

58 Joep Leerssen, "Oral Epic: The Nation Finds a Voice" in *Folklore and Nationalism in Europe during the Long Nineteenth Century*, ed. Timothy Baycroft and David Hopkin (Leiden, NL: Brill, 2012), 11–26.

59 Zoran Milutinović, *Getting Over Europe: The Construction of Europe in Serbian Culture* (Amsterdam: Rodopi, 2011), 16.

60 Anca Parvulescu and Manuela Boatcă, *Creolizing the Modern: Transylvania across Empires* (Ithaca, NY: Cornell University Press, 2022), 8.

61 Casanova, *The World Republic of Letters*; Moretti, "Conjectures on World Literature"; Jameson, "Third World Literature in the Era of Multinational Capitalism." On Jameson's place in the cross-fertilization of world systems theory and world literary theory, see James Christie, "Fredric Jameson and the Rise of World Literature: From World Systems Theory to Uneven and Combined Development," in *Cultures of Uneven Development: From International Relations to World Literature*, ed. James Christie and Nesrin Degirmencioglu (Leiden, NL: Brill, 2019), 199–223. A major exception here is Harsha Ram, whose work has engaged the place of spatial scale in the formation of a world literary field. See Ram, "The Scale of Global Modernisms: Imperial, National, Regional, Local," *PMLA* 131, no. 5 (October 2016): 1372–85.

62 Casanova, *The World Republic of Letters*, 45–8. In this sense, Casanova's argument parallels much of Jameson's interpretation of the Third World novel as a national allegory. See Jameson, "Third-World Literature in the Era of Multinational Capitalism."

63 The concept of mediating spaces also offers a corrective to Jameson's reading of the Third World novel as a national allegory, which, as Akhil Gupta notes, posits a "binary opposition between a first and third world … [that] leads to the over-valorization of nationalist ideology." Gupta, "The Song of the Nonaligned World: Transnational Identities and the Reinscription of Space in Late Capitalism," *Cultural Anthropology* 7, no. 1 (February 1992): 75. For an elaboration of this argument, see Aijaz Ahmad, *In Theory: Classes, Nations, Literatures* (London: Verso, 2000), 43–71.

240 Notes to page 19

64 This critique leans heavily on Neil Brenner's analysis of the work of Immanuel Wallerstein in "The Space of the World: Beyond State-Centrism?" in *Immanuel Wallerstein and the Problem of World: System, Scale, Culture*, ed. David Palumbo-Liu, Bruce Robbins, and Nirvana Tanoukhi, (Durham, NC: Duke University Press, 2011), 117.

65 This perception of the geographical unevenness of world culture explains the preoccupation with cultural geographies in the work of so many writers on the Yugoslav Left. Consider, for instance, the proliferation of different geographies that animate Miroslav Krleža's short story with which this introduction opened. On the prominence of spatial concepts in Krleža's work, see Aleksandar Flaker, *Poetika osporavanja: avangarda i književna ljevica* (Zagreb: Školska knjiga, 1982), 142–54. Nor has the preoccupation with cultural geographies in Yugoslav literature been limited to writers of the Left. A number of recent works highlight this spatial dimension: Zoran Milutinović, "Territorial Trap: Danilo Kiš, Cultural Geography and Geopolitical Imagination," *East European Politics and Society* 28, no. 4 (November 2014): 715–38; Tyrus Miller, "Rethinking Central Europe: The Symbolic Geography of the Avant-Garde," *Modernism/Modernity* 10, no. 3 (September 2003): 559–67; Jessie Labov, *Transatlantic Central Europe: Contesting Geography and Redefining Culture beyond the Nation* (Budapest: Central European University Press, 2019); Dušan Bijelić, *Normalizing the Balkans: Geopolitics of Psychoanalysis and Psychiatry* (Farnham, GB: Ashgate, 2011); Milutinović, *Getting Over Europe*; Živković, *Literary Politics of Mitteleuropa*. Note also the frequent appearance of geographical terms in Marijeta Božović's "Introduction" to *After Yugoslavia: The Cultural Spaces of a Vanished Land*, ed. Radmila Gorup (Stanford, CA: Stanford University Press, 2013), 1–22.

66 James M. Robertson, "Dispatches from the Appendix of Europe: Miroslav Krleža's Abject Modernism," *Papers on Language and Literature* 55, no. 3 (Summer 2019): 227–55.

67 August Cesarec, "Annamu na Balkanu," *Plamen*, 12 (1919): 211–5.

68 Marko Ristić, "O modernom i o modernizmu, opet" *Delo* 1, no. 1 (March 1955): 51–71.

69 Stavrianos, *Balkan Federation*; Roudometof, *Nationalism, Globalization and Orthodoxy*; Dejan Đokić, *Elusive Compromise: A History of Interwar Yugoslavia* (New York: Columbia University Press, 2007); Đilas, *The Contested Country*; Sabrina Ramet, *Nationalism and Federalism in Yugoslavia, 1962–1991* (Bloomington: Indiana University Press, 1992); Andrew Wachtel, *Making a Nation, Breaking a Nation: Literature and*

Cultural Politics in Yugoslavia (Stanford, CA: Stanford University Press, 1998); Hilde Katrine Haug, *Creating a Socialist Yugoslavia: Tito, Communist Leadership and the National Question* (London: IB Tauris, 2012); Dejan Jović, *Yugoslavia: A State that Withered Away* (West Lafayette, IN: Purdue University Press, 2009). One notable exception, which aims to look at regional federalism outside of its reference to the national question, is Pavlos Hatzopoulos, *The Balkans beyond Nationalism and Identity: International Relations and Ideology* (London: IB Tauris, 2008).

70 The major exception to this tendency is the work of revisionist historians of the Yugoslav self-management system, who have foregrounded the international context of the development of Yugoslav socialism. See Susan Woodward, *Socialist Unemployment: The Political Economy of Yugoslavia, 1945–1990* (Princeton, NJ: Princeton University Press, 1995) and Vladimir Unkovski-Korica, *The Economic Struggle for Power in Tito's Yugoslavia: From World War II to Non-Alignment* (London: IB Tauris, 2016).

71 Ivo Banac, *The National Question in Yugoslavia: Origins, History, Politics* (Ithaca, NY: Cornell University Press, 1984), 70–114; Dennison Rusinow, "The Yugoslav Idea before Yugoslavia" in *Yugoslavism: Histories of a Failed Idea, 1918–1992*, ed. Dejan Đokić (London: Hurst and Co., 2003), 11–26; and Wachtel, *Making a Nation*, 19–53. For an account of how these nationalist ambitions played out through claims to the space of Bosnia and Herzegovina, see Edin Hajdarpašić, *Whose Bosnia? Nationalism and Political Imagination in the Balkans, 1840–1914* (Ithaca, NY: Cornell University Press, 2015).

72 On the tension between unitarist and supranationalist models of Yugoslavism, see Banac, *The National Question in Yugoslavia*; Wachtel, *Making a Nation*.

73 The significance of the global economic restructuring of the 1970s has been expertly demonstrated by Fritz Bartel in *The Triumph of Broken Promises: The End of the Cold War and the Rise of Neoliberalism* (Cambridge, MA: Harvard University Press, 2022).

74 Todorova, *Imagining the Balkans*.

75 Helpfully, Todorova has since produced an excellent study of the movement for Balkan federalism in Bulgaria in *The Lost World of Socialists at Europe's Margins: Imagining Utopia, 1870s–1920s* (London: Bloomsbury Academic Publishing, 2020).

76 Bakić-Hayden, "Nestling Orientalisms"; Wolff, *Inventing Eastern Europe*; Todorova, *Imagining the Balkans*.

242   Notes to pages 25–7

CHAPTER ONE

1   On the history of Italian-Ottoman imperial rivalry in Africa, see Mostafa
    Minawi, *The Ottoman Scramble for Africa: Empire and Diplomacy in the
    Sahara and the Hijaz* (Stanford, CA: Stanford University Press, 2016),
    61–79; Ali Abdullatif Ahmida, "State and Class Formation and
    Collaboration in Colonial Libya," in *Italian Colonialism*, ed. Ruth Ben-
    Ghiat and Mia Fuller (New York: Palgrave Macmillan, 2005), 59–72.
2   Francesco Caccamo, "Italy, Libya and the Balkans," in *The Wars before
    the Great War: Conflict and International Politics before the Outbreak of
    the First World War*, ed. William Mulligan, Andreas Rose, and Dominick
    Geppert (Cambridge: Cambridge University Press, 2016), 21–40.
3   Quoted in L.S. Stavrianos, "The Balkan Federation Movement: A Neglected
    Aspect," *The American Historical Review* 48, no. 1 (1942): 31–2.
4   "Protest protiv rata: miting od 23 Oktobra," *Radničke novine*,
    25 October 1911, 2.
5   Both Rebecca Karl and Nicole CuUnjieng Aboitiz point to the ways in
    which early anticolonial movements conceived of political and cultural
    affiliation through geographical frames of reference: Karl, *Staging the
    World: Chinese Nationalism at the Turn of the Twentieth Century*
    (Durham, NC: Duke University Press, 2002) and CuUnjieng Aboitiz, *Asian
    Place, Filipino Nation: A Global Intellectual History of the Philippine
    Revolution, 1887–1912* (New York: Columbia University Press, 2020).
    See also Sebastian Conrad and Dominic Sachsenmaier, "Introduction," in
    *Competing Visions of World Order: Global Moments and Movements,
    1880s–1930s*, ed. Sebastian Conrad and Dominic Sachsenmaier (New
    York: Palgrave Macmillan, 2007), 11–12; Michael Goebel, *Overlapping
    Geographies of Belonging: Migrations, Regions, and Nations in the
    Western South Atlantic* (Washington, DC: American Historical
    Association, 2013). In this regard, we can also point to the rise of geopol-
    itics as an interdisciplinary approach to world politics that foregrounded
    geographic factors in determining the dynamics of state formation, expan-
    sion, and decline. See John Agnew and Luca Muscarà, *Making Political
    Geography* (Lanham, MD: Rowman and Littlefield, 2012), 61–72; David
    Thomas Murphy, *The Heroic Earth: Geopolitical Thought in Weimar
    Germany* (Kent, OH: Kent State University Press, 1997), 2–8. Vanessa
    Ogle also notes a similar tendency to think in terms of geographic regions
    when it comes to mapping the temporal divisions of world space. Ogle,
    The Global Transformation of Time, 1870–1950 (Cambridge, MA:
    Harvard University Press, 2015), 27–8.

Notes to pages 28–30

6 Giovanni Arrighi, *The Long Twentieth Century: Money, Power and the Origins of Our Times* (London: Verso, 2010), 272–5.

7 Jürgen Osterhammel, *The Transformation of the World: A Global History of the Nineteenth Century*, trans. Patrick Camiller (Princeton, NJ: Princeton University Press, 2014), 107–8.

8 John Komlos, *The Habsburg Monarchy as a Customs Union: Economic Development in Austria-Hungary in the Nineteenth Century* (Princeton, NJ: Princeton University Press, 1983), 5; John Lampe and Marvin Jackson, *Balkan Economic History, 1550–1950: From Imperial Borderlands to Developing Nations* (Bloomington: Indiana University Press, 1982), 124, 128.

9 W.O. Henderson, *Genesis of the Common Market* (London: Frank Cass, 1962), 56–63; Ivan Berend, *History Derailed: Central and Eastern Europe in the Long Nineteenth Century* (Berkeley: University of California Press, 2005), 138.

10 Manu Goswami, *Producing India: From Colonial Economy to National Space* (Chicago, IL: University of Chicago Press, 2004), 42.

11 Barbara Jelavich, *History of the Balkans: Eighteenth and Nineteenth Centuries* (Cambridge: Cambridge University Press, 1983), 244; Gale Stokes, *Politics as Development: The Emergence of Political Parties in Nineteenth-Century Serbia* (Durham, NC: Duke University Press, 1990), 11; Dimitrije Đorđević, "Ottoman Heritage versus Modernization: Symbiosis in Serbia during the Nineteenth Century," *Serbian Studies* 13 (1999): 36.

12 Lampe and Jackson, *Balkan Economic History*, 121–5.

13 Ibid., 130–1.

14 Jelavich, *History of the Balkans*, 244–5.

15 Dušan Bataković, *The Foreign Policy of Serbia (1844–1867): Ilija Garašanin's* Načertanije (Belgrade: Institute for Balkan Studies, 2014), 254–8.

16 Arrighi, *The Long Twentieth Century*, 273; Cornelius Torp, *The Challenges of Globalization: Economy and Politics in Germany, 1860–1914*, trans. Alex Skinner (New York: Berghahn, 2014), 112–13.

17 Arrighi, *The Long Twentieth Century*, 273–5; Sebastian Conrad, *Globalisation and the Nation in Imperial Germany*, trans. Sorcha O'Hagan (Cambridge: Cambridge University Press, 2010), 67–9.

18 The Pig Wars were a series of trade embargoes imposed by Austria-Hungary on Serbian hog exports in response to Serbian efforts to form a customs union with Bulgaria. The embargoes remain a pointed example of the weaponization of trade policy in service to geopolitical ends. Lampe and Jackson, *Balkan Economic History*, 175–6.

244 Notes to pages 30–4

19 Ibid., *Balkan Economic History*, 211.
20 Augusta Dimou, *Entangled Paths towards Modernity: Contextualizing Socialism and Nationalism in the Balkans* (Budapest: Central European University Press, 2009), 93–4.
21 Ibid., 138.
22 Stokes, *Politics as Development*, 197.
23 Ibid., 197–8, 201–2, 207–16.
24 Loukianos Hassiotis, "The Ideal of Balkan Unity from a European Perspective (1789–1945)," *Balcanica* 41 (2010): 209–29.
25 Latinka Perović, *Srpski socijalisti 19. veka, II: ideje i pokret Svetozara Markovića* (Beograd: Rad, 1985), 335. On the longer influence of the Swiss model for ideas of Balkan federalism, see Vladislav Lilić, "Balkan Intellectuals and Plans for a Balkan Federation in the 1860s and 1870s: American and Swiss Models in the Political Thought of Vladimir Jovanović and Lyuben Karavelov" (Master's thesis, Universität Wien, 2016).
26 Dimou, *Entangled Paths towards Modernity*, 17–37.
27 Stavrianos, *Balkan Federation*, 115–16; Perović, *Srpski socijalisti 19. veka: II*, 333–7; Woodford McClellan, *Svetozar Marković and the Origins of Balkan Socialism* (Princeton, NJ: Princeton University Press, 1964), 184–6.
28 An intriguing examination of the legal and temporal politics of the states rights argument is Natasha Wheatley's "Legal Pluralism as Temporal Pluralism: Historical Rights, Legal Vitalism, and Non-Synchronous Sovereignty" in *Power and Time: Temporalities in Conflict and the Making of History*, ed. Dan Edelstein, Stefanos Geroulanos, and Natasha Wheatley (Chicago: University of Chicago Press, 2020), 53–79.
29 Svetozar Marković, "Slovenska Austrija i srpsko jedinstvo," in *Celokupna dela V*, ed. Radomir Lukić (Beograd: Zavod za udžbenike i nastavna sredstva, 1995), 97.
30 Svetozar Marković, "Manjina i većina" in *Celokupna dela I*, ed. Radomir Lukić (Beograd: Narodna knjiga, 1987), 193.
31 Ibid., 193.
32 Leszek Kołakowski, *Main Currents of Marxism*, trans. P.S. Falla (New York: W.W. Norton, 2005), 605–7.
33 Svetozar Marković, "Srbija na istoku" in *Celokupna dela VIII*, ed. Radomir Lukić (Beograd: Zavod za udžbenike i nastavna sredstva, 1995), 16–19.
34 Ibid., 29.
35 Ibid., 42, 68.
36 Ibid., 69.

Notes to pages 34–8

37 Ibid., 70–1.
38 Ibid., 75.
39 Ibid., 19, 73.
40 Ibid., 84.
41 As McClellan notes, in taking this approach, Marković was closely aligned with the thinking of his Russian contemporary, Nikolai Chernyshevskii, and both presaged the later Marxist arguments of Parvus and Leon Trotsky. See McClellan, *Svetozar Marković*, 198–9.
42 Marković, "Srbija na istoku," 97.
43 Branko Nadoveza, *Balkanski socialisti i balkanska federacija* (Belgrade: Zadužbina Andrejević, 1997), 13; Stokes, *Politics as Development*, 221–4.
44 The most thorough study of Tucović's social thought to date is Desanka Savićević, *Društvena i politička teorija i kritika u radovima Dimitrija Tucovića* (Belgrade: Rad, 1972).
45 On the influence of German social democracy among Serbian and Bulgarian socialists, see Georges Haupt, *Aspects of International Socialism, 1871–1914* (Cambridge: Cambridge University Press, 1986), 48–80; Maria Todorova, *The Lost World of Socialists at Europe's Margins: Imagining Utopia, 1870s–1920s* (London: Bloomsbury Academic Publishing, 2020), 31–3.
46 Blagovest Njagulov, "Early Socialism in the Balkans: Ideas and Practices in Serbia, Romania and Albania," in *Entangled Histories of the Balkans: Volume Two: Transfers of Political Ideologies and Institutions*, ed. Roumen Daskalov and Diana Mishkova (Leiden, NL: Brill, 2014), 234.
47 Haupt, *Aspects of International Socialism*, 63.
48 In addition to major studies such as John Hobson's *Imperialism: A Study* (1902), Rudolf Hilferding's *Finance Capital* (1910), Rosa Luxemburg's *Accumulation of Capital* (1913), Vladimir Lenin's *Imperialism, the Highest Stage of Capitalism* (1916), and Nikolai Bukharin's *Imperialism and World Economy* (1917), leading socialist theoreticians including Karl Kautsky, Otto Bauer, Max Beer, Julian Marchlewski, and Karl Radek set out to grapple with the changing nature of capitalism in the age of imperialism. An excellent anthology of texts on the question by theorists of the Second International can be found in Richard B. Day and Daniel Gaido, ed., *Discovering Imperialism: Social Democracy to World War I* (Leiden, NL: Brill, 2012). For a historical overview of this question, see Alex Callinicos, *Imperialism and Global Political Economy* (Cambridge: Polity Press, 2009), 23–67.
49 Dimitrije Tucović, "Govor na zboru u beogradu, 26 Avgusta (8 Septembra) 1912. godine. o 'događajima na balkanu i socijalnoj demokratiji,'" in *Sabrana dela 6* (Belgrade: Rad, 1980), 516.

246 Notes to pages 38–42

50 The quotation is from the final resolution of the First Balkan Social Democratic Conference, which Tucović himself helped to draft. See "Resolution of the First Balkan Social Democratic Conference," trans. Andreja Živković, in *The Balkan Socialist Tradition*, ed. Andreja Živković and Dragan Plavšić (London: Porcupine Press, 2003), 164–5.

51 Dimitrije Tucović, *Srbija i Arbanija* (Belgrade: Kultura, 1946), 111–12.

52 Ibid., 112. Italics in the original.

53 Todorova, *The Lost World of Socialists at Europe's Margins*, 56.

54 Dmitrije Tucović, "Politički momenat u borbi oko trgovinskoga ugovora između Srbije i Austro-Ugarske," *Sabrana dela* 7 (Belgrade: Rad, 1980), 421–6.

55 Dimitrije Tucović, "What We Say," trans. Dragan Plavšić and Andreja Živković, in *The Balkan Socialist Tradition*, 144–5.

56 As Rebecca Karl has demonstrated, this ability to draw equivalences across broad geographic expanses was critical to the formation of anti-colonial and nationalist thought. See Karl, *Staging the World*. Harry Harootunian has also highlighted the ways in which such modes of geographical comparison were made possible through a new temporal order that emerged from this era of global capitalist integration and imperialist expansion. Harootunian, "Remembering the Historical Present," *Critical Inquiry* 33, no. 3 (Spring 2007): 478–84.

57 Dmitrije Tucović, "Kad gori oko nas, smemo li ćutati?" in *Sabrana dela* 6, 507–8.

58 On the notion of quasi-sovereignty, see Robert Jackson, *Quasi-States: Sovereignty, International Relations, and the Third World* (Cambridge: Cambridge University Press, 1990).

59 Haupt, *Aspects of International Socialism*, 74–5; G.D.H. Cole, *A History of Socialist Thought: Volume 3, Part 2: The Second International, 1889–1914* (London: MacMillan, 1960), 554–8; Pieter Judson, *The Habsburg Empire: A New History* (Cambridge, MA: Harvard University Press, 2016), 372–4.

60 Todorova, *The Lost World of Socialists at Europe's Margins*, 57–9.

61 Karl Kautsky, "The National Tasks of the Socialists among the Balkan Slavs," trans. Barbara Rampoldi, in *The Balkan Socialist Tradition*, 157–63.

62 Todorova, *The Lost World of Socialists at Europe's Margins*, 59.

63 On the place of Macedonia in the emerging Ottoman capitalist economy, see Costas Lapavitsas and Pinar Cakiroglu-Bournos, *Capitalism in the Ottoman Balkans: Industrialization and Modernity in Macedonia* (London: IB Tauris, 2021).

Notes to pages 42–5

64 Tucović, *Srbija I Arbanija*, 117. On the use of violence in the Balkan Wars, see Siniša Malešević, *Grounded Nationalisms: A Sociological Analysis* (Cambridge: Cambridge University Press, 2019), 166–72.
65 Tucović, *Srbija i Arbanija*, 118–19.
66 Ibid., 111.
67 Ibid.
68 See, for instance, Dragiša Lapčević, "Against War: Speech in Serbian parliament, 31 July 1914," trans. Dragan Plavšić, in *The Balkan Socialist Tradition*, 234.

CHAPTER TWO

1 Jakub Beneš, "The Green Cadres and the Collapse of Austria-Hungary in 1918," *Past and Present* 236, no. 1 (August 2017): 207–41.
2 Ivo Banac, *The National Question in Yugoslavia: Origins, History, Politics* (Ithaca, NY: Cornell University Press, 1984), 127, 248–60, 291–327; Miranda Vickers, *Between Serb and Albanian: A History of Kosovo* (New York: Columbia University Press, 1998), 99–102.
3 Ivan Očak, "Povratnici iz sovjetske rusije u borbi za stvaranje ilegalnih komunističkih organizacija uoči prvog kongresa SRPJ(k)," *Historijski zbornik* 27–8 (1974–75): 1–26. The short-lived Hungarian Soviet Republic also served as an important training ground for early Yugoslav communists, giving them concrete experience in organizing revolution. See András Siklós, *Revolution in Hungary and the Dissolution of the Multinational State* (Budapest: Akadémiai Kiadó, 1988), 138; Milan Vesović, *Revolucionarna štampa u kraljevini srba, hrvata i slovenaca, 1918–1929* (Belgrade: Institut za savremenu istoriju, 1979), 25; Vujica Kovačev, *Na zajedničkom frontu revolucije: veze između jugoslovenskih i mađarskih komunista 1918–1919 i učešće jugoslovena u mađarskoj revoluciji 1919* (Belgrade: Institut za savremenu istoriju, 1987); Očak, "Povratnici iz sovjetske rusije," 16.
4 Aleksa Đilas, *The Contested Country: Yugoslav Unity and Communist Revolution, 1919–1953* (Cambridge, MA: Harvard University Press, 1991), 63; Banac, *The National Question in Yugoslavia*, 328–32.
5 Klaus Richter, *Fragmentation in East Central Europe: Poland and the Baltics, 1915–1929* (Oxford: Oxford University Press, 2020).
6 Nicole Jordan, *The Popular Front and Central Europe: The Dilemmas of French Impotence, 1918–1940* (Cambridge: Cambridge University Press, 1992).

248 Notes to pages 45–50

7 Quoted in Ivan Avakumović, *History of the Communist Party of Yugoslavia, Volume I* (Aberdeen, GB: Aberdeen University Press, 1964), 50–1.

8 John Riddell, ed., *To See the Dawn: Baku, 1920, First Congress of the Peoples of the East* (New York: Pathfinder Press, 1993), 121.

9 Pavlos Hatzopoulos, *The Balkans beyond Nationalism and Identity: International Relations and Ideology* (London: IB Tauris, 2008), 69–96.

10 Slavoljub Cvetković, "Balkanska komunistička federacija i makedonsko nacionalno pitanje," *Istorija 20. Veka*, 12, no. 2 (1994): 49–59.

11 L.S. Stavrianos, *Balkan Federation: A History of the Movement towards Balkan Unity in Modern Times* (Hamden, CT: Archon Books, 1964), 196–223. Stefan Gužvica's forthcoming manuscript, *Sickle without a Hammer: Communism and Nation-Building in the Balkans, 1900–1930s*, promises a rich account of interwar communism's Balkan federalism. On the relationship between the Stamboliiski government and the Comintern, see Alex Toshkov's *Agrarianism as Modernity in Twentieth-Century Europe: The Golden Age of the Peasantry* (London: Bloomsbury, 2019).

12 Maria Todorova, *Imagining the Balkans* (Oxford: Oxford University Press, 2009), 38–43; Zoran Milutinović, *Getting over Europe: The Construction of Europe in Serbian Culture* (Amsterdam: Rodopi, 2011); Vladimir Gvozden, "Writing Difference/Claiming General Validity: Jovan Dučić's *Cities and Chimaeras* and the West," in *Balkan Departures: Travel Writing from Southeastern Europe*, ed. Wendy Bracewell and Alex Drace-Frances (New York: Berghahn Books, 2009), 75–86.

13 Avakumović, *History of the Communist Party of Yugoslavia*, 54–6.

14 Vesović, *Revolucionarna štampa*, 83–6; Mladen Iveković, *Hrvatska lijeva inteligencija, 1918–1945* (Zagreb: Naprijed, 1970), 105–6.

15 Steven Lee, *The Ethnic Avant-Garde: Minority Cultures and World Revolution* (New York: Columbia University Press, 2015), 2.

16 On Krleža's relationship with the interwar communist movement, see Ivan Očak, *Krleža-partija: Miroslav Krleža u radničkom i komunističkom pokretu, 1917–1941* (Zagreb: Spektar, 1982).

17 Stanko Lasić, *Krleža, kronologija života i rada* (Zagreb: Grafički zavod hrvatske, 1982), 83, 148–9.

18 Ibid., 95.

19 Ibid., 103–5.

20 Quoted in ibid., 117.

21 The title of "ban" corresponded to that of viceroy. Zorica Stipetić, *Argumenti za revoluciju – August Cesarec* (Zagreb: Centar društvenih djelatnosti, 1982), 26–8, 37–8.

22 Ibid., 48.

Notes to pages 50–5   249

23 Ibid., 76–7.
24 Lasić, *Krleža*, 148.
25 Krleža, "Hrvatska književna laž," *Plamen* 1 (1919): 39.
26 Ibid., 32.
27 Ibid., 34.
28 Ibid., 36. Many thanks to Ellen Elias-Bursać for her help in translating this passage.
29 Ibid., 38.
30 On the influence of Nietzsche on Krleža's work, see Jan Wierzbicki, *Miroslav Krleža* (Zagreb: Liber, 1980).
31 Krleža, "Hrvatska književna laž," 40.
32 Ibid., 40.
33 "Internationala aeterna," *Plamen* 5–6 (1919): 239.
34 August Cesarec, "Annamu na Balkanu," *Plamen* 12 (1919): 213.
35 Ibid., 213.
36 There is an impressive body of scholarship on the history of *Zenit* in English: Vidosava Golubović, "The *Zenit* Periodical (1921–1926)" in *Zenit, 1921–1926*, ed. Vidosava Golubović and Irina Subotić (Belgrade: Narodna Biblioteka Srbije, 2008), 469–76; Aleš Erjavec, "The Three Avant-Gardes and Their Context: The Early, the Neo, and the Postmodern," in *Impossible Histories: Historical Avant-Gardes, Neo-Avant-Gardes, and Post-Avant-Gardes in Yugoslavia, 1918–1991*, ed. Dubravka Đurić and Miško Šuvaković (Cambridge, MA: MIT Press, 2003), 36–62; Igor Marjanović, "*Zenit*: Peripatetic Discourses of Ljubomir Micić and Branko Ve Poljanski," in *On the Very Edge: Modernism and Modernity in the Arts and Architecture of Interwar Serbia (1918–1941)*, ed. Jelena Bogdanović, Lilien Filipovitch Robinson, and Igor Marjanović (Leuven, BE: Leuven University Press, 2014), 63–84; Marijeta Božović, "*Zenit* Rising: Return to a Balkan Avant-Garde," in *After Yugoslavia: The Cultural Spaces of a Vanished Land*, ed. Radmila Gorup (Stanford, CA: Stanford University Press, 2013), 135–48; Andreas Kramer, "Europa Minor: Yvan and Claire Goll's Europe," in *Europa! Europa?: The Avant-Garde, Modernism and the Fate of a Continent*, ed. Sascha Bru et al. (Berlin: De Gruyter, 2009), 126–37.
37 Ljubomir Micić, "Savremeno novo i slučeno slikarstvo," *Zenit* 10 (Decembar 1921): 11.
38 Branko Ve Poljanski, "Alarm," *Zenit* 21 (February 1923): 5.
39 On the question of *Zenit*'s critique of Europeanism as anachronistic, see Radomir Konstantinović, "Ko je barbarogenije," *Treći program* (Spring 1969): 9–21.

250 Notes to pages 56–60

40 Ljubomir Micić, "Delo zenitizma," *Zenit* 8 (October 1921): 2.

41 Todorova, *Imagining the Balkans*, 17–18.

42 Ljubomir Micić, "Zenitist Manifesto," trans. Maja Starčević, in *Between Worlds: A Sourcebook of Central European Avant-Gardes, 1910-1930*, ed. Timothy O. Benson and Eva Foracs (Cambridge, MA: MIT Press, 2002), 284.

43 Konstantinović makes this point in "Ko je barbarogenije," 11–12.

44 Elazar Barkan and Ronald Bush, ed., *Prehistories of the Future: The Primitivist Project and the Culture of Modernism* (Stanford, CA: Stanford University Press, 1995); Sieglinde Lemke, *Primitivist Modernism: Black Culture and the Origins of Transatlantic Modernism* (Oxford: Oxford University Press, 1998); Carole Sweeney, *From Fetish to Subject: Race, Modernism, and Primitivism, 1919–1935* (Westport, CT: Praeger, 2004); Frances C. Connelly, *The Sleep of Reason: Primitivism in Modern European Art and Aesthetics, 1725–1907* (Philadelphia: Pennsylvania State University Press, 1995).

45 Timothy Brennan, "Postcolonial Studies between the European Wars: An Intellectual History," in *Marxism, Modernity, and Postcolonial Studies*, ed. Crystal Bartolovich and Neil Lazarus (Cambridge: Cambridge University Press, 2004), 189.

46 Ivan Goll, "Zenitist Manifesto," trans. Maja Starčević, in *Between Worlds*, 289.

47 Goll's move parallels earlier efforts of revolutionary nationalists in the Philippines to translate ideas of regional geographic affiliation into a language of racial community. Nicole CuUnjieng Aboitiz, *Asian Place, Filipino Nation: A Global Intellectual History of the Philippine Revolution, 1887–1912* (New York: Columbia University Press, 2020), 55–65.

48 Ljubomir Micić, "Zenithosophy: Or the Energetics of Creative Zenithism," trans. Maja Starčević, in *Between Worlds*, 517.

49 Micić, "Zenitist Manifesto," 284.

50 Dubravka Đurić, "Radical Poetic Practices: Concrete and Visual Poetry in the Avant-Garde and Neo-Avant-Garde," in *Impossible Histories*, 66, 74.

51 Stevan Živanović, "Brsadino mia ligna vieno," *Zenit* 15 (June 1922): 35. For one of the few histories of Esperanto and its adoption among the revolutionary Left, see Gregor Benton, *Chinese Migrants and Internationalism: Forgotten Histories, 1917–1945* (Abingdon, GB: Routledge, 2002).

52 Vlado Martelanc, "Panait Istrati, glasnik Balkana," *Mladina* 3, nos. 9–10 (1926–27): 224.

Notes to pages 60–4

53 Ivan Graho, "Panevropa," *Mladina* 2, nos. 6–7 (1925–27): 133.

54 This dimension of Kosovel's work has been explored by Ana Jelnikar in *Universalist Hopes in India and Europe: The Worlds of Rabindranath Tagore and Srečko Kosovel* (New Delhi: Oxford University Press, 2016).

55 Janez Vrečko, *Srečko Kosovel: monografija* (Ljubljana: Založba ZRC, 2011), 18–20.

56 Peter Stih, Vasko Simoniti, and Peter Vodopivec, *A Slovene History: Society, Politics, Culture* (Ljubljana: Inštitut za novejšo zgodovino, 2008), 397.

57 Glenda Sluga, *The Problem of Trieste and the Italo-Yugoslav Border: Difference, Identity and Sovereignty in Twentieth-Century Europe* (Albany: State University of New York Press, 2001), 44.

58 Vrečko, *Srečko Kosovel*, 9–10.

59 As Tyrus Miller notes, the zenitists also pointed to Italy's annexations and persecution of its Slavic minorities to aggressively assert the autonomy of their Balkan primitivism from its absorption by Italian futurism. Miller, "A Geography of Dispersion: Central Europe and the Symbolic Spaces of the Avant-Garde" *International Yearbook of Aesthetics* 14 (2010): 191–4.

60 Letter to Fanica Obidova, 27 July 1925, in *Izbrana pisma*, ed. Ludwig Hartinger (Ljubljana: Mladinska knjiga, 2006), 223–4.

61 Letter to Vinko Kosak, 15 August 1925, in *Izbrana pisma*, 230.

62 Letter to Pavla Hočevar, 25 April 1925, in *Izbrana pisma*, 205.

63 Letter to Fanica Obidova, 8 May 1925, in *Izbrana pisma*, 207.

64 Srečko Kosovel, "Ecstasy of Death" in *Look Back, Look Ahead: The Selected Poems of Srečko Kosovel*, ed. and trans. Ana Jelnikar and Barbara Siegel Carlson (Brooklyn, NY: Ugly Duckling Presse, 2010), 150–3.

65 Srečko Kosovel, "Ljubljana Is Asleep," in *Look Back, Look Ahead*, 123.

66 Sluga, *The Problem of Trieste*, 44.

67 Richard Jackson, "Being a Lamp: Srečko Kosovel," in *Look Back, Look Ahead*, xi–xii.

68 See, for instance, the opening stanzas of "Ej, hej" ("Hey hey"): Srečko Kosovel, *Integrali* (Sarajevo: Krug 99, 2003), 55.

69 Srečko Kosovel, "The Syphilitic Captain," in Srečko Kosovel, *The Golden Boat: Selected Poems of Srečko Kosovel*, trans. Bert Pribac and David Brooks (Cambridge: Salt Publishing, 2008), 139. See also Janez Vrečko, "Barbarogenij, barbarsko in fašizem," *Primerjalna književnost* 35, no. 3 (2012): 266–7.

70 Srečko Kosovel, "Gray," in *Look Back, Look Ahead*, 140–1.

252 Notes to pages 64–7

71 Ana Jelnikar, "Srečko Kosovel and Rabindranath Tagore: Points of Departure and Identification," *Asian and African Studies* 14, no. 1 (2010): 84.

72 Očak, *Krleža-partija*, 97–111.

73 Stipetić, *Argumenti za revoluciju*, 153–4.

74 The two authors noted this more restrained spirit in an editorial in the first issue of the magazine: "Napomena uredništva," *Književna republika* 1, no. 1 (1923): 38–9.

75 The text that prompted the ban was Ljubomir Micić, "Zenitizma kroz prizmu marksizma," *Zenit* 43 (December 1926): 12–15.

76 Srečko Kosovel, "The Ninth Country," in *The Golden Boat*, 48.

77 Kreft's account of Kosovel's funeral can be found in Vrečko, *Srečko Kosovel*, 28–31.

CHAPTER THREE

1 Dejan Đokić, *Elusive Compromise: A History of Interwar Yugoslavia* (New York: Columbia University Press, 2007), 67.

2 Mladen Iveković, *Hrvatska lijeva inteligencija 1918–1945* (Zagreb: Naprijed, 1970), 153–5.

3 Đokić, *Elusive Compromise*, 69–70.

4 Ibid., 83–5; Alex Dragnich, *The First Yugoslavia: Search for a Viable Political System* (Stanford, CA: Hoover Institution Press, 1983), 76–9; John Lampe, *Yugoslavia as History: Twice There Was a Country* (Cambridge: Cambridge University Press, 1996), 169.

5 Dragnich, *The First Yugoslavia*, 76–7.

6 The party changed its name from the Socialist Workers Party of Yugoslavia (communist) to the Communist Party of Yugoslavia in June 1920. Aleksa Đilas, *The Contested Country: Yugoslav Unity and Communist Revolution, 1919–1953* (Cambridge, MA: Harvard University Press, 1991), 58–63.

7 Kevin McDermott and Jeremy Agnew, *The Comintern: A History of International Communism from Lenin to Stalin* (Basingstoke, GB: Macmillan Press, 1996), 68–119.

8 Ivan Avakumović, *History of the Communist Party of Yugoslavia* (Aberdeen, GB: Aberdeen University Press, 1967), 94.

9 Lampe, *Yugoslavia as History*, 174. See also Ivan Očak, *Krleža-Partija: Miroslav Krleža u radničkom i komunističkom pokretu 1917–1941* (Zagreb: Spektar, 1982), 184; Avakumović, *History of the Communist Party of Yugoslavia*, 96.

Notes to pages 68–70

10 Adam Tooze, *The Deluge: The Great War, America and the Remaking of the Global Order* (New York: Penguin Books, 2015).

11 Ivan Berend, *Decades of Crisis: Central and Eastern Europe before World War II* (Berkeley: University of California Press, 1998), 255–9.

12 Ibid., 259–61.

13 On Manoilescu's thought, see Joseph LeRoy Love, *Crafting the Third World: Theorizing Underdevelopment in Rumania and Brazil* (Stanford, CA: Stanford University Press, 1996).

14 Sunyoung Park points to a similar process of the politicization of literature during this period in colonial Korea. See *The Proletarian Wave: Literature and Leftist Culture in Colonial Korea, 1910–1945* (Cambridge, MA: Harvard University Asian Center, 2015), 37.

15 Iveković, *Hrvatska lijeva inteligencija*, 219–41; Stanko Lasić, *Sukob na književnoj ljevici 1928–1953* (Zagreb: Liber, 1970); Vlado Mađarević, *Književnost i revolucija: prilog analizi sukoba na književnoj ljevici* (Zagreb: August Cesarec, 1974); Vasilije Kalezić, *Pokret socijalne literature: književna studija* (Belgrade: Petar Kočić, 1975); Predrag Matvejević, *Književnost i njezina društvena funkcija: od književne tendencije do sukoba na ljevici* (Novi Sad, RS: Radivoj Ćirpanov, 1977); Zorica Stipetić, "O pojmu lijeve inteligencije u Hrvatskoj u tridesetim godinama," *Časopis za suvremenu povijest* 11, no. 1 (1979): 113–29; Aleksandar Flaker, *Poetika osporavanja: avangarda i književna ljevica* (Zagreb: Školska knjiga, 1982); Ralph Bogert, *The Writer as Naysayer: Miroslav Krleža and the Aesthetic of Interwar Central Europe* (Columbus, OH: Slavica, 1990), 82–147; Ivana Perica, "'Social Literature Swindlers': The R/Evolutionary Controversy in Interwar Yugoslav Literature," *Neohelicon* 45 (2018): 249–80.

16 Ivo Brnčić, "Generacija pred zaprtimi vrati," in *Generacija pred zaprtimi vrati: izbor, esejev in kritik*, ed. Mitja Mejak (Ljubljana: Cankarjeva založba, 1951), 9–19; Ervin Dolenc, "'Generation before Closed Doors': Slovenian Intellectual Issues between the Two World Wars," *Slovene Studies* 23, nos. 1–2 (2001): 15–25.

17 This generation included, for instance, the trio of activists that Josip Broz Tito would appoint to the central committee during his reorganization of the KPJ in 1937: Milovan Đilas, Edvard Kardelj, and Aleksandar Ranković. It also included figures such as the Montenegrin partisan general Svetozar Vukmanović-Tempo, the poet Radovan Zogović, the architect of the postwar self-management economy, Boris Kidrič, and the future diplomat Aleš Bebler, to name only a few.

254 Notes to pages 70–1

18 Djagalov notes a similar phenomenon with regards to the popularity of Russian realist literature among Asian and African anticolonial writers in the early twentieth century. Rossen Djagalov, *From Internationalism to Post-colonialism: Literature and Cinema between the Second and Third Worlds* (Montreal and Kingston: McGill-Queen's University Press, 2020), 37–42.

19 Perica, "'Social Literature Swindlers.'" The influence of social literature on members of this generation is evidenced in their memoirs. See, for instance: Milovan Đilas, *Memoir of a Revolutionary*, trans. Drenka Willen (New York: Harcourt, Brace and Jovanovich, 1973), 20–1, 83; Radovan Zogović, *Postajanje i postojanje* (Novi Sad, RS: Matica Srpska, 1993), 8–13; Svetozar Vukmanović Tempo, *Revolucija koja teče: memoari* (Belgrade: Komunist, 1971), 13–23.

20 Michael Denning, *The Cultural Front: The Laboring of American Culture in the Twentieth Century* (London: Verso, 1997); Barbara Foley, *Radical Representations: Politics and Form in U.S. Proletarian Fiction 1929–1941* (Durham, NC: Duke University Press, 1993); James Murphy, *The Proletarian Moment: The Controversy over Leftism in Literature* (Urbana: University of Illinois Press, 1991); Park, *The Proletarian Wave*; Sheila Fitzpatrick, *The Cultural Front: Power and Culture in Revolutionary Russia* (Ithaca, NY: Cornell University Press, 1992); Katerina Clark, *Eurasia without Borders: The Dream of a Leftist Literary Commons, 1919–1943* (Cambridge, MA: Harvard University Press, 2021); Djagalov, *From Internationalism to Post-colonialism*; Anna Björk Einarsdóttir, "Comintern Aesthetics in the Andes: The Indigenous Revolutionary," *Science and Society* 85, no. 4 (October 2021): 443–73.

21 *Proletkult* was an abbreviation for the movement for proletarian culture that developed in the Soviet Union between the revolution of 1917 and the state's consolidation of cultural institutions in the early 1930s. Lynn Mally, *Culture of the Future: The Proletkult Movement in Revolutionary Russia* (Berkeley: University of California Press, 1990); Edward James Brown, *The Proletarian Episode in Russian Literature, 1928–1932* (New York: Octagon Books, 1971).

22 On the debate over naturalism and reportage in the Soviet and German movements, see Murphy, *The Proletarian Moment*, 36–54; Marla Zubel, "The Object or the Fact? The Political Aesthetics of Interwar Reportage," *Genre* 49, no. 3 (2016): 407–29. A key figure in the German debate was the Hungarian Marxist Georg Lukács, whose arguments rejecting naturalism and advancing a classical mode of realism would gain greater traction in Comintern cultural circles during the years of the Popular Front. These

Notes to pages 71–9

views were best set out in his essay, "Narrate or Describe?" republished in *Writer and Critic and Other Essays*, ed. and trans. Arthur Kahn (New York: Merlin Press, 1970), 110–48.

23 The notion of *partiinost* was first formulated by Lenin in 1905 and became a contested term during the intense literary debates of the 1920s in the Soviet Union and Germany. For a succinct definition of the concept and its use by Soviet theorists, see Herman Ermolaev, "Partiinost,'" in *Handbook of Russian Literature*, ed. Victor Terras (New Haven, CT: Yale University Press, 1985), 331. For a genealogy of the concept in Soviet and German debates, see C. Vaughan James, *Soviet Socialist Realism: Origins and Theory* (London: Palgrave MacMillan, 1973), 15–27; Murphy, *The Proletarian Moment*, 49–51.

24 Pascale Casanova, *The World Republic of Letters*, trans. M.B. DeBevoise (Cambridge, MA: Harvard University Press, 2004), 12.

25 Djagalov, *From Internationalism to Postcolonialism*, 21–2.

26 Kalezić, *Pokret socijalne literature*, 75.

27 A detailed survey of these journals can be found in Vasilije Kalezić, *U Krležinom savježdu* (Zagreb: August Cesarec, 1982), 15–23.

28 Although Denning emphasizes the genuine internationalism and geographic diversity of the proletarian literary canon, this was not reflected in the texts that made their way into Yugoslav social literature. Michael Denning, *Culture in the Age of Three Worlds* (London: Verso, 2004), 58.

29 "Intelektualci Evrope čitaocima Jugoslavije," *Nova literatura* 1, no. 1 (December 1928): 3.

30 Bratko Kreft, "Tempo ... Tempo ..." *Stožer* 4, no. 3 (December 1933): 117.

31 Harry Harootunian, "Remembering the Historical Present," *Critical Inquiry* 33, no. 3 (Spring 2007): 489.

32 Oto Bihalj, "Istok, Zapad, i akrobati duha," *Nova literatura* 1, no. 1 (December 1928): 15.

33 See the entire issue of *Nova literatura* 1, no. 4 (March 1929).

34 *Stožer* 3, nos. 10–12 (December 1932): 296, 301, 316.

35 The following year, Aragon published a collection of poetry inspired by this journey to the Urals. See Louis Aragon, *Hourra l'Oural* (Paris: Denoel et Steele, 1934). On Aragon's trip to the USSR, see T.V. Viktorova, "'Strana nasiliia i prekrasnyh glaz": Lui Aragon o poseshchenii sovietskogo Urala' *Noveishaia istoriia Rossii* 3 (2012): 157–70.

36 On Žicina's novel, see Jelena Petrović, *Women's Authorship in Interwar Yugoslavia: The Politics of Love and Struggle* (Cham, CH: Palgrave Macmillan, 2019), 223–6.

256 Notes to pages 79–84

37 Miloš Pantić, "Epopeja kolektiviziranih seljaka u S.S.S.R." *Stožer* 5, nos. 4–5 (January–February 1934): 164.

38 Much as the Marxist notion of primary accumulation refers to the initial appropriation of resources that sets the cycle of capital production in motion, "translation-accumulation" refers to the effort to sharpen a national literature's competitive edge in the world literary field through the translation of the "great universal texts which are recognized as universal capital in the literary universe." Pascale Casanova, "Consecration and Accumulation of Literary Capital: Translation as Unequal Exchange," in *Critical Readings in Translation Studies*, ed. Mona Baker (London: Routledge, 2010), 290–1.

39 Oto Bihalji-Merin, "'Naša' i 'strana' knjiga," *Stožer* 3, no. 4 (April 1932): 119.

40 Even within the political borders of the Kingdom of Yugoslavia, the presumed audience of Serbo-Croatian readers would have excluded those minorities that spoke other languages such as Slovene, Macedonian, Hungarian, or Albanian.

41 Giovanni Arrighi, *The Long Twentieth Century: Money, Power and the Origins of Our Times* (London: Verso, 2010), 282–3; Tooze, *The Deluge*, 511–15.

42 Miloš Crnjanski, "Mi postajemo kolonija strane knjige (I)," *Vreme*, 3 March 1932, 2.

43 Crnjanski was one of a generation of diplomat-litterateurs that presided over and helped form what Suzana Vuljević has described as a transnational cultural-diplomatic network in the interwar Balkans. See Suzana Vuljević, "The Crisis of Spirit: Pan-Balkan Idealism, Transnational Cultural-Diplomatic Networks and Intellectual Cooperation in Interwar Southeast Europe, 1930–1941" (PhD diss., Columbia University, 2020).

44 One of the few biographies of Crnjanski available is Radovan Popović, *Život Miloša Crnjanskog* (Belgrade: Prosveta, 1980). For a background of the polemic, see Kalezić, *Pokret socijalne literature*, 165–82.

45 Crnjanski, "Mi postajemo kolonija strane knjige (I)," 2.

46 See Miloš Crnjanski, ed. *Antologija kineske lirike* (Belgrade: Napredak, 1923); "Predgovor" in Oskar Uajld, *Slika Dorijana Greja* (Vukovar, HR: Nova doba, 1920), 3–13.

47 Miloš Crnjanski, "Mi postajemo kolonija strane knjige (II)," *Vreme*, 12 March 1932, 2.

48 Miloš Crnjanski, "Panika oko naše knjige," *Vreme*, 22 March 1932, 7. The italics are mine – JR.

Notes to pages 86–9

49 My interpretation of Krleža's arguments is indebted to Nirvana Tanoukhi's essay, "The Scale of World Literature," in *Immanuel Wallerstein and the Problem of the World*, ed. David Palumbo-Liu, Bruce Robbins, and Nirvana Tanoukhi (Durham, NC: Duke University Press, 2011), 78–98.

50 Irina Subotić, "Concerning Art and Politics in Yugoslavia during the 1930s," *Art Journal* 52 (1993): 69–71; Bojana Videkanić, "The Long Durée of Yugoslav Socially Engaged Art and its Continued Life in the Non-Aligned World," in *Socialist Yugoslavia and the Non-Aligned Movement*, ed. Paul Stubbs (Montreal and Kingston: McGill-Queen's University Press, 2023), 136–41. For a more detailed examination of Hegedušić's views, see Ivana Hanaček, "Đuro Tiljak i Krsto Hegedušić: skica za povijest jednog (ne)prijateljstva kroz prizmu odnosa prema socijalno angažiranoj umjetnosti," *Ars Adriatica* 11 (2021): 365–82.

51 On Krleža's role in the conflict on the literary Left, see Lasić, *Sukob na književnoj lijevici*; Kalezić, *U Krležinom Savježdu*; Stanko Lasić, *Krležologija ili povijest kritičke misli o Miroslavu Krleži: knjiga prva: kritička literature o Miroslavu Krleži od 1914. do 1941* (Zagreb: Globus, 1989), 91–359.

52 In this sense, the Yugoslav polemics bore similarities to other disputes within Left literary cultures at this time. See, for example, Murphy, *The Proletarian Moment*; John Zammito, *The Great Debate: "Bolshevism" and the Literary Left in Germany, 1917–1930* (New York: Peter Lang, 1984).

53 Fitzpatrick, *The Cultural Front*, 115–48. Milovan Đilas relates the dynamics of this radicalization and division of literature into "bourgeois" and "proletarian" camps in *Memoir of a Revolutionary*, 86–9.

54 On Breton's critique of the Soviet Union, see Pierre Taminiaux, "Breton and Trotsky: The Revolutionary Memory of Surrealism," *Yale French Studies* 109 (2006): 52–66.

55 Miroslav Krleža, "Foreword to Krsto Hegedušić's *The Drava Valley Motifs*," trans. Vladislav Beronja, *Journal of Croatian Studies* 44 (2003): 167. See also Jan Wierzbicki, *Miroslav Krleža* (Zagreb: Liber, 1980), 83.

56 Krleža, "Foreword," 169.

57 Ibid., 170.

58 Ibid., 180.

59 Krleža had explored this theory of culture as the subjective expression of the material landscape a few years earlier in his writing on German expressionism. See, for instance, Miroslav Krleža, "O nemirima današnje njemačke lirike," *Hrvatska Revija* 11 (1931): 600–14.

258 Notes to pages 90–100

60 Krleža, "Foreword," 189.

61 Ibid., 189.

62 Georg Lukács, *The Historical Novel*, trans. Hannah Mitchell and Stanley Mitchell (Lincoln: University of Nebraska Press, 2010). Also see Clark's discussion of Lukács's place within 1930s Soviet cultural debates in Katerina Clark, *Moscow, the Fourth Rome: Stalinism, Cosmopolitanism and the Evolution of Soviet Culture, 1931–1941* (Cambridge, MA: Harvard University Press, 2011), 163–8.

63 This reading is in tension with that proposed by Andrew Wachtel, who interprets *Povratak* as an allegory for Yugoslav national cultural development. Wachtel, *Making a Nation, Breaking a Nation: Literature and Cultural Politics in Yugoslavia* (Stanford, CA: Stanford University Press, 2000), 123. For an extended discussion of this argument, see James M. Robertson, "Dispatches from the Appendix of Europe: Miroslav Krleža's Abject Modernism," *Papers on Literature and Language* 55, no. 3 (Summer 2019): 227–55.

64 Miroslav Krleža, *The Return of Philip Latinowicz*, translated by Zora Depolo (Evanston, IL: Northwestern University Press, 1995), 60–1.

65 Such scatological imagery was a recurring theme in Krleža's descriptions of the region. In his 1933 story "Cvrčak pod vodopadom" ("The Cricket beneath the Waterfall", trans. Frank S. Lambasa), the author used the figure of a cricket living in a public urinal as a metaphor for the life of an intellectual in a provincial Pannonian village. Miroslav Krleža, *The Cricket beneath the Waterfall and Other Stories*, ed. Branko Lenski (New York: The Vanguard Press, 1972), 35–68. In that same year, after relocating to Belgrade, he also wrote to a friend describing the "muddy, yellow (light-yellow) waters of the Danube (which looks like children's diarrhea)." Miroslav Krleža, Letter to Julija Benešić, 16 December 1933 in *Pisma* (Sarajevo: Oslobođenje, 1988), 50.

66 Tooze, *The Deluge*, 511–15.

CHAPTER FOUR

1 Quoted in Branko Matan, *Speak Now or Never: The 1933 Dubrovnik PEN Club Congress* (Zagreb: Croatian PEN Centre, 1993), 50.

2 Lisa Pine, *Education in Nazi Germany* (Oxford: Berg, 2010), 34.

3 Mladen Iveković, *Hrvatska lijeva inteligencija 1918–1945* (Zagreb: Naprijed, 1970), 187.

4 Hilde Katrine Haug, *Creating a Socialist Yugoslavia: Tito, Communist Leadership and the National Question* (London: IB Tauris, 2012), 56–7;

Notes to pages 100–5

Aleksa Đilas, *The Contested Country: Yugoslav Unity and Communist Revolution, 1919–1953* (Cambridge, MA: Harvard University Press, 1991), 89–97.

5 Rossen Djagalov, *From Internationalism to Post-colonialism: Literature and Cinema between the Second and Third Worlds* (Montreal and Kingston: McGill-Queen's University Press, 2020), 59.

6 Johann Chapoutot, *Greeks, Romans, Germans: How the Nazis Usurped Europe's Classical Past*, trans. Richard R. Nybakken (Berkeley: University of California Press, 2016), 166–7.

7 On the history of post-World War I diplomacy in Eastern Europe, see Piotr Wandycz, *The Twilight of French Eastern Alliances, 1926–1936: French-Czechoslovak-Polish Relations from Locarno to the Remilitarization of the Rhineland* (Princeton, NJ: Princeton University Press, 1988).

8 Stephen Gross, *Export Empire: German Soft Power in Southeastern Europe, 1890–1945* (Cambridge: Cambridge University Press, 2015), 290–1.

9 Ibid., 288–90.

10 Benjamin Martin, *The Nazi-Fascist New Order for European Culture* (Cambridge, MA: Harvard University Press, 2016), 6, 8.

11 Ibid., 5.

12 Kevin McDermott and Jeremy Agnew, *The Comintern: A History of International Communism from Lenin to Stalin* (Basingstoke, GB: Macmillan Press, 1996), 127–9.

13 Ibid., 123–7.

14 Ibid., 129–30.

15 Đilas, *The Contested Country*, 85.

16 Ibid., 93–4; Haug, *Creating a Socialist Yugoslavia*, 37–42.

17 On Yugoslav émigrés in Europe, see Mira Kolar-Dimitrijević, "Odnos KPJ prema Jugoslavenskoj radničkoj emigranciji u međuratnom razdoblju," *Časopis za suvremenu povijest* 16, no. 2 (1984): 71–83; Stefan Gužvica, "Books and Rifles: The Political Activity of Yugoslav Communist Students in Prague from 1927 until 1937," *Slovanský přehled* 1 (2017): 65–103 (part one); and *Slovanský přehled* 2 (2017): 343–71 (part two).

18 On Yugoslav participation in the Spanish Civil War, see Savo Pešić, *Španjolski građanski rat i KPJ* (Rijeka, HR: Izdavački centar Rijeka, 1990).

19 Margot Heinemann, "*Left Review, New Writing* and the Broad Alliance against Fascism," in *Vision and Blueprints: Avant-Garde Culture and Radical Politics in Early Twentieth-Century Europe*, ed. Edward Timms and Peter Collier (Manchester, GB: Manchester University Press, 1988), 115.

260   Notes to pages 105–10

20 Herbert Lottman, *The Left Bank: Writers, Artists, and Politics from the Popular Front to the Cold War* (Chicago, IL: University of Chicago Press, 1998), 63.

21 Nexø's speech was reprinted in Russian translation in *Mezhdunarodnyi kongress pisatelei v zashchitu kultury, Parizh iiun 1935: doklady i vystupleniia*, ed. Ivan Luppol (Moscow: Khudozhestvennaia literatura, 1936), 151–2.

22 As Rossen Djagalov notes of this period, the Soviet Republic of Letters became synonymous with the World Republic of Letters identified by Casanova. Djagalov, *From Internationalism to Post-colonialism*, 59.

23 On the renewed interest of Soviet culture in the classical literary tradition of Europe, see Katerina Clark, *Moscow, the Fourth Rome: Stalinism, Cosmopolitanism and the Evolution of Soviet Culture, 1931–1941* (Cambridge, MA: Harvard University Press, 2011), 169–209.

24 Karl Radek, "Contemporary World Literature and the Tasks of the Proletarian Art," in *Problems of Soviet Literature: Reports and Speeches at the First Soviet Writers' Congress*, ed. H.G. Scott (New York: International Publishers, 1935), 173.

25 George Dimitrov, "Revolutionary Literature and the Struggle against Fascism," trans. D. Kogan, *International Literature* 4 (1935): 55.

26 Georg Lukács, "Narrate or Describe?" in *Writer and Critic: and Other Essays*, ed. and trans. Arthur Kahn (Lincoln, NE: Iuniverse, 2005), 110–48.

27 Ibid., 143. On Lukács's theory of historical action, see Tyrus Miller, *Georg Lukács and Critical Theory: Aesthetics, History, Utopia* (Edinburgh, GB: Edinburgh University Press, 2022), 55–80.

28 Clark, *Moscow, the Fourth Rome*, 312–13.

29 Georg Lukács, *The Historical Novel*, trans. Hannah Mitchell and Stanley Mitchell (Lincoln: University of Nebraska Press, 1962), 48–9.

30 Ibid., 47.

31 McDermott and Agnew, *The Comintern*, 131.

32 Georgi Dimitrov, "The Fascist Offensive and the Tasks of the Communist International in the Struggle of the Working Class against Fascism," in Georgi Dimitrov, *Selected Speeches and Articles* (London: Lawrence and Wishart, 1951), 100.

33 McDermott and Agnew, *The Comintern*, 135.

34 Several essays by Radovan Zogović feature citations of Lukács's work: for example, the critical review "Osude bez prizive," *Naša stvarnost* 15–16 (June 1938): 19–38, republished in *Zli volšebnici*, vol. 3, ed. Gojko Tešić (Beograd: Slovo ljubve, 1983), 359–76. Hereafter all citations for this

Notes to pages 110–14

essay will be to the Tešić collection. A translation of Lukács's essay "Friedrich Engels als Literaturtheoretiker und Literaturkritiker" was serialized in the Zagreb-based new realist journal *Književni savremenik*: G. Lukács, "Engels kao književni teoretičar i kritičar' *Književni savremenik* 10 (October 1936): 139–44; 11 (November 1936): 187–92; and 12 (December 1936): 219–28. The young Bosnian Muslim Avdo Humo also notes a familiarity with Lukács's work among those on the Belgrade literary Left. Humo, *Moja generacija* (Sarajevo: Svjetnost, 1984), 395.

35 Đilas and Jovanović had actually served time together at the notorious Sremska Mitrovica prison during the period of the Karađorđević dictatorship.

36 Vladimir Velmar-Janković, *Pogled s Kalemegdana - ogled o beogradskom čoveku* (Belgrade: Biblioteka grada Beograda, 1991). On the thematic links between Janković and the early avant-gardes, see Rory Yeomans, "Of 'Yugoslav Barbarians' and Croatian Gentlemen Scholars: Nationalist Ideology and Racial Anthropology in Interwar Yugoslavia," in *"Blood and Homeland": Eugenics and Racial Nationalism in Central and Southeast Europe, 1900–1940*, ed. Marius Turda and Paul J. Weindling (Budapest: Central European University Press, 2007), 98–101.

37 For a fuller exploration of these themes among right-wing intellectuals in interwar South East Europe, see Keith Hitchins, "Interwar Southeastern Europe Confronts the West," *Angelaki: Journal of the Theoretical Humanities* 15, no. 3 (2010): 9–26.

38 Đorđe Daničić [Jovanović], "Kalemegdanski pogled na nas," in *Zli volšebnici*, 407.

39 Đorđe Jovanović, "Ugrožena kultura," *Književni savremenik* 1, no. 12 (December 1936): 217.

40 Milovan Đilas, "Problemi naše književnosti," in Milovan Đilas, *Problemi naše književnosti* (Cetinje, ME: Crnogorsko društvo nezavisnih književnika, 2009), 125.

41 Ibid., 128.

42 Radovan Zogović, *Tri članka o srpskom eposu* (Belgrade: Naša stvarnost, 1937), 21–2.

43 Ibid., 36.

44 Zogović, "Osude bez prizive," 376.

45 Dušan Moravec, "Bratko Kreft: (Ne)jubilejni pogledi na njegovo delo," *Sodobnost* 33, no. 2 (1985): 113.

46 Fran Petre, "Proletarski odri v Ljubljani in okolici med obema vojnama" in *Delavski oder na Slovenskem*, ed. Ferdo Delak (Ljubljana: Mestno gledališče ljubljasko, 1964), 22; Milan Vesović, *Revolucionarna štampa u*

262 Notes to pages 114–16

kraljevini srba, hrvata i slovenaca, 1918–1929 (Belgrade: Institut za savremenu istoriju, 1979), 120.

47 Petre, "Proletarski odri," 24.

48 For an insight into Kreft's views on the theater during this period, see Bratko Kreft, "Problemi današnjega kazališta," *Književnik* 3, no. 4 (April 1930): 144–7.

49 Vaso Bogdanović (writing under the pseudonym N. Kostin), an important figure in the social literature movement, included an essay on the 1573 rebellion in his collection *Suvremeni književni i kulturni problemi* (Zagreb: Nakladna knjižara Epoha, 1935), 5–19. A year later, an article in *Književni savremenik* sought to defend the legacy of the rebellion from appropriation by the Far Right. M.S., "Dvije knjige o hrvatskoj seljačkoj buni 1573," *Književni savremenik* 11 (November 1936): 177–83.

50 The Croatian language is divided into three major dialects: Štokavian, Kajkavian, and Čakavian. After Štokavian was selected as the basis for modern Croatian owing to its similarity with the dialects spoken in Bosnia and Herzegovina, Serbia, and Montenegro, Kajkavian and Čakavian became marginalized within Croatian literature. Krleža's decision to compose the *Balade* in Kajkavian was twofold: on the one hand, it was the dialect spoken in the lands of the 1573 revolt; on the other, it was a provocation to proponents of a homogeneous Croatian national culture. On the place of the 1573 revolt in this work, see Mladen Kuzmanović, "Odjeci seljačke bune 1573. u *Balade Petrice Kerempuha* Miroslava Krleže," *Radovi Zavoda za hrvatsku povijest* 5, no. 1 (1973): 227–35.

51 For an overview of the critical reception of *Balade* in Yugoslavia at the time, see Stanko Lasić, *Krležologija: kritička literature o Miroslavu Krleži od 1914–1941* (Zagreb: Globus, 1989), 244–58.

52 The convoluted publication of the *Balade* is recounted in Stanko Lasić, *Krleža, kronologija života i rada* (Zagreb: Grafički zavod hrvatske, 1982), 258–60.

53 For an excellent history of the notorious uskoks, see Wendy Bracewell, *The Uskoks of Senj: Piracy, Banditry, and Holy War in the Sixteenth-Century Adriatic* (Ithaca, NY: Cornell University Press, 1992).

54 An account of the social, political, and religious tensions that shaped the revolt can be found in Peter Stih, Vasko Simoniti, and Peter Vodopivec, eds., *A Slovene History: Society, Politics, Culture* (Ljubljana: Institut za novejšo zgodovino, 2008), 167–70.

55 Bratko Kreft, "Velika puntarija," in Bratko Kreft, *Celjske grofje, Velika puntarija, Krajnski komedijanti* (Ljubljana: Mladinska knjiga, 1967), 119–20.

Notes to pages 117–24

56 Ibid., 123–7.

57 Ibid., 128.

58 Ibid., 137.

59 Zorica Stipetić, *Argumenti za revoluciju: August Cesarec* (Zagreb: Centar društvenih djelatnosti Saveza socijalističke omladine Hrvatske, 1982), 238–44.

60 Ibid., 267–76.

61 Ibid., 327–51.

62 Jelena Subotić, *Yellow Star, Red Star: Holocaust Remembrance after Communism* (Ithaca, NY: Cornell University Press, 2019), 97–9.

63 Stipetić, *Argumenti za revoluciju*, 330.

64 Ibid., 418.

65 Ibid., 414–15.

66 Ibid., 412–13; Nevenko Bartulin, *The Racial Idea in the Independent State of Croatia: Origins and Theory* (Leiden, NE: Brill, 2014), 155–6; Rory Yeomans, *Visions of Annihilation: The Ustasha Regime and the Cultural Politics of Fascism, 1941–1945* (Pittsburgh, PA: University of Pittsburgh Press, 2013), 272.

67 August Cesarec, *Sin domovine: životna drama Eugena Kvaternika* (Zagreb: Dom i svijet, 1997), 54–5.

68 Ibid., 61.

69 Ibid., 55.

70 Ibid., 49.

71 Ibid., 69.

72 Quoted in Stipetić, *Argumenti za revoluciju*, 414.

73 Cesarec, *Sin domovine*, 81.

74 Included in this group were Božidar Adžija, the philosopher Ognjen Prica, the journalist and social literary critic Otokar Keršovani, and Zvonimir Richtmann.

75 Stipetić, *Argumenti za revoluciju*, 438–41.

76 Milovan Đilas, *Wartime*, trans. Michael Boro Petrovich, (New York: Harcourt Brace Jovanovich, 1977), 10.

77 For an analysis of cultural production during the Yugoslav partisan war, see Miloš Miletić and Mirjana Radovanović, ed., *Lekcije o odbrani: prilozi za analizu kulturne delatnosti* NOP-*a* (Belgrade: KURS, 2016).

264   Notes to pages 126–30

CHAPTER FIVE

1 Mark Wheeler, "Pariahs to Partisans: The Communist Party of Yugoslavia," in *Resistance and Revolution in Mediterranean Europe, 1939–1948*, ed. Tony Judt (London: Routledge, 1989), 126.
2 Melissa Feinberg, *Communism in Eastern Europe* (New York: Routledge, 2022), 27–34.
3 Hilde Katrine Haug, *Creating a Socialist Yugoslavia: Tito, Communist Leadership and the National Question* (London: IB Tauris, 2012), 115.
4 Ibid., 88–92.
5 Ibid., 117.
6 This chapter leans on Robert Niebuhr's persuasive argument that Tito's regime relied heavily on its foreign policy prestige to boost its domestic legitimacy. Niebuhr, *The Search for a Cold War Legitimacy: Foreign Policy and Tito's Yugoslavia* (Leiden, NE: Brill, 2018). See also Branko Petranović, *Balkanska federacija, 1943–1948* (Belgrade: Edicija svedočanstva, 1991), 137–9.
7 Ivo Banac, *With Stalin against Tito: Cominformist Splits in Yugoslav Communism* (Ithaca, NY: Cornell University Press, 1988), 28–43.
8 Adamantios Skordos, "Vom 'grossrussischen Panslavismus' zum 'sowjetischen Slavokommunismus': Das Slaventum als Feindbild bei Deutschen, Österreichern, Italienern und Griechen," in *Post-Panslavismus: Slavizität, Slavische Idee und Antislavismus im 20. und 21. Jahrhundert*, ed. Agnieszka Gąsior, Lars Karl, and Stefan Troebst (Gottingen, DE: Wallstein Verlag, 2014), 421–3.
9 Carol Lilly, *Power and Persuasion: Ideology and Rhetoric in Communist Yugoslavia, 1944–1953* (Boulder, CO: Westview Press, 2001), 38–41.
10 Benedict Anderson, *Imagined Communities: Reflections on the Origin and Spread of Nationalism* (London: Verso, 2006).
11 Jan Claas Behrends, "Stalins slavischer Volkskrieg: Mobilisierung und Propaganda zwischen Weltkrieg und Kaltem Krieg (1941–1949)" in *Post-Panslavismus*, 86–8.
12 Edward Jan Paul Pawlowski, "Pan-Slavism during World War II" (PhD diss. Georgetown University, 1968), 56–63, 101–16; Nikolai Kikeshev, *Slaviane protiv fashizma* (Moscow: Rossiiskaia akademiia nauk, 2005), 13–15.
13 Stefan Troebst, "Schwanengesang gesamtslavischer 'Einheit und Brüderlichkeit': Der Slavenkongress in Belgrad 1946" in *Post-Panslavismus*, 47.
14 Hans Kohn, *Pan-Slavism, Its History and Ideology* (New York: Vintage, 1960), 301.

Notes to pages 130–3   265

15 Kohn, *Pan-Slavism,* 301; Pawlowski, "Pan-Slavism during World War II," 104; Kikeshev, *Slaviane protiv fashizma,* 74–7. For an example of the diaspora work of the movement, see the pamphlet *The Slavic Peoples against Hitler: A Report on the Slavic Conference in Moscow, August 1 and 11, 1941 and its Effects on Slavic Communities throughout the World* (New York: American Council on Soviet Relations, 1941).

16 Troebst, "Schwanengesang gesamtslavischer 'Einheit und Brüderlichkeit,'" 47.

17 Behrends, "Stalins slavischer Volkskrieg," 88–90.

18 These messianic themes were pithily captured by Iaroslavskii in 1941: "Without Russia, there can be no Slavdom." Quoted in Behrends, "Stalins slavischer Volkskrieg," 88.

19 Pawlowski, "Pan-Slavism during World War II," 110.

20 Behrends, "Stalins slavischer Volkskrieg," 99–103.

21 Troebst, "Schwanengesang gesamtslavischer 'Einheit und Brüderlichkeit,'" 47–8.

22 Behrends, "Stalins slavischer Volkskrieg," 103. A good example of the ways in which Yugoslav intellectuals deployed this Slavic idea to justify their territorial claims is Ljubo Drndić, "Značaj i perspektive krajeva Julijske krajine priključenih FNR Jugoslavije," *Republika* 3, no. 11 (1947): 849.

23 Haug, *Creating a Socialist Yugoslavia,* 56–7; Aleksa Đilas, *The Contested Country: Yugoslav Unity and Communist Revolution, 1919–1953* (Cambridge, MA: Harvard University Press, 1991), 89–97.

24 Haug, *Creating a Socialist Yugoslavia,* 96–101.

25 Petranović, *Balkanska federacija,* 121–2.

26 Ibid., 157–60; Niebuhr, *The Search for a Cold War Legitimacy,* 44–50.

27 Petranović, *Balkanska federacija,* 193–5; Banac, *With Stalin against Tito,* 32–6.

28 Troebst, "Schwanengesang gesamtslavischer 'Einheit und Brüderlichkeit,'" 47–8; Behrends, "Stalins slavischer Volkskrieg," 95; Kohn, *Pan-Slavism,* 303.

29 Recent scholarship has demonstrated that Soviet intellectual culture was informed by distinct understandings of race, albeit understandings that identified "degrees of kinship" rather than notions of genetic difference. David Rainbow, "Race as Ideology: An Approach" in *Ideologies of Race: Imperial Russia and the Soviet Union in Global Context,* ed. David Rainbow (Montreal and Kingston: McGill-Queen's University Press, 2019), 8. See also Francine Hirsch, "Race Without the Practice of Racial Politics," *Slavic Review* 61, no. 1 (Spring 2002): 30–43.

266 Notes to pages 133–9

30 Troebst, "Schwanengesang gesamtslavischer 'Einheit und Brüderlichkeit,'" 48–9.

31 Jože Pirjevec, *Tito and His Comrades* (Madison: University of Wisconsin Press, 2018), 68–70. See also Svetozar Vukmanović Tempo's account of the 5 July 1941 meeting of the KPJ's politbureau in *Revolucija koja teče: memoari* (Belgrade: Komunist, 1971), 185–9. A good example of the messianic rhetoric with which KPJ officials often spoke of the Soviet Union is Milovan Đilas's 1943 article, "Crvena armija spasilac čovječanstva," reprinted in *Članci, 1941–1946* (Belgrade: Kultura, 1947), 72–7.

32 Arhiv Jugoslavije, Fond 507, Centralni komitet Komunističke partije Jugoslavije, 1942–112. 1942. III. 7. "Naprednim slojevima Bugarske vojske."

33 Arhiv Jugoslavije, Fond 507, Centralni komitet Komunističke partije Jugoslavije, 1941–133. *Vjesnik: hrvatske jedinstvene nacionalno oslobodilačke fronte*, XII 1941, br. 9, "Ruski partizani naši učitelji," 4–6.

34 Arhiv Jugoslavije, Fond 507, Centralni komitet Komunističke partije Jugoslavije, 1941–113. *Bilten: komunističke partije jugoslavije za Bosnu i Herzegovinu*, br. 1, 18 December 1941, 6.

35 John Enyeart, *Death to Fascism: Louis Adamič's Fight for Democracy* (Urbana: University of Illinois Press, 2019), 71–2.

36 Louis Adamič, *My Native Land* (New York: Harper and Brothers, 1943), 447–8, 466.

37 Ibid., 448.

38 Ibid., 208–9.

39 Ibid., 465–6.

40 Arhiv Jugoslavije, Fond 507, Centralni komitet Komunističke partije Jugoslavije, 1942. XI, 3-5. 1942. "Narodu Crne Gore i Boke."

41 Andrew Wachtel, *Making a Nation, Breaking a Nation: Literature and Cultural Politics in Yugoslavia* (Stanford, CA: Stanford University Press, 1998), 149–50.

42 Haug, *Creating a Socialist Yugoslavia*, 75–82. For a detailed account of the Serb-Croat dynamics within the wartime KPJ, see Filip Erdeljac, "After Indifference: Non-Elite Engagement with National Politics in the Interwar Yugoslav Kingdom, World War II Croatia and Socialist Yugoslavia, 1934–1948" (PhD diss., New York University, 2016), 309–400.

43 Arhiv Jugoslavije, Fond 507, Centralni komitet Komunističke partije Jugoslavije, 1943, "Poruka Dalmatincima," April 1943.

44 Vladimir Nazor, *S partizanima, 1943–1944* (Belgrade: Državni izdavački zavod Jugoslavije, 1945), 78.

45 Ibid., 37.

Notes to pages 139–43

46 On the intellectual genealogy of the Ustasha's racial ideology, see Nevenko Bartulin, *The Racial Idea in the Independent State of Croatia* (Leiden, NE: Brill, 2014).

47 Petranović, *Balkanska federacija*, 58–9.

48 Ibid., 65.

49 Accounts of why Tito rejected the plans differ. While Tempo's later memoirs clearly suggest that Tito, correctly, worried about his strategic differences with the Greek and Bulgarian communists over the necessity of guerilla struggle and the revolutionary transfer of power, Milovan Đilas chalked it up to Tito's concerns over the influence of the British on the Greek resistance. Meanwhile, the historian Branko Petranović cites Tito's fears that any steps towards a wider Balkan federation would alienate the British who, in the summer of 1943, appeared amenable to arming Yugoslav partisans. Tempo, *Revolucija koja teče*, 361; Milovan Đilas, *Wartime*, trans. Michael Boro Petrovich (New York: Harcourt, Brace, Jovanovich, 1977), 350; Petranović, *Balkanska federacija*, 65–8.

50 Tempo, *Revolucija koja teče*, 360.

51 Petranović, *Balkanska federacija*, 98.

52 Tempo, *Revolucija koja teče*, 354.

53 Ibid., 369–70.

54 Ibid., 380.

55 Christine Lavrence has conveniently coined the term "Balkan time" to mark this notion of cyclical temporality: "Beyond Balkan Time: Memory, Monument and Agency in Belgrade," (PhD diss., York University, 2005). This concept obviously builds on earlier theoretical scholarship, including Maria Todorova, *Imagining the Balkans* (Oxford: Oxford University Press, 2009) and Tomislav Longinović, *Vampire Nation: Violence as Cultural Imaginary* (Durham, NC: Duke University Press, 2011).

56 Haug, *Creating a Socialist Yugoslavia*, 116–19; Melissa Bokovoy, *Peasants and Communists: Politics and Ideology in the Yugoslav Countryside, 1941–1953* (Pittsburgh, PA: University of Pittsburgh Press, 1998), 29–79; Vladimir Unkovski-Korica, *The Economic Struggle for Power in Tito's Yugoslavia: From World War II to Non-Alignment* (London: IB Tauris, 2016), 22–56.

57 Niebuhr, *The Search for a Cold War Legitimacy*, 20–2, 48–50; Banac, *With Stalin against Tito*, 28–43.

58 Geoffrey Swain, "The Cominform: Tito's International?" *The Historical Journal* 35, no. 3 (September 1992): 641–63; Unkovski-Korica, *The Economic Struggle for Power in Tito's Yugoslavia*, 56–9.

268   Notes to pages 143–4

59 See, for example, Milovan Đilas's description of Tito's first postwar visit
    to Czechoslovakia in March 1946 in *Rise and Fall*, trans. John F. Loud
    (London: MacMillan, 1985), 11–25. Also, Troebst, "Schwanengesang
    gesamtslavischer 'Einheit und Brüderlichkeit,'" 45–6.
60 Petranović, *Balkanska federacija*, 154–5; Pirjevec, *Tito and his Comrades*,
    168–74.
61 Pawlowski, "Pan-Slavism During World War II," 304–5; Troebst,
    "Schwanengesang gesamtslavischer 'Einheit und Brüderlichkeit,'" 51–2.
62 Hrvoje Klasić, "Sveslavenski kongres u beogradu 1946. i njegova
    percepcija u hrvatskom tisku," *Historijski Zbornik* 58 (2005): 176.
63 Čedomir Minderović, "O neposrednim zadacima naše književnosti i naši
    književnih radnika," *Mladost* 3, no. 12 (Decembar 1947): 6.
64 Arhiv Jugoslavije, Fond 498, Savez književnika Jugoslavije, 12. Zapisnik,
    18.III.1947, 2.
65 A good overview of some of this translation work can be found in
    "Bibliografija," *Naša književnost* 1, no. 1 (January 1946): 146–9, which
    details recent publications, including foreign translations. To give just a
    sense of the volume of translations of Slavic literatures published during
    this time, consider the following: Over 1946–47, the first three volumes of
    Sholokhov's *Quiet Flows the Don* were published in both Serbo-Croatian
    by the Belgrade-based publisher, Kultura, and in Slovene by the Ljubljana
    house, Cankarjeva založba. Other works by Sholokhov were also trans-
    lated during this period, including *Uzorana ledina*, trans. Ivana
    Anđelković (Belgrade: Kultura, 1945), and *Oni su se borili za otadžbinu*,
    trans. Ivana Anđelković (Sarajevo: Svjetlost, 1945). Other publications
    from Soviet literature included Aleksej Tolstoj: *Članci: 1942–1943*, trans.
    Mirjana Obrenović Šimanski (Zagreb: Nakladni zavod Hrvatske, 1945);
    Junaci (Belgrade: Prosveta, 1945); *Novele i pripovetke, 1910–1943*, trans.
    Svetozar Matić, Vera Stojić, and Kiril Taranovski (Belgrade: Državni
    izdavački zavod jugoslavije, 1945); *Hleb* (Belgrade: Kultura, 1946);
    Moreplovci, trans. Jelena Jovanović (Belgrade: Prosveta, 1946);
    Aleksandar Fadejev: *Lenjingrad u danima blokade*, trans. Zoraida
    Mihailvić (Belgrade: Prosveta, 1945); *Poraz*, trans. Ružica Bonači-Janović
    (Belgrade: Kultura, 1946); *Metelica*, trans. Nikola Ivančević (Novi Sad,
    RS: Matica Srpska, 1947); *Mlada garda*, trans. Slavka Dimić-Piškin and
    Milica Dajović (Belgrade: Novo pokolenje, 1947); Mihail Iljin: *Crnim po
    belom*, trans. Radovan Teodosić (Belgrade: NOPOK, 1945); *Kako je čovjek
    postao divom*, trans. Stjepan Kranjčević (Zagreb, Nakladni zavod
    hrvatske, 1945); *Priče o stvarima*, trans. Tatjana Šeremet and Stjepan
    Kranjčević (Belgrade: Kultura, 1946); *Priroda i ljudi*, trans. Z. and J.

Aljančić (Belgrade: NOPOK, 1946); *Čovek i stihija*, trans. M. Cvetanović i V. Vasić (Belgrade: Novo pokolenje, 1948); Vasilij Grossman: *Narod je besmrtan*, trans. Milica Latković (Belgrade: Prosveta, 1944); *Staljingradske crtice* (Moskva: Izdavačko preduzeće literature na inostranim jezicima, 1944); *Život: pripovijest*, Đuro Čajkovski (Zagreb: Nakladni zavod Hrvatske, 1946); Ilja Erenburg: *Dani slave* (Novi Sad, RS: Knjižara budućnost, 1945); *Ratni dnevnik*, trans. Milica Čolaković (Belgrade: Prosveta, 1945); *Lav na trgu*, trans. Nina Kožemjakin (Sarajevo: Radnik, 1948); Nikolaj Ostrovski: *Rođeni u buri*, trans. Miloš Moskovljević (Belgrade: NOPOK, 1945); *Kako se kalio čelik* (Belgrade: NOPOK, 1945); *Kako se je kalilo jeklo*, trans. Vladimir Levstik (Ljubljana: Mladinska knjiga, 1945); and Jurij Janovskij: *Zemlja otaca*, trans. Nana Bogdanović (Belgrade: Prosveta, 1945). Translations from Polish literature included Jerzy Andrzejewski, *Pepeo i alem-kamen*, trans. Julije Benešić (Zagreb: Matica hrvatska, 1948); Zofja Nalkovska, "Profesor Španer," *Naša književnost* 1, no. 12 (December 1946): 538–44; Zofia Nałkowska, *Medaljoni*, trans. Julije Benešić (Zagreb: Nakladni zavod hrvatski, 1948); Seweryna Szmaglewska, *Dim nad logorom Birkenau*, trans. Julije Benešić (Zagreb: Kultura, 1947); Marija Šćepanska, "Meseci," *Naša književnost* 1, no. 4 (April 1946): 565–85; as well as an overview of contemporary cultural life in the country by S.S., "Kulturni život u Poljskoj," *Naša književnost* 1, no. 2 (February 1946): 297–9. From Czech literature, the most translated writer was Ivan Olbracht: *Izgnanici u dolini*, trans. Krešimir Georgijević (Novi Sad, RS: Budućnost, 1946); *Ogledalo s rešetkama*, trans. Ljudevit Jonke (Zagreb: Matica hrvatske, 1946); *Ana proleterka*, trans. Ljudevit Jonke (Zagreb: Kultura, 1947); *Hajduk Nikola Šuhaj*, trans. Ljudevit Jonke (Zagreb: Nakladni zavod hrvatske, 1947); as well as Julius Fučík: *Zapisci s vješala*, trans. Ljudevit Jonke (Zagreb: Nakladni zavod hrvatske, 1946); *Zapiski izpod vešal*, trans. Viktor Smolej (Ljubljana: Slovenski knjižni zavod, 1947); "Reportaža pisana s omčom o vratu," *Naša književnost* 1, no. 4 (April 1946): 546–64. Other Czech translations included Petr Bezruč, *Šleske pjesme*, trans. Gustav Krklec (Zagreb: Nakladni zavod hrvatske, 1948); Marie Majerová, *Sirena*, trans. Ljudevit Jonke (Zagreb: Nakladni zavod hrvatske, 1948); Božena Němcová, *Bakica: slike iz seoskoga života*, trans. Ljudevit Jonke (Zagreb: Nakladni zavod hrvatske, 1946); and brief reports on Czech culture in articles such as "Kulturne pojave u Češkoj," *Naša književnost* 1, no. 4 (April 1946): 619–20, and N.L. "Češki spev o našim borbama i patnjama," *Naša književnost* 1, no. 2 (February 1946): 299–300. The Slovak writer Peter Jilemnicky was translated in "U tuđini," *Naša književnost* 1,

270   Notes to pages 144–8

no. 12 (December 1946): 552–60, and his *Neorano polje* translated into Serbo-Croatian by Krešimir Georgijević (Belgrade: Prosveta, 1948) and Slovene by Viktor Smolej (Ljubljana: Cankarjeva založba, 1947); while Yugoslav writers commemorated the death of the leftist poet Janko Jesenski in Z.B., "Smrt slovačkoga pisca Janka Jesenskoga," *Naša književnost* 1, no. 2 (February 1946): 314–15. Finally, translations from contemporary Bulgarian literature included Georgi Karaslavov, *Tatula*, trans. Petar St Bešević (Belgrade: Iproz, 1945); *Povesti sa sela* (Belgrade: Zadružna knjiga, 1948); Ljudmil Stojanov, *Mehmed Sinap: povijest jednog ustanka*, trans. Ivan Davorinov (Zagreb: Nakladni zavod hrvatske, 1948); and the collection of short stories *Milosrđe boga Marsa: pripovetke nove Bugarske*, trans. Dušan Kostić and Đoka Ignjatović (Belgrade: Prosveta, 1945). This is far from an exhaustive list of the hundreds of translations from Slavic literatures into Serbo-Croatian and Slovene (to say nothing of Macedonian) from 1945–48, but it goes some way to demonstrating the emphasis publishers placed on orienting Yugoslav readers to a broader Slavic cultural world.

66 Miodrag Popović, "Više pažnje prevodnoj poeziji," *Mladost* 3, no. 12 (December 1947): 105.

67 Dušan Pirjevec, "Most," *Novi Svet* 5–7 (1946): 464.

68 On the link between Greater Russian nationalism and the new Slavic movement, see Behrends, "Stalins slavischer Volkskrieg," 95.

69 Igo Gruden, "Sofija," *Novi Svet* 5–7 (1946): 325.

70 Miško Kranjec, *Pesem gora* (Ljubljana: Slovenski knjižni zavod, 1946), 124–5.

71 Ibid., 411.

72 Dimitrije Tucović, *Srbija i Arbanija* (Belgrade: Kultura, 1946).

73 Dimitar Mitrev, "Dimo hadži Dimov: po slučaj 21 godina od negovata smrt," *Novi Den*, 1 (October 1945): 42.

74 Milan Bogdanović, "Stogodišnjica rođenja Svetozara Markovića," *Naša književnost* 1, no. 9 (September 1946): 5–8; Jovan Popović, "Svetozareva buktinja i našom književnošću," *Naša književnost* 1, no. 9 (September 1946): 9–25; Oskar Davičo, "Pesme u spomen na tamnovanje i smrt Svetozara Markovića," *Naša književnost* 1, no. 9 (September 1946): 45–52; Dušan Matić, "Svetozar Marković i naša kultura," *Naša književnost* 1, no. 9 (September 1946): 53–65; Todor Pavlov, "Svetozar Marković," *Naša književnost* 1, no. 2 (February 1947): 161–77; Marin Franičević, "Svetozar Marković," *Republika* 2, nos. 9–10 (1946): 697–711.

75 Niebuhr, *The Search for a Cold War Legitimacy*, 44–50.

Notes to pages 149–50

76 Petranović, *Balkanska federacija*, 154–5. Also see Edvard Kardelj's speech from the conference: "Zgodovinski opomin Edvarda Kardelja na mirovni konferenci," *Novi Svet* 9 (1946): i–vii.

77 Petranović, *Balkanska federacija*, 159–61.

78 "Republika federative popullore e Jugosllavis dhe Republika Popullore e Shqipnis vendosen ne nenshkruaj paktin miqesin dhe ndihmën reciproke," *Zani i Rinisë*, 2, no. 16 (1946): 1; "Rroftë miqsija Jugosllavo-Shqiptare," *Flaka e vllaznimit* 3, no. 56 (12 July 1947): 2.

79 Vladimir Dedijer, *Tito Speaks: His Self Portrait and Struggle with Stalin* (London: Weidenfeld and Nicolson, 1953), 311–12.

80 D. Dragutinoviq, "Si jetojmë na ..." *Zani i Rinisë* 2, no. 19 (2 October 1946): 3.

81 See the report of the general secretary of the Union of Writers of Yugoslavia from November 1947: Minderović, "O neposrednim zadacima naše književnosti i naši književnih radnika," 1–7. An example of this was the visit of the Albanian writer Aleks Çaçi to Belgrade in May 1948: "Albanski književnik Aleks Ćaći u Beogradu," *Književne novine*, 4 May 1948, 2.

82 Aleks Ćaći, "Pismo iz Albanije," *Književne novine*, 11 May 1948, 4: Dimiter Šuterići, "Albanska književnost," *Naša književnost* 1, no. 1 (January 1946): 113–18; Vehbi Bala, "Pred jurišem" and "Selo," *Republika* 3, no. 5 (1947): 336–7; Jusuf Alibali, "Ram Sula," *Mladost* 3, no. 10 (October 1947): 52–8. The fact that Shuteriqi's text was based on a French translation and Alibali's on a Russian translation suggests Yugoslav intellectuals' lack of familiarity with the Albanian language.

83 Arhiv Jugoslavije, Fond 507, CK KPJ, Ideološka komisija to CK KP Hrvatske Agit-Prop, 17 January 1947, 4.

84 These often reflected the underlying prejudices and paternalism of Yugoslav intellectuals with regards to their comrades to the south. See, for instance, Marjan Mušič, "Albanske študije," *Novi Svet* 2, no. 7 (1947): 488–96.

85 Marijan Jurković, "Bilješke iz Albanije," *Književne novine*, 25 May 1948, 4.

86 Radovan Zogović, *Žilama za kamen* (Titograd: Grafički zavod, 1969), 101–28.

87 Ibid., 143–54.

88 He returned to this theme during the war in his 1944 text, "Bratstvo po oslobodilačkom oružju" (Brotherhood by armed liberation), which cele-brated the joint campaign of Yugoslav and Albanian partisans in Kosovo.

272   Notes to pages 150–3

Radovan Zogović, *Na poprištu: književni i politički članci, književne krit-ike, polemike, marginalije* (Belgrade: Kultura, 1947), 323–6.

89 Radovan Zogović, "Okoli Skadra" and "Srpasti mesec za mejo zasužnjene albanije," trans. Pavel Golia, *Novi Svet* 3, no. 4 (1948): 250–1.

90 Dušan Kostić, "Pismo sa Kosova i Metohije," *Književne novine*, 11 May 1948, 3.

91 Whether this account is accurate or not, it speaks to the image that socialist intellectuals hoped to cultivate of Zogović as an important Yugoslav interlocutor with Albania. Jurković, "Bilješke iz Albanije," 4.

92 Venko Markovski, "Zheleznicata," *Novi Den* 9–10 (November–December 1946): 29–30.

93 Mira Alečković, "Snovi neimara Rada," *Mladost* 3, no. 3 (March 1947): 45–6.

94 This reading is buttressed by the fact that, in her reportage from the work brigades, Alečković made a point of referencing the young volunteers from Albania and Greece who joined the Yugoslav youth in constructing the new socialist countryside. Mira Alečković, "Novoj pruzi naš pozdrav i naša vernost," *Mladost* 3, no. 4 (April 1947): 1–6.

95 Banac, *With Stalin against Tito*, 32–8; Andrew Rossos, "Incompatible Allies: Greek Communism and Macedonian Nationalism in the Civil War in Greece, 1943–1949," *Journal of Modern History* 69, no. 1 (March 1977): 42–76.

96 "Rroftë miqsija Jugosllavo-Shqiptare," *Flaka e vllaznimit* 3, no. 56 (12 July 1947): 2.

97 Rossos, "Incompatible allies."

98 Jane Sapozhnikov, "Nepokoreni," *Novi den* 1–2 (January–February 1947): 48–52.

99 Blazhe Koneski, "Na granica," *Novi den* 4–5 (April–May 1947): 47–8.

100 The commission was, however, frequently called upon by members of the communist states to also investigate opposition accusations of the Greek government's persecution of political opponents. Thanasis D. Sfikas, "Britain, the United States and the Soviet Union in the United Nations Commission of Investigation in Greece, January–May 1947," *Contemporary European History* 2, no. 3 (1993): 250–5.

101 *Med Markosovimi partizani* (Ljubljana: Slovenski knjižni zavod, 1948); *Mezhdu partizanite na Markos*, trans. Liliia Katskova (Sofiia: Bŭlgarskata rabotnicheska partiia, 1948); *Hellász sziklái között*, trans. István Kovács (Budapest: Szikra, 1948); *Hos Markos' partisaner*, trans. S. Suzin (Oslo: Falken, 1948); *Fī Ziyārat ansār Mārkūs* (Beirut: Dār al-Qāri' al-'Arabī, 1948).

Notes to pages 153–9

102 Oskar Davičo, *Među Markosovim partizanima* (Belgrade: Prosveta, 1969), 55, 58, 274.

103 Ibid., 68–9, 123.

104 Ibid., 96.

105 On Rhigas and the Balkan Enlightenment, see Paschalis Kitromilides, "An Enlightenment Perspective on Balkan Cultural Pluralism: The Republican Vision of Rhigas Velestinlis," *History of Political Thought* 24, no. 3 (Autumn 2003): 465–79.

106 Davičo, *Među Markosovim partizanima*, 265–6.

107 Ibid., 66, 123–6, 227, 364–7.

108 Ibid., 61–2.

109 Arhiv Jugoslavije, Fond 507, Centralni komitet Komunističke partije Jugoslavije, 1943, Kutija 22 "Sedmonovembarski govor druga Milovana Đilasa," 1.

110 Ibid., 2.

111 Ibid., 3.

CHAPTER SIX

1 Ivo Banac, *With Stalin against Tito: Cominformist Splits in Yugoslav communism* (Ithaca, NY: Cornell University Press, 1988).

2 Dennison Rusinow, *The Yugoslav Experiment, 1948–74* (Berkeley: University of California Press, 1977).

3 John Lampe, Russell Prickett, and Ljubiša Adamović, *Yugoslav-American Economic Relations since World War II* (Durham, NC: Duke University Press, 1990), 35; John Lampe, *Yugoslavia as History: Twice There Was a Country* (Cambridge: Cambridge University Press, 1996), 250–6; Susan Woodward, *Socialist Unemployment: The Political Economy of Yugoslavia, 1945–1990* (Princeton, NJ: Princeton University Press, 1995), 145–6; Lorraine Lees, *Keeping Tito Afloat: The United States, Yugoslavia, and the Cold War* (University Park: Pennsylvania State University Press, 1997), 76–9.

4 As revisionist historians of Yugoslavia have demonstrated, from the mid-1950s onwards the country became dependent on loans and investment from the US and Western Europe. See Woodward, *Socialist Unemployment*, 222–4; Vladimir Unkovski-Korica, *The Economic Struggle for Power in Tito's Yugoslavia: From World War II to Non-Alignment* (London: IB Tauris, 2017), 220–1.

5 Rusinow, *The Yugoslav Experiment*; Fred Warner Neal, *Titoism in Action: The Reforms in Yugoslavia after 1948* (Berkeley: University of California Press, 1958); Goran Musić, "Yugoslavia: Workers' Self-Management as

274 Notes to pages 159–61

State Paradigm" in *Ours to Master and to Own: Workers' Control from the Commune to the Present*, ed. Immanuel Ness and Dario Azzellini (Chicago, IL: Haymarket Books, 2011), 172–90.

6 The process of decentralization and its long-term consequences for the internal coherence of the Yugoslav federation are unpacked in Dejan Jović, *Yugoslavia: A State that Withered Away* (West Lafayette, IN: Purdue University Press, 2009).

7 Unkovski-Korica, *The Economic Struggle for Power in Tito's Yugoslavia*, 94.

8 Banac, *With Stalin against Tito*, 28–43; Rinna Kullaa, *Non-Alignment and Its Origins in Cold War Europe: Yugoslavia, Finland and the Soviet Union* (London: IB Tauris, 2012), 29–33.

9 Robert Niebuhr, *The Search for a Cold War Legitimacy: Foreign Policy and Tito's Yugoslavia* (Leiden, NE: Brill, 2018), 15; Jürgen Dinkel, *The Non-Aligned Movement: Genesis, Organization and Politics (1927–1992)*, trans. Alex Skinner (Leiden, NE: Brill, 2019).

10 On the early origins of Yugoslav non-alignment, see Alvin Rubinstein, *Yugoslavia and the Nonaligned World* (Princeton, NJ: Princeton University Press, 1970), 15–21; Niebuhr, *The Search for a Cold War Legitimacy*, 92–5; Jovan Čavoški, "Arming Nonalignment: Yugoslavia's Relations with Burma and the Cold War in Asia (1950–1955)" *Cold War International History Project*, Working Paper 61 (April 2010).

11 Vijay Prashad, *The Darker Nations: A People's History of the Third World* (New York: New Press, 2007), 95–104.

12 Dinkel, *The Non-Aligned Movement*, 105–7.

13 Svetozar Rajak, "In Search of a Life outside the Two Blocs: Yugoslavia's Road to Non-Alignment" in *Velike sile i male države u hladnom ratu 1945–1955: slučaj Jugoslavije*, ed. Ljubodrag Dimić (Belgrade: Katedra za istoriju Jugoslavije, 2005), 84–105; Tvrtko Jakovina, *Treća strana hladnog rata* (Zagreb: Fraktura, 2011); Kullaa, *Non-Alignment and Its Origins in Cold War Europe*; Niebuhr, *The Search for a Cold War Legitimacy*; Radina Vučetić and Paul Betts, eds., *Tito in Africa: Picturing Solidarity* (Belgrade: Museum of Yugoslavia, 2017).

14 Dinkel, *The Non-Aligned Movement*, 96; Paul Stubbs, "Introduction: Socialist Yugoslavia and the Non-Aligned Movement: Contradictions and Contestations," in *Socialist Yugoslavia and the Non-Aligned Movement*, ed. Paul Stubbs (Montreal and Kinsgton: McGill-Queen's University Press, 2023), 11.

15 These international conferences were often part of a wider media strategy to shore up postcolonial states' newly won sovereignty. Dinkel, *The Non-Aligned Movement*, 53–8.

Notes to pages 161–4 275

16 As the late Aijaz Ahmad argued, the appeal of non-alignment for many postcolonial leaders lay in its potential to resolve the contradictions of domestic politics. Ahmad, *In Theory: Classes, Nations, and Literatures* (London: Verso, 1992), 297–304.

17 Dinkel, *The Non-Aligned Movement*, 64, 89; and Niebuhr, *The Search for a Cold War Legitimacy*, 102–11.

18 Prashad, *The Darker Nations*, xv.

19 Nemanja Radonjić, "A Non-Aligned Continent: Africa in the Global Imaginary of Socialist Yugoslavia," in *Socialist Yugoslavia and the Non-Aligned Movement*, 306–7.

20 An excellent overview of how Yugoslav non-aligned diplomacy was covered in the Yugoslav press is Vučetić and Betts, *Tito in Africa: Picturing Solidarity*.

21 On the symbolic geographies of non-alignment, see Radonjić, "A Non-Aligned Continent," 302–28; and Ljiljiana Kolešnik, "Practices of Yugoslav Cultural Exchange with Non-Aligned Countries," in *Socialist Yugoslavia and the Non-Aligned Movement*, 178–9.

22 Dinkel, *The Non-Aligned Movement*; Agustín Cosovschi, "From Santiago to Mexico: The Yugoslav Mission in Latin America during the Cold War and the Limits of Non-Alignment," in *Socialist Yugoslavia and the Non-Aligned Movement*, 283–301.

23 Theodora Dragostinova, *The Cold War from the Margins: A Small Socialist State on the Global Cultural Scene* (Ithaca, NY: Cornell University Press, 2021), 8.

24 In this sense, I follow Robert Niebuhr's insistence on the parallels between socialist Yugoslavia's Balkan-oriented brinksmanship during the 1940s and its non-aligned foreign policy in the 1950s–60s. Niebuhr, *The Search for a Cold War Legitimacy*, 51–2.

25 Glenda Sluga, *Internationalism in the Age of Nationalism* (Philadelphia: University of Pennsylvania Press, 2013), 105; Glenda Sluga, "UNESCO and the (One) World of Julian Huxley," *Journal of World History* 21, no. 3 (September 2010): 393–418. Nancy Jachec traces what seems to be a key conceptual morphology of one-worldism in her history of the notion of a "civilization of the universal" that came to animate figures around UNESCO in the 1950s. See Nancy Jachec, *Europe's Intellectuals and the Cold War: The European Society of Culture, Postwar Politics and International Relations* (London: IB Tauris, 2015), 71–96.

26 For an account of the ways imperial legacies shaped the construction of postwar international institutions, see Sluga, "UNESCO and the (One) World of Julian Huxley"; Mark Mazower, *Governing the World: The*

276 Notes to pages 164–7

History of an Idea, 1815 to the Present (New York: Penguin Press, 2012), 191–243. Other scholars, however, have pointed to the ways in which postwar conceptions of one-worldism challenged imperial logics of cultural difference. See Erez Manela, "Visions of One World" in *The Cambridge History of America and the World: The Perils of Interdependence*, ed. Brooke Blower and Andrew Preston (Cambridge: Cambridge University Press, 2022), 3: 702–22; Todd Shepard, "Algeria, France, Mexico, UNESCO: A Transnational History of Anti-Racism and Decolonization, 1932–1962" *Journal of Global History* 6, no. 2 (July 2011): 273–97; François Hartog, *Regimes of Historicity: Presentism and the Experience of Time*, trans. Saskia Brown (New York: Columbia University Press, 2015), 24–7.

27 Quoted in James Sewell, UNESCO *and World Politics: Engaging in International Relations* (Princeton, NJ: Princeton University Press, 1975), 114. See also, Sluga "UNESCO and the (One) World of Julian Huxley," 397.

28 This postwar reframing of the global had downstream effects. As Perrin Selcer has demonstrated, the emergence of postwar international govern-ance led to an explosion of new scalar arrangements around the world as a globally active caste of technocrats set out to reframe a myriad of regu-lative problems or research programs at scales that often transcended or cut through state borders. Perrin Selcer, *The Postwar Origins of the Global Environment: How the United Nations Built Spaceship Earth* (New York: Columbia University Press, 2018), 8–10.

29 Dinkel, *The Non-Aligned Movement*, 108–9; Tvrtko Jakovina, "'Not Like a Modern Day Jesus Christ': Pragmatism and Idealism in Yugoslav Non-Alignment," in *Socialist Yugoslavia and the Non-Aligned Movement*, 113; Manu Bhagavan, *The Peacemakers: India and the Quest for One World* (Noida, IN: HarperCollins India, 2012).

30 Bojana Videkanić, *Nonaligned Modernism: Socialist Post-colonial Aesthetics in Yugoslavia, 1945–1985* (Montreal and Kingston: McGill-Queen's University Press, 2019), 109.

31 Stubbs, "Introduction," 12–13.

32 Ješa Denegri, "Inside or Outside 'Socialist Modernism'? Radical Views on the Yugoslav Art Scene," in *Impossible Histories: Historical Avant-Gardes, Neo-Avant-Gardes and Post-Avant-Gardes in Yugoslavia, 1918–1991*, ed. Dubravka Đurić and Miško Šuvaković (Cambridge, MA: MIT Press, 2003), 170–208; Radina Vučetić, *Coca Cola Socialism: Americanization of Yugoslav Culture in the Sixties*, trans. John K. Cox (Budapest: Central European University Press, 2018), 137–43; Borislav

Jakovljević, *Alienation Effects: Performance and Self-Management in Yugoslavia, 1945–91* (Ann Arbor: University of Michigan Press, 2016), 83–98; Sveta Lukić, *Contemporary Yugoslav Literature: A Sociopolitical Approach*, trans. Pola Triandis (Urbana: University of Illinois Press, 1972), 13–19, 35–7.

33 Videkanić, *Nonaligned Modernism*, 7–10.

34 Stanko Lasić has demonstrated how the debates in 1950 returned to several questions that had driven the conflict on the literary Left of the 1930s. Stanko Lasić, *Sukob na književnoj ljevici 1928–1953* (Zagreb: Liber, 1970), 245–92.

35 On Ristić's role in the European Society of Culture, see Jachec, *Europe's Intellectuals and the Cold War.*

36 Kolešnik, "Practices of Yugoslav Cultural Exchange with Non-Aligned Countries," 179; Videkanić, *Nonaligned Modernism*, 105; Jachec, *Europe's Intellectuals and the Cold War*, 108–9.

37 Marko Ristić, *Politička književnost: za ovu Jugoslaviju, 1944–1958* (Sarajevo: Oslobođenje, 1977), 252.

38 Ibid.

39 Ibid.

40 Ibid., 256. In this he echoed a similar argument by Jawaharlal Nehru, who framed the Indian federation in a similar light. Sluga, *Internationalism in the Age of Nationalism*, 85.

41 Miroslav Krleža, "Govor na kongresu jugoslavenskih književnika u Ljubljani 1952" in *Programi i manifesti u hrvatskoj književnosti*, ed. Miroslav Šicel (Zagreb: Liber, 1972), 326.

42 Miroslav Krleža, *Eseji: knjiga šesta* (Zagreb: Zora, 1967), 227.

43 Eric Weitz, "Self-Determination: How a German Enlightenment Idea Became the Slogan of National Liberation and a Human Right," *The American Historical Review* 120, no. 2 (April 2015): 462–96; James M. Robertson, "Navigating the Postwar Liberal Order: Autonomy, Creativity and Modernism in Socialist Yugoslavia," *Modern Intellectual History* 17, no. 2 (June 2020): 385–412.

44 Oskar Davičo, "Marginalije povodom jednog vekovnog ljudskog sna i današnjih pregovora o primirju," *Književne novine*, 10 July 1951, 3.

45 Weitz, "Self-determination," 470–1.

46 Ibid., 489–95; Adom Getachew, *Worldmaking after Empire: The Rise and Fall of Self-Determination* (New York: Columbia University Press, 2019), 87–92; Roland Burke, *Decolonization and the Evolution of International Human Rights* (Philadelphia: University of Pennsylvania Press, 2010), 35–58.

278   Notes to pages 170–2

47 Predrag Milojević, "Veliki i mali: od objekta imperijalizma do subjekta svetske politike," *Književne novine*, 1–15 May 1955, 2.

48 Christoph Kalter, *The Discovery of the Third World: Decolonization and the Rise of the New Left in France c. 1950–1976*, trans. Thomas Dunlap (Cambridge: Cambridge University Press, 2016), 201–2, 214–27.

49 Bojana Videkanić, "The Long Durée of Yugoslav Socially Engaged Art and its Continued Life in the Non-Aligned World," in *Socialist Yugoslavia and the Non-Aligned Movement*, 134–5.

50 Videkanić, *Nonaligned Modernism*, 55–7.

51 Krleža, "Govor na kongresu," 330.

52 Ristić, *Politička književnost*, 252–3.

53 Vladimir Petrić, "Kabuki nekad i sad," *Književne novine*, 3 June 1954, 7; B. Marinković-Rakić, "Poznanstvo s Afrikom," *Književne novine*, 12 August 1954, 8; U Nu, "O suvremenoj burmanskoj književnosti," *Republika* 12, no. 3 (May 1956): 63; "Njihova umetnost prodrla je u svet," *Književne novine*, 15 February 1955, 5; Novak Simić, "Arapska umetnost danas," *Republika* 12, no. 6 (December 1956): 38–40; Vera Ilić, "Svet i pozorište," *Književne novine*, 1–15 August 1955, 8–9.

54 Svetozar Petrović, "Jugoslaveni i Indija," *Republika* 11, no. 6 (1955): 382–99; Milica Tomić and Vanessa Vasić-Janeković, "Socialist Friendship," in *Red Africa: Affective Communities and the Cold War*, ed. Mark Nash (London: Black Dog Publishing, 2016), 153–64; Mila Turajlić, "Film as the Memory Site of the 1961 Belgrade Conference of Non-Aligned States," in *Socialist Yugoslavia and the Non-Aligned Movement*, 203–31.

55 Mao Ce-Tung, *Govori i članci* (Belgrade: Borba, 1949); "Razgovor Mao Ce Tunga s kineskim književnicima (I)," *Književne novine*, 11 January 1949, 2; "Razgovor Mao Ce Tunga s kineskim književnicima (II)," *Književne novine*, 18 January 1949, 2; "Borba za stvaranje narodne književnosti Nove Kine," *Književne novine*, 9 August 1949, 2–3; Lu Šin, *Istinita istorija a-keja i druge pripovetke*, trans. Desanka Maksimović (Belgrade: Prosveta, 1950); Lao Še, *Mjesečev srp*, trans. Nikola Sokolovski and Momčilo Ristić (Sarajevo: Svjetlost, 1956); *Djevojka sa jezera Tung Ting: kineske novele*, trans. Vladislav Kostić (Sarajevo: Veselin Masleša, 1954).

56 Ejmos Tutuola, *Pijač palmina vina*, trans. Antun Šoljan and Ivan Slamnig (Zagreb: Zora, 1954); *Crni Orfej: izbor iz suvremene crnačke i madagaskarske poezije*, ed. and trans. Božo Kukolja (Zagreb: Epoha, 1955); Vojin Dramušić, ed., *Crnačka poezija*, trans. Drago Ivanišević and Šime Balen (Sarajevo: Narodna prosvjeta, 1956); Leo Frobenius, ed., *Afričke*

Notes to pages 173–4

pripovetke, trans. Mirko Cvetkov (Novi Sad, RS: Matica srpska, 1953). See also the regular translations of and reports on African and Caribbean literature in *Književne novine*: Z. Tomičić, "Autoportre Afrike," 13 May 1954, 6–7; "Poezija crnaca iz Francuskih kolonija," 1 July 1954, 2; "Njihova umetnost prodrla je u svet," 15 February 1955, 5; Zoran Žujović, "Sada je red na Afriku …," 14 October 1956, 6.

57 Mirko Cvetkov, ed., *Indijske pripovetke* (Novi Sad, RS: Matica srpska, 1958); Džainendra Kumar, *Ostavka* (Belgrade: Nolit, 1958); Natsume Soseki, *Kokoro* (Zagreb: Zora, 1953); Natsume Soseki, *Botchan* (Belgrade: Narodna knjiiga, 1957); Nakagava Joiči, *Duge godine* (Sarajevo: Svjetlost, 1957); Jakup Kadri Karaosmanoglu, *Kuća pod najam* (Sarajevo: Svjetlost 1958); Halide Edib Adivar, *Rabija* (Sarajevo: Svjetlost, 1959); "Etiopske narodne priče," *Književne novine*, 22 July 1954, 1; "Stvaranje čoveka," *Književne novine*, 10 June 1954, 3; "Duboko učvršćena mudrost," *Književne novine*, 17 June 1954, 8; "Govor ljubavnika," *Književne novine*, 3 June 1954, 4.

58 Pandit Džavaharlal Nehru, *Otkriće Indije*, (Belgrade: Rad, 1952); Džavaharlal Nehru, *Odkritje Indije* (Ljubljana: Državna založba Slovenije, 1956); Gamal Abdel Naser, *Filozofija revolucije* (Sarajevo: Džepna knjiga,1956).

59 Aleš Bebler, *Putovanje po sunčanim zemljama* (Belgrade: Udruženje novinara Srbije, 1954); Radoljub Čolaković, *Utisci iz Indije* (Novi Sad, RS: Bratstvo-Jedinstvo, 1954).

60 Živko Milić, *Koraci po vatri* (Belgrade: Kosmos, 1956); Fadil Hadžić, *Budha me lijepo primio* (Zagreb: Vjesnik, 1955); Mahmud Konjhodžić, *Video sam Egipat* (Zagreb: Sloga, 1956); Josip Kirigin, *Palma Misira* (Zagreb: Kultura, 1956); and *Tišine pod Himalajama* (Sarajevo: Narodna prosvjeta, 1956).

61 Zuko Džumhur, *Pisma iz Azije* (Mostar, BA: Prva književna zadruga, 1973); *Pisma iz Afrike i Evrope* (Sarajevo: Oslobođenje, 1991); Čedomir Minderović, *Tragovi Indije* (Sarajevo: Veselin Masleša, 1966).

62 By the early 1960s, arguably, writers like Minderović and Džumhur had successfully transcended the orientalist framework of this genre, and their travelogues placed less emphasis on an exoticized otherness and more on the Third World as a space of contradictions ripe for reflecting on the human condition.

63 Josip Kirigin, "Bijel sam ali nisam bijelac," *Republika* 12, no. 2 (1956): 27.

64 Videkanić, *Nonaligned Modernism*, 55–8. On the history of these discourses, see Larry Wolff, *Inventing Eastern Europe: The Map of*

280 Notes to pages 175–6

Civilization on the Mind of the Enlightenment (Stanford, CA: Stanford University Press, 1996); Maria Todorova, *Imagining the Balkans* (Oxford: Oxford University Press, 1997).

65 Rubinstein, *Yugoslavia and the Nonaligned World*, 43–5.

66 On the politics of race in socialist Yugoslavia, see Catherine Baker, *Race and the Yugoslav Region: Postsocialist, Post-Conflict, Post-colonial?* (Manchester, GB: Manchester University Press, 2018); Peter Wright, "'Are There Racists in Yugoslavia?': Debating Racism and Anti-Blackness in Socialist Yugoslavia," *Slavic Review* 81, no. 2 (Summer 2022): 418–41; Sunnie Rucker-Chang, "(Re)Imagining Solidarities, (Re)Imagining Serbia: South-South Student Mobility and the 'World in Serbia' Project," in *Cultures of Mobility and Alterity: Crossing the Balkans and Beyond*, ed. Yana Hashamova, Oana Popescu-Sandu, and Sunnie Rucker-Chang (Liverpool, GB: Liverpool University Press, 2022), 19–34.

67 Radina Vučetić notes a similar trace of the legacy of European colonialism in the photography of Tito's numerous diplomatic visits from the 1950s and 1960s. Radina Vučetić, "Tito's Africa: Representations of Power during Tito's African Journeys," in *Tito in Africa*, 45.

68 Ristić, *Politička književnost*, 253.

69 Given Ristić's surrealist past, his close ties to interwar Parisian intellectual circles, and his diplomatic postings to France in the postwar years, it is safe to assume that he was aware of these trends within French anthropology. On Leiris's views, see Stefanos Geroulanos, *Transparency in Postwar France: A Critical History of the Present* (Stanford, CA: Stanford University Press, 2017), 101–10.

70 As Dragostinova notes in the case of Bulgaria, the discourse of "grand world civilizations," which similarly foregrounded the importance of premodern cultural heritage, facilitated cultural affiliations between the Second and Third worlds. See Dragostinova, *The Cold War from the Margins*, 162–94.

71 Stefanos Geroulanos, "Polyschematic Prehistory at the Dusk of Colonialism: Internationalism, Racism, and Science in Henri Breuil and Jan Smuts," *Res: Anthropology and Aesthetics* 69–70 (Spring–Autumn 2018): 138.

72 This idea was clearly expressed in, for instance, UNESCO's early interest in composing a global history of mankind, as well as the priority it accorded the preservation of cultural heritage. See Poul Duedahl, "Selling Mankind: UNESCO and the Invention of Global History," *Journal of World History* 22, no. 1 (March 2011): 107; Lynn Meskell, *A Future in Ruins: UNESCO, World Heritage, and the Dream of Peace* (New York: Oxford University Press, 2018), 3.

Notes to pages 176–8

73 Two very different visions of UNESCO's one-worldism, written by intellectuals close to the institution, are Julian Huxley, UNESCO: *Its Purpose and Its Philosophy* (Washington, DC: Public Affairs Press, 1948); and Claude Lévi-Strauss, *Race and History* (Paris: UNESCO, 1952). On the history of postwar humanism, see Erika Lorraine Milam, *Creatures of Cain: The Hunt for Human Nature in Cold War America* (Princeton, NJ: Princeton University Press, 2019); Geroulanos, *Transparency in Postwar France*, 91–111; Charles King, *Gods of the Upper Air: How a Circle of Renegade Anthropologists Reinvented Race, Sex, and Gender in the Twentieth Century* (New York: Doubleday, 2019); Jane Hiddleston, *Decolonising the Intellectual: Politics, Culture, and Humanism at the End of the French Empire* (Liverpool, GB: Liverpool University Press, 2014).

74 On Yugoslavia's enthusiastic integration into UNESCO, see Miroslav Perišić, *Od Staljina ka Sartru: formiranje jugoslovenske inteligencije na evropskim univerzitetima, 1945–1958* (Belgrade: Zavod za udžbenike, 2012), 350–1.

75 Ristić, *Politička književnost*, 253.

76 The "Herder effect" refers to the principle, most commonly attributed to Johann Gottfried Herder, that posited an equivalence between nation and language. Pascale Casanova, *The World Republic of Letters*, trans. M.B. DeBevoise (Cambridge, MA: Harvard University Press, 2004), 75–9.

77 On the fears of national extinction in Eastern European cultures, see John Connelly, *From Peoples into Nations: A History of Eastern Europe* (Princeton, NJ: Princeton University Press, 2020), 23–5.

78 Eli Finci, "Duh naše renesansne književnosti," *Književne novine*, 12 September 1950, 1; Miroslav Krleža, "Bogumilski mramorovi," *Književne novine*, 3 June 1954, 1–2; Milutin Garašanin, "Značaj neolita Srbije za proučavanje praistorije Evrope," *Književne novine*, 25 March 1954, 5. It is also likely that this concern with earlier eras of the region's cultural history was related to what Sveta Lukić characterized as the "conformist literary formula" of the Yugoslav reform era, according to which "the further into the past and away from the present the better." Lukić, *Contemporary Yugoslav Literature*, 105.

79 Meskell, *A Future in Ruins*. On the temporal structure of heritage, see Hartog, *Regimes of Historicity*, 149–92.

80 Perišić, *Od Staljina ka Sartru*, 361, Oskar Davičo, "Svetovnost i jedinstvo," *Književne novine*, 27 March 1951, 1, 3. See also the UNESCO publication of this exhibition: Svetozar Radojčić and David Talbot Rice, *Yugoslavia: Mediaeval Frescoes* (Greenwich, CT: New York Graphic Society, 1954).

Notes to pages 178–80

81 Kolešnik, "Practices of Yugoslav Cultural Exchange with Non-Aligned Countries," 184.

82 Bebler, *Putovanje po sunčanim zemljama*, 71, 91, 99, 102–4, 146.

83 Ibid., 183–4.

84 "Duboko učvršćena mudrost," 8; "Govor ljubavnika," 4; "Stvaranje čoveka," 3; "Mit acteka o postanku čoveka," *Književne novine*, 26 August, 1954, 6; "Kina o kraju života," *Književne novine*, 24 June 1954, 3; "Polinezanski mit of zadobijanju besmrtnosti," *Književne novine*, 2 September 1954, 4.

85 Čedomil Veljačić, "Život i nauka Gotama Bude," *Republika* 12, no. 3 (May 1956): 40–1; "Iz 'Dhammapade' – antologije indijskog morala," *Republika* 11, nos. 2–3 (1955): 121–7; "Rig-Veda," *Republika* 12, no. 1 (February 1956): 36–7.

86 See, for instance, Oto Bihalji-Merin's introduction to an Ancient Egyptian poem, "Govor ljubavnika," 4.

87 Josip Kirigin, "U grobnici Tutankamona," *Republika* 12, no. 4 (July 1956): 30–1; Veljačić, "Život i nauka Gotama Bude," 40–1; M.M., "Etrusko slikarstvo," *Književne novine*, 1 April 1956, 6; Ivica Degmedžić, "Otkrivena jedna vrst kretsko-mikenskog pisma," *Republika* 12, no. 5 (October 1956): 48–9; Milan Bartoš, "Pravo nacija na arheološke objekte," *Književne novine*, 10 June 1956, 1, 3.

88 Ristić himself was one of those who had advocated for an exploration of the aesthetic possibilities offered by "primitive" cultures. In his 1931 surrealist manifesto, *Nacrt za jednu fenomenologiju iracionalnog (Schema for a Phenomenology of the Irrational)*, he and his younger collaborator, Koča Popović, developed a Freudian-Marxist theory to argue that the mythical and mystical thinking of so-called "primitive" cultures presented a more immediate and direct connection to the unconscious mind than that of Western European philosophy. Koča Popović and Marko Ristić, *Nacrt za jednu fenomenologiju iracionalnog i Hronika lumbaga ili slavenska binda* (Belgrade: Prosveta, 1985), 40–2.

89 Irina Subotić, "Concerning Art and Politics in Yugoslavia during the 1930s," *Art Journal* 52 (1993): 69–71.

90 In 1952, for instance, the Gallery of Peasant Art (renamed the Gallery of Primitive Art four years later) was founded in Zagreb, where it exhibited the interwar and contemporary work of this movement.

91 I.F. "Izložba seljačke umetnosti," *Književne novine*, 22 July 1954, 8.

92 See, for instance, the feature on "our primitives" "Naši 'primitivci'" *Književne novine*, 23 December 1956, 7.

Notes to pages 180–5

93 Examples of Yugoslav exoticism of non-European cultures include: Zvonimir Golob, "Poezija 'primitivnih' naroda," *Književne novine*, 1–15 June 1955, 10; Predrag Perović, "Crna plastika: povodom Kongresa književnika i umetnika Crnaca," *Književne novine*, 30 September 1956, 1, 9; Zika Bogdanović, "Putnici i pesnici," *Književne novine*, 28 October 1956, 4; Tomičić, "Autoportre Afrike," 6–7.

94 Karl Marx, *The Eighteenth Brumaire of Louis Bonaparte* (New York: Cosimo, 2008), 1.

95 For an example of this realist position in art, see Ljubo Babić, "O progresu i tradiciji na likovnom području," *Republika* 10, no. 5 (May 1955): 369–73. On the debate between modernists and realists in postwar Serbian literature, see Predrag Palavestra, *Posleratna srpska književnost, 1945–1970* (Belgrade: Prosveta, 1972), 11–6, 58–60.

96 Marko Ristić, "O modernom i o modernizmu, opet," *Delo* 1. no. 1 (March 1955): 60.

97 Ibid., 60.

98 Bojana Videkanić identifies a similar temporal and geographical eclecticism at play in the 1966 "Peace, Humanism and Friendship" exhibition. Videkanić, "The Long Durée of Yugoslav Socially Engaged Art," 149–50.

99 Once again, this was a vision of world culture perfectly in tune with the turn being taken within UNESCO by leading French intellectuals. Consider, for instance, Lévi-Strauss's critique of social evolutionism, or Michel Leiris's arguments concerning cross-cultural exchange. Lévi-Strauss, *Race and History*, 11–23; Michel Leiris, *Race and Culture* (Paris: UNESCO, 1951), 25–35; Hartog, *Regimes of Historicity*, 23–8.

100 Li Kung-Co, "Upravitelj južne vazalne države," *Republika*, 12, no. 3 (May 1956): 21–3.

101 *Književne novine*, 15 February 1955, 1.

102 Niebuhr, *The Search for a Cold War Legitimacy*, 73; Vučetić, "Tito's Africa," 19; Rubenstein, *Yugoslavia and the Nonaligned World*, 209–11; James Mark et al., *1989: A Global History of Eastern Europe* (Cambridge: Cambridge University Press, 2019), 32; Łukasz Stanek, *Architecture in Global Socialism: Eastern Europe, West Africa, and the Middle East in the Cold War* (Princeton, NJ: Princeton University Press, 2020), 148–9.

103 By 1968, around 3,400 foreign students were studying at Yugoslav universities, the bulk of whom were from Africa and the Middle East. Miodrag Džuverović, "Foreign Citizens Studying in Yugoslavia," *Yugoslav Survey* 9, no. 3 (August 1968): 109. See also Leonora Dugonjić-Rodwin and Ivica

284 Notes to pages 185–7

Mladenović, "Transnational Education Strategies during the Cold War: Students from the Global South in Socialist Yugoslavia, 1961–91," in *Socialist Yugoslavia and the Non-Aligned Movement*, 331–59.

104 In 1960, for instance, students at the University of Ljubljana formed an "Anti-colonial Club," which organized around anti-imperial and anti-apartheid solidarity. Arhiv Jugoslavije, Savez studenata Jugoslavije, Fond 145, Folder 64, "Pravilnik antikolonialnega kluba," 1960. Likewise, in 1969 the Club of International Friendship at the University of Belgrade organized a day-long study group that included a focus on guerilla struggles in Asia, Africa, and Latin America. Arhiv Jugoslavije, Savez studenata Jugoslavije, Fond 145, Folder 33, 123–134, 22–23 March 1969, "II seminar marksističkih kružoka klubova međunarodnog prijateljstva u jugoslaviji."

105 "Izveštaj komisije UK SKS" in *Jun-Lipanj 1968: Dokumenti* (Zagreb: Hrvatsko filozofsko društvo, 1971), 25–6. On the impact of the 1966 protests on antigovernment sentiment in Yugoslavia, see Boris Kanzleiter, "1968 in Yugoslavia: Student Revolt between East and West," in *Between Prague Spring and French May: Opposition and Revolt in Europe, 1960–1980*, ed. Martin Klimke, Jacco Pekelder, and Joachim Scharloth (New York: Berghahn, 2011), 90–1; and Hrvoje Klasić, *1968: Jugoslavija i svijet* (Zagreb: Ljevak, 2012), 102–5.

106 Arhiv Jugoslavije, Savez studenata Jugoslavije, Fond 145, Folder 28, 915–918, Budo Lazović, "Informacija o razgovoru delegacije SSJ sa delegacijama studentskih organizacija Vijetnama."

107 "O čemu su govorili delegate i gosti," *Studentski list*, 17 January 1967, 5.

108 Notes from the conference discussion can be found in Arhiv Jugoslavije, Savez studenata Jugoslavije, Fond 145, Folder 7, 406–21.

109 Ralph Pervan, *Tito and the Students: The University and the University Student in Self-Managing Yugoslavia* (Nedlands: University of Western Australia Press, 1978); Boris Kanzleiter, *Die "Rote Universität": Studentenbewegung und Linksopposition in Belgrad, 1964–1975* (Hamburg, DE: VSA, 2011).

110 For an account of the student protests of June 1968, see Klasić, *1968*; Kanzleiter, "1968 in Yugoslavia"; Madigan Fichter, "Yugoslav Protest: Student Rebellion in Belgrade, Zagreb, and Sarajevo in 1968," *Slavic Review* 75, no. 1 (Spring 2016): 99–121.

111 On the importance of the anti-Vietnam War protests of the mid-1960s for shaping youth counterculture in Yugoslavia, see Madigan Fichter's forthcoming book, *Strange Forest: The Global 1960s in the Socialist Balkans* (Oxford: Oxford University Press).

Notes to pages 189–90

CHAPTER SEVEN

1 Revisionist historians of Yugoslavia have emphasized the dynamics of global capitalism and the role of international institutions, rather than local actors, in bringing about the violent collapse of the country in the 1990s. Susan Woodward, *Balkan Tragedy: Chaos and Dissolution after the Cold War* (Washington DC: Brookings Institute, 1995); Vladimir Unkovski-Korica, *The Economic Struggle for Power in Tito's Yugoslavia* (London: IB Tauris, 2017); Andreja Živković, "From the Market ... to the Market: The Debt Economy after Yugoslavia," in *Welcome to the Desert of Post-Socialism: Radical Politics after Yugoslavia*, ed. Srećko Horvat and Igor Štiks (London: Verso, 2015), 45–64.

2 In this sense, the chapter expands on critical accounts of this idea such as that of Maria Todorova in *Imagining the Balkans* (Oxford: Oxford University Press, 2009), 140–60, and Nataša Kovačević, *Narrating Post/Communism: Colonial Discourse and Europe's Borderline Civilization* (London: Routledge, 2008).

3 On Second-Third world ties, see James Mark et al., *1989: A Global History of Eastern Europe* (Cambridge: Cambridge University Press, 2019); Kristen Ghodsee, *Second World, Second Sex: Socialist Women's Activism and Global Solidarity during the Cold War* (Durham, NC: Duke University Press, 2019); Rossen Djagalov, *From Internationalism to Postcolonialism: Literature and Cinema between the Second and Third Worlds* (Montreal and Kingston: McGill-Queen's University Press, 2020); Łukasz Stanek, *Architecture in Global Socialism: Eastern Europe, West Africa, and the Middle East in the Cold War* (Princeton, NJ: Princeton University Press, 2020).

4 Nicholas Miller, *The Nonconformists: Culture, Politics and Nationalism in a Serbian Intellectual Circle, 1944–1991* (Budapest: Central European University Press, 2013); Jasna Dragović-Soso, *Saviours of the Nation: Serbia's Intellectual Opposition and the Revival of Nationalism* (Montreal and Kingston: McGill-Queen's University Press, 2002).

5 Jeffry Frieden, *Global Capitalism: Its Rise and Fall in the Twentieth Century* (New York: W.W. Norton, 2006), 363–72.

6 Fritz Bartel, *The Triumph of Broken Promises: The End of the Cold War and the Rise of Neoliberalism* (Cambridge, MA: Harvard University Press, 2022), 15.

7 Ibid., 372–6.

8 Ibid., 398–400. For a more detailed discussion of the intellectual contours of neoliberal globalization, see David Harvey, *A Brief History of*

286 Notes to pages 191–4

Neoliberalism (Oxford: Oxford University Press, 2005); Quinn Slobodian, *Globalists: The End of Empire and the Birth of Neoliberalism* (Cambridge, MA: Harvard University Press, 2018).

9 Bartel, *The Triumph of Broken Promises*, 12–13, 184–90.

10 For an overview of the geographic dynamics of post-1970s globalization, see Neil Brenner, *New State Spaces: Urban Governance and the Rescaling of Statehood* (Oxford: Oxford University Press, 2004), 27–68, 161–71.

11 Paul Stubbs, "Introduction: Socialist Yugoslavia and the Non-Aligned Movement: Contradictions and Contestations," in *Socialist Yugoslavia and the Non-Aligned Movement: Social, Cultural, Political, and Economic Imaginaries*, ed. Paul Stubbs (Montreal and Kingston: McGill-Queen's University Press, 2023), 17.

12 Frieden, *Global Capitalism*, 373–6.

13 Sam Gindin and Leo Panitch, *The Making of Global Capitalism: The Political Economy of American Empire* (London: Verso, 2013), 213–6; Jerome Roos, *Why Not Default? The Political Economy of Sovereign Debt* (Princeton, NJ: Princeton University Press), 126–8.

14 Bret Benjamin, "Developmental Aspirations at the End of Accumulation," *Mediations*, 32, no. 1 (Spring 2018): 53–4; Harvey, *A Brief History of Neoliberalism*, 73–5.

15 Bartel, *The Triumph of Broken Promises*, 127–33.

16 Dubravka Sekulić, "'The Sun Never Sets on Energoprojekt ... until It Does': The Yugoslav Construction Industry in the Non-Aligned World," in *Socialist Yugoslavia and the Non-Aligned Movement*, 272.

17 Frieden, *Global Capitalism*, 286–7.

18 Tony Judt, *Postwar: A History of Europe since 1945* (London: Penguin, 2006), 461–2; Christopher Bickerton, *European Integration: From Nation-States to Member States* (Oxford: Oxford University Press, 2012), 93–4; Giovanni Arrighi, *The Long Twentieth Century: Money, Power and the Origins of Our Times* (London: Verso, 2010), 328–9; Ashoka Mody, *EuroTragedy: A Drama in Nine Acts* (New York: Oxford University Press, 2018), 52–9.

19 While Bartel overlooks the role of European integration in his account of the institutionalization of neoliberal policies in the late Cold War, Christopher Bickerton makes a strong case that a crucial impetus for this process was the effort by national governments to limit their own sovereignty in order to realize unpopular liberalizing reforms. Bickerton, *European Integration*, 90–109. On the relationship between European integration and the new mode of post-1970s globalization, see Frieden,

Notes to pages 194–6

Global Capitalism, 383–4; Gindin and Panitch, The Making of Global Capitalism, 196–203.

20 Mark et al., 1989: A Global History of Eastern Europe, 133.

21 Benedetto Zaccaria, The EEC's Yugoslav Policy in Cold War Europe, 1968–1980 (London: Palgrave Macmillan, 2016); Branislav Radeljić, "Cooperation despite Stark Scepticism: The European Economic Community and Socialist Yugoslavia in the 1970s" in Breaking Down Bipolarity: Yugoslavia's Foreign Relations during the Cold War, ed. Martin Previšić (Berlin: De Gruyter, 2021), 229–48.

22 See Tvrtko Jakovina, "'Not Like a Modern Day Jesus Christ': Pragmatism and Idealism in Yugoslav Non-Alignment," in Socialist Yugoslavia and the Non-Aligned Movement, 121; Jure Ramšak, "Shades of North-South Economic Detente: Non-Aligned Yugoslavia and Neutral Austria Compared," in Socialist Yugoslavia and the Non-Aligned Movement, 247.

23 Dejan Jović, Yugoslavia: A State that Withered Away (West Lafayette, IN: Purdue University Press, 2009), 95–140; Hilde Katrine Haug, Creating a Socialist Yugoslavia: Tito, Communist Leadership and the National Question (London: IB Tauris, 2012), 195–212.

24 In a sense, we might consider Edvard Kardelj's policies as a specifically Yugoslav mode of the politics of breaking promises, as they attempted to devolve social responsibilities away from central government and embed them in markets. Indeed, Johanna Bockman has argued that Yugoslavia's experiment with self-management socialism, which was largely shaped by Kardelj's theories, prefigured many of the ideological themes and economic policies that would later animate neoliberal theory in the West. Bockman, Markets in the Name of Socialism: The Left-Wing Origins of Neoliberalism (Stanford, CA: Stanford University Press, 2011).

25 Jović, Yugoslavia, 141–7.

26 Woodward, Balkan Tragedy, 40, 47–8; Zaccaria, The EEC's Yugoslav Policy in Cold War Europe, 81.

27 Woodward, Balkan Tragedy, 47–81; Jović, Yugoslavia, 141–59; Vladimir Unkovski-Korica, "Self-Management, Development and Debt: The Rise and Fall of the 'Yugoslav Experiment,'" in Welcome to the Desert of Post-Socialism, 21–43.

28 This divergence in the country was noted by foreign observers. It is significant that by the early 1980s, EEC officials were making distinctions between the northern and southern republics of the federation and some even started to negotiate with individual republican governments, bypassing the federal state. Radeljić, "Cooperation despite Stark Skepticism," 241, 246.

288 Notes to pages 196–9

29 Jović, *Yugoslavia*, 147–59; Woodward, *Balkan Tragedy*, 47–63.
30 On the (complex) link between economic crisis and nationalist mobilization in Yugoslavia during the late 1980s, see Goran Musić, *Making and Breaking the Yugoslav Working Class: The Story of Two Self-Managed Factories* (Budapest: Central European University Press, 2021).
31 Živković, "From the Market ... to the Market," 49.
32 Woodward, *Balkan Tragedy*, 99–100.
33 Slobodan Milošević, *Godine raspleta* (Belgrade: Beogradski izdavački zavod, 1989), 242.
34 Milošević, *Godine raspleta*, 241.
35 Tony Judt, for instance, pointed to the expansion and increasing integration of the European Communities as a key factor in the growing receptivity of Western intellectuals to the notion of Central Europe. Judt, "The Rediscovery of Central Europe," *Daedalus*, 119, no. 1 (Winter 1990): 40–1. This idea clearly built on the revival of Europeanist discourses during the era of détente. Mark et al., *1989*, 132–6.
36 Mark et al., *1989*, 146–9.
37 On the reception of the Central Europe idea in Yugoslavia, see Maria Todorova, *Imagining the Balkans* (Oxford: Oxford University Press, 2009), 140–60; Vladimir Zorić, "The Mirror and the Map: Central Europe in the Late Prose of Danilo Kiš," *Književna istorija* 46, no. 153 (2014): 505–24; Vladimir Zorić, "*Discordia Concors*: Central Europe in Post-Yugoslav Discourses" in *After Yugoslavia: The Cultural Spaces of a Vanished Land*, ed. Radmila Gorup (Stanford, CA: Stanford University Press, 2013), 88–114; Jessie Labov, *Transatlantic Central Europe: Contesting Geography and Redefining Culture beyond the Nation* (Budapest: Central European University Press, 2019), 89–108; Yvonne Živković, *The Literary Politics of Mitteleuropa: Reconfiguring Spatial Memory in Austrian and Yugoslav Literature after 1945* (Rochester, NY: Camden House, 2021).
38 Živković, *The Literary Politics of Mitteleuropa*, 68.
39 Predrag Matvejević, *Razgovori s Krležom* (Belgrade: Beogradski izdavački-grafički zavod, 1987), 74.
40 As Živković notes, for instance, among Croat intellectuals of the 1980s the concept had little purchase, and was often criticized as being culturally passé or politically retrograde. Živković, *The Literary Politics of Mitteleuropa*, 166–7.
41 On the Central Europe concept in the writings of Danilo Kiš, see Živković, *The Literary Politics of Mitteleuropa*, 172–201; Zorić, "The Mirror and the Map"; Labov, *Transatlantic Central Europe*, 101–8.

Notes to pages 199–205

42 Živković, *The Literary Politics of Mitteleuropa*, 80.

43 For the ways in which Central Europe came to be deployed against a Yugoslav project, see Zorić, "The Mirror and the Map," 506–7.

44 Taras Kermauner, *Pisma srbskemu prijatelju* (Celovec, AU: Založba Drava, 1989), 157. The origins of this idea can be traced back to the French-Russian philosopher, Nikolai Berdiaev, whose work was an important influence on the interwar Catholic personalists of Slovenia.

45 Ibid., 25–6, 70, 161–5.

46 Ibid., 69, 137–8.

47 Ibid., 266.

48 Ibid., 161.

49 Ibid., 162–3.

50 Živković, *The Literary Politics of Mitteleuropa*, 171–2.

51 Kermauner, *Pisma srbskemu prijatelju*, 150–1.

52 In describing his divergence from the Marxist humanism of his contemporaries, Kermauner noted the role of Milton Friedman in shaping his own intellectual trajectory, suggesting an underlying conceptual affinity between his ideas of Central Europe and the new paradigm of neoliberalism. See Kermauner, *Pisma srbskemu prijatelju*, 62.

53 Ibid., 76.

54 Ibid., 176

55 As Mark and his co-authors note, the rethinking of Europe in Eastern Europe during the 1970s and 1980s was a process of producing new boundaries and exclusions. Mark et al., *1989*, 129–30.

56 On the Praxis movement, see Gerson Sher, *Praxis: Marxist Criticism and Dissent in Socialist Yugoslavia* (Bloomington: Indiana University Press, 1977).

57 A collection of Matvejević's protest letters was published as *Otvorena pisma: morale vježbe* (Belgrade: Nova 12, 1986).

58 Predrag Matvejević, *Jugoslovenstvo danas: pitanje kulture* (Zagreb: Globus, 1982), 39

59 Ibid., 56.

60 Ibid., 47; see also 52.

61 Ibid., 59.

62 On Matvejević's theory of the Yugoslav national question, see Igor Štiks and Andrew Wachtel, "Squaring the South Slavic Circle: Ethnicity, Nationhood, and Citizenship in Yugoslavia," in *Civic Nationalisms in a Global Perspective*, ed. Jasper Trautsch (London: Routledge, 2019), 54–69.

63 The title of the English translation, which will be cited here as a reference for non-Serbo-Croatian speakers, is *Mediterranean: A Cultural*

290 Notes to pages 205–8

Landscape, trans. Michael Henry Heim (Berkeley: University of California Press, 1999). This book opened Matvejević up to a wider readership beyond Yugoslavia, led to his being made a vice president of PEN International, and gave him access to some of the most prestigious universities in Europe. Zdenko Lešić, "Predrag Matvejević," *Dijalog; Časopis za filozofiju i društvenu teoriju* 1-2 (2017): 28. The text has been translated into over twenty languages, including Spanish (1991), French (1992), Italian (1993), German (1993), Dutch (1994), Japanese (1997), Greek (1998), Turkish (1999), Arabic (1999), English (1999), Hebrew (2001), Macedonian (2002), Czech (2002), Finnish (2003), Polish (2003), Hungarian (2006), Esperanto (2007) and Slovene (2008).

64 Vicko Krstulović, *Jadranska orijentacija* (Zagreb: Vjesnik, 1967). On the rivalries between "Adriatic" and "Danubian" conceptions of Yugoslavia in the 1960s, see Dennison Rusinow, *The Yugoslav Experiment, 1948–1974* (Berkeley: University of California Press, 1977), 133.

65 Zaccaria, *The EEC's Yugoslav Policy in Cold War Europe*, 60.

66 Matvejević's views were outlined in his essay "Central Europe Seen from the East of Europe," republished in *In Search of Central Europe*, ed. George Schöpflin and Nancy Wood (Cambridge: Polity Press, 1989), 183–90.

67 Yvonne Živković, for instance, sharply differentiates early-twentieth-century notions of Central Europe as a geopolitical category from the 1980s dissident conceptions of it as "a community of the arts." Živković, *The Literary Politics of Mitteleuropa*, 44. Similarly, Jessie Labov notes that the importance Kundera placed on the Jewish legacy of the region symbolized all that was "profoundly intellectual about his vision of Central Europe." Labov, *Transatlantic Central Europe*, 74.

68 Matvejević, *Mediterranean*, 85–6.

69 Ibid., 190.

70 Ibid., 85.

71 Ibid., 199.

72 Matvejević's strategy of breaking up the space of Yugoslavia along regional-civilizational spaces, rather than nationality, recalled the strategy of communist intellectuals of the 1950s, who briefly sought to promote subnational regionalisms to foster a stronger Yugoslav sense of identity. James Robertson, "Small Socialism: The Scales of Self-Management Culture in Postwar Yugoslavia," *Slavic Review* 80, no. 3 (Fall 2021): 563–84. This strategy also resonated with his earlier arguments warning against the homogenizing effects of nationalist culture. Matvejević, *Jugoslavenstvo danas*, 32.

Notes to pages 208–12 291

73 Matvejević, *Mediterranean*, 198.

74 Ibid., 10.

75 Ibid., 109–15, 142.

76 Ibid., 42, 149–53.

77 See, for instance, Matvejević's criticism of the prominent literary theorist and cultural official, Josip Vidmar, for his efforts to strictly delimit a Slovene national culture from a wider Yugoslav culture. Matvejević, *Otvorena pisma*, 75–6.

78 Anna Botta, "Predrag Matvejević's *Mediterranean Breviary*: Nostalgia for an 'Ex-World' or a Breviary for a New Community?," *California Italian Studies* 1, no. 1 (2010): 12.

79 Matvejević, *Mediterranean*, 25.

80 See Jacques Derrida's 1990 essay on Paul Valéry and the "Mediterranean spirit" of Europe, later published as *The Other Heading: Reflections on Today's Europe*, trans. Pascale-Ann Brault and Michael B. Naas (Bloomington: Indiana University Press, 1992). For an effort to situate Matvejević within this Mediterranean turn, see Botta, "Predrag Matvejević's *Mediterranean Breviary*."

81 See, for instance, Matvejević, *Otvorena pisma*.

82 Mila Orlić, "Od postkomunizma do postjugoslavenstva: Udruženje za jugoslavensku demokratsku inicijativu," *Politička misao* 48, no. 4 (2011): 98–112.

83 On Ugrešić's early biography, see David Williams, *Writing Postcommunism: Towards a Literature of the East European Ruins* (London: Palgrave Macmillan, 2013), 40–2.

84 Dragana Obradović, *Writing the Yugoslav Wars: Literature, Postmodernism, and the Ethics of Representation* (Toronto: University of Toronto Press, 2016), 89. On the concept of commercial nationalism in the former Yugoslavia, see Zala Volčič and Mark Andrejević, "Nation Branding in the Era of Commercial Nationalism," *International Journal of Communication* 5 (2011): 598–618.

85 Dubravka Ugrešić, *The Culture of Lies: Antipolitical Essays*, trans. Celia Hawkesworth (London: Phoenix, 1999), 40–1.

86 The more egregious and, one might suggest, disingenuous critiques of Ugrešić's postmodern fiction are discussed in Williams, *Writing Postcommunism*, 42–5. A more nuanced version of this argument is laid out in Gordana Crnković, "Women Writers in Croatian and Serbian Literature," in *Gender Politics in the Western Balkans: Women and Society in Yugoslavia and the Yugoslav Successor States*, ed. Sabrina Ramet (University Park: Pennsylvania State University Press, 1999),

292 Notes to pages 212–20

239–41. See also: Vedrana Veličković, "'Justabit-Racist': Dubravka Ugrešić, Cosmopolitanism and the Post-Yugoslav Condition," in *Postmodern Literature and Race*, ed. Len Platt and Sara Upstone (New York: Cambridge University Press, 2015), 145–6. Andrew Wachtel offers an alternative account in his excellent reading of Milorad Pavić's *The Dictionary of the Khazars*, which suggests postmodern literature was more complicit in fostering nationalism than scholars have typically believed. Andrew Wachtel, *Making a Nation, Breaking a Nation: Literature and Cultural Politics in Yugoslavia* (Stanford, CA: Stanford University Press, 1998), 210–18.

87 Dragana Obradović has offered one of the most forceful arguments against the tendency to periodize Ugrešić's pre- and postwar writings. See Obradović, *Writing the Yugoslav Wars*, 68.

88 Pascale Casanova, *The World Republic of Letters*, trans. M.B. DeBevoise (Cambridge, MA: Harvard University Press, 2004).

89 Dubravka Ugrešić, *Fording the Stream of Consciousness* trans. Michael Henry Heim (Evanston, IL: Northwestern University Press, 1993), 184.

90 Ugrešić set up this parallel in her opening chapter. In response to letters from friends in Zagreb describing the inflation and shortages prompted by the IMF's structural adjustment program, she commented: "Reading their letters made me love my country because it's so small. I feel sorry for it." A few pages later, when asked to justify her decision to write a novel about writers, she responded: "I love writers; they are so small and pitiful." Ugrešić, *Fording the Stream of Consciousness*, 6, 10.

91 Ibid., 187.

92 Ibid., 89.

93 The cynical use of the "Central Europe" category would reappear in Ugrešić's 1990s writings, where she satirized the anxiety with which Yugoslav writers obsessed over which of the "marketable political labels" Western journalists and publishers placed on them. Ugrešić, *The Culture of Lies*, 35.

94 Ugrešić, *Fording the Stream of Consciousness*, 5.

95 Ibid., 8.

96 Dubravka Ugrešić, "Parrots and Priests," *Partisan Review* 59, no. 4 (1992): 676–83. The talk was later republished in *The Culture of Lies*, and it is to this publication that I will refer.

97 Ugrešić, *The Culture of Lies*, 38.

98 Ibid., 35.

99 Natasa Kovačević, "Storming the EU Fortress: Communities of Disagreement in Dubravka Ugrešić," *Cultural Critique* 83 (Winter 2013): 63–86.

Notes to pages 222–8

CONCLUSION

1 On the fascinating history of McDonald's in Serbia, see Lily Lynch, "I'm Lovin' It (Most of the Time): A Brief History of McDonald's in Serbia," *Balkanist*, 27 August 2014, http://balkanist.net/im-lovin-it-mcdonalds-serbia.

2 Samuel Moyn, "Fantasies of Federalism," *Dissent*, Winter 2015, https://www.dissentmagazine.org/article/fantasies-of-federalism.

3 Andrew Wachtel, *Making a Nation, Breaking a Nation: Literature and Cultural Politics in Yugoslavia* (Stanford, CA: Stanford University Press, 1998), 227–48.

4 Predrag Matvejević, *Jugoslovenstvo danas: pitanje kulture* (Zagreb: Globus, 1982), 47.

5 As Rogers Brubaker argues with regard to the Soviet Union, far from eroding it, the country's model of socialist federalism in fact institutionalized the nation state. Brubaker, *Nationalism Reframed: Nationhood and the National Question in the New Europe* (Cambridge: Cambridge University Press, 2004), 23–54.

6 Adom Getachew presents a similar account of the failure of supranationalism in her analysis of the federalist debates in postcolonial Africa and the Eastern Caribbean. Getachew, *Worldmaking after Empire: The Rise and Fall of Self-Determination* (New York: Columbia University Press, 2019), 107–41.

7 Dejan Jović, *Yugoslavia: A State that Withered Away* (West Lafayette, IN: Purdue University Press, 2009), 63.

8 Ivo Banac, *With Stalin against Tito: Cominformist Splits in Yugoslav Communism* (Ithaca, NY: Cornell University Press, 1988), 31–2.

9 Paul Niland, "Making Sense of Minsk: Decentralization, Special Status, and Federalism," *Atlantic Council*, 27 January 2016, https://www.atlanticcouncil.org/blogs/ukrainealert/making-sense-of-minsk-decentralization-special-status-and-federalism.

10 Christopher Bickerton, *European Integration: From Nation-States to Member States* (Oxford: Oxford University Press, 2012), 113–50; Philip Cunliffe et al., *Taking Control: Sovereignty and Democracy after Brexit* (Cambridge: Polity Press, 2023). Quinn Slobodian has demonstrated that many neoliberal theorists were in favour of supranational federalism precisely because it offered a means for limiting the scope of democratic contestation. Slobodian, *Globalists: The End of Empire and the Birth of Neoliberalism* (Cambridge, MA: Harvard University Press, 2018), 91–120.

294 Notes to pages 228–9

11 To that end, consider Srećko Horvat and Igor Štiks's rather dour comments regarding Croatia's entry to the EU: Srećko Horvat and Igor Štiks, "Croatia Has Become the Latest Member of the EU Periphery," *The Guardian*, 1 July 2013, https://www.theguardian.com/commentis free/2013/jul/01/croatia-latest-member-eu-periphery.

12 Georges Canguilhem, *Knowledge of Life*, trans. Stefanos Geroulanos and Daniela Ginsburg (New York: Fordham University Press, 2008), 29.

Index

Adamič, Louis, 135–7
Adriatic, 29, 42, 138, 160, 205
Adžija, Božidar, 72, 263n74
Africa, 25–7, 39, 41, 172–5, 192, 195, 201–2, 208, 216
Albania, 7, 26, 42–3, 128, 131–4, 140–1, 148–51, 153, 160; treaty of friendship with Yugoslavia, 133, 149
anarchism, 12, 15, 32
anticolonialism, 21, 27, 46, 51, 53, 57, 64, 160, 168, 170, 172–5, 187, 201, 216, 219, 284n104
anticommunism, 45–6, 83, 200
antifascism, 22, 99–100, 103–8, 111, 123, 129, 138, 153–4
Antifascist Council for the National Liberation of Yugoslavia (AVNOJ), 126
Anti-imperialism, 24, 37–43, 48, 141–2, 147, 151, 164, 184–7
antiracism, 136, 175–6
anti-Semitism, 83, 102, 104
anti-Stalinism, 49, 69, 86–7, 159, 163, 167, 169–70, 173, 195, 200–2, 205, 227
apartheid, 160, 284n104
Arabs, 153, 172, 201, 208

Aragon, Louis, 79, 105, 255n35
Association for the Yugoslav Democratic Initiative, 203, 209–11
austerity, 191, 194, 196–7, 202
Austria, 29, 51, 68, 92, 101, 115, 120
Austro-Marxism, 8, 41–2
Averbakh, Leopold, 72, 79

Baillon, André, 73, 79
Balkan command, 140–1, 267n49
Balkan Communist Federation, 46, 131–3
Balkan federalism, 5–6, 26, 33, 35, 37–43, 63, 97, 103–4, 122, 127–8, 131–4, 136, 140–3, 148–56, 160, 164–5, 199, 223–4, 226–8
Balkanism, 22, 24, 65, 86, 104, 111, 118, 142
Balkanization, 7, 98, 105; of Europe, 44, 57–8, 60
Balkan Wars, 4, 25–6, 38–9, 42–3, 140, 152
Balzac, Honoré de, 105, 107, 109, 113
Bandung Conference, 170

Index

Barbaro-genius, 56, 58, 101, 110–11
Barbusse, Henri, 72, 73, 105
Bebler, Aleš, 173, 178, 253n17
Belgrade, 5, 26, 65, 82, 101, 110–11, 125, 140, 143–4, 152, 160, 167, 185, 222
Berlin, 5, 37, 72, 82, 101, 107, 122; Congress of, 29
Bihalji-Merin, Oto, 72, 73, 75, 79, 80
Bogumils, 53, 178
bolshevism, 5–6, 49, 45, 51, 60, 101
Bosnia and Herzegovina, 122, 126, 135, 138, 140, 156, 188; Habsburg annexation of, 26, 30, 39
Bretton Woods, 23, 189, 190, 195
Britain, 22, 28, 30, 41, 46, 67, 74–5, 96, 101, 105, 107–9, 113, 117, 126, 137, 151, 153, 184, 191
Brnčič, Ivo, 70, 72
Bruegel, Pieter, 86, 89
Budapest, 5, 50, 101, 171
Buddha, 54, 173, 179, 184
Bulgaria, 7, 20, 25, 33, 35, 59, 101, 122, 125, 129, 135–6, 140, 144, 151, 153–4, 160; greater, 140, 33; radical politics in, 8, 26, 32, 36, 38, 42, 46, 50, 148; union with Yugoslavia, 33, 131–4, 146–7, 156, 228

čakavian dialect, 138, 262n50
canonization, 17–18, 71–73, 80, 106–7, 109, 112–13, 179, 182, 213, 255n28

Casanova, Pascale, 17–19, 71, 80, 177, 212
Central Europe, 28, 53, 56, 101, 107; dissident concept of, 23, 189, 198–203, 205–9, 212, 215–16, 218–19
Cesarec, August, 19, 50, 53–4, 72, 114, 118–23; collaboration with Krleža, 21, 49–51, 54, 59, 64–5, 70; *Sin domovine* (*Son of the Homeland*), 114, 118–22
China, 39, 83, 102, 125, 186; literature of, 83, 172, 182
Cold War, 159–60, 162, 165, 171, 176, 184–7, 192, 194–5, 198
Comintern, 21–2, 46, 49, 55, 69, 75, 87, 97, 100, 103–8, 113–14, 118–19, 122; Third Period of, 67, 100, 102–3, 108
Commission for Foreign Cultural Relations, 167, 180
communism, 5–6, 45, 51, 53, 70, 79, 91, 102, 106, 126–127, 200–1, 217
constructivism, 49, 60
Crnjanski, Miloš, 66, 69, 82–6, 92, 96, 102, 110, 177
Croatia, 3–5, 20, 33, 49–51, 53, 55, 86, 92, 119–22, 126, 135, 137–9, 149, 190, 194–5, 201, 207, 210–11, 213, 228; Independent State of, 122, 125
Cuba, 160, 216
cultural development, 6, 16–19, 21–2, 68–9, 73–5, 79–87, 89, 92, 94, 96, 112–13, 168, 175–6, 178
cultural exchange, 23, 85, 102, 128, 133, 144–5, 149, 178, 204,

Index

208. *See also* cultural internationalism

cultural internationalism, 163–5, 167–8, 172–3

Czechoslovakia, 92, 101, 108, 129, 1434, 198, 213

dadaism, 54, 59

Dalmatia, 98, 120, 137–9, 152, 178, 207

Danube, 8, 28, 101, 258n65, 290n64

Davičo, Oskar, 152–5, 169–70; *Među Markosovim partizanima* (*Among Markos's Partisans*), 153–5

decolonization, 165, 168–71, 173–6, 178

détente, 194, 288n35, 253n17, 254n19, 257n53, 261n35, 267n49

Dimitrov, Georgi, 103, 106, 108, 119

Drašković, Milorad, 45–6, 56

Dubrovnik, 98–9

Engels, Friedrich, 17, 32, 38, 107

Esperanto, 59Ethiopia, 173–5

ethnic cleansing, 42, 140, 188

Eurasia, 21, 102, 125, 138, 146, 198

European Communities, 188, 189, 226, 228, 287n28

European Economic Community, 11, 191–6

European integration, 22, 24, 34, 104, 113, 165, 188–90, 192–5, 197, 218, 222, 224, 226, 228, 286–7n19

European Union, 10, 188, 197, 219, 221, 228

fascism, 22, 65, 68, 82, 99–100, 102–6, 108–11, 118–23, 125, 130, 137, 138, 144, 171

federalism, 14–15, 32, 223, 228. *See also* Balkan federalism; Yugoslavism; supranationalism

fédération balkanique, La, 46, 114, 118

France, 22, 46, 101, 103, 105, 108–9, 113, 119–20, 144, 182, 184

French Revolution, the, 39, 105, 107, 116–17, 181

futurism, 60, 251n59

Garašanin, Ilija, 29, 31

geography: cultural, 100, 105, 109, 111, 113, 144, 165, 189, 208, 215; imagined, 16, 56, 156, 189, 229; of kinship 23, 133–4, 145–6; of non–alignment, 23, 162–3, 169, 172; symbolic, 48, 63, 226; uneven, 13–14, 19, 38, 68, 80–1, 85–6, 89, 91–2, 95, 97, 127, 134, 195, 225, 238n42, 240n65

geopoetics, 21, 48, 58–9, 63, 69, 86, 100, 109, 111, 122, 225–6

Germany, 14, 22, 28, 30, 37, 71, 96, 99–102, 105, 109, 113, 117–18, 129, 121–2, 125, 129–30, 135, 139

Ghana, 172, 216–17

globalization, 6–7, 10–15, 17, 20, 27–30, 36, 38, 67–9, 74–5, 81, 96, 165, 168, 191–2, 198, 202, 204–5, 211–15, 217–19, 225

298 Index

Goll, Yvan, 54, 57, 250n47
Gorkii, Maksim, 70, 72–3, 79
Grahor, Ivo, 60, 65, 114
great depression, the, 21, 67–9, 71, 75, 80–1, 83, 85, 95–6, 101
Greece, 7, 25–6, 32, 35, 101, 105, 128, 131, 133–4, 136, 141, 194, 228, 272n94; Civil War in, 131, 151–5; Communist Party of, 46, 151, 158; Democratic Army of, 133, 143, 150–1, 267n49
Grosz, George, 72, 86, 89

Habsburg Empire, the, 4–5, 8, 15, 20, 26, 29–30, 32, 34, 36, 39, 41–2, 44, 51, 60, 83, 115, 118–21, 147, 171, 198–9, 201–2, 215
Hegedušić, Krsto, 86, 89–92
heritage, 17, 55, 95, 120, 138, 184; European, 99–101, 105–7, 110, 114, 118, 198, 200; world 176–9, 280n70
historical materialism, 75, 79, 91, 117, 120, 176–7, 179, 180–2
Hitler, Adolf, 22, 99, 102–3, 125, 129
Hlebine, 86, 179
humanism, 106–9, 100–11, 118, 176; Marxist, 15, 187, 200, 203–4
Hungary, 92, 101, 107, 117, 122, 125, 144

Illyrian movement, the, 5, 20, 51, 112
imperialism, 7–9, 12, 14, 21, 26–7, 31, 36–9, 41–2, 51, 58, 63, 83, 102, 104, 121, 151, 156, 169–71, 185, 225, 245n48

India, 39, 41, 57, 64, 74–5, 160, 172–4, 178–9, 184
International Monetary Fund, 192, 196, 202
International Writers' Congress for the Defense of Culture, 98, 105
Italy, 25–7, 30, 39, 42, 60–3, 65, 82, 102, 104, 119–22, 125, 141, 150, 152, 175

Japan, 14, 30, 37, 73, 96, 125, 172, 173, 204
Jews, 123, 152, 182, 198, 206
Jovanović, Đorđe, 110–11, 113, 261n35

kajkavian dialect, 115, 262n50
Karađorđević, Aleksandar, 44, 67–8, 72, 82, 103, 115, 201
Kardelj, Edvard, , 159, 195, 253n17, 287n24
Kautsky, Karl, 36–7, 42
Kermauner, Taras, 188, 200–2, 207–8
Kidrič, Boris, 159, 253n17
Kirigin, Josip, 173–5
Kiš, Danilo, 199, 215
Kisch, Egon Erwin, 72, 79
kitsch, 51, 211, 217–18
Klopčič, Mile, 72, 115
Književna republika (Literary Republic), 49, 65
Književne novine (Literary Newspaper), 149, 172, 178, 182–3
Konrád, György, 198–9, 215
Kosovel, Srečko, 21, 49, 59–65, 70, 114, 118
Kosovo, 42–4, 128, 131, 140, 150, 197, 221–2, 228, 271n88

Kranjec, Miško, 147
Kreft, Bratko, 65, 72, 74, 114–18, 120, 122; *Velika puntarija* (*The Great Rebellion*), 114–18
Krleža, Miroslav, 19, 21, 49, 54–7, 59, 61, 64, 69–70, 82, 96, 115–16, 118–19, 167, 169–71, 174, 199, 219; critique of social literature, 85–9; early biography, 3–6, 49–51; "Hrvatska književna laž" ("The Croatian Literary Lie"), 51–3; *Podravi motivi* (*The Drava Valley Motifs*), 89–92; *Povratak Filipa Latinowicza* (*The Return of Filip Latinowicz*), 92–5
Kundera, Milan, 198–9, 215
Kvaternik, Eugen, 112, 119–22

Lenin, Vladimir, 50, 52, 70, 72, 79, 187, 255n23
literary left, 18, 97, 99–100, 110, 118; polemics on the, 22, 68–9, 72. *See also* Krleža, Miroslav: critique of social literature
Ljubljana, 60–3, 65, 72, 83, 116, 169–71, 200
longue durée, 23, 163, 176, 180, 208
Lukács, Georg, 22, 91, 107–8, 113, 119, 254–5n22
Luxemburg, Rosa, 37, 41

Macedonia, 15, 33, 36, 38, 39, 42–4, 50, 72, 104, 126, 128, 131, 140–1, 148, 150–5
Manoilescu, Mihail, 68, 85, 96
Marković, Svetozar, 20, 27, 30, 32–7, 55, 148; *Srbija na istoku* (*Serbia in the East*), 33–6

Marx, Karl, 17, 32, 38, 50, 52, 70, 107, 181, 187
Marxism, 31–2, 36–7, 89, 91, 107, 167, 169–80, 187, 200, 256n38
Matvejević, Predrag, 190, 203–10, 211, 219, 224; *Mediteranski brevijar* (*Mediterranean Breviary*), 203–10
Mediterranean, 188, 194, 203–9, 219, 227
Micić, Ljubomir, 21, 44, 49, 54–9, 61–2, 65, 110–11
Middle East, 30, 173, 178, 195, 216
Milošević, Slobodan, 196–7, 201, 221
minor literature, 214–15
modernism, 3, 18–19, 22–3, 39, 49, 57, 62, 69, 71, 82, 85–7, 91, 110, 115, 174, 179–82; socialist, 167, 179
Molière, 99, 105, 114, 118
Montenegro, 25, 126, 137
Morocco, 39, 41
Moscow, 5, 22, 46, 67, 71, 85, 89, 103, 106–7, 119–20, 122, 129–30, 145

Nasser, Gamal Abdel, 160, 173
national developmentalism, 14, 30–1, 36–7, 39, 68–9, 83, 85, 95–6, 192
national question, 7, 12, 19, 33, 37, 41–2, 64, 100, 103, 108, 119, 121, 140–1, 168, 225
naturalism, 71, 79, 107, 254–5n22
Nazism, 99–102, 108, 139
Nazor, Vladimir, 137–9, 142
Nehru, Jawaharlal, 160, 173, 183–4, 277n40

neoliberalism, 189, 191–2, 196–7, 202, 286–7n19, 287n24, 289n52, 293n10

New Slavic Movement, 11, 22–3, 127–39, 142, 144–7, 151, 154, 156–7, 224, 227–8

New York, 17, 67, 71, 114, 118

Nexø, Martin Anderson, 98, 105, 110

Nietzsche, Friedrich, 50, 52, 58, 89, 94

non-alignment, 6, 11–12, 23, 159, 160–7, 169, 172, 184–7, 191–2, 194, 201, 208–9, 216, 223–7

North Africa, 25–7

Nova literatura (New Literature), 72–3, 75–8

one-worldism, 23, 163–5, 167–9, 171, 176–8, 180, 184, 186–7, 209

orientalism, 11, 17, 24, 53, 64, 111, 173–5, 180, 279n62

Ottoman Empire, the, 7, 15, 25–7, 29, 32, 36, 38–9, 42, 59, 83, 112, 152, 171, 176, 199, 201

Pannonia, 11, 92–5, 96

pan-Slavism, 8, 33, 129–30, 135. *See also* New Slavic Movement, Yugoslavism

Paris, 3–5, 17, 32, 65, 67, 71, 85–6, 89, 101, 104–6, 119–20, 122, 179, 187, 200, 210

Party of Rights, 119–20

Pašić, Nikola, 25, 30–1

People's Radical Party, 30, 36, 66

Persia, 39, 41, 208

Pirjevec, Dušan, 125, 146

Piscator, Erwin, 72, 114

Plamen (The Flame), 3, 49–54, 59, 63–4

Poland, 120–1, 129, 131, 144, 153, 198

popular front, 22, 97, 100, 102–6, 108–10, 112–13, 115, 117–19, 122–3, 131, 165, 227

Prague, 54, 67, 101, 104, 122, 145

Praxis, 200, 204

Prica, Ognjen, 87, 263n74

primitivism, 55–7, 59–60, 65, 110–11, 174–5, 179–80, 251n59

proletarian culture, 22, 69, 71–3, 75–6, 85–7, 100, 106–7, 109, 176, 254n21

quasi-state, 7, 41, 233n13

race, 57, 64, 80, 94, 120, 125, 127–9, 131, 133–4, 136, 138–9, 146–7, 151, 154–5, 164, 174–5, 250n47, 265n29

Ranković, Aleksandar, 195, 253n17

realism, 18, 22, 71, 79–80, 86–7, 89, 91, 94, 100, 107, 113, 181–2; new, 100, 109–14, 176; socialist, 106, 167, 176, 179

Red Army, 134, 142, 146

reportage 71, 79, 84, 153, 175, 254–5n22

Republika, 172, 179, 182

Ristić, Marko, 19, 167–8, 172, 175, 177–8, 181–2, 280n69, 282n88

Romania, 7, 32, 46, 68, 85, 92, 101, 117, 231–2n7

romanticism, 52, 70, 80, 84, 169

Rome, 53, 82, 101

Russia, 30, 32, 34, 37, 39, 41, 119,

130, 137, 145–6, 148, 203, 206, 222, 228; as defender of Slavdom, 129–30, 135–6, 142, 146–7; literature of, 109, 113, 144
Russian Revolution, the, 5, 21, 43–5, 49, 54–5, 87, 156, 169

Said, Edward. *See* orientalism
scalar politics, 4, 9–10, 22, 165
scale, 4, 6, 8–10, 12–15, 18–19, 21–2, 33, 35, 37–8, 46, 54, 69, 82, 86–7, 92, 96, 113–14, 122, 133, 137, 159–61, 164–5, 176, 186, 191, 205, 207–8, 212, 214–15, 217–8, 223–6, 218
Second International, 37, 41–2
self-management socialism, 159, 178, 195, 287n24
Serbia, 4, 7–8, 15, 20–1, 25–7, 32–3, 37, 42–3, 50, 59, 65–6, 122, 126, 135, 151, 154, 190, 196–7, 200–1, 210–11, 221–3; greater, 29, 31, 33, 103, 131, 138, 197, 202, 227; literature of, 18, 50, 69, 82–4, 110–13, 176, 181; state development of, 28–31, 34–5, 38–9
Serbian Revolution, the, 28–9, 33–4
Sholokhov, Mikhail, 79, 268–70n65
Sinclair, Upton, 72–3, 75, 79
Slovene-Croatian Peasant Rebellion, the, 112, 115–17, 120, 262n49
Slovenia, 49, 59–61, 63–5, 66, 72, 74, 83, 112, 114–18, 126, 131, 136, 146–7, 150, 178, 190, 194–7, 200–2, 207, 228, 289n44, 291n77

social democracy, 15, 26, 40–2, 46, 67, 73, 80, 100, 246n50; in Croatia, 72; in Germany, 36–7; in Serbia, 20, 27, 31, 36–8, 43, 50, 53, 227
social literature, 22, 68–73, 75, 79–87, 89, 94, 96–7, 99–100, 109–11, 113–14, 118–19, 123, 173
socialist modernism. *See* modernism
socialist realism. *See* realism
Sofia, 46, 101, 145
Soviet Republic of Letters, 71, 96, 260n22
Soviet Union, 50, 55, 75, 113, 119, 139, 153, 156, 167, 172, 180, 186, 191, 198, 213, 293n5; geopolitics of, 22, 45, 69, 102–3, 126, 129–30, 134, 137, 142, 145, 161, 228; literature of, 71–3, 78–9, 87, 105–7, 144, 268–70n65; relations with Yugoslavia, 23, 84, 127–8, 135, 143, 158–60, 187, 195, 201
Spain, 32, 104, 119, 194
Stalin, Joseph, 139, 158, 160, 228
Stalinism, 22, 49, 69, 86, 143, 159, 167, 169–71, 173, 195, 200–1, 205, 213, 227
Starčević, Ante, 112, 119
Stožer (*The Pole*), 72, 79
St Petersburg, 5, 32
Strossmayer, Josip Juraj, 20, 121
supranationalism, 6–12, 16, 20–3, 27, 31, 33, 37–8, 43, 124, 127–8, 131–4, 143, 157, 160–2, 165, 198, 202, 205, 218, 223–9; in literature, 16, 18–19, 48–49, 58–9, 81–2, 86–7, 92, 96–7,

108, 138, 163. *See also* Balkan federalism; federalism; New Slavic Movement; Yugoslavism

surrealism, 19, 86–7, 110, 152, 167, 169, 177, 181, 280n69, 282n88

Switzerland, 32, 244n25

Tempo, Svetozar Vukmanović, 140–2, 253n17, 254n19, 267n49

temporality, 19, 73–5, 79–80, 91, 113, 139, 176–7, 180–2, 208–9, 246n56

territorialization, 8, 14, 28, 42, 69, 73, 80, 82, 84–5, 87, 97, 109, 170

Thessaloniki, 4, 26, 153

Third-Worldism, 23–4, 160, 162–3, 165, 169–70, 173–5, 185–7, 191–2, 199, 201–2, 208, 216–17, 219–20, 226, 279n62

Tito, Josip Broz, 125, 139–40, 143, 158–62, 174, 183–4, 187, 228, 253n17, 267n49

Tito-Stalin split, 23, 127–8, 157–60, 164, 167, 201, 227

Toller, Ernst, 79, 99, 105

Tolstoi, Lev, 50, 70, 105, 107, 109, 113

translation, 18, 23, 59, 66, 69, 72–3, 75, 79–81, 82–4, 97, 102, 144, 149–50, 172–3, 178–9, 182, 217, 256n38, 268–70n65

travelogues, 23, 79, 173–5, 178, 279n62

Trieste, 60, 125, 131, 146, 158

Tripoli, 25–7, 39

Tucović, Dimitrije, 20, 27, 36–43, 50, 148–9; Turkey, 141, 173

Ugrešić, Dubravka, 3, 190, 203, 210–19; ; UNESCO, 164, 167–8, 175–6, 178

Union of Writers, 144, 149, 169, 171, 179

United Nations, 152–4, 160–1, 165, 221

United States (US), 67, 75–6, 96, 101, 126, 135–6, 151, 153, 161, 184–6, 190–2, 196, 216–17, 222

Ustasha, 104, 119, 122–3, 139

Ve Poljanski, Branko, 54–5, 61

Vienna, 5, 46, 67, 101, 104, 107, 114, 116, 122, 171

Vietnam, 53–4, 184–7

Volcker shock, 23, 190

world literature, 17, 19, 22, 69, 71, 79, 99, 105, 182; world literary field, 16, 85, 214; world literary system, 17–18, 69, 71, 84, 95, 113–14, 212, 214, 218

World War I, 5, 20–1, 27–8, 43, 45, 48, 50, 59–60, 62, 82, 86, 95, 120, 147, 227

World War II, 22, 70, 122, 126, 131, 147–8, 151, 153–4, 164, 169, 175, 190, 226–7

Yugoslav Communist Party (KPJ), 22, 67, 70, 86, 97, 100, 103, 110, 119, 122–3, 126–8, 131, 134–5, 137, 140, 143, 148–9, 152, 156–7

Yugoslavia: Kingdom of Serbs, Croats, and Slovenes, 5, 15, 44–6, 59, 64, 66, 118; Federal People's Republic of, 126, 143, 158; Socialist Federative

Republic of, 11, 188, 218, 224, 226

Yugoslavism, 19–21, 48, 67, 103–4, 126, 131, 136, 191, 199, 201, 204, 224, 227

zadruga, 34–5, 37, 55

Zagreb, 4, 49–50, 54–5, 59, 66, 72, 83, 119–20, 123, 138, 185–6, 204, 211–12, 216

Zedong, Mao, 125, 172, 221

Zemlja art collective, 86, 179

Zenit, 54–5, 59–61, 63–5

zenitism, 49, 55–8, 60–4, 70, 111, 251n59

Zogović, Radovan, 72, 87, 110, 112–13, 150, 176, 253n17, 254n19, 272n91